Hon. B. B. WINBORNE,
January, 1901.

The Colonial and State Political History of Hertford County North Carolina

BENJAMIN B. WINBORNE
MURFREESBORO, N.C.
Author of *The Winborne Family*, and
The Historical Brief of Political Economy.

God bless our native land!
Firm may she ever stand
Through storm and night;
When the wild tempests rave,
Ruler of wind and wave,
Do thou our country save
By thy great might!

HERITAGE BOOKS
2012

HERITAGE BOOKS
AN IMPRINT OF HERITAGE BOOKS, INC.

Books, CDs, and more—Worldwide

For our listing of thousands of titles see our website
at
www.HeritageBooks.com

A Facsimile Reprint
Published 2012 by
HERITAGE BOOKS, INC.
Publishing Division
100 Railroad Ave. #104
Westminster, Maryland 21157

Copyright © 1998 Heritage Books, Inc.

Originally printed for the author by
Edwards & Broughton
1906

— Publisher's Notice —
In reprints such as this, it is often not possible to remove blemishes from the original. We feel the contents of this book warrant its reissue despite these blemishes and hope you will agree and read it with pleasure.

International Standard Book Numbers
Paperbound: 978-0-7884-0949-3
Clothbound: 978-0-7884-9407-9

DEDICATION.

I DEDICATE THIS BOOK TO THE MEMORY OF THE DEPARTED WORTHIES OF HERTFORD COUNTY, AND THE DESCENDANTS OF THOSE NOBLE PEOPLE.

BENJ. BRODIE WINBORNE.

May, 1906.

INTRODUCTION.

Hertford County is rich in the character of her families, and in the acts and deeds of her sons, in war and in peace, but poor in her records.

On the night of August 22, 1830, the entire records of the county were destroyed by fire. One Wright Allen was indicted in our Superior Court for forging the name of Timothy Ridley, of Maney's Neck, and thinking that the note was in the court-house, and that by burning the same he could destroy the evidence of his guilt, he touched the torch to the building, and quickly the court-house and all the records of the county, from its foundation, were consumed by the flames. The records of seventy years of the county's history were within a few hours blotted from human eyes. Again on February 20, 1862, the records of this splendid county, together with the court-house, were ruthlessly burned by the Union soldiers during the cruel war between the American States. The date of this fire is hard to determine. I find reliable authorities fixing it February 20, March 20, and May 20. It is, however, immaterial. The will books since 1830, and a few of the old record books of the Court of Pleas and Quarter Sessions, which happened to be in Murfreesboro, where the Clerk resided, were saved. Hence appears the reason why I have undertaken the Herculean task of trying to reproduce some of the past history of the county. I have been practicing law in the county since 1875, and I have so often felt the dire need for these lost records.

I beg that my imperfect history may be read with sympathy for its author. Much of my information I secured from old deeds among my father's papers. His deeds carry me back to 1812, and one as far back as 1762, and gives the name of the first Clerk of the County Court. The deeds and old wills and copies of records of other families, which have been kindly furnished me, have enabled me, with the old Colonial and State Records of North Carolina, to bring together this imperfect history of a noble people.

BENJ. B. WINBORNE.

May, A. D. 1906.

The Colonial and State Political History of Hertford County, N. C.

PUBLIC PRIDE.

For centuries and ages, nations and sub-divisions of nations, and governments, have honored their heroic and noble dead. Monuments, statues, histories, and other records have been resorted to as far back as recorded time to commemorate and perpetuate the deeds, the acts, the successes and the mistakes of prominent and leading characters. Not only that those in the future may live and profit by the noble deeds of the past, and shun the ignoble deeds and mistakes of a preceding generation, but to gratify and perpetuate their pride of their great dead.

We have been unable to find in recorded history of the civilized world any nation, any government, any state, any county, or any political division of a territory, that was not proud of its noble men and women; and in some way were willing to hand down to future generations the history of the proud deeds of its subjects and its sublime characters.

Such is the history of religion, of the science of governments, of literature, of philosophy, of the science of war, and everything else. What we know and enjoy to-day is due to our knowledge of the past. Our Christianity, our civilization is, to-day, the acme of our knowledge of the past. We are all the time building on the past, without which we could not obtain a solid foundation, but would be building on a sandy foundation. What would we know about our Savior and the sufferings of Jesus of Nazareth on the cross, and the beauties and attractions of Heaven, but for the recorded words in the Holy Bible? What would we know of the world, and its great men, its inventions, its advancements in civilization, and the progress of mankind in everything, were it not for the histories, the monuments, statues and other pyramids, written and erected for the guidance of those to come afterwards?

A nation, a country, a state, a county that has not pride of its noble dead, is composed of a mankind fit only for "treason, strategem, and spoils," and for the habitation of Hell. We have been often asked why we should be interested in writing a history of the by-gone days of Hertford County. Why, they are the most glorious days of our life! All the sunshine, all the hopes, and all the beauties of life are in those days. Ancestors, parents, friends, and other noble men and women, help to make the grand history of this old political subdivision of the State. We are proud of its history; proud of its dead. We love to sing the songs of its praises. A being who has no love for his county and the noble deeds of its dead has no soul. He is like the "lean and hungry Cassius"—dangerous. Let us remember—let us love until the end of time.

When we think of the true and devoted sons of the Colonial days, of the brave and loyal sons of the Revolutionary times, of the determined and self-sacrificing sons of the infant days of the State and Republic, and the gallant and courageous soldiers of the county whenever the liberties, rights and freedom of the people of the States were involved, and the part its great men took in shaping the laws of the country and in the perpetuation of its institutions, we feel like exclaiming, "O, fortunate country, who had such sons to be the herald of thy fame!"

AMERICA.

To know well the child we should know its parents.

Columbus discovered America—the New World—the unknown land—in the year 1492. It was a beautiful part of Nature's landscape. Its coasts, its level lands, its hills and valleys, its magnificent forests, and its grand and placid streams of water filled the hearts and souls of Columbus and his companions with untold and indescribable joy. It was uninhabited, except by wild beasts and savage tribes of Indians. Where the Indians came from we do not know. They seemed to be indigenous to the soil. The Great God of Nature created and placed them here, as he did the beasts of the forest. Columbus returned to the Old World, his native land, and told of the New World he had discovered. He told them of its beauties and its attractions. The popular mind soon became emblazoned with imaginary pictures and pent-up glories and blessings of this fairy land beyond the broad and deep waters. The whole of Europe became excited. Soon, voyages began to be made, in crude crafts, across the billows of the mighty oceans to reach the new land of flowers and take possession of it and make it the home of the free, and the asylum of the oppressed. Old England quickly proceeded to profit by the discovery of Columbus and take possession of this new and far-off land, about which the Old World had become so much aroused by the reports of Columbus, a native of Italy, the land of valor and beauty.

Bancroft's History of the United States is the most delightful treatise on the early and primeval days of the Western Continent the reader can obtain. Of the discoveries of the lands along the musical and poetic borders of the Rio Grande and of the mighty Mississippi Valley, the widespreading lap of the Western Continent, the reader can find no more pleasing and fascinating accounts than Prescott's Histories of Mexico and Peru. Ridpath's recent History of the United States is, also, written in a most interesting style. Its rhetoric is ornate and easy.

The early settlers of the New World experienced great troubles with the native Indians, and many of them were murdered by these wild, barbaric natives. The New World was called America in honor of Amerigo Vespucci, which was an undeserved honor.

CAROLINA.

On the 25th day of March, 1584, Queen Elizabeth of England granted to Sir Walter Raleigh a charter authorizing him to take possession of an extensive territory of land in America, extending from the 33d to the 40th parallel of north latitude, and to people it, and organize a state, to be governed by Raleigh, as lord-proprietor. This territory was called *Carolina*. The granting of this charter was the first step in the work of English colonization in America. Five voyages were made under it, but without success in establishing a permanent settlement. Raleigh's vessels landed at Roanoke Island, where he landed his colonists and attempted to effect a settlement, but the hostility of the Indians was too great. One of his colonies left on the island, consisting of 108, were lost, and no account of them has ever been given. It is known as the "lost colony." The Indians evidently destroyed them. On the 18th day of August, 1585, Virginia Dare was born on this island. She was the first English white child ever born in the New World.

Raleigh finally abandoned his efforts.

Again, on the 20th day of March, 1663, King Charles, the Second, granted a charter for *Carolina* to Edward, Earl of Clarendon, George, Duke of Albemarle, William, Lord Craven, John, Lord Berkley, Anthony, Lord Ashley, Sir George Carteret, Sir William Berkley, and Sir John Colleton, to be known as the Lords Proprietors of *Carolina*. They were granted all the land extending from the north end of the island called Lucke Island, in the southern Virginia seas, and with six and thirty degrees of the north latitude, and to the west as far as the South Seas, and southerly as far as St. Matthias River, on the coast of Florida. The territory of country was not named Carolina in honor of Charles II., as some writers have it, but it was named "Carolina" by John Ribault, a French navigator, as early as 1562.

The Lords Proprietors were invested with power to set up a form of government of their own, to make laws for the government of the people, to hold courts, and do all acts and exercise all other powers desired to gratify their lordships.

The first permanent settlement in *Carolina* is stated by Bancroft to have been made immediately after the expulsion of the Quakers from Virginia in 1662.

On July 30, 1665, King Charles II. granted the same Lords Proprietors a second grant, extending the boundaries of *Carolina* north and eastward as far as the north end of Currituck River, upon a straight westerly line to Wyanoke Creek and so on.

The area of Carolina, under this charter, was a million of square miles, and included a large part of Mexico, all of Texas, all our territory south of 36 deg. 30 min. and west of Arkansas, and the lands now embraced in the States of North and South Carolina, Georgia, Tennessee, Arkansas, Alabama, Mississippi, Louisiana. But the grantees only had possession of a small part of the territory.

In 1669, John Lock, of England, wrote the first constitution for the Proprietary government of *Carolina*. Ashley Cooper, one of the Lords Proprietors, afterwards wrote an amendment to it. But the framework of the whole fabric was too impracticable and metaphysical, and it was never fully put in operation. It was finally abrogated, in 1693, by the Lords Proprietors.

On September 8th, 1663, Sir William Berkley, Governor of Virginia, and one of the Lords Proprietors of the Province of *Carolina*, was directed to visit the settlement on Albemarle, and organize a regular government. He did so. George Drummond was appointed Governor, and a council of six was also appointed, and thus was formed the infant colony thereafter known as *the County of Albemarle*.

NORTH CAROLINA.

In the year 1697 that portion of Carolina lying north of the Santee River became known and recognized as North Carolina, and the southern portion as South Carolina. The County of Albemarle was in North Carolina. Later this colony became subdivided into three counties.

Hertford County was not one of the original subdivisions of the territory of the colony of North Carolina. At the close of the Indian War of 1711, North Carolina was divided into three counties—Albemarle, Bath, and Clarendon. These counties were subdivided into precincts. Albemarle was divided into Currituck, Pasquotank, Perquimans, Chowan, Bertie, and Tyrrell precincts. Bath was divided into Beaufort, Hyde, Craven, and Carteret precincts. Clarendon County had only one precinct, New Hanover. Bertie precinct was carved out of Albemarle County territory in 1722. Northampton County was formed in 1741 from a portion of the territory of Bertie.

GOVERNORS OF THE COUNTY OF ALBEMARLE.

Geo. Drummond, appointed in fall 1663.

Samuel Stevens, appointed in October, 1667; died early in 1674.

Sir Geo. Cartwright, President of the Council, 1674. He returned to England in 1676.

Thomas Miller, appointed, to fill vacancy, in 1677.

CULPEPPER'S REBELLION.

In Nov., 1777, Sir Geo. Eastchurch was appointed Governor of the County of Albemarle, and left England, but when he reached the West Indies he fell in love with a beautiful girl and lingered there. After making known his devotion they were married. He then renewed his journey to North Carolina. When he reached the shores of the new country he found that one Culpepper had, in December, 1677, usurped the government and proclaimed himself governor. Eastchurch tried to suppress Culpepper's usurpation, and secured the aid of the Governor of Virginia, but failed, and thereby by the simple act of a lover, lost his government, and also his life, as he was killed in his effort to assert his authority. Lovers should not neglect their business, as they may lose all, is the lesson here taught.

John Harvey was appointed President of Council in 1680.

John Jenkins, appointed Governor, June, 1680, and died December, 1681.

Henry Wilkinson, appointed Governor February, 1681.

Seth Sothel, appointed Governor 1683. This man, Seth Sothel, was a great rascal. He was expelled as Governor of the County of Albemarle shortly after his appointment. He then went to Charleston, in South Carolina, and, in 1690, was elected Governor of that county, and was there impeached and expelled. An honest public servant is a prize to any people. No mean, insincere, selfish, and untrue man ought ever to be allowed to hold any office or place of trust.

Philip Ludwell, appointed Governor 1689.

Alexander Lillington, appointed deputy Governor 1693.

Thomas Harvey, appointed deputy Governor 1693.

From April, 1693, to 1712, North and South Carolina had the same governors.

Philip Ludwell, appointed 1693.

Thomas Smith, appointed 1693.

Joseph Blake, appointed 1694.

John Archdale, appointed 1695.

Joseph Blake, appointed 1696.

James Moore, appointed 1700.

Nath'l Johnson, appointed 1703.

Edward Tynte, appointed 1706.

Robert Gibbes, appointed 1710.

THE GOVERNORS OF NORTH CAROLINA UNDER THE PROPRIETARY GOVERNMENT FROM 1699 TO 1729.

They took the oath of office as follows:
Henderson Walker, President of the Council, 1699.
Robert Daniel, Deputy Governor, 1704.
Thos. Carey, Deputy Governor, 1705.
William Glover, President of the Council, May, 1709.
Edward Hyde, President of the Council, August, 1710.
Edward Hyde, appointed Governor January 24, 1712.
Thomas Pollock, President of Council, September 12, 1712.
Charles Eden, appointed Governor May 28, 1714, and died March 26, 1722.
Thomas Pollock, President of Council March 30, 1722, and died August 30, 1722.
William Reed, President of Council, September 7, 1722.
George Burrington, Governor, January 15, 1724.
Sir Richard Everard, Governor, July 17, 1725.

Governor Everard remained in office until the Lords Proprietors (excepting John Lord Carteret) sold their interests in the soil and the rights acquired under the charters from King Charles II. to the Crown of England, and thus ended the Proprietary Government of the Carolinas.

THE BRITISH GOVERNORS OF NORTH CAROLINA FROM 1731 TO THE FREEDOM OF THE COLONIES IN 1776.

The dates refer to the time they took the oath of office.
George Burrington, February 25, 1731.
Nathaniel Rice, April 17, 1734.
Gabriel Johnson, November 2, 1734.
Nathaniel Rice, February 1, 1752.
Matthew Roman, February 1, 1753.
Arthur Dobbs, November 1, 1754.
William Tryon, October 27, 1764.
James Hassel, July 1, 1771.
Josiah Martin, August, 1771.

All the governors since Governor Martin have held their offices under the Constitutions of the State of North Carolina.

PRELUDE TO HERTFORD.

The histories of Bertie and Northampton counties constitute a part of the primeval history of Hertford County. So, to truly understand the history of Hertford, we must understand the histories of its mother counties. We want to know the men, the families, who controlled and shaped the destinies and affairs of these mother counties. Many of our ancestors occupied official positions in those counties. We speak of counties. There were only three counties in North Carolina, until 1738. The other sub-divisions of the territory were called precincts. In 1738 the precincts were dignified by the names of counties.

BERTIE PRECINCT.

In 1722, Bertie Precinct was carved out of Albemarle County by the Lords Proprietors under their charters from King Charles the Second. The boundaries were as follows:

"That part of Albemarle County lying on the west side of Chowan River, being a part of Chowan Precinct. Bounded to the northward by the line dividing the government from Virginia, and to the southward by the Albemarle Sound and Moratuck River, as far up as Welsh's Creek, and then including both sides of said river and the branches thereof, and as far as the limits of the government, be, and the same is hereby declared to be erected into a precinct by the name of Bertie Precinct, in Albemarle County."

Later, in 1729, the boundaries of Bertie Precinct were fixed as follows: The Roanoke on the south and west, the State line between Virginia and North Carolina on the north, the Chowan River and Albemarle Sound on the east.

During the governorship of old Gabriel Johnson, some writers put it in 1741 and some in 1743, another act of the Royal General Assembly was passed, establishing out of the territory of Bertie County, the county of Northampton.

The representatives of Bertie County in the Colonial Assembly from the ending of the Proprietary Government in 1729 to the formation of Hertford County in December, 1759, were as follows:

1731-2. Arthur Williams, James Castellow, Col. Thos. Pollock, Isaac Hill, Capt. George Wynns.

1733. The same members, except William Kinchen in place of Col. Thomas Pollock.

1734. Castellow, Williams, Capt. G. Wynns, John Lawson, and John Harrell.

1735-6. The same as above, except John Hodgson and John Harrell represented one vote.

1737-8. Thomas Bryant, John Dawson, John Hodgson, Benj. Hill, James Castellow and Arthur Williams.

1739-40. Benj. Hill, James Castellow, Thos. Bryant, John Dawson and John Browne.

1741-2. Not given.

Northampton is now formed, and Bertie given three members and Northampton two.

BERTIE'S REPRESENTATIVES.

1743. Benj. Hill, James Castellow, and Thos. Bryant.
1744. Benj. Hill, James Castellow, and Thos. Barker.
1745. Benj. Hill, James Castellow, and Thos. Barker.
1746. John Wynns, ———, ———.

Here the colonial records show that there was a breach between Gov. Gabriel Johnson, which had been brewing for sometime, when some of the northeastern counties—Chowan, Perquimans, Tyrrell, Bertie, and others in the east—refused to send members to the Assembly, or rather their members elect would not attend, and the Governor could not get a quorum to transact business. Gov. Gabriel Johnson was an arbitrary and unpopular ruler. His trouble with his eastern counties was that he wanted to deprive them of their proper representation. He met with the same rebellious spirit as did later King George the Third, when he and his aristocracy tried to crush the American colonies and deprive them of proper representation. This deplorable condition continued about ten years. In 1746, John Wynns was the only member of Bertie who appeared. The Governor issued his mandates that the members must attend the sessions and represent the freeholders. But they defied the commands.

The next time we find Bertie and the other indignant counties being represented in full was in 1754.

Bertie sends in 1754-5-6-7-8-9, John Campbell, Thomas Whitnel, and Benj. Wynns.

John Campbell was Speaker of the House for two or more years. He did not attend in 1756 on account of sickness. He lived at Coleraine in Bertie County, and was one of the most distinguished men in the State in his day.

In 1760, after Hertford County was formed, Bertie's members were William Williams and John Hill.

The justices of the peace appointed for Bertie in 1739 were Benj. Hill, Esq., Needham Bryan, Wm. Cathcart, William Kinchen, Peter West, Thos. Bryan, Thos. Handsford, Rowland Williams, Thos. Whitnel, John Prat, James Castellow, John Dawson, and John Edwards.

In 1746, the list of justices of the peace of Bertie County was revised, and George Gould, Wm. Cathcart, James Castellow, Benj. Hill, John Harrell, Needham Bryant, George Lockhart, John Brown, Samuel Scally, Samuel Ormes, George Patterson, Robert Hunter, and Edward Bryan were appointed.

In May, 1759, the list was again revised, and Robert Sumner, Lillington Lockhart, Peter West, Thos. Slater, and James Moore were added to the list.

Thos. Barker, Needham Bryant, Thos. Whitnel, Edward Bryan, and Thos. Turner had become citizens of Northampton County, and could not serve. John Harrell, Jr., had died, and John Harrell, Sr., Robert Hunter, Robert Sumner, William Wynns, Jacob Blount, Robert Hardy, and Peter

2

18   HISTORY OF HERTFORD COUNTY, N. C.

West had been cut off into Hertford County, and were dropped from the list.

Benj. Wynns, Clerk of the Court, was also cut off into Hertford County, and his place was declared vacant. In 1754 the Clerk of the Court of Bertie County was Samuel Ormes. John Prat was Sheriff in 1739.

CHOWAN COUNTY'S REPRESENTATIVES IN THE ASSEMBLY.

1744-5. James Anderson, Henry Baker, and Dempsey Sumner.

1746-7. Peter Payne, Joseph Blount, James Anderson, and John Benbury.

1757-9. Dempsey Sumner, Joseph Blount, Timothy Walton, Joseph Heron and Edwin Vail.

1754-9. Thomas Barker, for Edenton.

1760. Thomas Child, Thomas Barker, Francis Corbin, Samuel Johnston, and Edwin Vail.

JUSTICES OF THE PEACE.

1746. John Montgomery, Esq., James Anderson, Thomas Garrett, Henry Baker, John Sumner, Dempsey Sumner, and William Hunter.

CLERK OF COURT.

1754. William Halsey.

NORTHAMPTON COUNTY.

This county was carved out of Bertie County in 1741-3, and for about twenty years a portion of Hertford County was within her borders, hence we are interested in her political history during that period when we were nursing partly at her breast. Northampton County's first representation in the Colonial Assembly began, so far as we can find from the record, in 1744. Her members being as follows (she was entitled to two):

1744. Samuel Taylor and John Dawson.
1745. John Dawson and James Washington.
1746. Benj. Hill and James McDowell.

HISTORY OF HERTFORD COUNTY, N. C.   19

1747. John Dawson and James Washington.
1748. John Dawson and James Washington.
1749. John Dawson and James Washington.

The same interregnum in the legislative branch of the government was participated in by this county, as in the other counties heretofore mentioned.

Gov. Gabriel Johnson had made himself extremely offensive to the people in the east and their representatives. He was an arbitrary and bad man. In 1754 James Washington and Robert Jones, Jr., were the representatives.

1755. James Washington and Robert Jones, Jr.
1756. James Washington and Robert Jones, Jr.
1757. James Washington and Robert Jones, Jr.
1758. William Murfree and Robert Jones, Jr.
1759. William Murfree and Robert Jones, Jr.

After the passage of the bill creating Hertford County, the county was represented in 1760 by James Washington and Robert Jones, Jr.

The justices of the peace in Northampton County during the twenty years next preceding the establishing of Hertford County were: William Cathcart, William Kinchen, John Dawson, Roland Williams, James Washington, James Maney, William Short, John DeBerry, John Moore, John Drew, Nathan Williams, John Duke, John Gilliam, Osborn Jeffries, John Lamon, William Battle, and Arthur Harris.

SHERIFFS.

1741-52. John Jones.
1752-3.   John Luke.
1754-5.   Nathan Williams.
1755-60. John Jones.

CLERKS OF COURT.

1741-4.   John Edwards.
1744-6.   Robert Foster.
1746-8.   John Hooker.
1748-65. John Edwards.

PUBLIC REGISTER.

James Dancy.

Northampton County was known as the Northwest Parish. But on account of its great length it was, in 1758, divided, by virtue of an act of the Colonial Assembly, into two parishes, namely, Northwest and St. George.

The following vestrymen were named for the Northwest Parish: William Murfree, James Washington, James Turner, Samuel Thomas, Joseph Sykes, Charles Skinner, William Battle, Joseph Smith, Benj. DeBerry, Robert Warren, James Maney, and John Figures.

The vestrymen of St. George were: William Cathcart, John Jones, William Allen, Harwood Jones, Thomas Barrett, William Winborne, Green Hill, John Dukes, William Pace, Thomas Winborne, and William Short.—*State Rec. of N. C., vol. 23—499.*

This new county included all that part of Bertie County bounded as follows: "All that part of Bertie lying north and west of Sandy Run and a direct line from the head of said Run to the head of Beaver Dam Swamp and Meherrin Creek and River." This included the Menola section of St. John's Township, the most of Murfreesboro Township, and the whole of Maney's Neck Township, now in Hertford County, in the boundaries of the new county of Northampton.

HERTFORD COUNTY.

On the 12th day of December, 1758, John Campbell, a member from Bertie in the Colonial General Assembly of North Carolina, presented a petition asking for the erection of Hertford County from the territory of Chowan, Bertie, and Northampton. On the 18th day of December, 1759, Benj. Wynns, one of the members from Bertie, was ordered to prepare and bring in a bill pusuant to the prayer of the petition, which he did, and the same was presented and passed and sent to the Council. On December 19, 1759, it was endorsed and sent to the upper house, where it was first read and passed. The bill was finally passed December 29, 1759, and the county given two members in the General Assembly. The boundary being as follows:

Beginning in Bertie County at the first high land on the northwest side of Mare Branch on Chowan River Pocosin, running thence by a direct line to Thos. Outlaw's plantation, near Stony Creek, thence by a direct line to Northampton County line at the plantation whereon James Rutland formerly lived, then along Northampton County line to the head of Beaver Dam Swamp, then by a line direct to the easternmost part of Kirby Creek, thence down the creek to the Meherrin River; then up the Meherrin River to the Virginia line; then easterly along the Virginia line to Bennett's Creek; then down Bennett's Creek to Chowan River; then across the river to the mouth of the said Mare Branch; and up the branch to the beginning, and all of said territory shall be known as Hertford County, and parish of St. Barnabas.

In 1764 the line between Hertford and Northampton was changed, as follows:

"Beginning on Kirby's Creek, where the dividing line joins said creek, running thence up the creek to the fork thereof (which is in the fork of the Vaughan Mill Pond), then up Turkey Creek to Maple Fork; then by a direct south course till it intersects the present dividing line."

DECADE I.

1760–1770.

Having traced the history of the discovery of America, the settlement of Carolina, the division of Carolina into North and South Carolina, the subdivision of North Carolina into counties and precincts, then precincts into counties, and the establishment of Hertford County, which received its name in honor of Francis Seymour, Marquis of Hertford, a great friend of liberty and of the American Colonies, and who introduced in the House of Lords in 1765 a bill to repeal the infamous Stamp Act; we will now proceed to briefly notice the prominent events in the history of this little but illustrious county of Hertford, and its people who figured in shaping its destiny and perpetuating its fame. This is not to be a general history of the State, but purely a county history. The reader must read other works for general historical information. For convenience, the writer will divide his writings into Decades instead of Chapters.

Arthur Dobbs was made Governor of the Province of North Carolina November 1, 1754, and remained in office until October, 1764, when he was succeeded by William Tryon, October 27, 1764, and who remained in office until he was appointed Governor of New York, June 1, 1771.

The citizenship of the county was of a high type, many of its men had been educated in the schools and universites of the old countries. Its women were beautiful and attractive. Its early settlers were French, Irish, Scotch, and Scotch-Irish principally. Col. James Jones, of Hertford County, was a member of Governor Dobbs' Council and one of the leading men of the Province. He aided greatly in securing the establishment of the loyal and graceful little county of Hertford.

On May 9, 1760, an order for an election of members to represent Hertford County in the General Assembly was

Decade I.—1760–1770.

issued by the Clerk of the Crown. Notwithstanding the writ of election was issued in May, 1760, we find no record showing any representation from Hertford County in the General Assembly until 1762.

The list of the members elected to first represent Hertford County in the General Assembly is given on page 801, vol. 6, Col. Rec., by Col. Wm. L. Saunders, the compiler, as being Messrs. Benj. Wynns and William Murfree; but this is a mistake. The records do not show that Benj. Wynns was ever sworn in or ever took part in the deliberations of the body. Benj. Wynns was during this time Clerk of the Court. The records do show that William Murfree and Henry Winborne presented certificates of election from Hertford County, and they were sworn in and seated as the first members in the Colonial General Assembly of North Carolina from Hertford County. Col. Rec., vol. 6, pages 810 and 916. When the county was formed, Benj. Wynns lived in Winton and was one of the representatives from Bertie, and William Murfree lived near the present site of Murfreesboro, and was one of the members from Northampton. Both of these distinguished gentlemen were cut off from their respective counties and embraced in the territory of Hertford.

The laws of the Colony were enacted by an Assembly composed of freeholders, elected in the several counties. The member was required to be the owner of at least one hundred acres of land, and the voter was required to own in fee at least fifty acres of land, and the King's Council, which was referred to as the Upper House or Council. The Councilmen were appointed by the King, generally upon the recommendation of the royal governor of the Province, and the Council was presided over by the Governor, and sometimes by the Chief Justice.

Hertford County was represented in the Council for some years in the person of Col. James Jones. The colonial members of the Assembly or House were:

1762-63. Henry Winborne, William Murfree.

1764-65.   Benj. Wynns, Robert Sumner.
1766-68.   Benj. Wynns, Matthias Brickle.
1768-70.   Peter Wynns, Edward Hare.
1770-72.   Benj. Wynns, Edward Hare.
1772-74.   Benj. Wynns, Sr., Benj. Wynns, Jr.
1775.   Wm. Murfree, George Wynns.

The Assembly was dissolved, or prorogued, at the will of the Governor. The bills, after passing the House, were sent generally by two members of the House, appointed by the Speaker, to the Upper House or Council. Bills after passing both branches, if of any political importance, were still subject to the approval or disapproval of the King, speaking through his Governor. We will speak briefly now of these representative citizens.

Wm. Murfree was a former citizen of Northampton County, living in that part of Northampton where the present town of Murfreesboro is located, when Hertford County was formed. He first appeared in the Assembly from Northampton as the successor of James Washington, resigned, in 1757, and continued as a member of that body until Hertford was formed, when he became a citizen of Hertford County. Being a man of ability and experience, his new county made no mistake in returning him to the Assembly. He married Mary Moore, of Northampton, and they were the parents of the great warrior and patriot, Col. Hardy Murfree, of Hertford County. He was the second colonial sheriff of this county, and served several years after his return from the Assembly.

Henry Winborne, a substantial planter, living in the central part of the county, was his collegue in the House. Winborne came to the county from Nansemond County, Va., in 1742, with his companion, Bryan Hare, from the same county. They bought from Daniel Hough, of Bertie, 400 acres of land on Meherrin (now Potecasi) Creek, December 8, 1742. A certified copy of the old deed is now in the possession of the author. He was the great-grandfather of the late Maj. S. D. Winborne, of this county.

Decade I.—1760-1770. 25

This was his first entrance in political life. He was a man with a strong and vigorous intellect and was an active and useful member of the House. He was one of the colonial justices of the peace of the county, and served his county well as the presiding member of the Court of Pleas and Quarter Sessions, which was the chief court of the people in those days. He married Sarah Hare, a Quaker lady of Nansemond County, Va. She died about 1759, and they left, as is known, two sons, William and Thomas, and one daughter, Sarah. There may have been other children.

Henry Winborne's daughter, Sarah, married the first Starkey Sharp, and they had two daughters, Sarah and Elizabeth, and one son, Jacob. Sarah married Thos. E. Hare, Elizabeth married Nathan Harrell, and Jacob married a Miss Hunter of Gates County. His son William Winborne and his wife Judith were the parents of the late John Winborne, who lived below Harrellsville. His son Thomas married Sarah Copeland, aunt of James Copeland, who represented the county in the House and Senate in the seventh decade, and they were the parents of Elisha Winborne and Sarah A. Winborne. Elisha married Martha Warren, of Southampton County, Va., and they were the grandparents of the author. Sarah married John Gurley, and their descendants are now living in Mississippi. The author's book, "The Winborne Family," published in 1905, gives a full history of all the old Winborne families in North Carolina. Henry had a brother by the name of Thomas, and probably others, in Northampton County.

Henry Winborne was one of the first two representatives in the legislature from the new county, and his direct descendant, Robert Warren Winborne, was the first Democrat elected in the county, in 1884, to the legislature, after the days of reconstruction and the enfranchisement of the negro in 1868. Another of his direct descendants, B. B. Winborne, the author of this book, represented the chivalrous little county of Hertford in the legislature in 1895 and again in

1905. The first and last stand 143 years apart on the roll. He still has younger descendants in North Carolina and Virginia, bearing his family name to do him honor. Micajah T. Winborne of Alabama, the late Maj. S. D. Winborne of this county, Dr. Robert H. Winborne of Chowan County, Mrs. Britton Moore late of Murfreesboro, and Richard Winborne late of Tennessee, were his great-grandchildren. The old representative and chairman of the county court owned about 1,200 acres of land in the central part of the county, in and around the present town of Union.

Benj. Wynns was a member of the Assembly in 1759 from Bertie, when Hertford was formed. He lived where the town of Winton is now located, and had been a member of the House of Commons from Bertie constantly since 1754, and was a man of great wealth, long experience as a public officer and legislator. He drew the bill to create Hertford County, and was also the author of the bill to incorporate the town of Winton. Before Hertford was formed Mr. Wynns, in 1754, introduced a bill to locate and incorporate a town on his land at Barfields. That failed, and ten years later, while a member from the new county of Hertford, he, in 1764, introduced a bill to establish a town on his land, where the town of Winton is located. The bill passed in 1768, and he donated 150 acres of land for the town, which was named Winton in his honor. Henry Hill, Wm. Murfree, John Baker, Matthias Brickle, Joseph Dickinson, Henry King, and Benj. Wynns were appointed commissioners in the act, to have the town laid off, the streets named, lots numbered, and a map made of the town. Fifty acres were to be set apart for town commons. Godwin Cotton surveyed and plotted the town. This was the first incorporated town in the county, and stood alone in its glory for twenty years. It soon became the centre and the Mecca of Hertford's dignitaries. Benj. Wynns owned all the land and river front from Folly Branch to Hare's mill-race, besides other large bodies of land in the county. He was the first Clerk of the

MICAJAH T. WINBORNE,
Great Grandson of Henry Winborne.
Died in 1843 in Mobile, Ala., of Yellow Fever, aged 23 years.

Decade I.—1760-1770.   27

Court in the county, from 1760-1764, as appears from old deeds found among the papers of the late Maj. S. D. Winborne, and of Oris Parker, Esq., the grandson of the first Peter Parker. John A. Wynns, of Winton, was also very probably the son of Benj. Wynns, Jr.

Benj. Wynns and John Wynns were men of prominence in Bertie Precinct as far back as 1735. They were deputy surveyors under the Surveyor-General of the Crown in 1844, and their depositions were taken on behalf of the Crown to prove charges of corruption against Gov. Gabriel Johnson, for violating the land-grant laws. The offices held by Benj. and John Wynns were of great importance in those days, and only worthy and efficient men were selected to fill them. Both of them were freeholders and on the jury list of Bertie in 1740. John Wynns was Deputy Clerk of the Court of that county in 1741, aged 39. Col. Rec., vol. 4, p. 1117. George Wynns, who was still older, was prominent in Bertie as far back as 1719.

At the General Court for Chowan Precinct, held at Queen Anne's Creek, (Edenton), July 28, 1719, Geo. *Winns* was a member of the grand jury. In 1723 he was a witness in a land suit tried in court, held at A-hot-sky (Ahoskie). April 9, 1724, Winns was appointed a justice of the peace for Bertie Precinct. Was Clerk of the Court of his county, and in 1728 is mentioned in the Colonial Records as captain in the militia. He represented Bertie Precinct, after the Lords Proprietors surrendered their charter rights to the Crown, in the Assembly of the Province in 1731-2-3-4-5-6. John Wynns was in the Assembly from Bertie in 1746. William Wynns was a justice of the peace in Bertie six years prior to the formation of Hertford, and was also a justice in Hertford. George Wynns, Jr., was made Major in the colonial militia in 1764, and entered the Continental Army in 1777. In 1780 he was captured by the British and carried to London and held

---

Note.—Geo. Winns and wife Rose conveyed 150 acres of land on Wiccacon Creek to John Early, July 14, 1714.

as a prisoner of war until the close of hostilities, when he returned to his native county of Hertford. He was a member from his county in the convention of the State in 1788, to consider the ratification of the United States constitution. The Americanized Encyclopædia Britannica has it that Gen. Thomas Wynns was the prisoner. That is a mistake. The General was never a prisoner.

The Wynnses lived in and around Winton, except George Wynns, who lived on the farm on which Dr. R. P. Thomas now resides. Benjamin, John, William and George, Jr. (who was made major in 1764), must have been sons of George Wynns, Sr. Benj. Wynns had a son of the same name, who was Public Register of the county from 1760-64, and Clerk of the Court from 1764-72, and again in 1802, and a member of the Assembly in 1773-74. We do not find John Wynns mentioned in public life after 1746. Peter Wynns was in the Assembly in 1769-70, but after this we lose trace of him.

Benj. Wynns, Jr., left four sons—Benjamin, George, William, and Thomas. The latter was the youngest, and was born about 1758 or 1759, according to the notice of his death, published in the *Raleigh Register* in 1825. His age was given in the *Register* at his death as being about 66 years.

BENJ. WYNNS
The Third.

Benj. Wynns III., left four sons—Benjamin IV., Thomas, James Dean, and William B. Wynns. The U. S. Census of 1790 shows that at that time John A. Wynns, Matthew Wynns, Maj. George Wynns, and Gen. Thos. Wynns, and Wm. Wynns were living in this county and were heads of families. The others had died previous to that date, except Benj.

III. The Wynns families were among the oldest and most

prominent in the county in those days. The official record of the county indicates how they were regarded by their fellow-citizens. The name is printed in various ways in the old colonial and State records. We find it spelt Winn, Wynn, and Wynns. But the old members spelt it Wynns, as shown by their signatures seen by the writer. The name is spelt in the charter of Virginia of 1609, Wynne. Capt. Thomas Wynne, Capt. Peter Wynne, and Capt. Edmond Wynne are there mentioned in the list of grantees in the charter from King Charles II. Of this illustrious family, Col. James M. Wynns, of Murfreesboro, the only surviving son of William B. Wynns, is the only survivor of the older Wynns. He and his brother, the late Thomas P. Wynns, have children living in this county and in Virginia. Col. J. M. Wynns' uncle, Benjamin, has descendants in Florida.

Robert Sumner was a wealthy old bachelor, who lived and enjoyed life at St. John's, where courts in olden times were held. He dressed well, drove fine horses, drank the finest liquors, enjoyed the standard literature of the times, as well as the current news, and was fond of entertaining his friends. He had figured much in public life and was regarded as probably the strongest and ablest of his compeers in Hertford. He was the grand-old-man on all public occasions. Moses and Josiah Sumner, also, lived in that part of the county, and each served as Sheriff of the county at a later period. He was in the first list of justices of the peace for the county, and the presiding officer at one time of the old court of the county. In the next decade the reader will learn more of this lofty old gentleman.

Matthias Brickle lived at the old Daniel Valentine place, near Winton, which is sometimes called Oak Villa. He was one of Hertford's most worthy and valued citizens. He came to the county before its formation. He vied with Col. Robert Sumner for the mastery in the county. He had a liberal education as well as Sumner. He had the advantage of Sumner, however, in that he was the head of a most interesting and intelligent family of sons and daughters. His father, Rev. Matthias Brickle, of Bertie, was the first resident preacher west of the Chowan River. He entered upon his mission about 1730, and preached with great power at old St. John's and at old St. Luke's chapels. The latter chapel was near the present church Buckhorn. Rev. Brickle died about 1758, and Rev. Wm. Gurley succeeded him in his grand work. His son, Col. Matthias Brickle, first married, on November 6, 1748, Rachel Noailles, of a French Huguenot family. By this marriage he reared several children: Sally, who became the wife of Col. Hardy Murfree; James Noailles Brickle, who became a notable physician and a distinguished soldier and legislator. The latter died in Tennessee and was buried by the side of his brother-in-law, Colonel Murfree. William and Matthias Brickle, Jr., were also sons of this marriage. He had several other daughters by this marriage. One of whom married Maj. John Brown, a retired British navy officer, who had located in this county near old St. John's, long prior to the war of 1776. The late James L. Anderson owned the place where Major Brown lived and died. William and Matthias both rose to prominence and distinction in the county and State. Colonel Brickle was the first High Sheriff of the county up to 1766, preceding in that office his worthy contemporary, William Murfree, who was in the office from 1766-1771. Colonel Brickle's wife, Rachel, died February 17, 1770, and some time after that he married Mrs. Nannie Jones, the widow of the second James Jones, of Pitch Landing, and reared several children from this marriage. One of his daughters by his first marriage, married Dr. Bryant Bembury, a celebrated physician, who emigrated to America in 1783, from Clonmel County, Ireland, and located in Hertford County, where his father and his family had preceded him. Dr. Bembury died in Murfreesboro, October 15, 1809, and is buried in Winton in the family burying-ground, between the court-house square and the river. Dr. John Brickle, a noted physician in Edenton,

Decade I.—1760–1770.

a ripe scholar, a philosopher, and an historian, was uncle to Colonel Brickle. Miss Levinia Bembury Brickle, a granddaughter of Colonel Brickle, died in Murfreesboro, July 27, 1799, and was buried in Winton. Godwin Cotton, of Hertford, married Sarah Brown, the daughter of Maj. Jno. Brown, and granddaughter of Colonel Brickle. Maj. John Brown and his wife, Sarah, were also the grandparents of the late John A. Anderson, of Winton, Eliza Brown, wife of the late James M. Trader, of Murfreesboro, Mrs. Polly Everett, who lived near old St. John's, and Dr. Godwin C. Moore. Col. Matthias Brickle died October 17, 1788.

Capt. Arthur Cotton, son of John Cotton of Bertie, whose will was probated in 1727, married Elizabeth Rutland, daughter of James Rutland, who built the house where the boundary lines of Hertford and Northampton corner, and they were the parents of Godwin Cotton, who married Sarah Brown. Godwin Cotton, by his marriage with Miss Brown, reared several children. Their daughter Betsey married Col. John Johnson, once prominent in Bertie, but moved to Hertford County before his death, and died at Mulberry Grove in 1807, near St. John's. They left two children— Rev. Dr. Samuel Iredell Johnson, and Sally Johnson, who afterwards married James D. Wynns, of Hertford County, and uncle to our Col. James M. Wynns. Their other daughter married James Wright Moore, and they were the parents of the late Dr. Godwin C. Moore, the late Mrs. Sallie M. Westray, of Nash County, and the late Mrs. Emeline Le Vert, wife of Dr. Henry B. Le Vert, of Mobile, Ala. It was this distinguished physician, Dr. Le Vert, and his good wife who administered to the comfort of young Micajah T. Winborne, uncle of the writer, during his last illness in 1843, in Mobile, away from his loved ones. He was buried in their private burying ground, and a beautiful monument was erected at his grave by this noble lady and his other friends in his distant home. The goodness in our fellow-man excites admiration. It makes us love to say:

> "There is so much bad in the best of us,
> And so much good in the worst of us,
> That it hardly behooves any of us
> To talk about the rest of us."

Edward Hare, one of the representatives from the county from 1768-72, lived in Maney's Neck, where the late J. W. Barnes resided, and belonged to the prominent Hare family of the county. He and Moses Hare lived in Chowan County in 1740, and afterwards moved to Hertford. Jesse Hare, his brother, was one of the colonial magistrates of the county. Moses Hare lived in the county prior to the Revolution of 1776, and was the father of Jamima Hare, the second wife of Starkey Sharp, the first, (1743-1791). Since writing "The Winborne Family," a further investigation enables the writer to give more information of the Hare family. It is there stated that Thos. E. Hare, son of Edward Hare, who married Henry Winborne's granddaughter, Sarah Sharp, left no children. This was a mistake. They left several sons—John, Jacob, and Starkey S. Hare. John lived in Murfreesboro and often served as an election officer. He married Elizabeth R., the daughter of Lewis Meredith, and left several children—Thomas, John, Emma, Francis, and Eliza E. Hare. Jacob married a Miss Ware, and served the county in the Senate in 1830. Starkey S. Hare first married Mary A. Askew, sister to the late John O. Askew, and after her death he married Mary E. Askew, sister to the late Dr. A. J. Askew, of Bertie. They left two sons—Starkey S. Hare, Jr., and Thomas E. Hare. The former married Susan Brown. These families emigrated to Fayette County, Tenn. The old colonial law-maker, Wm. Haywood, of Edgecombe County, N. C., married Charity Hare, of this county, daughter of Moses Hare. In 1790, Moses Hare, Sr., and Moses Hare, Jr., resided in that part of Gates County which was formerly a part of Hertford.

NOTE.—Edward Hare's will dated May 16, 1772. Bryan Hare, Benj. Wynns, Jr., Isaac Pipkin. and many others, are mentioned. He was the son of Edward Hare of Chowan and wife Mary Scott.

Decade I.—1760–1770.

Col. William Haywood was a colonel in the War of 1776, and married Charity Hare, of Hertford County, in March, 1754. John Haywood (1755-1827), who was State Treasurer for forty years; Sherwood Haywood (1762-1829), U. S. Commissioner of Loans; Wm. H. Haywood (1770-1857), Clerk U. S. District Court, and father of the U. S. Senator, Wm. H. Haywood, Jr.; and Stephen Haywood (1772-1824), planter and State Senator, were sons of this marriage.

PUBLIC LANDINGS.

The King's public landings and places of inspection of flax seed, pork, beef, rice, flour, indigo, butter, tar, pitch and turpentine, staves, headings, lumber, shingles, and other commodities, for sale or export, in the county, were, at the large "warehouses" on Chowan River. Vanpelt's, on Wycacon Creek, and Catharine Creek; Hill's Ferry and Murfree's Landing, on the Meherrin River; Maney's Landing, on Chowan River; Bennet's Creek Bridge; at Mt. Sion, and at Winton, on the Chowan. There were warehouses at each of the above places and an inspector appointed and kept at each place. This was kept up for many years after the War of 1776. The inspectors were appointed annually by the old County Courts up to a short time prior to the Civil War of 1861-'5.

COURT OF PLEAS AND QUARTER SESSIONS.

This Court was abolished in North Carolina by the Canby Constitution in 1868. It existed in England, it was the principal court of the people in Colonial times, and was continued by the State. It was presided over by the justices of the peace of the county. When Hertford County was established in 1759 the act provided that this court should be held by the justices of the Peace on the fourth Tuesdays of May, August, November and February of each year, at Cotton's Ferry, on Chowan River, which is now known as Bar-

3

field. Under the colonial laws, it had jurisdiction to try and determine all criminal offenses, not punishable with death, and to try and determine all civil actions not involving the title to land, and where the amount involved did not exceed forty shillings, proclamation money, all matters pertaining to the settlement of estates, the proof of conveyances, wills and the like.

JUSTICES OF THE PEACE.

The colonial justices of the peace appointed for Hertford County after its formation were: Scarbrook Wilson, Henry King, Jesse Hare, John Brown, John Baker, Henry Hill, John Brickle, Robert Sumner, Henry Winborne, Peter West, and Robert Hardy.

They were appointed by the General Assembly for life or during good behavior, as were all justices of the peace in North Carolina prior to 1868. Whenever any important county business was to be transacted, such as levying taxes, electing county officers, and accepting their bonds, making contracts for the county, and the like, a majority of the justices were required to be present and preside. But other business could be transacted by three justices.

The office of justice of the peace has its origin in ancient times, and has always been regarded as a dignified, honorable and important position. Peace is the very end and foundation of civil society, as Blackstone writes, and the common law of England, as well as the American law, has ever had a special care and regard for the preservation of the peace of society. This officer has been found necessary, through the ages, and is to-day, an indispensable officer in the administration of justice and the orderly enforcement of the laws of society. It is a position of great honor and importance, and every man should feel highly honored when clothed with the dignified and important powers and authority of a justice of the peace. *At common law a justice of the peace had the power, when a felony or a breach of the peace had been committed in his presence, to personally arrest the offender, or command others to do so, and had the same power to prevent a breach of the peace, which was about to take place in his presence. If, however, the crime was not committed in the presence of the justice, he could not arrest or order an arrest, except by his written warrant, based upon oath or affirmation. Such is still the law wherever this office exists.* The Constitution of the United States directs that "no warrant shall issue but upon probable cause, supported by oath or affirmation."

The justice or magistrate was the king's main reliance for the preservation of order, and in America he has been the principal officer in the administration of the laws of organized society.

CONSTABLES.

The office of constable is another important office, finding its origin in the remote days of antiquity. The constable has always been the ministerial officer of the justice's court. He must act whenever commanded by the justice, when acting within his jurisdiction.

In North Carolina, prior to 1868, the counties were divided into military districts, called captain's districts, and in each district was a militia captain, and a constable, appointed by the justices of the peace of the county.

It has been impossible to ascertain the names of any of the constables during this decade. But the other county officers may be found in the "List of Officers" in the back part of this book.

SOME INTERESTING FACTS.

During the colonial times the Assembly selected a list of persons, in each county, qualified for jury service, and only freeholders were selected. In 1740 the following persons were selected for Bertie, some of whom were cut off in 1759 into Hertford, and became ancestors of many of our citizens, viz.: Thomas Jenkins, John Worrell, Benj. Hill, Daniel Dickinson, Edw. Harrell, Abner Harrell, William Hines,

Thomas Barfield, John Taylor, Nich. Tyner, Jr., John Brown, Samuel Harrell, Patrick Carter, Isaac Parker, Edw. Harrell, Jr., William Barfield, John Bird, Edward Bird, William Rosberry, William Jordan, William Boon, James Rutland, Sr., Peter West, Thomas Hayes, James Barfield, Benj. Wynne, Richard Barfield, Thomas Banks, John Griffin, John Beverly, Henry Jones, James Maney, Joseph Bridgers, Nathan Joyner, John Vanpelt, Daniel Vanpelt, Robert Lawrence, James Jones, Benj. Bridges, William Whitley; James Dukes, Josiah Liverman, David Legatt, John Harrell, Sr., and John Harrell, Jr. In Chowan County there were on the jury list of same date, John Vann, William Vann, Edw. Hare, Moses Hare, Henry Baker, and Michael Slaughter. The last four became citizens of Hertford County. Most of these names are familiar names in Hertford County to-day.

COLONIAL MINISTERS.

Rev. Matthias Brickle, Rev. Wm. Gurley, and Rev. John Alexander, of whom King George II. wrote, "He is a curious and eccentric genious, but true to his church."

MILITIA IN HERTFORD.

In 1766, there were in Hertford County 1,393 white men over 18 years of age, capable of bearing arms. At the general muster of the Hertford Reg. of Militia, May 28, 1772, Col. Benj. Wynns made the following report:

"Since last muster day, Lt.-Col. Henry Hill, Capt. Michael Ward, and Capt. Emelius Deming have died. Capt. Sam. Cryer has removed from the county. Commissioned officers in the regiment are: Benj. Wynns, Col.; John Baker, Maj.; James Boon, Capt.; John Harrell, Lt.; Benj. Wynns, Jr., Ens.; Edw. Hare, Capt.; Henry King, Lt.; Isaac Pipkin, Ens.; Robert Sumner, Capt.; John Speight, Lt.; James Hooker, Ens.; Moses Sumner, Capt.; Willis Nichols, Lt.; Gilstrap Williams, Ens.; Benj. Brown, Lt.; George Wynns,

Ens.; Jeremiah Brown, Capt.; Ely Eley, Lt.; Abram Jones, Ens.; James Riddick, Capt.; John Benton, Lt.; Demsey Parker, Ens.; Lawrence Baker, Capt.; Jethro Harrell, Lt.; Jesse Harrell, Ens.; Jesse Williams, Lt.; Hardy Murfree, Ens.; Robert Carr, Lt.; Wm. Stephen, Ens. Officers recommended to vacancies: John Baker, Lt.-Col.; Matthias Brickle, Maj.; Benj. Brown, Capt.; George Wynns, Lt.; Benj. Brown, Jr., Ens.; Jesse Williams, Capt.; Hardy Murfree, Lt.; James Moore, Ens.; Robert Carr, Capt.; William Stevens, Lt.; William Battle, Ens. Non-commissioned officers: 30 sergeants, 30 corporals. 10 drummers, 621 privates, 10 companies."

DECADE II.

1770-1780.

From 1770 to 1775 the Province was in a state of the greatest excitement. The colonists felt that the mother country was cruel and oppressive. Governor Tryon had been a most tyrannical ruler. His previous cruelty to the Cherokee Indians won for him the appellation of the "Great Wolf of North Carolina." The colonists began to entertain the same notion of him. When the English Parliament insisted upon enforcing the Stamp Act in the colonies, and refused to listen to the eloquent appeals of William Pitt (Lord Chatham) in behalf of the colonies, who were being taxed without their consent, and when it became known in North Carolina, the Assembly was in session. The excitement among the members became intense and threatening. Governor Tryon, recognizing the fury ahead, prorogued the Assembly at once. The act was finally repealed, but the feeling between the mother country, the Governor and the colony was such that war was inevitable. The King and Parliament continued their cruelty and refused to listen to the just appeals of the colonies. They began to prepare for war. In 1773, John Harvey, Speaker of the House of Commons, laid before the House resolutions from Virginia and several other Provinces, asking that a committee be appointed to inquire into the encroachments upon the rights and liberties of the colonies by the British Government. The Assembly did so. In August, 1774, Governor Martin protested against these meetings. But the people refused to listen to tyrants, and on August 25, 1774, the first Congress of the people, independent of the King, met at New Bern, composed of delegates from most of the counties. Hertford did not send delegates to this congress. When the delegates assembled, they recognized His Majesty, George III., as the lawful King of Great Britain, and declared their true and faithful

DECADE II.—1770-1780.   39

allegiance to him as their sovereign. But protested in twenty-seven resolutions adopted against their treatment by the mother country, and proclaimed that the very essence of the British constitution was that no subject should be taxed but by his own consent, freely given by himself in person or by his legal representative. The work of this convention was a profound warning to the British Government, that the American colonies, while they claimed no more rights than other Englishmen, yet those rights they intended to enjoy. The resolutions were sent to the King, who paid no attention to them. The colonies seeing that British tyranny would continue, councils of safety were at once provided for the whole Province, and for the several districts. Gen. Lawrence Baker and Day Ridley, of Hertford County, were appointed on the Committee of Safety for the Edenton District. The preparations and preliminaries for a bloody and determined war at once began on both sides. For the resolutions, the reader is referred to vol. 9, Col. Rec., pp. 1043 *et seq*. Edgecombe, Guilford, Surry and Wake counties, and the towns of Hillsboro, Brunswick and Campbelton (now Fayetteville), also, failed to send delegates to this congress or convention.

The next congress or convention of delegates of the people was held at Hillsboro, August 21, 1775. Hertford sent to this convention an able and patriotic delegation, who were, Wm. Murfree, Lawrence Baker, Matthias Brickle, Day Ridley, and George Wynns. Active preparations for war were made. Maurice Moore, William Hooper, Richard Caswell, Joseph Hewes, and Robert Howe were appointed a committee to prepare an address to the inhabitants of the Province, calling upon them to unite in defence of American liberty, and take up arms and assume control of the militia. Col. Rec., vol. 10, p. 164. On September, 1775, the following persons were appointed by this congress, officers from Hertford County: Benjamin Wynns, Colonel; Matthias Brickle, Lt.-Col.; Lawrence Baker, 1st Maj.; George Little, 2d Maj.; Hardy Murfree, Capt. During the war, Major Baker was promoted to the rank of general, and Captain Murfree promoted to the rank of major and later to colonel.

The Provincial Congress next met in the town of Halifax, on April 4, 1776. In that body Hertford was represented by Robert Sumner, Col. Matthias Brickle, Maj. Lawrence Baker, William Murfree, and Day Ridley. Col. Rec., vol. 10, p. 523. Vast preparations were made by this body for the war, and members were pledged to secrecy as to the acts and discussions in congress, under penalty of being expelled and considered an enemy to America. The officers appointed in the provincial militia by the congress of August, 1775, were re-appointed by this congress with same rank. This congress called upon the people to elect delegates to a congress to meet November 12, 1776, to prepare a Bill of Rights and a constitution for the independent and sovereign State of North Carolina.

Hertford County sent to this congress Maj. Lawrence Baker, William Murfree, Robert Sumner, Day Ridley, and James Wright. Col. Rec., vol. 10, p. 913. A committee to draft the Bill of Rights and a constitution reported, and the same was adopted by the congress, and it is a lasting monument to the wisdom, patriotism, and ability of the patriots of North Carolina in those trying and exciting days. Col. Rec., vol. 10, p. 1006.

The war was against tyranny and for liberty, and had been raging for over a year. The first battle was fought at Lexington, Mass., April 18, 1775, which was won by the British, and they moved on to Concord. The country was wild with excitement. Americans were determined and loyal to the cause of liberty. Disloyalty was promptly crushed. The patriotic call to arms was sounded throughout the borders of the colonies, and the patriotic hosts of America responded with all the courage and determination of true lovers of lib-

---

NOTE.—Col. Day Ridley's will dated March 9, 1777, and recorded in Edenton. He speaks of his wife and two sons, Timothy Sharp Ridley and Nathaniel Ridley. Timothy Sharp and Richard Taylor were his executors.

DECADE II.—1770-1780. 41

erty. Little Hertford was not asleep. She furnished her quota of as brave soldiers as ever followed the flag of liberty. Who wrote the Constitution of North Carolina which was adopted by the congress of November, 1776, has been an unsettled question. On the 6th day of December, 1776, Thomas Jones, of Chowan, reported that the form of the constitution was ready. Mr. Wheeler, in his history of the State, says: "It was *believed* to be the production of Thomas Jones, Thomas Burke, and Richard Caswell. But this is disputed by Hardy Murfree Banks, of the Murfree family. He sternly claims that it was written by William Murfree, one of the members from Hertford County, although he was not a member of the committee of the congress to draw a constitution. The Provincial Congress of the State assembled at Halifax in April, 1776, appointed a committee to prepare a civil constitution, and an election was ordered to be held October 15, 1776, to elect delegates to a congress to meet November 12, 1776, at Halifax, to adopt a constitution and form of government. It was during this interval, it is claimed, that William Murfree prepared his form of a constitution. Others did the same. All of them were submitted to the congress when it met. It is claimed by this distinguished gentleman that all the forms submitted were rejected except the one drawn by William Murfree, and that one was finally adopted by the congress.

SOME OF THE HERTFORD COUNTY OFFICERS AND SOLDIERS IN THE WAR FOR INDEPENDENCE IN ADDITION TO THOSE ALREADY NAMED.

Godwin Cotton, aide-de-camp of Col. Howe, of Chowan; Col. Thomas Wynns, Maj. George Wynns; Maj. George Little; Capt. Abner Perry, of St. John's; Capt. Joseph Walker, of Murfreesboro; Capt. Isaac Carter; Capt. Thomas Coleman, of Maney's Neck; Capt. Thomas Brickle, of Winton; Capt. James Jones, of Pitch Landing; Capt. Samuel Jones, of St. John's; Capt. Harry Hill, of Maney's Neck; Lt. John

Winborne, of Winton; Lt. John Baker, of Harrellsville; Henry Winborne, of Winton; Joseph Dickinson, of Winton; Lt. Wm. Murray, Capt. John McGlaughon, Lt. John Harrell.

There were other officers from the county. Some were killed, and others advanced in rank. Some who entered as privates were promoted. It is impossible to give the names of all of Hertford's sons, as the old records do not name the counties from which the soldiers enlisted.

The following are a few additional names, contained in one of Col. Hardy Murfree's reports: Matthias Brickle, Ens.; John Burton, Adjt.; Benj. Baker, David Boon, William Butler, Giles Carter, Cæsar Chavis, John Duke, Thomas Davidson, Boble Gay, Thomas Green, James Hall, Kinchen Hollomon, Richard Johnson, Barnaby Johnson, Jesse Knight, William Knott, Thomas Lassiter, Jacob Lassiter, Dr. William Lewis, Lewis Lilly, John Morgan, Moses Manley, Michæl McKeel, Nottingham Monk, Southam Manley, Marmaduke Moore, James Morgan, Thomas Pierce, Exum Powell, James Pierce, Stephen Ray.

Hertford County furnished ten companies of true soldiers to the war. The county should seek to have a complete roster of her troops.

The American people were true and loyal subjects to the mother country. They loved the old land, its traditions, its history, and its families. But they could not supinely submit to the wrongs and exactions of a bigoted aristocracy. The colonies took up arms against the old country because they were forced to do so. The American people did not belong to a servile race. They breathed the spirit of liberty and of freedom. The courage, bravery, valor, suffering, and love of freedom of the Continental soldiers have never been surpassed in the history of the world. They were the true sons of liberty. Patrick Henry, of Virginia—the immortal Patrick!—when he exclaimed just before the battle of Lexington, Mass., which was the first battle of the war, that "the war is inevitable and let it come. The next gale that sweeps from the north will bring to our ears the clash of resounding arms," etc.—met with a hearty echo and re-echo in the hearts of the American people. These patriots looked to God for help. And while the ways of God are mysterious, yet when they attack, they are like a thunderbolt. Quoting from Ridpath: "The love of freedom was intense, and hostility to tyranny a universal passion" with North Carolinians. In the time of Sothel, it was said of the North Carolinians "that they would not pay tribute *even* to Cæsar."

The soldiers in the War of 1776-1782 from Hertford made a proud record. There were Tories within our borders, as in other counties, but her true sons won laurels on the fields of battle, in the war for freedom from the British yoke of oppression.

William Murfree, of whom we have written, was a gentleman of great prominence and experience in governmental affairs during the colonial days, leading up to the war, and a patriot. He furnished to his county, his State, and to the American army, a son, who made a record that will perpetuate the fame of Hertford County until the end of historic time. This son was Col. Hardy Murfree, who entered the Continental Army as captain, afterwards promoted to the rank of major, and later to colonel, on account of the most gallant service to his country. The revolutionary history of North Carolina, yea, of America, would be incomplete without the sublime military record of this great man. He was in command of the North Carolina troops in some of the most bloody and decisive battles of the war. He was in command of the troops in the campaigns in Pennsylvania and New York in 1778 and 1779. After the Americans had been defeated in the first engagement at Stony Point on the Hudson, in New York, General Wayne determined to make an effort to retake it from the enemy. It looked like a hopeless task, and to attempt it would be like walking in the mouth of hell. The fort was thoroughly fortified and garrisoned, and with a full-armed force on the inside. General Wayne called for Col. Hardy Murfree, with his North Carolina band of patriots to make the assault. Col. Hardy Murfree agreed to lead in the forlorn hope of attacking the fort in the dark hours of the night. General Wayne was about a mile off. Major Murfree, with forty brave and undaunted North Carolinians, advanced along the deadly causeway and hillside to reach the side of the fort where the enemy were not on the lookout. Shortly before midnight, with unloaded guns and fixed bayonets, through a storm of cannon shot and musketry, the gallant band of continentals, with Murfree in the lead, without firing a gun, scaled the heights of the fort and quietly entered the fort and captured every British soldier who had not been bayonetted in the assault. General Wayne and the body of his army was about a mile off, and he received a wound in the head. Some few of Murfree's brave band were also wounded. This was one of the most brilliant feats of arms during the whole war, and filled both armies and the two countries with wonder and admiration. Major Murfree's heroic conduct, gallantry, and soldierly daring on this occasion is referred to by General Wayne in a letter to John Jay, with great appreciation. Major Murfree and his brave and fearless soldiers were like the Saxons, of whom Sidonius, the Bishop of Clermont, wrote as follows: "They overcome all who have the courage to oppose them. They surprise all who are so imprudent as not to be prepared for their attack. When they pursue, they inevitably overtake: when they are pursued, their escape is certain. They despise danger. Tempests, which to others are dreadful, to them are subjects of joy."

Murfree was commissioned lieutenant-colonel, April 1, 1778. Lt. John Winborne, of Hertford County, who was under the command of Colonel Murfree and was one of the brave forty continentals, died from a wound received in this

---

* NOTE.—Some writers fix the number at 80. While Maj. Murfree was moving in the rear Gen. Wayne and Col. DeFleury assaulted the Fort from other directions. The British lost in the engagement 63 killed and 543 captured. The Americans lost 15 killed and 83 wounded.

miraculous feat of daring soldiers. Henry Winborne, of the same county, the oldest known North Carolina Winborne, and the great-grandfather of Maj. S. D. Winborne, and who enlisted in the Continental Army in Capt. Jos. Walker's company, May 24, 1777, was also one of the immortal forty, who was willing to throw himself in the jaws of death to save the honor of his country. He came out, with his leader, Colonel Murfree, unhurt. We imagine that we can see this strong, courageous and patriotic old private, climbing the heights of the fort, and with his bayonet-spiked rifle, weeding his way through the enemy.

Colonel Murfree, who lived in Murfreesboro, married, February 17, 1780, Sarah, the accomplished daughter of Col. Matthias Brickle, of Hertford County, and reared three children—one daughter, who married a Mr. Burton, and two sons, Matthias Brickle Murfree and William Hardy Murfree.

Mrs. Burton and her husband, and Matthias B. Murfree, moved to Tennessee, where they settled. William H. Murfree married Elizabeth M. Maney, of Murfreesboro, his native town, remained in Murfreesboro until about 1823, when he moved to Tennessee.

Maj. John Brown, of St. John's, a retired British navy officer, immigrated to America some years before the war, and settled in the St. John's section in Hertford County, and married before the war another of the daughters of Col. Matthias Brickle. He was an uncompromising Tory. He was too old to enter the war, but had several sons. His son John Brown, Jr., did not share his father's sentiments, but was a loyal and patriotic continental. His father was so bitter in his opposition to his son's sympathies, that the latter went to Virginia and joined a Virginia company, and fought under the command of Gen. La Fayette. When the war was over he returned to his father's home, but the old gentleman was so unforgiving and so unreconstructed, that young John Brown left and made his home in Georgia, and is the ancestor of some of Georgia's most distinguished people.

During the earlier days of the war, Col. Benj. Wynns, of Hertford County, the great-grandfather of our Col. James M. Wynns, was in command of the continental troops at Norfolk, Va., and there met Governor Dunmore, the former British governor of Virginia, who was in command of the British forces. In a conflict between the two armies, Colonel Wynns succeeded in driving Dunmore back in a speedy retreat. After the victorious campaign of Colonel Wynns' forces around Norfolk, he returned through the Albemarle section, which had been in a great state of excitement on account of the threatened invasion of that section by the unscrupulous Dunmore and his army, and he (Colonel Wynns) was met with great rejoicing among the people and was rewarded with the unbounded praises of the Americans along his route. Our Hertford County soldiers fought for the cause of liberty, not only on the soil of Pennsylvania, New York, and Virginia, but also on the soil of South Carolina, on her own soil, and finally at Yorktown, when Cornwallis surrendered his arms.

The war ended in 1782. But the British were still mad. God was with the oppressed, and it seems that He has touched the Stars and Stripes with His holy hand.

The war between the British Government and the American colonies for liberation of the colonies from the British Crown was the most important war and produced grander results than all the previous wars of recorded time. It was the Greater Magna Charter of the world.

The Americans were taught to beware of the Englishmen. Eternal vigilance became the watchword of the American people. A strong militia was kept organized, and the best navy that the government was able to support was kept equipped, for action against the old enemy. It was during this period when the American victories were being closely guarded, that some of her younger sons were advanced in her well-organized militia and State troops, and received their military titles.

DECADE II.—1770-1780.   47

While the war was raging, the State of North Carolina kept up the legislative branch of its government. Richard Caswell was elected Governor of the State by the convention of November, 1776, and continued in office until 1779. Hertford was represented in the Senate in 1777, 1778 and 1779 by her grand old bachelor of St. John's, Robert Sumner. And in the House of Commons in 1777 by Joseph Dickinson, an Irishman, who came among us in 1740, and the father of the late eminent son of the county, Gen. Joseph F. Dickinson, and by Joseph Garrett, who lived on the north side of Chowan River, and who represented Gates County in the House in 1780. In 1778, by William Baker, a brother of Gen. Lawrence Baker, and James Maney, the second, of Maney's Neck. And in 1779 by William Wynns, a great-uncle of James M. Wynns. William Wynns lived west of Winton, at the James Jordan place, the parental home of Mrs. A. I. Parker, of Winton, and by Nathan Cotton, who also lived near Winton. These sessions of the General Assembly were held under the new Bill of Rights and new Constitution, adopted in November, 1776. The Constitution provided for a General Assembly, to be composed of a Senate and a House of Commons. It will not be amiss to copy a few sections of this famous document.

"1. That the legislative authority shall be vested in two distinct branches, both dependent on the people, to-wit, a Senate and a House of Commons.

"2. That the Senate shall be composed of representatives, annually chosen by ballot, one from each county in the State.

"3. That the House of Commons shall be composed of representatives annually chosen by ballot, two from each county, and one for each of the towns of Edenton, New Bern, Wilmington, Salisbury, Hillsborough, and Halifax."

A senator was required to have usually resided in the county for at least one year immediately preceding his election, and the owner of 300 acres of land in fee.

NOTE.—William Wynns married Zilpha Blanchard January 2, 1752.

A member of the House was required to have usually resided in the county for at least one year preceding his election, and have possessed 100 acres of land in fee for at least six months prior to his election.

Only freeholders, 21 years of age, owning 50 acres of land, and who had been citizens of the county for twelve months immediately preceding the day of election, were allowed to vote for a senator. All freemen, 21 years of age, who had resided in the county 12 months immediately preceding election day, and who had paid his taxes were allowed to vote for a member of the House of Commons.

The General Assembly elected the Governor and other State officers, and appointed the Justices of the Peace for the counties, who held their offices for life or during good behavior. In 1779 the county of Gates was formed out of Hertford, Chowan and Perquimans. All that part of Hertford County bounded by Bennett's Creek, the southern boundary of Virginia, and the Chowan River was made a part of Gates, and all of Chowan and Perquimans counties lying north of Catharine and Warwick Creeks was, also, placed in the new county of Gates.

By this use of the political knife, Hertford County lost some of her most valued citizens. For the county officers during this period, see List of Officers of the county, in the back of the volume.

JUSTICES OF THE PEACE.

After North Carolina became a sovereign State the General Assembly, on December 28, 1778, appointed the following justices of the peace for Hertford County: Col. Matthias Brickle, Maj. George Little, Gen. Lawrence Baker, James Wright, William Murfree, James Boone, John Harrell, John Northcott, James Riddick, Edward Hare, Josiah Sumner, and Benj. Brown, Esquires.

GATES COUNTY.

In the year 1779 the county of Gates was carved out of Hertford, Chowan and Perquimans counties, taking from Hertford all that part of her territory lying north of Chowan River, and between said river, the southern boundary of Virginia, and Bennett's Creek. This took from Hertford County some of her distinguished men, such as Gen. Lawrence Baker, John B. Baker, James Garrett, and many others of her most distinguished families, and men who had given luster to her history. Thereafter William Wynns and Henry Winborne were added to the list of the justices for Hertford County. Wynns resigned in 1783, and Thomas Winborne, the son of Henry Winborne, was appointed. In 1789, Henry Winborne and his son, Thomas Winborne, were among the justices selected to hold the county courts. Henry was then in his 69th year and Thomas in his 32d year.

COURTS OF GENERAL JURISDICTION.

In 1774, the colonial assembly established in the Province a Court of Oyer and Terminer, to be presided over by the Chief Justice and two other justices of the Province. This court was given general jurisdiction to try all matters and to hear appeals from other courts. The terms of this court for Chowan, Perquimans, Pasquotank, Currituck, Bertie, Tyrrell, Hertford, and Martin counties, were held in Edenton on the first days of July and January of each year. Hon. John Montgomery, of Tyrrell, who was for a long while Attorney-General in the Province, was appointed Chief Justice by the King to succeed Chief Justice Wm. Smith in 1740, who had returned to England. Montgomery was succeeded as Attorney-General by Jos. Anderson, Esq., of Chowan, and as Chief Justice by Geo. Berry. The latter in 1767 was succeeded by Martin Howard. Chief Justice Maurice Moore and Richard Henderson as Associate Justice presided at the sessions of the new court. This court was superseded, in 1806, by the Superior Court, two terms of which were required to be held annually at the court-house in each county. The first term of the Superior Court ever held in Hertford County, was held in Winton in September, 1806, and presided over by Judge David Stone, of Bertie County. Prior to the establishment in 1774 of the Court of Oyer and Terminer, there was no court of general jurisdiction in the Province. The former Superior Court was abolished in 1773, on account of trouble between Governor Josiah Martin and the Assembly. The Superior Court for each county still exists in North Carolina, presided over by a district judge, and the criminal docket prosecuted on behalf of the State by a district solicitor, except that the attorney-general of the State was required to perform the duties of solicitor in the third district, in which Wake County was located, up to 1868. After that date a solicitor was required to be elected in each district. W. N. H. Smith, of Hertford County, succeeded David Outlaw, of Bertie County, as Solicitor of the district in 1847, and Smith was succeeded in 1857 by Elias C. Hines of Chowan. Hines was succeeded in 1863 by Jesse J. Yeates, of Hertford, and Yeates was succeeded in 1867 by Mills L. Eure, of Gates. The judges and solicitors, prior to 1868, were elected by the General Assembly; since that date they have been elected by the people. The Superior Court judges have always been required in North Carolina to rotate and hold the courts of a different district each spring and fall, except the period between July, 1868, and 1876. Since 1868, Hertford County has not been allowed to remain in any judicial district long enough for any of her sons to aspire to judicial honors in the district.

From 1773 until after the Revolutionary War, there were but little court facilities for the people. The country was in a state of chaos and uncertainty, as it was during the Civil War between the States, from 1861-1866, that trials of civil matters between citizens were almost absolutely suspended, and only matters pertaining to the public welfare occupied the attention of the people.

RICHARD WINBORNE.
Youngest Son of Elisha Winborne, and Grandson of Thomas Winborne,
and great grandson of Henry Winborne.
Died in 1862 in LaGrange, Tenn, aged 33.

DECADE II.—1770-1780.

GEN. LAWRENCE BAKER.

GEN. LAURENCE S. BAKER.
1861-5.

In the colonial and Revolutionary times of the American colonies, Hertford County's sons ranked with the best of the land. If space would permit it would afford the author wonderful pride to write the biography of each of her great men. He has read so much about these patriots, that he feels that he lived with them and saw them in all their grandeur. But we are compelled to content ourselves with a brief notice of them.

Among that galaxy of patriots and high-born gentlemen, none stood out more prominent than Gen. Lawrence Baker, whose principal home and plantation was located in that part of Hertford County lying north of Chowan River, at Buckland, not far from the present town of Gatesville.

Gen. Lawrence Baker sprang from a long line of noble ancestors. In 1644, Lawrence Baker came from the old country and settled in Surry County, Va. He served in the House of Burgesses from 1660-1676, and died in 1681, leaving a son, Henry, who settled in Isle of Wight County, Va., and there died in 1712, leaving also a son, Henry, who lived at Buckland, in Chowan County, N. C., but which was cut off into Hertford County when it was established in 1759. His wife was Miss Angelico Bray. At his death in 1739, his son Henry became the owner of Buckland. This Henry married Katharine Booth, of Southampton County, Va., and also lived and died, in 1770, at the old Buckland homestead, leaving surviving four sons—William, Henry, Bray, and Lawrence. Henry and Bray died young without ever marrying, so far as we can learn. William, under the old law of primogeniture, inherited the old home, Buckland; and married Judith Norfleet, the daughter of our oldest Marmaduke Norfleet. They left children. Lawrence Baker became the owner of "Cole's Hill" plantation, not far from Buckland, then in Hertford County, and married Anne Jones, daughter of Capt. Albrighton Jones, of Southampton County, Va. Captain Jones came from Wales and married the daughter of Col. Charles Simmons, of England. Gen. Lawrence Baker left one son by this marriage, Dr. Simmons J. Baker, who afterwards became distinguished in this State as Senator from Martin County, and two daughters—Elizabeth and Agatha. His first wife having died, he married Maria Burgess, a daughter of Rev. Thomas Burgess, an Englishman, who lived in this country at different times, in Southampton and Nansemond Counties, Va., and in Halifax County, N. C. General Baker left by this marriage one son, Dr. John Burgess Baker, and one daughter, Martha Susanna Baker. While the General's plantation and home was at "Cole's Hill," he spent much of his time around Murfree's Landing. After he was cut off into Gates County in 1779, he continued his visits to the old place of his many joys in the palmy days of his useful manhood.

Buckland was first claimed by Nansemond or Upper Norfolk County, Va., but the survey of the boundary line between the Provinces of Virginia and North Carolina in 1727 threw it in Chowan Precinct, N. C. In 1759 it was in Hertford, and in 1779 it was included in the boundaries of Gates County.

General Baker was one of Hertford's delegates to the Hillsboro Convention of August 21, 1775, and he and Day Ridley, of Hertford, were appointed on the Committee of Safety in the Edenton District. He was also one of her delegates to the Halifax Congress of April 4, 1776, and by that body appointed First Major in the Continental Army, and was again a delegate from his county in the Congress of November 12, 1776, that framed and adopted the first Bill of

Decade II.—1770-1780. 53

Rights and first Constitution of the State. In all of these important patriotic bodies his wise counsel was of the greatest value. During the session of the Congress of November, 1776, he was excused from further service, that he might engage in the active duties of an officer on the battle fields. In 1778 he, with other such men, was named by the Assembly of his State as one of the Justices of the Peace of his county. The best men in these days filled these places. He much regretted being cut off from his native county. He loved the name of Hertford.

After the war he was made General in the State Troops, which office he held for some years. The last office he filled was Clerk of the Court in Gates County, which office he was filling when he died, about 1806. During the same time Gen. Isaac Pipkin, of Gates, was Public Register. He still has a granddaughter, Mrs. Susan J. Myrick, living in Murfreesboro, and grandsons, Dr. Richard Baker, of Hickory, N. C., and Gen. Lawrence S. Baker, of Suffolk, Va., whose likeness appears above. The latter was one of the famous generals of the late Confederate States Army, and a granddaughter, Mrs. Edw. Neal, now of Washington, N. C.; all of whom are over 84 years of age and yet are active and in full possession of all of their faculties. His grandson, William J. Baker, late of Norfolk, Va., has children living in that city.

Dr. Simmons J. Baker resided in Martin County, N. C. He was educated in Scotland, and was an eminent physician and a wise and intelligent legislator from that county. He was in the House of Commons from Martin County in 1814 and 1815, and in the Senate in 1816, 1817 and 1818.

Dr. John B. Baker married Mary Wynns Gregory, and resided at his father's place in Gates County, and represented that county in the House of Commons in 1811 and in the Senate in 1818, 1820 and 1822.

DECADE III.

1780-1790.

The war is still raging. General Cornwallis, with his army in South Carolina, is winning victories over the Continentals, under the command of General Gates. Cruel Tarleton is murdering prisoners. The American nation is almost bankrupted; the Continental soldiers are poorly clad and fed, and they are gloomy. General Greene is put in command of the Continentals in the South, in place of General Gates. South Carolina and Georgia are in possession of the British, who are cruel and oppressive to the people. The British next invade North Carolina. The first battle occurs October 7, 1780, on King's Mountain, and Colonel Campbell, with his Continentals, wins a great victory. This encouraged the Americans. Active war then ceased for two or three months. The Continentals rested and became ready to renew the conflict. Benedict Arnold, who had been made Major-General by Congress in 1777, after the battles of "Bemis' Heights," turned traitor, was court-martialed, convicted and severely reprimanded by General Washington. Afterwards he was allowed to command the American troops at West Point. He soon again traitorously arranged with Sir Henry Clinton to surrender West Point, its garrisons and stores, to the British, in consideration of 10,000 pounds and a promise of being made a Brigadier-General in the British Army. His plans were frustrated, but he made his escape on the *Vulture,* an English war vessel. Great Britain was not only involved in trouble with the Colonies, but was in disfavor with France, and also became involved in trouble with the Dutch government. General Greene, after the battle of King's Mountain, and after resting his men and recruiting his army, divided it into two divisions: the Western Division was placed under the command of General Morgan, who proceeded to pursue Cornwallis and Colonel Tarleton in South Carolina, and the British met inglorious defeat in every engagement. The two armies next encountered at Guilford Court-house, and the Americans again won.

Cornwallis becoming disheartened, leaves for Virginia soil. The Continentals continue the pursuit and struggle until Cornwallis, on October 18, 1781, surrendered to the triumphant Continental Army. On the next day the terms of surrender were signed, and General Cornwallis led the whole British Army out of the trenches around Yorktown into an open field, "where, in the presence of the allied ranks of France and America, 7,247 English and Hessian soldiers and 840 sailors laid down their arms, delivered their standard and became prisoners of war." The British still have control of South Carolina and Georgia. The King's army evacuated Savannah July 11, 1782, and Charleston December 14, 1782. Thus ended the great war for liberty.

Preliminary Articles of Peace between Great Britain and the United States were executed November 30, 1782, at Paris. On September 3, 1783, a final treaty of peace was entered into at Paris between all the warring nations. In "The Treaty of 1783" the American States were recognized as independent sovereign States. Great Britain re-ceded Florida to Spain, and all the remaining territory east of the Mississippi River and south of the Great Lakes was surrendered to the United States. The boundaries of the Carolinas extended from the Atlantic to the Mississippi River. The thirteen original States covered all of this territory. This territory of land has been subdivided into States, until we now have embraced within the borders of the first thirteen States the following additional States: Tennessee, Mississippi, Alabama, Kentucky, Illinois, Wisconsin, Michigan, Ohio, Indiana, West Virginia, Vermont and Maine. The State of Florida was ceded to the United States by Spain in 1819.

56   HISTORY OF HERTFORD COUNTY, N. C.

After the Treaty of Peace there arose the momentous questions with the victorious Americans of securing and retaining the results of their struggles, and of forming a general government between the States for their mutual protection.

Liberty, like the Goddess of Justice, needs to be guarded. Eternal vigilance is to be the watchword of the God-favored Americans. The property of the Tories and traitors is to be seized to help pay the great war debt with which the country was burdened. The wisest statesmanship was needed. The old Articles of Confederation between the States were too loosely drawn in 1776 to afford the protection needed by the States. The sovereign States were willing to join in a close compact, but were jealous of the plans of some of the leaders. They had been once pinioned to the British government, and they were careful how they pledged their rights. The Congress of the United States, which was holding its sessions under the Articles of Confederation, drew up a Declaration of Rights and a Constitution for the thirteen American States, and submitted it to the States for adoption.

As before stated, this is not intended to be a general history, so the reader should refer to some general history for a more accurate detail of the movements of the country during this period.

North Carolina called a convention to meet in Hillsborough on the 21st day of July, 1788, to consider the Bill of Rights and Constitution, drawn for the American States to adopt and ratify. This convention was composed of 288 members. Hertford County sent as her delegates Maj. George Wynns, Gen. Thomas Wynns, Rev. Lemuel Burkitt, Maj. William Little and Maj. Samuel Harrell. After an exciting session, the Convention refused to adopt the Bill of Rights and the Constitution, and adjourned, members returning home to consult their constituents.

The State in 1789 called another convention to meet in Fayetteville, on the 2d day of November, 1789, to again

Decade III.—1780-1790.

consider whether North Carolina would join the Union. The delegates met. Many of the objections that existed to the Bill of Rights and Constitution, submitted in 1788, had been removed by amendments, and this Convention ratified and adopted the same, and North Carolina became a devoted member of the Union. Hertford County sent to this Convention some of her ablest statesmen—Gen. Thomas Wynns, Robert Montgomery, Esq., Col. Hardy Murfree, Henry Hill, Esq., and Henry Baker, Esq. North Carolina was next to the last of the thirteen original States to join the Union. Gov. Samuel Johnson, of Chowan County, was president of both conventions. Maj. George Wynns and Gen. Thomas Wynns were brothers, and also brothers of Benjamin Wynns, Jr., and William Wynns. Thomas was the youngest of the four brothers, and was colonel in the latter part of the War of 1776-'82. He was made general in the State troops after the war. George was first made Major in 1764, in the Colonial militia.

Rev. Lemuel Burkitt was a profound and eloquent Kehukee Baptist divine, and was one of the ablest men in the Convention. He was well versed in the history of the long struggles of the Baptists and Quakers for Higher Liberty and freedom of conscience, and he pointed out the dangers that might follow by an adoption of the Bill of Rights and Constitution as then submitted. This grand old man lived near old St. John's. Some of his writings on the Old Testament are at this day referred to as among the clearest explanations of that Great Book. We are unable to give his ancestry. We find, however, in 1720 and 1721 and later, the names of John Burkitt, Sr., and John Burkitt, Jr., mentioned among the inhabitants of the Albemarle section.

Maj. Samuel Harrell was on the jury list in Bertie in 1740, and had often served his county in the capacity as Clerk of the Court, and was made major in the State troops after the war, and resigned the office in 1783. The old veteran private soldier, Henry Winborne, who was one of the immortal forty that climbed the walls of the fort at Stony Point, was appointed major to succeed Samuel Harrell. William Little was brother of Maj. George Little, of Maney's Neck. Of this family we write in the 5th Decade. A new delegation was sent to the second Convention in 1789, except Gen. Thomas Wynns.

Robert Montgomery lived near Montgomery's Mill, in this county, and was the owner of that mill. He and his wife are buried there at his old homestead. He was a lawyer of splendid ability. He was a descendant of John Montgomery, of Tyrrell County, and afterwards of Edenton. John Montgomery was Attorney-General under the King for a number of years, and succeeded William Smith as Chief Justice about 1740.

Col. Hardy Murfree was the hero of Stony Point, and a great man. He had served his country gallantly in war. He served his State as Commissioner of Confiscated Property in the Edenton District for ten or more years after the war, and was holding this office when he was in the Convention. This was his first civil office. He was an able member of the Convention, and was said to be one of the handsomest men of his day, and was regarded by his State as one of its greatest soldiers, statesmen, and patriots. He was appointed also by the Legislature of 1784 as one of the commissioners to have the Albemarle Sound cleaned out to lessen the dangers of commerce. He lived on the hill in Murfreesboro, near the river. In 1790 he was the largest slave-holder in the county, and his friend, Maj. Henry Winborne, was the second (See Census of 1790). For some years they worked their slaves together in subduing the forest and cultivating the soil, and making and selling tar, pitch, turpentine, and tobacco, which were the most profitable enterprises in those primeval days of American Statehood. Colonel Murfree, who had received grants of large bodies of land in the territory, which afterwards were embraced in the State of Tennessee, moved to that State from Murfreesboro, in Hertford

County, in 1807, and settled on Murfree's Fork of West Harpeth River, near the town of Franklin, Tenn. His wife died five years before he left Hertford County, and he only lived about two years after reaching Tennessee. He died in 1809, and was buried in his adopted soil with great Masonic and military form and ceremony.

On this occasion Gov. Felix Gundy, of Kentucky, delivered a most eloquent oration on the life, character, and public services of this great American. The Nashville papers, in speaking of the occasion, said: "The surrounding hills were covered with vast numbers of people, and the awful silence which pervaded such an immense crowd evinced the feelings of the spectators for the memory and virtues of the deceased. Colonel Murfree was said to be really the last survivor who commanded a regiment during the Revolutionary War."

He was the eldest child of William Murfree and wife, Mary Murfree, *nee* Moore. Colonel Murfree's eldest son, William Hardy Murfree, remained in Murfreesboro, N. C., and married Miss Elizabeth M. Maney. To this distinguished man we may again make reference.

Henry Hill lived at his father's old home at Hill's Ferry, on the Meherrin River. His and his father's names, the author has found, were sometimes spelt *Harry Hill*. His grandfather was Harry Hill. He owned a large landed estate reaching far down the river, taking in the farm of Miss Sallie Warren. He had served his people before and after this time in places of public trust. He had only one child, a daughter, who married a lawyer, Harry W. Long, who were the maternal grandparents of our George Cowper, Esq., of Winton.

Henry Baker was a brother of John Baker, and they were sons of William Baker, of Buckland, nephews of Gen. Lawrence Baker, and lived in Winton. Both were strong and able men, and ranked with the best. The Bakers of the lower part of our county are descendants of these men.

Pleasant Jordan, who represented the county in the Senate in 1780, lived near Winton, and was the father of Abner Jordan and David Jordan, and the grandfather of the later Col. Pleasant Jordan, of Winton. One of his daughters married Capt. Abner Perry, of revolutionary fame, and another one married Capt. James Frazier, the Tory, of Frazier's Cross Roads, and father of John Hamilton Frazier.

Abner Jordan by his marriage left two sons, William and James. David Jordan married a Miss Kinsey, and they left two sons, Kinsey Jordan and Pleasant Jordan, and one daughter, Matilda. Kinsey Jordan was for a long time a justice of the peace in the county. He was a large and portly old bachelor, and greatly enjoyed entertaining his gentlemen friends. Pleasant Jordan, the second, married the daughter of Thomas Weston, of Northampton County. They were the parents of the late Dr. Joseph Perry Jordan, Mrs. Geo. R. Branch, of Northampton County, and Mrs. Etta P. Deloatch, of Northampton, widow of the late James I. Deloatch. James Jordan married Miss Mary Williams, and they left four sons—Joseph J. Jordan, the late Sheriff of the county; Richard Jordan, who died in Florida; John Jordan, who was killed some years ago by the falling of a tree, and William Jordan, of Winton, and two daughters—Pattie, the wife of A. I. Parker, Esq., of Winton, one of the County Commissioners, a justice of the peace, president of the Farmers and Merchants Bank of Winton, and the pleasant and accommodating hotelist at the county seat. This hotel has had for its proprietors Joseph F. Dickinson, James Copeland, W. F. Bynum, Pleasant Jordan, and Joseph J. Jordan.

James Jordan's other daughter, Mary, married Wade H. Garriss, of Murfreesboro. They are both dead, but have two daughters living—Mrs. Susan R. Deloatch, of Jackson, N. C., and Mrs. John P. Mitchell, of Winton, the parents of James R. Mitchell, Esq., a young attorney in the county.

David Jordan's daughter Matilda married William Shaw, who moved from Bertie County to Hertford about 1830 and settled near Bethlehem Church. They are dead, but have two sons living in the county—John S. Shaw and William P. Shaw, merchants in Winton.

W. P. SHAW, ESQ.

W. P. Shaw, Esq., is one of our most prominent citizens, and has been for a number of years a leading and useful man in the county. He was born October 13, 1842. His parents were not able to give him the educational advantages they desired, but he made good use of his opportunities. He attended the public schools in his neighborhood, and the Union Male Academy at Harrellsville, in his native county, a school of high standing, and for years presided over by Prof. Edwin Everts, a cultured and scholarly gentleman from New Hampshire as principal, and Prof. C. F. Lyon as assistant. Shaw was a gallant Confederate soldier for three years and lieutenant in Capt. William Sharp's Co. D, Fourth North Carolina Cavalry. He was with his company in the Army of Northern Virginia in many of the bloody engagements of the war, 1861-'65, and remained in the thickest of the fight until his great leader, the immortal R. E. Lee, surrendered at Appomattox. When he returned in 1865 from the war he located in Coleraine, in Bertie County, where he was engaged in the mercantile business for four years. In September, 1869, he married Mary R. Askew, daughter of John O. and Sarah A. Askew, at Pitch Landing, in his native county, and returned to Hertford County and located in Winton, where he and his brother John have since been engaged in the mercantile pursuits. Lieutenant Shaw has three children—W. P. Shaw, Jr., Mrs. D. R. Britton, and John A. Shaw, by his marriage. In politics Lieutenant Shaw has always been an unwavering Democrat. He was Mayor of his town from 1873 to 1877, when he resigned to accept the position of one of the presiding officers of the Inferior Court of his county—a court of limited criminal jurisdiction—which position he held with much credit to himself and his county until 1886. He was one of the two Senators in the General Assembly of the State from the First Senatorial District from 1886 to 1890, where he served on a number of the most important committees and as chairman of the Committee on Education. He was one of the promoters of the State Normal College at Greensboro, and for several years was one of its directors. As chairman of the Board of Education of his county for several years and as one of the trustees of the Chowan Baptist Female Institute, he has succeeded in making himself a recognized leader in his county. Mr. Shaw after the war began the study of law, but abandoned it without obtaining license. He is a refined and courteous gentleman.

STATE OF FRANKLAND.

Not long after the close of the War of Independence, North Carolina found herself involved in a serious rebellious trouble with some of her own citizens. I have heretofore spoken of the three political divisions of the State, one of which was Clarendon, with only one precinct, New Hanover. This county of Clarendon embraced the whole western part of North Carolina, and the present State of Tennessee to the Mississippi River. A great portion of the land was unknown and was only inhabited by savages and wild beasts. At the close of the Revolutionary War the United States found themselves burdened with a heavy debt, and their creditors were somewhat impatient. So Congress called on the States to surrender to Congress their unoccupied lands, that they might be sold to settlers and granted to creditors, in payment of their debts. North Carolina responded to this patriotic call.

In April, 1784, the General Assembly at Hillsborough passed an act authorizing her delegates in Congress to offer a deed for North Carolina's western territory, to help discharge these obligations. Some of her citizens objected, and in August 23, 1784, a convention of the discontents met in Jonesboro to take some action about the matter. John Sevier was chosen president, and Langdon Coster was clerk of the Convention. This body promptly dispatched a messenger to Congress to get it to accept the offer of the State and to make an independent State of the territory.

The General Assembly met in October, 1784, and repealed the offer to Congress. This exasperated Sevier and his followers, so they met again at Jonesboro December 14, 1784. They formed a resolution seceding from North Carolina, and forming the State of Frankland, at once adopted a Constitution, had at once a General Assembly organized, declared themselves independent, and defied North Carolina. John Sevier was made Governor, and Judges and other State officers elected, and the like.

Governor Caswell, in April, 1785, issued his proclamation "against this lawless thirst for power," and went vigorously at work to crush out the rebellion. After about two years the State of Frankland was conquered, the conspirators captured, and its rise and fall became a matter of history. And, strange to say, this same man Sevier was forgiven and was in Congress afterwards from the State. North Carolina granted to her soldiers lands in this territory for services in the late war. Many of her people went out there to live, and when the State of Tennessee was organized and admitted into the Union in 1796, it was controlled by former North Carolinians. Hertford County furnished her part of the best citizenship of the new State.

John Brickle, who was in the Senate from the county in 1782, and Thomas Brickle, who was one of the members in the House in 1781, 1782, 1783, 1784 and 1786, were brothers, and sons of John Brickle, to whom Henry Winborne conveyed, October 15, 1754, 200 acres of land on Meherrin Creek. These Brickles were the ancestors of the Brickles of Hertford in recent years.

William Hill, one of the members in the House in 1784 and 1786, was the elder brother of Henry Hill, who was in the House in 1788, and for several years following. They were the sons of Capt. Harry Hill, of Maney's Neck, an officer in the Revolutionary War. William died in Fayetteville in December, 1786, while a member of the House.

James Maney, one of the members in the House in 1785, was a member of the Maney family, whose first settlement in this county was at Maney's Ferry on the Chowan River. A sketch of this gentleman and his family and his ancestors is to be found in Decade VI.

Col. Hardy Murfree, on his return from the war, was honored with a grand ball at the house of Capt. Lewis Meredith in Murfreesboro. He had won lasting laurels in the war. He was spoken of and written about as a most gallant military officer, patriot, and a great man. The Legislature of 1784 passed an act directing the Commissioners of Confiscated Lands to proceed to sell the same. Colonel Murfree, the Commissioner in the Edenton District, showed great wisdom and wonderful discrimination in these cases. The Legislatures conferred and consulted with him about these matters in the State. He moulded public thought throughout the State on the many complicated questions growing out of the changed conditions of things.

About December 1, 1790, Sarah Long, of Hertford County, widow of the then late Nehemiah Long, of the same county, appealed to the Legislature for relief, and through the great magnanimity of this great man, Colonel Murfree, she obtained her relief. The author wonders if they were the parents of the old attorney, Harry W. Long?

In 1787 the Legislature enacted many important laws. Among them were acts against gambling; trading with slaves; for correcting and collating the statutes and laws, by Judge

Decade III.—1780-1790.

Iredell; for recording deeds for lands, and so on; for improving the navigation of Albemarle and Pamlico Sounds by opening Nag's Head Inlet, and to cut the Raleigh Canal in Tyrrell County. The commissioners for this purpose were Governor Johnson, of Chowan; Whitmel Hill, John Skinner, Josiah Collins, Demsey Connor, Col. Hardy Murfree and Gen. Lawrence Baker, of Hertford County, Charles Johnson, Gen. Isaac Gregory, and others.

The latter part of this decade records some interesting events. Winton, the colonial town and the capital of the county, situated on the beautiful Chowan River, about two miles below the mouth of the historic Meherrin, which had enjoyed the distinction of being the only incorporated town in the county for twenty years, was destined to lose much of its importance, wealth, and many of its prominent citizens by the establishing of the new town of Murfreesborough, at Murfree's Landing on the Meherrin River. Restless nature in the formation of the earth's crust, prepared at the latter place a most beautiful and ideal elevated plateau of land for a town, with natural drains and pure water. This beautiful spot on nature's landscape was the home of William Murfree, a legislator of State reputation and renown. Near him resided many others. It was a thickly-settled neighborhood of a high order of citizenship. Mr. Murfree donated 97 acres of land for a town at Murfree's Landing; and the General Assembly of the State, on January 6, 1787, passed an act incorporating the town of Murfreesborough on said land. In the act William Murfree, Patrick Brown, Redmond Hackett, William Vaughan and John Parker were appointed Commissioners and Trustees of said town, and they were empowered to have the same laid off, sell the lots, and apply the money in the improvement of the streets and the like. Soon the flag of the new and young rival of Winton floated triumphantly, as the leading town in the East. It drew heavily from the population of Winton. The county capital soon lost its Wheelers, Gurleys, Brickles, Browns, Dickinsons, Bemburys, Morgans, and other families, who made their homes in the new town on the high hills. Its attractions were soon heralded throughout the Northern States, and its population was being constantly increased by wealthy and educated people from Virginia and the more Northern States, who were seeking their abode in a place where the climate and hygienic conditions were attractive. It was soon made the centre of education and excellent schools, and churches. From its infancy to the present time it has been noted for its schools and refined and intelligent citizenship. Even in this age of religio-politico—commercial and money-loving statesmanship, the town retains its divine reverence and many of its older charms and attractions.

The beginning of its charter is as follows:

"An Act for establishing a town on the lands of William Murfree on Meherrin River, in the County of Hertford."

"Whereas, it has been represented to the General Assembly that on the lands of William Murfree, at Murfree's Landing on the Meherrin River, there is a very proper situation for a town; that the place is remarkably healthy and convenient to a country which produces large supplies of tobacco, naval stores, corn, pork, and lumber, for exportation, and that the convenience for shipping produce at this landing is greatly superior to what is generally found at other landings; and;

"Whereas, a great number of citizens of this State, inhabitants of the counties of Hertford, Northampton, Halifax, Warren, Edgecombe, Bertie, Gates, and Chowan, have prayed that a town may be erected at this place, and William Murfree, the proprietor of the soil, hath consented that ninety-seven acres of the land adjoining to the river, which has been surveyed and laid off, shall be appropriated to this use:

"Be it therefore enacted by the General Assembly of the

State of North Carolina, and it is hereby enacted by the authority of the same, that the said ninety-seven acres of land shall be laid out in lots of half an acre, with convenient streets, and the same are hereby constituted and established a town, and shall be called by the name of Murfreesborough.

"Ratified the 6th day of January, 1787." (Acts 1787, page 166.)

The General Assembly of the State, on the same day it incorporated Murfreesborough, also incorporated the town of Princeton, on the lands of Matthew Figures, in Northampton County, about four or five miles up the river from Murfreesborough. The act appointed Howell Edmunds, James Vaughan, Matthew Figures, Nehemiah Long, Nicholas Edmonds, Henry DeBerry and Benjamin Cokeley, Commissioners and Trustees for designing and keeping up of said town. The Commissioners were all influential and prominent men. James Vaughan was a captain in the Revolutionary War, and won distinction as a soldier, and after the war he and Howell Edmonds became leaders as legislators from Northampton.

The new town was established and soon became the home of several families of prominence. Col. James Washington, the old colonial legislator of Northampton, became a resident; Capt. James Vaughan, Howell Peebles, Capt. Robt. Peebles, Benj. Williamson, and others, took up their abode in the new town. But Princeton did not flourish long. The dreams of its promoters were not realized. Its rival on the hills a few miles below on the Meherrin possessed too many advantages. Finally the charter was surrendered, the buildings taken down and removed, its inhabitants became denizens of other

---

NOTE.—Bartholomew Figures Moore, the great North Carolina lawyer was the grandson of Bartholomew Figures, of Northampton County, N. C., and grand nephew of Matthew Figures of that county, and of William Figures of Hertford County. B. F. Moore was born January 29, 1801, and was related to William Law Murfree, of Tennessee, whose great-grandmother, wife of William Murfree, was Mary Moore, of Northampton County, N. C. Nathaniel and Thomas Figures were younger members of this family.

places, and its beautiful streets and decorated and handsome residences and lots became parts of a magnificent plantation, which still bears the name of Princeton, and is now owned by T. J. and Uriah Vaughan, of Murfreesborough, the great-grandsons of William Vaughan, one of the original commissioners of Murfreesborough.

Murfreesborough, from its establishment, has been the home of a wealthy and high class of citizenship, and members of its old families are scattered throughout the States.

George Ganey's patent in 1713 embraced all the lands in and around the town on the hill. The stream of water from the E. C. Worrell grist-mill, just east of the town, to the river, was in olden times known as Ganey's Creek.

During this decade Col. Benjamin Wynns, Col. Robert Sumner, Col. Mathias Brickles, Edward Hare, Nathan Cotton, William Winborne, and many others, fall in the arms of death.

The Hillsboro Convention of 1788, by ordinance, located the Capital of the State and fixed the seat of the State government on the land of Joel Lane, in Wake County, and there established the present city of Raleigh. The capitol was located in Union Square, situate in the centre of the land purchased from Lane. The capitol and other State buildings were erected on this land. In 1831 the first capitol was destroyed by fire, and the present capitol was built soon thereafter, at a cost of $520,000. This building is found at the present time insufficient to meet the demands of the State, and it is now being mooted and advocated that the capitol building be enlarged at a cost of about $400,000.

In 1789 the University of North Carolina was established by the General Assembly, and in 1792 the institution was located at Chapel Hill. In October, 1793, the corner-stone was laid, and in 1795 the school was opened for students. It has made for the State a proud record.

DECADE IV.

1790—1800.

We will begin the Fourth Decade with the first census of the United States, that we may see what families lived in the county in 1790, and the number of males and females in each family, and the number of slaves in the county, and by whom owned.

The writer is struck with the great similarity of the names of families then and now, in the historic county of Hertford. Its citizenship has certainly maintained its purity through the ages.

As far back as 1725 we find James Howard, a land-owner on Ahoskie Ridge. His descendants still inhabit that section. So Jonathan Sears, who was a land-owner in November, 1715, on the Meherrin River and Creek. The Searses of to-day are still land-owners in that same territory. The descendants of William, Henry and John Willoughby, of the 17th Century, and of Gov. John Jenkins, are still to be found in our midst.

The first column contains the heads of families, the second the number of free white males over 16 years, including the heads of families, the third the number of free white males under 16 years, the fourth the number of free white females, including heads of families, the fifth the number of free negroes, and the sixth the number of slaves owned by the several families:

1	2	3	4	5	6
Askew, James	..	2	2	1	6
Askew, Aaron	..	2	4	..	8
Askew, Cullen	1	1	4	..	1
Archer, Armstrong	..	..	..	4	..
Archer, Evans	..	..	..	3	..
Archer, Jacob	..	..	..	8	..
Archer, Wm.	..	..	1	..	5
Archer, Peggy	..	..	..	2	..
Archer, Caleb	..	..	..	5	..
Askew, Wm.	1	1	2	..	3
Askew, Mary	1	1	2	..	1

	1	2	3	4	5	6
Askew, Zack		1	5	3	..	2
Askew, Priscilla		1	1	3	..	..
Askew, Shadrack		1	..	1	..	17
Archer, Thomas		..	..	..	5	..
Alexander, Tibbs		1	1	5	..	..
Askew, Charnady		1	5	..	1	5
Andrews, Richard		1	1	4	..	..
Askew, James		1	2	2	1	6
Brickle, Aaron		1	1	7	..	29
Benthall, Joseph		1	3	4	..	9
Brown, James		1	..	2	..	..
Battle, John		1	..	2	..	3
Battle, Martha		1	2	4	..	9
Bolton, Thomas		2	..	3	..	..
Bell, James		1	..	..	..	..
Banner, William		1	..	..	..	..
Boone, Arthur		..	..	..	6	..
Bailey, Wm.		..	..	1	6	..
Beaman, Cullin		1	..	1	..	..
Brown, Francis		1	2	2	..	3
Beaman, John		2	..	2	..	1
Beaman, Manning		1	..	3	..	1
Brown, Jeremiah		2	..	5	..	23
Best, Wm.		1	1	3	..	..
Brown, Thomas		2	..	3	..	..
Brown, John		1	..	2	..	1
Batton, John		1	2	1	..	..
Bishop, John		1	..	2	..	8
Bishop, Jesse		1	3	3	..	..
Bolton, Jane		2	..	3	..	..
Brickle, John, dc'd by Jordan Pearce		..	..	1	..	10
Bell, Francis		1	1	3	..	3
Brown, Samuel		2	..	1	..	4
Boutwell, Adam		1	1	2	..	11
Bird, Mary		..	1	4	..	..
Bacon, James		1	4	3	1	5
Boroughs, Hardy		1	1	1	..	..
Boroughs, Sarah		3	..	2	..	..
Baker, Benj.		2	2	2	..	..
Boroughs, Sam.		1	2	2	..	..
Byram, Jno.		2	1	2	..	..
Byram, Thos.		1	1	2	..	..
Brown, Lewis		1	3	5	..	5
Brown, Lewis		1	3	5	5	6
Benberry, Bryan		1	..	4	..	11

Decade IV.—1790-1800. 71

1	2	3	4	5	6
Brown, Patrick	1	..	..	..	..
Bowser, Thomas	..	..	..	9	..
Brown, Stephen	1	2	4	..	..
Britton, Benj.	1	1	1	..	3
Brown, Sophia	..	3	2	..	..
Bayer, John	2	2	3	..	2
Blanchard, Miles	1	2	2	..	7
Baker, Zadoc	1	..	4	..	3
Brown, Benj.	3	..	2	..	10
Belch, Elisha	1	1	4	..	..
Banks, Benj.	1	3	2	..	9
Banks, Alex'r	3	..	2	..	11
Benson, Ezekel	1	3	2	..	3
Blake, Ellis Gray	1	..	..	..	..
Brewer, Jesse	1	1	3	..	..
Baley, Wm.	2	2	..	1	..
Boone, Allen	1	3	3	..	2
Britt, Thomas	2	4	3	..	7
Britt, Joseph	4	..	2	1	..
Basset, Eliz.	..	3	1	1	..
Best, Thomas	1	1	2	..	1
Best, Henry	1	1	1	..	..
Best, Mary	..	..	3	..	3
Benthall, Daniel	2	..	5	..	4
Bass, Willis	..	..	..	4	..
Best, David R.	1	2	3	..	5
Bridger, Joseph	3	1	4	..	5
Brown, Rhoderick	1	..	2	2	3
Bizell, Solo.	..	..	..	11	..
Boone, Mary	1	2	2	..	3
Barrow, John	2	2	4	..	..
Barnes, Randolph	3	1	3	..	..
Britt, James	1	3	4	..	10
Britt, Abram	1	2	2	..	1
Britt, Benj.	1	3	2	..	..
Britt, Martin	1	4	3	..	..
Boone, Nicholas	1	2	3	1	4
Barden, Wm.	2	1	2	..	1
Barden, James	1	1	1	..	..
Britt, Silas	1	2	2	..	1
Britt, Arthur	1	..	..	..	..
Brown, Elizabeth	2	..	2	..	12
Bruse, Abram	1	..	2	..	1
Bruse, Bennet	1	3	2	..	1
Burton, John	1	..	..	..	..
Brickle, Thos. N	1	1	3	..	3

History of Hertford County, N. C.

1	2	3	4	5	6
Blake, Eliz.	..	1	3	..	..
Brickle, Matthias	2	1	3	..	11
Brickle, Wm.	1	..	2	..	8
Baker, Blake	2	2	7	..	3
Brantley, Benj.	2	2	4	..	5
Brown, Fred.	1	..	2	..	3
Brickle, Jonathan	1	1	1	..	..
Bird, Robert	1	1	2	..	..
Brown, Lewis	1	1	3	..	1
Brown, Richard	1	..	2	..	2
Brown, Sarah	1	..	2	..	1
Cail, Jeremiah	1	3	1	..	..
Cornelius, Martha	..	1	2	..	..
Cretchilor, Providence	..	1	5	..	..
Carr, Robert	3	4	4	..	14
Carr, Matthew	3	..	4	..	11
Carr, Lawrence	2	1	2	..	4
Calf, James	1	5	3	..	7
Christia, James	1	..	1	..	..
Cook, Charles	1	1	2	..	..
Cooke, Benj.	1	1	1	..	..
Chritenton, Eliz.	..	1	5	..	10
Carter, Lewis	1	3	4	..	6
Carter, Isaac	2	1	1	..	28
Canidy, John	1	1	4	..	..
Cotton, Godwin	1	..	6	..	9
Cotton, Wm.	2	3	3	..	2
Cherry, James	1	1	2	..	5
Cotton, Sam	1	..	3	..	7
Cotton, Noah	1	..	..	..	2
Cruger, James	1	..	1	..	..
Christia, David	1	..	..	..	..
Cross, Stephens	1	..	..	..	..
Cotton, James	1	..	1	..	2
Cotton, Thomas	2	4	3	..	3
Carter, Isaac	3	3	3	..	23
Copeland, Mary	3	..	1	..	4
Copeland, Thomas	1	1	1	..	1
Copeland, John	1	4	2	..	1
Copeland, Hollowell	1	2	2	..	..
Copeland, Eli	1	1	5	..	2
Clark, Stephen	1	1	1	..	1
Clarke, Kerney	1	..	1	..	..
Coleman, Thomas	1	3	2	..	1
Clarke, Wm.	2	1	2	..	..
Copeland, Thos.	2	..	2	..	7

Decade IV.—1790-1800.

1	2	3	4	5	6
Copeland, James	2	..	..	..	3
Copeland, Stephen	1	..	1	1	2
Cook, Daniel	2	1	3	..	..
Carter, Martha	1	..	2	..	2
Carter, James	1	3	3	..	..
Crow, Eliz.	..	..	1	..	..
Daughtry, Eliz.	2	1	2	..	10
Darden, Willis	1	3	3	..	5
Darden, John	2	3	2	2	5
Darden, Elisha	1	1	4	..	4
Darden, David	4	..	1	..	8
Dilday, Joseph	1	4	4	..	..
Darden, Elisha	1	3	6	..	9
Darden, Allen	1	..	..	..	..
Darden, Henry	1	1	2	2	1
Driver, Sam	1	1	2	..	8
Drew, Richard	1	..	..	..	8
Davis, Luke	1	..	2	..	..
Dunn, George	1	2	..	..	12
Dunning, Sam	1	2	1	..	1
Driver, Martha	1	..	1	..	7
Driver, John	2	3	3	..	13
Denton, Polly	..	1	1	..	2
Downing, Wm.	2	3	3	..	3
Deanes, Daniel	3	2	4	1	7
Duer, Ann	1	..	1	..	..
Dennis, Littleton	2	..	..	..	..
Darden, Jethro	1	1	1	..	11
Darden, Jet	1	1	..	..	7
Deanes, James	1	1	3	..	7
Deanes, Wm.	1	2	1	..	4
Davis, Mary	..	1	2	..	..
Daughtie, James	1	..	2	..	..
Daughtie, Wm.	1	..	4	..	..
Daughtie, Jethro	2	..	1	..	..
Daniel, Joseph	3	..	2	2	..
Deanes, Thomas	1	..	1	..	4
Denton, James	3	..	3	..	3
Davis, Sam	2	2	5	..	10
Dickerson, John	1	2	6	..	..
Davis, Blake	1	1	2	..	1
Evans, Benj.	3	3	5	..	5
Evans, Cornelius	2	2	3	..	3
Evans, Wm.	2	1	3	..	3
Eley, Michael	1	..	4	..	9
Eley, Edward	1	1	1	..	13

	1	2	3	4	5	6
Evans, Peter		1	2	3	..	..
Evans, Robert		2	2	4	..	..
Everett, James		1	..	2	..	6
Evans, Wm.		1	..	1	..	5
Ezell, Benj.		2	3	5	..	..
Evans, Francis		2	3	5	..	..
Evans, Thomas		1	1	3	..	..
Edes, Stephen		1	..	..	..	..
Freeman, Josiah		1	..	..	..	2
Foster, James		1	..	1	1	5
Felton, Elisha		2	4	2	..	16
Figures, Thomas		1	..	1	..	..
Figures, Wm.		1	3	6	..	16
Figures, Thomas		1	1	..	..	19
Fairless, Robert		1	2	1	..	..
Fells, Edw.		2	1	2	..	..
Fairless, Wm.		2	1	2	..	..
Fauney, Wm.		1	..	3	..	..
Fawn, Ann		1	..	1	..	4
Fairlen, Zadoc		1	..	..	..	..
Flower, Rand		2	..	2	..	..
Goodman, David		2	..	..	..	3
Ganes, Anthony		..	..	..	2	..
Gatling, James		1	2	3	..	2
Garvey, Patrick		5	..	2	..	6
Grantham, James		2	1	6	..	..
Graham, Chancey		1	2	3	..	2
Gay, James		1	1	5	2	..
Griffith, Jno.		1	4	2	..	4
Green, Joseph		2	2	2	..	..
Gay, John		1	2	3	..	..
Godwin, Barney		1	..	2	..	..
Godwin, John		1	..	..	..	..
Gliston, Daniel		2	1	..	..	2
Gatling, Arthur		2	2	4	..	5
Gatling, Edw.		1	3	4	..	..
Gatling, Wm.		1	..	..	..	..
Griffith, Bunnell		1	..	3	..	2
Griffith, Hartwell		1	..	..	..	..
Gatling, Rachel		..	..	2	..	..
Gatling, David		2	..	2	..	1
Gatling, Hardy		1	6	6	..	..
Godwin, Kerney		3	1	5	..	10
Godwin, Barney		3	..	3	..	..
Gatling, Jethro		2	1	2	..	3
Glover, Wm.		2	4	5	..	9

Decade IV.—1790-1800.

	1	2	3	4	5	6
Harrell, Mary	1	1	3	..	11
Harrell, Wm.	1	..	..	..	7
Hill, Charles	1	1	1	..	4
Hobbs, Elisha	..	..	1	..	..
Holloman, Hanche	2	1	3	..	..
Hobbs, Wm.	1	..	1	..	2
Hobbs, Jacob	2	2	3	..	..
Hill, Henry	2	..	..	..	23
Hayes, Joseph	1	4	4	..	5
Hobbs, Abram	1	1	1	..	..
Hutchins, Wm.	2	1	3	1	3
Hart, John	1	..	..	..	7
Hutchins, ——	2	1	3	..	1
Howard, Luke	2	3	2	..	7
Handcock, Nehemiah	1	3	3	..	..
Howard, Moses	2	..	3	..	3
Horton, Hugh	2	6	3	..	7
Humphry, Wm.	2	3	5	1	1
Howard, Elisha	1	2	4	..	..
Harrell, Elijah	3	..	2	..	..
Horton, Matthew	3	..	5	..	..
Hipton, Wm.	1	5	1	..	..
Horton, Eliz.	..	..	3	..	..
Hutchins, Aaron	1	..	1	..	..
Hayes, Marmaduke	2	..	..	..	5
Horton, Williford	2	..	3	..	4
Harrison, James	1	2	2	..	3
Holland, Thos.	1	2	1	..	21
Holloman, Malichi	1	4	6	..	..
Holloman, Samuel	2	2	2	..	..
Holloman, Silvia	2	..	2	..	..
Holloman, Aaron	3	..	6	..	..
Holloman, David	1	4	4	..	1
Hill, John	1	..	..	..	13
Hill, Hardy	1	4	1	..	..
Hill, Michael	2	..	3	..	..
Hare, John	1	3	2	..	..
Hayes, Ezekel	1	..	1	..	3
Harrison, Thos.	1	3	3	..	..
Hitchborne, John	4	..	..	..	2
Holloman, Christopher	2	2	5	..	2
Hill, Whitmell	1	1	3	..	..
Holloman, John	1	2	4	..	3
Harrell, Jesse	1	3	3	..	..
Haine, Benj.	1	1	2	..	17
Holloman, Cornelius	1	1	1	..	1

1	2	3	4	5	6
Haine, Jesse	1	..	..	..	7
Hobbs, Sarah	1	2	3	..	..
Harrison, Wm.	2	1	1	..	..
Horton, Wm.	1	3	4	..	..
Howell, John	1	..	2	..	..
Hill, Joseph	2	1	4	..	10
Hayes, Wm.	1	..	1	..	..
Hall, Mary	..	..	..	6	..
Harrell, Nathan	1	2	3	..	11
Holland, Hezekiah	..	4	2	..	..
Hale, Fereby	..	1	2	1	..
Jackson, Lon	1	2	1	..	1
Jordan, Wm.	1	..	..	..	2
Ives, Sam	2	3	3	..	1
Ireland, Grofton	2	1	1	..	4
Jones, Wm.	1	..	..	..	6
Jiggitts, Edw.	1	1	3	..	7
Jackson, Isaac	1	3	2	..	..
Jones, Sarah	..	..	3	..	3
Jones, James	1	..	2	..	7
Jones, Amilescent	..	..	1	..	2
Jernigan, Needham	1	3	3	..	7
Jiggitts, Wm.	1	4	1	..	..
Joyner, Charles	1	2	3	..	..
Jernigan, John	1	3	5	..	..
Jenkins, Charles	1	1	4	..	9
Jenkins, Webb	1	1	5	..	2
Johnson, Anna	1	..	2	..	..
Jenkins, Wm.	2	..	2	..	1
Jenkins, Dempsey	1	1	2	..	4
Jenkins, Samuel	1	1	1	..	2
Jenkins, Winborne	1	5	4	..	5
Jenkins, Henry	2	1	2	..	17
Jenkins, Benj.	1	1	2	..	3
Jordan, Eliz.	1	1	4	..	15
Kelley, Delphia	..	1	2	..	..
Knight, Wm.	1	1	3	..	2
Knight, Dempsey	1	3	4	..	..
Keene, Jacob	2	1	5	..	..
Knox, James	1	..	4	..	1
King, Jesse	1	..	..	..	2
Keele, Jacob	2	1	5	..	..
Long, Jno.	1	1	2	..	..
Lee, James	1	1	1	..	..
Lewis, Edw.	2	..	5	..	..
Luton, Sam	2	..	3	..	2
Luton, Thos.	2	2	3	..	2

Decade IV.—1790-1800.

1	2	3	4	5	6
Langston, Luke	1	2	4	..	2
Little, George	3	..	2	..	36
Lewis, Luke	1	1	8	..	3
Lawed, Margaret	..	..	4	..	..
Lassiter, Jason	1	..	3	..	1
Lintal, Joseph	1	2	1	..	..
Langston, John	1	3	2	..	2
Langston, Martha	1	..	3	..	12
Lawrence, Exum	2	3	2	..	4
Liverman, Edmond	1	1	4	..	..
Lassiter, Zadoc	1	..	..	..	34
Lassiter, Wm.	1	..	..	1	18
Land, Bird	2	..	1	..	9
McFarlane, Walter	1	2	6	..	..
Moore, James	4	3	2	..	39
Moore, James	1	3	4	..	23
Mullen, Wm.	4	4	6	..	10
Mullen, James	1	1	3	..	7
Magget, John	1	2	5	..	17
Mullen, Jno.	1	2	..	..	1
Matthews, Farmer	1	..	..	..	..
Mayne, Robert	2	2	5	..	4
Morgan, Jacob	1	..	..	..	..
Marsh, Geo.	1	4	4	..	..
Moore, Willis	2	2	4	..	8
Moore, Aaron	3	..	3	..	13
McGlauhon, Elisha	1	..	2	..	..
McGlaughon, Geo.	1	..	2	..	1
McGlaughon, James	1	..	1	..	2
Modlin, Dempsey	1	3	3	..	..
Morgan, Willis	1	..	3	..	..
Manley, Gabriel	..	..	..	2	..
Mashborn, Wm.	1	3	3	..	..
Mitchell, Wm.	1	2	2	..	..
Masongill, Daniel	3	4	5	..	3
Miller, Jno.	2	2	2	..	1
Murfree, Wm.	2	..	1	..	20
Murfree, Hardy	5	3	5	..	45
Maney, James	1	1	3	..	39
Maney, Peggy	..	2	2	..	7
Morgan, Eliz.	..	1	1	..	..
Moore, Wm.	1	1	1	..	17
Morgan, Hardy	1	2	1	..	..
Moore, Lawrence	2	3	1	..	10
Macon, Wm.	3	4	2	..	..
Mashborn, Matt.	1	1	6	..	1

	1	2	3	4	5	6
Matthews, Edmond	1	..	2		..	1
Moore, Edward	1	3	3		..	21
Matthews, Giles	1	4	2		..	..
Mashborn, Charity	..	4	3		..	..
Morgan, James	2	3	2		..	1
Montgomery, Robert	1	2	5		..	17
Montgomery, Elinder	..	1	2		..	1
Moore, Wm.	1	1	2		..	..
Morgan, James	1	2	2		..	..
Meredith, Lewis	3	1	2		..	19
Nichols, Wm.	1	3	2		..	1
Nichols, Jno.	2	3	4		..	..
Newsom, Joel	1	..	4		..	2
Newsom, Charles	1	..	3		..	5
Newsom, Hosea	4	2	7		..	14
Newsom, John	1	..	1		..	1
Northcott, John	1	..	2		..	..
Northcott, John	2	1	4		..	1
Nickins, Malichi	..	..	..		5	..
Nowell, Dempsey	2	2	3		..	1
Norvell, Benj.	1	..	5		..	2
Norvell, Mary	1	1	3		..	..
Northcott, Anthony	1	1	2		..	1
Nichols, Nat.	1	1	4		..	..
Nickins, James	..	..	3		..	..
Outlaw, Wm.	3	4	3		..	19
Outlaw, Thomas	1	3	5		..	4
Outlaw, Lewis	1	1	2		..	1
Overton, James	1	1	2		..	..
Overton, Nath'l	1	3	5		..	..
Odom, Jacob	1	..	2	1		..
Orange, Henry	..	..	..	3		..
Perry, Abner	1	..	4		..	10
Porter, Abram	1	4	3		..	18
Parten, Hubbon	1	..	3		..	2
Parten, Henry	1	..	1		..	1
Powell, Shadrick	2	..	..		..	5
Perry Simeon	2	3	4		..	8
Perry, Ezekel	2	1	3		..	10
Powell, Anna	..	1	1		..	2
Powell, Dempsey	1	1	6		..	4
Pruet, Mary	..	..	4		..	4
Peal, Edw.	2	3	3		..	..
Peal, Dempsey	1	4	1		..	..
Peal, Ann	..	3	2		..	..
Peal, Thomas	1	3	3		..	1

Decade IV.—1790-1800.   79

1	2	3	4	5	6
Pinner, Rachel	1	1	3	..	1
Pearce, Daniel	1	7	4	..	7
Porter, Wm.	1	2	4	..	10
Porter, Jno.	1	..	..	..	4
Pinner, Milbry	..	1	1	..	1
Perry, Wm.	1	..	2	..	4
Peal, Daniel	1	2	1	..	1
Perry, James	1	3	2	..	7
Parker, Sam	2	2	3	..	..
Pearce, Job	1	1	3	..	..
Perry, Celia	1	1	2	..	21
Parker, Abigail	..	..	1	..	..
Powell, Charles	3	3	1	..	20
Pender, Jethro	1	2	1	..	..
Parker, Wm.	1	..	1	..	5
Parker, Wm.	2	..	4	..	3
Parker, Jno.	1	4	3	..	8
Parker, Silas	2	2	6	..	1
Parker, Peter	3	4	5	..	1
Parker, Ephraim	1	1	3	..	1
Parker, Daniel	1	1	3	..	..
Panter, Edw.	..	..	..	..	2
Perry, Elisha	1	3	4	..	1
Phelps, Dempsey	1	1	1	..	..
Perry, Wm.	1	2	2	..	3
Pearce, Jordan	1	..	..	..	..
Quemby, Jesse	2	3	3	..	7
Reynolds, Thomas	1	..	..	..	..
Read, Hamilton	2	1	..	..	3
Rawles, Wm.	1	2	3	..	12
Raby, Joel	1	3	2	..	..
Rhoads, Abram	3	1	6	..	6
Rasberry, Wm.	1	..	2	..	..
Rawls, Mariah	1	..	3	..	..
Reynolds, Jesse	..	..	..	11	..
Rasberry, Margaret	2	2	3	..	..
Russell, Thomas	1	..	1	..	3
Rooks, Dempsey	1	2	3	..	..
Rooks, Joseph	1	1	2	..	1
Rea, Wm.	1	..	..	..	1
Roberts, Wm.	1	2	1	..	5
Ridley, Thomas	2	..	..	..	11
Rindal, Joseph	1	1	2	..	1
Riley, Benj.	1	1	5	..	2
Rea, Wm.	2	..	3	..	8
Rutland, Wm.	1	2	3	..	4

1	2	3	4	5	6
Riley, Wm.	1	1	1	..	..
Rascoe, Alex.	1	..	1	..	..
Rawles, Absalom	2	1	2	..	6
Roads, Wm.	1	..	4	..	..
Rogers, Jonathan	1	2	3	..	15
Revel, Matthews	2	2	3	..	..
Revel, Silas	1	1	1	..	..
Rider, Nancy	..	..	3	..	..
Rogers, James	2	2	7	..	..
Rawles, Jesse	1	5	4	..	2
Rayner, Amos	3	..	..	..	5
Starkey, John	2	2	4	..	..
Sanderford, James	1	2	1	..	1
Story, John	1	1	4	..	..
Sanderford, Nancy	1	1	5	..	2
Sanderford, John	1	1	5	..	3
Sanders, John P.	1	3	3	..	..
Smith, James	..	..	..	6	..
Smith, Abram	1	1	3	..	..
Smith, John	1	1	2	..	..
Sumner, Mary	1	4	8	..	15
Spires, Elisha	1	..	..	..	1
Spires, Absalom	2	2	1	..	2
Scull, Edw.	1	2	3	..	..
Sessoms, Ann	2	3	2	..	14
Sumner, Moses	2	5	4	..	28
Sanders, Nathan	1	..	3	..	..
Spicey, Daniel	1	2	1	..	..
Simons, Joshua	2	1	3	..	13
Sewell, Dempsey	1	1	..	..	2
Scull, John	1	1	6	..	3
Sharp, Gemona	1	1	4	..	16
Sessoms, Rachel	2	..	2	..	6
Scull, Elisha	1	..	4	..	11
Shepherd, Providence	1	2	5	..	..
Skinner, James	1	2	3	..	35
Strickland, Drew	1	..	4	..	1
Shewinaft, Wm.	..	..	8	..	..
Sears, John	1	..	..	8	..
Spikes, Thomas	3	1	3	..	..
Sanders, David	1	1	2	..	..
Saunders, Wm.	1	2	2	..	..
Sumner, Eliz.	1	..	2	..	..
Stephens, Ann	..	5	2	..	..
Sewell, Wm.	3	1	4	..	..
Simons, Obediah	1	..	3	..	..

Decade IV.—1790-1800.

1	2	3	4	5	6
Sorrell, James	..	..	..	..	8
Sewell, Richard	1	1	2	..	..
Sharp, Isaac	..	..	..	..	5
Sharp, Starkey	..	..	..	..	5
Scott, John	1	2	4	..	18
Sorrell, Wm.	1	2	5	..	..
Smith, Thomas	1	3	6	..	..
Tyler, Hellen	1	5	2	..	14
Tifton, John B.	1	1	3	..	7
Thomas, Isaac	1	..	1	..	..
Thomas, Josiah	1	..	..	..	..
Thomas, Benj.	1	..	1	..	..
Tiley, John	1	1	1	1	1
Tritt, Thos.	4	2	1	..	13
Trader, Rachel	1	1	3	..	..
Tennessee, John	2	..	..	..	2
Tyler, Samuel	1	..	8	..	1
Thomson, Eliz.	..	..	4	..	1
Taylor, Miles	1	2	4	..	..
Taylor, Williford	1	4	..	..	4
Taylor, Boaz	1	1	1	..	..
Vassar, Robert	1	1	1	..	7
Vassar, Jesse	1	..	..	..	7
Vinson, Wm.	1	2	2	..	..
Vaughan, Wm.	2	3	4	..	..
Vinson, James	1	1	5	..	2
Vinson, Peter	1	2	2	..	..
Vanpelt, John	1	..	3	..	1
Vinson, Shad.	2	2	5	..	..
Vanpelt, Sarah	1	2	..	..	..
Vinson, Elisha	1	4	4	..	..
Vaughan, John	1	..	..	..	..
Valentine, Isaac	1	..	1	..	..
Valentine, David	2	2	3	..	2
Valentine, Alex.	2	1	4	..	1
Williford, John	3	4	2	..	8
Winborne, Josiah	1	..	..	..	3
Winborne, James	1	..	2	..	1
Winborne, John	1	..	1	..	5
Winborne, Henry	2	..	..	..	43
Winborne, Thomas	1	..	2	..	2
Wilkins, James	1	..	2	..	4
Williams, Charles	3	..	2	..	..
Weaks, Arthur	1	..	..	..	1

1	2	3	4	5	6
Willey, James	2	2	4	..	..
Williams, Richard	2	1	1	..	2
Weaks, Wm.	1	1	1	..	..
Whitley, Ann	1	3	4	..	..
Wilkins, Wm.	1	2	1	..	..
Wilkins, Richard	1	..	4	..	..
Wiggins, Wm.	1	4	3	..	2
Weaks, Julian	2	2	3	..	..
Whitley, James	3	..	3	..	..
Williams, William	1	..	2	..	6
Williams, Warner	1	2	1	..	..
Worrell, Richard	1	1	2	..	1
White, Henderson	4	1	3	..	12
Williams, Nathan	1	..	2	..	2
Williams, Gilstrap	1	1	1	..	..
Weaver, Ned	..	..	..	7	..
Webb, Benj.	3	4	2	..	2
Weston, Jordan	1	1	2	..	9
Weston, Jesse	2	3	2	..	..
Wiggins, Sarah	..	4	3	..	..
Ward, Isaac Hill	1	1	3	..	9
Williams, Ben.	1	..	1	..	2
Williams, Geo.	1	2	3	..	..
Williams, Whit	2	1	3	1	8
Watson, Micajah	1	..	..	..	..
Warren, Obediah	1	1	3	..	..
West, James	1	..	..	..	1
Worrell, Rhoda	..	1	1	..	1
Wilson, Matthew	2	4	4	..	21
Wiggins, Wright	2	..	2	2	..
West, John	1	2	..	..	3
Williams, Sarah	3	..	..	3	..
Worthington, Arcada	..	1	5	..	1
Worthington, Sarah	2	1	3	..	1
Willoughby, John	3	1	7	..	..
Wiggins, Sarah	..	..	..	8	..
Wiggins, Joshua	2	3	4	..	2
Warren, Jordan	1	1	1	..	..
Williams, Constant	..	..	..	1	..
Wright, Jane	1	..	3	..	14
Worthington, Mary	1	..	3	..	2
Williams, Eliz.	..	3	8	..	2
Walker, Patsy	..	1	5	..	11
Wright, Henry	1	1	1	..	11
White, Alex.	1	..	2	..	1
Wynns, Jno. A.	1	1	4	..	11

Decade IV.—1790-1800.

	1	2	3	4	5	6
Wynns, Matthew		1	1	3		1
Wynns, George		4		4		34
Wynns, Thomas		1		1		33
Wynns, William		2	1	5		29
Wiles, Joshua		1		3		26
Yeates, Sarah				1		6
Yeates, Jesse		1	1	4		7
Yealloby, Geo.		1	3	4		4

Josiah and James Winborne came to this county from Northampton, and emigrated to Edgecombe County about 1798. John Winborne was, also, of the Northampton family.

Gen. George Washington is still serving his first term as President of the United States. He is the idol of his country. The large majority of the people of Hertford County are Federalist in politics, which was the political faith of Washington. During this decade the country is tranquil in peace and the people happy and seeking out the pleasant places for homes. The young village of Murfreesborough becomes an attractive place to the home-seekers, and many find an abiding place within her borders. It soon becomes the centre of refinement, of education and of wealth.

The able, wealthy and benevolent Gen. Thomas Wynns, who was a member of the House of Commons of 1787, and of the Convention of 1789, begins his protracted service as State Senator from the county from 1790 to 1800, inclusive. He was the youngest of the four sons of Benjamin Wynns, and lived below Winton, at the place where the late Jackson B. Hare resided, and he built the house that now stands on the old hill. He also owned the Hare grist-mill. His wife was Susanna Maney, the daughter of James Maney II, of Maney's Neck. He was elected as Presidential Elector in 1801, and voted in the electoral college for Thomas Jefferson for President of the United States. Elected to Congress to succeed Charles Johnson, deceased, of Edenton, in 1802, and again elected to the Eighth and Ninth Congresses, ending March 4, 1807. He declined a further nomination for

Congress. Again elected by his countrymen a member of the State Senate, where he continued to serve his county until 1817, when he retired to private life. He was extremely fond of his nephews, Benjamin, Thomas, James D. and William B. Wynns. He had no children. His wife died in January, 1822, and he died in June, 1825. Both are buried on the old Maney plantation, near the present wharf at Riddicksville, in this county. He was made Major-General in the State Troops in the First Division, which position he held a number of years until he resigned to go to the Legislature in 1813. He was a great advocate of education, and was one of the first trustees of the State University. The *Raleigh Register* of 1825 speaks of him as a splendid and noble character and as one of the first men of the State. The paper also states that he had been frequently solicited to accept the nomination for Governor, but he invariably declined, although his nomination would have resulted in his election. He was a member of the electoral college in 1809, and voted for James Madison for President.

Robert Montgomery was another of the county's representative men. He was a lawyer of great ability, and took a leading part in shaping the legislation of the State. He was a direct descendant of John Montgomery, of Tyrrell County, who was for a long time Attorney-General in the Province, and succeeded William Smith as Chief Justice of the Province, about 1740. John Montgomery settled in Edenton while he was in office. Robert Montgomery married Mary Meredith, of Murfreesborough, and left several children, of whom we will write in Decade Seven. He died in Raleigh in 1808, while a member of the State Senate.

Henry Hill, a member of the House in 1788 to 1793, and again in 1795, lived in Murfreesborough, but owned a large landed estate in Maney's Neck, on the Meherrin River. He was the son of Capt. Harry (Henry) Hill, of Revolutionary fame, and who lived at Hill's Ferry, in Maney's Neck.

Decade IV.—1790-1800.

Henry Hill, Jr., was a lawyer and a man of ability. He married Sally Maget. His daughter married lawyer Harry W. Long, of this county.

James Jones, who represented, in part, the county in the House for twelve years, was the son of Col. James Jones, of Pitch Landing, and inherited a large estate from his father. He lived on his plantation near Pitch Landing. He was born in 1765 and died in 1816. He married Anne Walton, sister of Col. Isaac Walton and Timothy Walton. His widow and several children survived him. His sons were Dr. William Jones, James Sidney Jones, and Howell Jones. His granddaughter was the wife of Maj. John W. Moore. No county in the State was abler represented in 1791 than the patriotic little county of Hertford.

In 1793 Capt. Jethro Darden, of Maney's Neck, appeared for the first time in the House of Commons from Hertford. He served four terms, and was a man of intelligence and of large information, and was soon recognized as a leader, and reflected much credit on his county. He acquired his military title as captain in the militia service. On account of failing eyesight he was compelled to abandon public life, and finally, before his death in 1834, he became totally blind. He left several children—Edward R., John A., Penelope, wife of James Majette, Samuel A., Jethro R., and Sarah E. Darden. There was another citizen in the county during this decade by the name of Jet. Darden.

Nathan Harrell, who had been prominent in the county during the last decade, was still serving the people as Clerk of the Court during most of this decade. He married Elizabeth Sharp, daughter of Starkey Sharp and granddaughter of Maj. Henry Winborne. She was born in 1768 and died in 1840. He reared several children. Their daughter Nancy married Dr. William L. Smith, who had settled in the county from Connecticut, and William Nathan Harrell Smith, the late Chief Justice of the State, was the product of this marriage. Nathan Harrell died in 1802, leaving his widow and other children surviving him—Starkey Sharp Harrell and Sally Harrell. His widow married widower George Gordon, who afterwards became Public Register of the county, and then succeeding General Dickinson as Clerk of the Court. They left one child, Barsha Gordon. Dr. William L. Smith died in 1813, and his widow afterwards married James M. Yancey, formerly of Raleigh, but was later a citizen of Murfreesboro. They left one son, Antonio P. Yancey. Starkey S. Harrell, 1786-1830, married Elizabeth Simmons, 1788-1861, who were the parents of Mary, the wife of Lemuel R. Jernigan; of Nancy, the wife of Thomas Blount Sharp, and Starkey S. Harrell, Jr. Nathan Harrell's daughter, Sally, married G. H. Bond.

The grave robs the county, during this decade, of Henry Winborne, William Murfree, Maj. George Wynns, Starkey Sharp, the former Sheriff and Public Register, Maj. Samuel Harrell, the old Clerk of the Court, and many others.

In 1794 the General Assembly incorporated the Hertford Academy, which was located in the town of Murfreesboro. This was the first incorporated school in the county, though there had for a number of years existed schools in different parts of the county. Rev. Jonathan Otis Freeman was the first principal of the Academy, and he was aided by an able corps of assistants. The late Edmond B. Freeman, Clerk of the Supreme Court of North Carolina, was the son of Rev. J. O. Freeman. Rev. Freeman, as principal of the Academy in 1819, was succeeded by Thomas O'Brady, an impetuous and belligerent Irishman, who was a believer in the rod in the school-room. It is said of him that he was so pugnacious that he went on the street one day and engaged in a fight with one Drew Vinson, a brag fighter from the Canada section, and Vinson whipped him good. This so humiliated the Irish bully that he soon resigned and left the town.

O'Brady was succeeded as principal in 1822 by Rev. James Douglas, a Presbyterian divine, and a good man. Rev. Douglas was instrumental in establishing the old Presbyterian church in town, and O'Dwyer, in his diary of 1824, often speaks of his able discourses on the Bible. Douglas was principal of the department for boys and young men, and Miss Harriet Sketchly, afterwards Mrs. James Banks, was in charge of the female department of the school. In 1822 Mrs. James Banks purchased the Academy lot from John Wheeler, and for years conducted a flourishing high school for girls. The Male Academy was conducted after 1822 in another building. Rev. Douglas was succeeded several years thereafter as principal of the Male School by Rev. John Lamb Pritchard, and the latter was succeeded by A. T. Ackerman, a young man from New England, who later studied law and settled in Georgia to practice his profession. Ackerman became a distinguished lawyer and was appointed Attorney-General of the United States by President U. S. Grant during his first administration. This school was kept up until about twenty years ago, with able educators at its head.

DECADE V.

1800—1810.

The beginning of this decade found the county in great excitement. The Presidential election was to be held in November, 1800. There was great bitterness between the two political parties, the Federal and the Republican, and also factional divisions in each party. The Federalist candidates were John Adams, of Massachusetts, and C. C. Pinckney, of South Carolina; and the Republican candidates were Thomas Jefferson, of Virginia, and Aaron Burr, of New York. The electoral college failed to elect. Jefferson and Burr received 73 votes each, Adams 65, Pinckney 64, and Chief Justice Jay 1. Congress had to elect, and after a long and bitter fight in Congress, Jefferson was finally elected President and Burr Vice-President. Gen. Thomas Wynns was in the electoral college and voted for Jefferson for President and Burr for Vice-President.

The names of the old political parties in the United States did not represent the principles of the political parties bearing the same names to-day. The Whig party was the oldest political party in this country after the Revolution of 1776-'82. In the formation of the Union and the adoption of the Constitution of the United States in 1787 the American people became divided into two opposing political parties—Federalists and anti-Federalists. The Federalist was also composed of two elements—the extreme Federalists, as Alexander Hamilton, who favored a strong government, a national government with an aristocratic Upper House and Presidency, while the conservative Federalists, as George Washington, favored a Federal Constitution and government of the States without any aristocratic features. The extreme anti-Federalists, as Thomas Jefferson, wanted no Federal government of any kind, but favored simply a league like the old Articles of Confederation between the thirteen independent republics; and the great mass of the party opposed the adoption of the new Constitution submitted to the States in 1787. They divided, however, and the minority element joined the conservative Federalists in adopting the new Constitution, hoping that proper amendments would be adopted. And finally the whole anti-Federalists after a few years accepted the new Constitution and became the strict Constructionist party, confining the powers of the Federal government to the letter of the Constitution, whose principles have been the fundamental tenets of the Democratic party; while the principles contended for by the opposing party, known as the Loose Constructionists, the advocates of a national government and the subordination of State rights to the powers of the national government, with centralized tendencies, are now and have been since the battle of Appomattox in 1865, represented by the Republican party. The anti-Federalist party became known as the Strict Constructionists, and after the French Revolution they became known as the Democratic-Republican party, which has always been the official party name of the Democratic party up to the Civil War. It was in olden days spoken of as the Republican party. The old Federalist and Loose Constructionist became metamorphosed into the old Whig party, with many of its extreme notions eliminated, until the creation of the Republican party, of which Abraham Lincoln, W. H. Seward and others were the exponents. That is, the Republican party of to-day is the successor of the extreme Federalists and Loose Constructionists. The conservative Whigs and conservative Democrats after 1868 formed the present Democratic party, the modern representative of the Democratic-Republican party and Strict Constructionists.

GABRIEL'S INSURRECTION.

While the slave negroes of the South were kindly treated by their masters, who placed much value on them as profitable property, yet the savage treachery of their natures occasionally caused them to be guilty of brutality of the worst kind.

In August, 1800, Gabriel Prosser, a slave owned by a farmer near Richmond, Va., planned an "uprising" of the negroes to assassinate the whites, take charge of Richmond, and plunder the place. He armed his horde of bandits and set out on his wicked mission. But he was thwarted in his nefarious enterprise by a heavy storm of rainfall, which so swelled a creek in his pathway that he could not reach the city, and before he could surmount this difficulty his scheme was discovered, and he and his followers disbanded and took to the woods. They were finally captured and executed. Gabriel was hanged October 7, 1800. These occasional outbreaks of the negroes were invariably caused by some vicious negro who had been much favored by his white master and granted many liberties and privileges. They were generally negro preachers.

In 1801 William Hardy Murfree, of Murfreesboro, the son of Col. Hardy Murfree, the hero of Stony Point, graduated at the State University at Chapel Hill, and began the study of the law at Edenton, and was soon to begin to win laurels for himself and heap greater honors on his family, his county, his district and his State. After obtaining his law license he returned to his native town of Murfreesboro and opened his law office in the brick building between the Peter Williams lot and the ravine, on William street. He soon gave evidence of a great man. In 1805 he and James Jones represented the county in the House of Commons. Again in 1812 he was a member of the House, and then for four years a member of Congress from the Edenton District.

Robert Montgomery in 1801 begins to serve his county in the State Senate for seven terms, as successor of General Wynns. James Jones continues to serve in the House until 1807.

In 1801 Capt. Abner Perry, of Revolutionary fame, appears for the first time as a member of the House, and serves nine years. His gallant services in the War of the Revolution, and his estimable qualities as a man, made him a favor-

Decade V.—1800-1810. 91

ite with the people and an influential and useful member of the House. He lived near old St. John's, and married the daughter of Pleasant Jordan, who was in the Senate in 1780. He died in 1810 and left three sons—Abner J. Perry, Andrew T. Perry and John B. Perry. His daughter, Patsy, married John Dickinson, of Winton.

Thomas Deanes, who lived near Murfreesboro, serves the county as High Sheriff. In 1802 Joseph F. Dickinson begins to serve a long term of twenty years as Clerk of the County Court, and Mills Jernigan enters upon the duties of Public Register from 1800 to 1813. He was a county officer in the Third Decade.

In 1802 Gen. Thomas Wynns is elected to Congress, where he continues to serve his country for five years, and then returns in 1808 to his old place in the State Senate, where he continued until 1817.

Lewis Walters, of Winton, in 1807 makes his first appearance in public life as a member in the House. He served two terms, and was then defeated by Gen. Boone Felton.

The year of 1803 found the condition of the country in peace and prosperity, good-will prevailing among the people, in place of sectionalism and party strife. Murfreesboro was still the favorite place in the county. It was fast becoming the Mecca of the east. Over on the hill across the ravine leading to the river was the residence of Capt. Lewis Meredith. He was a man much valued in his day. He left no son, but several daughters. One of his daughters married James Maney, the mother of Judge Thomas Maney, and one married William Cowper, who was the mother of Lewis Meredith Cowper and Richard Greene Cowper and William Cowper, of Gates County, Mrs. Redmond R. Parker and Mrs. Weed. Another one of his daughters married Dr. Lewis Meredith Jiggetts, a physician of eminence, and a member of the House in 1822.

Col. Hardy Murfree was living at the late residence of his father, Wm. Murfree, on the hill on the opposite side of said ravine from Captain Meredith. Wm. H. Murfree had just opened his law office. Patrick Brown, of whom Major Moore speaks as being "a shrewd, honest and long-headed Scotchman," erected his home near the old Indian Queen Tavern, on the street now known as Broad street. He was an old bachelor and a merchant and a great writer. Dr. Thomas O'Dwyer, from Clonnel in Ireland, was also a bachelor, and lived on the same street near Brown. They were great cronies and succeeded in accumulating large estates by trading and note shaving. O'Dwyer died in 1834 in his 57th year, and was buried in Murfreesboro. He kept a diary which was a valuable document on account of the store of information it contained, but no copy can now be found except for the year 1824. Many other families settled in the town about this time from the Northern States, and afterwards became leading and eminent citizens in the county and State. Dr. O'Dwyer, while a speculator, was an honorable man, an eminent physician, a great philanthropist, an omniferous reader, and a believer in the religion of Christ, although not a communicant of any church. No one can read his writings without forming an exalted idea of the man. His frequent references to his mother and sister who were living in Edinburg in 1824, and to his native land, are sublime. He longs for home in the land of the shamrock.

> " O the shamrock, the green, immortal shamrock!
> Chosen leaf, of bard and chief,
> Old Erin's native shamrock."

But little is known of Walters.

General Felton was a man of considerable ability and courage. He descended from a noble and intellectual ancestry. He was a recognized leader in the House and Senate. He served six terms in the House and one in the Senate. He married the daughter of William White, of Raleigh, who was the sister of Governor Swain's wife, and granddaughter of Gov. Richard Caswell. General Felton died in Winton,

DECADE V.—1800-1810. 93

October 4, 1821, as appears from the *Raleigh Register* of November 2, 1821. He had been elected the second time to the Senate, just prior to his death. He owned what is known in the county as the "Cofield Land." Lewis Walters is returned to the House in 1810.

In 1805, Col. Hardy Murfree emigrated to Tennessee, where he owned a large landed estate, and died in 1809. We find on the death roll during this decade, Robert Montgomery, the able legislator; Nathan Harrell, Capt. Lewis Meredith, Thomas Winborne, the late chairman of the County Court, who left his widow and two minor children—Sarah Agatha and Elisha Winborne—surviving him. His widow married a Mr. Roberson, and they had one daughter who died in Mississippi in 1887 without marrying; his daughter, Sarah A., married John Gurley, of Murfreesboro. Their descendants live in Tennessee and Mississippi. Mrs. Rebecca Cowper, wife of Wm. Cowper, and Emily M. Hichborn, of Murfreesboro, and others. In 1809, Murfreesboro gained some valuable additions to her population; among them was Dr. Thomas Borland. John Scott, who lived near Harrellsville, was made general in the militia during this epoch.

DR. THOMAS BORLAND.

This high-minded citizen lived in Murfreesboro, on the lot now owned by James D. Babb. He was profound as a scholar, eminent as a physician, haughty and chivalrous in manner, strong in his love of country, and greatly respected by his neighbors. He was thoroughly familiar with all the classics and could read Greek and Latin fluently, and through life he enjoyed reading his Greek books. For a long while prior to his death, in 1830 or 1831, he was one of the wealthy and aristocratic justices of the county, and was often seen presiding over the court. Dr. Borland married Harriet Godwin and moved from Suffolk, Va., to Murfreesboro about 1809. They left the following sons: Euclid, Solon, and Roscius Cicero. Dr. Euclid Borland first married Elizabeth R. Moore. She died in January, 1850. A few years thereafter he married Lucy Wilkinson, daughter of Commodore Wilkinson of the U. S. Navy. He spent much of his time in Mississippi and Louisiana, where he owned large plantations, but his home was in Murfreesboro, until about 1856. For some years prior to his death, in April, 1881, this delightful and chivalrous old gentleman and his wife, Lucy, boarded at the Atlantic Hotel in Norfolk, Virginia. Like his father, he was fond of the classics, and especially of the Greek language and Greek characters. His son, General Euclid Borland, lived in New Orleans, La., and died September 26, 1896, in Norfolk, Va., at the age of 52, while on a visit to his relations.

Solon Borland emigrated from this county about 1842, to Arkansas, and became a United States Senator from that State, April, 1848, to April, 1853, and afterwards was Minister to Nicaragua, 1853 to 1854; General in the Confederate Army, and died in Texas, January 31, 1864.

We have written of Roscius Cicero Borland on other pages.

The Borlands were all brave, true, honorable and chivalrous people. Hertford for some reason never insisted upon the advancement of her noble and able sons for governmental honors. They were, however, always appreciated in their adopted homes.

Most of the Borlands and the members of their families are buried near Murfreesboro on the Ramsey farm, owned by the wife of the author.

Augustus Moore, who married Martha A. Bell, *nee* Ramsey, the widow of Samuel Bell, was born in 1784, near Murfree's Landing, in Hertford County, and died in Mississippi in 1843, where he was buried. Some years thereafter his body was exhumed to bring to the burying-ground near Murfreesboro. When taken up the body was found to be petrified and as hard as a rock. It was in this condition when it was reinterred at Ramsey.

Phogion A. Borland, son of Euclid, the first, by his first marriage, was a brave and daring soldier in the army of the Confederacy, and died August the 15th, 1863, from a wound received on the field of battle.

In addition to what we have said of the gentleman, the lawyer, and the chivalric Roscius C. Borland, we have learned that he stopped the practice of the law and left Hertford County to visit his brother Euclid in Mississippi on account of failing health. It is said that he was taken with measles while on this visit and died from it before returning, but this is contradicted by some, and the other account is that he returned to Murfreesboro from Mississippi and resided for a short while on the lot now occupied by E. C. Worrell, with his family, and there died. He died in 1847. But we find nothing to indicate that he was buried in the old family burying-ground, which is strong proof that he probably died in the South and was there buried. He married Miss Temperance Ramsey, of Hertford County, April 25, 1837, and left surviving him a daughter, Miss Harriott Godwin Borland, named for his mother, and a son Thomas Roscius Borland, named for his father and himself. His daughter married Mr. Thomas Smith, of Suffolk, Virginia, and his son was a prominent lawyer in Norfolk, Virginia, and U. S. District Attorney for the Eastern District of Virginia, and died while filling that office or shortly afterwards. The children of Roscius were born in Murfreesboro. He has a grandson, Armstead Borland, now living in Norfolk, Virginia, who is the last one of that name. Gen. Euclid Borland has two married daughters living in Louisiana.

GENERAL SCOTT.

John Scott appears in the census of Hertford County taken in 1790, as the head of a family of seven, and as the owner of eighteen slaves. In the early years of the nineteenth century, he was a militia general. He married a Miss Brett, the aunt of the late Elisha D. Brett, of Maney's Neck, and died January 30, 1812, leaving three sons, William, James and George. William lived in Maney's Neck, where W. H. Henderson now lives, near Riddicksville, when the author was a boy. He was the father of several children, one of whom now resides in the county, Winfield Scott. James, another son, married Martha Ann Rea, of Murfreesboro, and lived and died in Baltimore, Maryland. They were the parents of the late Mrs. H. T. Lassiter, of Murfreesboro, and of Mrs. Virginia Yeates, late wife of the Hon. Jesse J. Yeates. Another son, George, lived and died in Petersburg, Virginia. William had a son, Andrew, who was a general in the army of the Confederate States of America, from Florida.

William Little belonged to a family long famous for its virtues and patriotism in North Carolina. He was the son of William Little, of Chowan County, and who was Attorney-General and also Chief Justice under the government of the Lords Proprietors, and was also one of the commissioners for the Province of North Carolina in 1727 to settle the dividing line between the Provinces of Virginia and North Carolina. The mother of William Little, Jr., was the daughter of Chief Justice Gale. On November 4, 1790, Nathaniel Macon, a member of the House of Commons from Warren County, presented to the House of Commons the petition of William Little, of Hertford County, protesting against the election of Henry Hill of that county for the reason that his election was irregular and void. The petition was referred to a committee, whose report was adverse to Hill, and a new election was ordered. Hill and Little were again candidates, and Hill was duly elected. Both of the rival candidates were from Maney's Neck. This was the first contest from the noble little county of Hertford. His brother, George Little, of Hertford County, was a major in the militia during the Revolutionary War.

William Little, Jr., married Miss Mary Ann Person, sister of the famous Gen. Thomas Person, of Granville County, and left one son, William Person Little, who moved to Granville County and became a man of much prominence in the State. His daughter, Penelope, married Sharp Blount, a lawyer living in Winton.

Wm. P. Little married Ann Hawkins, the daughter of Philemon Hawkins, Jr., of Warren County. Their children were the late Col. George Little, of Raleigh, *aide-de-camp* to Governor Vance during the late Civil War; Thos. Person Little, of Hertford County, who was once chairman of the old County Court, Wm. P. Little, Jr., and Mrs. Dr. Charles Skinner, of Warren County. The daughter of Dr. Skinner married William Hutchings, of Hertford County, who resided where the Rev. H. B. Parker now resides, near Buckhorn. They were the parents of the late distinguished and gifted physician of Murfreesboro, Dr. Wm. H. Hutchings. Thos. P. Little never married. He lived in Maney's Neck on the farm known as Old Town, and was passionately fond of the sport of deer and fox hunting. In the correspondence between the Winborne brothers we frequently find a reference to the strong friendship of Thos. P. Little for the late Maj. S. D. Winborne. Wm. P. Little, Jr., died without leaving any male representative to perpetuate the family name. George Little, his brother, left two sons, William and George. The former was a distinguished surgeon in the late Confederate Army, and died in Raleigh in 1879. George Little, Jr., married Miss Momoiselle S. Vann, daughter of the late Tilman D. Vann, of Hertford County, and died in 1880. His widow and several daughters still survive him.

Among some of the prominent merchants in the county at the beginning of the last century were Daniel, William and Joseph G. Rea, of Murfreesboro, and James Rea, of Winton. They came from the North to this county, and for a number of years were among the leading business men in the county, and the descendants and connections of these people are large and extensive. The oldest of which we have any information was Daniel Rea, who lived North and married in 1764 Rachel Johnson, of New York, and their children, Daniel, Jr., William, Sally, James, Joseph G., Martha, and Sampson, all of whom became citizens of this county. Daniel Rea, Jr., married Sally, daughter of Alexander Banks, of this town. William Rea was married four times. His first wife was Margaret Wynns, of the old Wynns family of the county. She lived but a short time, when in 1797 he married Mary Wynns of the same family. His third wife was Mary Peck, a Northern lady, and his fourth wife was Julia Blackwell, of Blackwell's Island, N. Y. Mr. Rea lived on the lot where H. T. Lassiter now resides, and did business in the large brick building on the corner of Fourth and William streets. The late Col. U. Vaughan received his first lessons as clerk in Mr. Rea's store. He was a man of industry and great executive ability and business sagacity. He accumulated a large estate, and died in New York. No one was permitted to remain idle about him. When his clerks were not otherwise engaged, he made them empty nail kegs and count the nails, or rub hardware in the store, and the like. His brother and partner, Joseph G. Rea, married Nancy Canless in 1813, who was the aunt of Mrs. Lewis M. Cowper, who was Annis Collins, of Portsmouth, Virginia. He committed suicide by hanging himself in his garden. He lived at the place now owned by Lloyd J. Lawrence. He left no children. His widow long survived him. The writer, in 1888, qualified as administrator *de bonis non* on her estate, and made during the same year a final settlement. Their home was beautifully furnished with the most costly furniture and paintings. After his death, Lewis M. Cowper sold his place to Thomas N. Myrick, which is now owned by Uriah Vaughan, and moved with his family across the street to live with the widow, and that became the home of L. M. Cowper's family until their death.

Decade V.—1800-1810.

JAMES REA.

James Rea married Mourning Norfleet, of Gates County, in 1808, and was a prominent merchant in Winton. He died October 24, 1824, and his wife died March 24, 1842. They left one child, Hannah Peck Rea, who was the sole heir of his estate. She was greatly admired and much courted by the beaux of her day. She was greatly admired by W. D. Pruden, Sr., and his family, and they visited her up to her old age. Her father, James Rea, was born in Boston, Mass., October 9, 1779. Miss Rea married, in December, 1836, Jno.

JOHN V. LAWRENCE.

V. Lawrence, son of Elisha Lawrence of this county and his wife Polly Vaughan, a prominent and successful merchant in Murfreesboro. They reared eight children: Capt. L. C. Lawrence, who married, in 1867, Sue E. Southall, daughter of Jno. W. Southall; Mattie A., who married, in 1869, S. F. Pearce, of Camden County; James N. Lawrence, who married Bettie Pruden, in 1870, of Nansemond County, Virginia, and who are the parents of Lloyd J. Lawrence, Esq., one of the county's lawyers; Dr. John C. Lawrence, who married Tibbie Joynes in 1875, from Eastern Shore, Virginia. The Doctor was a very successful and reliable physician in his native town; he died in 1885, and his widow a few years thereafter married Judge Hance, of Baltimore City. The Doctor left no child. Charles A. Lawrence, married Anna Weirsdotz, of Norfolk, Virginia, in 1885, where they now live. Annie married, in 1872, her cousin, John N. Vaughan, a successful commission merchant of Norfolk, Va. Emily B. married, in 1876, Dr. Walter Reid, a celebrated physician in the U. S. Army. Dr. Reid died in 1904, leaving his wife and one daughter surviving him. Their oldest daughter, Ellen O., married the late Col. J. N. Harrell, November 5, 1863. Mr. Lawrence was for a long time an active justice of the peace in the county, and attended the terms of the County Court regularly. He was a man of strong character and was greatly esteemed in the county. For a number of years he and Col. Uriah Vaughan carried on a mercantile business as Lawrence & Vaughan, and met with much success. His children and grandchildren follow nearly all the avocations of life, and are well scattered. He died in 1870, and his wife died in 1904.

MRS. DR. WALTER REID.
nee EMILY LAWRENCE.

William Rea, son of Sampson, married Nancy Brown in 1818, and was the father of Margaret, the wife of the late B. T. Spiers, of Buckhorn, and of the late Sampson Rea, of Illinois. He died in 1825 and is buried in this town. His daughter Mary Ann married, in 1822, Col. Benj. B. Camp, of Murfreesboro, who was one of the old magistrates. Colonel Camp died October 9, 1833, and left one son, William, who went West and became a Methodist preacher. His widow married Jos. T. Liles and died in 1838. William Rea, Jr., married, in 1824, Nancy Cross, of this county. He soon died, and his widow married Garrison Smith in 1825. Smith also died early, and she married, in 1828, William T. Bynum, late of Maney's Neck, and was the mother of Bynum's daughters Mary and Annie. Bynum was married three times. One of his wives was a Stallings, of Gates, and

DECADE V.—1800-1810. 101

the last was the daughter of the late Jethro W. Barnes.
William Rea's daughter Fannie married King Parker, the
father of Rev. H. B. Parker and brother of Capt. Samuel
Moore's wife, of Buckhorn.

RETROSPECT 1810.

At the end of the first fifty years of the county's existence,
we find the United States on the verge of another war with
Great Britain. Let us look back and see what we have done
and the changes that have taken place since the birth of the
county. The Province has been transformed into an independent and sovereign State. The yoke of British authority
had been thrown off. We bow no longer at the altar of kings
and royal governors, nor suffer under arbitrary laws, but live
under a constitution adopted by our people, and governed by
officers of our choice. A compact had been entered into by
the thirteen original States for their mutual protection
against their common foes. A constitution for the government of the United States has been framed and adopted.
The number of States by this time had been increased to
seventeen. Schools had been established throughout the
States. The University of North Carolina had been established. The academy for boys and girls had been incorporated and established in Murfreesboro in 1794, and presided
over by able educators. The population of the county had
greatly increased by a highly educated Christian people, its
towns had become inhabited by a wealthy and energetic class
of business men and traders, while many of the old worthies
of the county had filled honorable graves, the living were
taking their places and rapidly advancing to places of great
honor and public trust in the State and country. Her sons
were widely known for their high character, patriotism and
eminent ability. Her daughters were the product of a lofty
and noble Christian civilization. Churches were dotted
throughout her borders and their pulpits filled by ministers
equal to those of the present day. Her profound Lemuel

Burkitt had been pleading for the Master and for Higher Liberty with burning eloquence and with great success. While her Samuel Wells, a follower of the Wesleys, had by his logic and wonderful discourses, fastened the Wesleyan Methodism in the hearts of many of her people and established the first Methodist church in Murfreesboro in 1806. With a high civilization and with her gifted sons and noble daughters, the county moved onward with beatific dreams for her future goal.

The thirteen original States were Delaware, Pennsylvania, New Jersey, Georgia, Connecticut, Massachusetts, Maryland, South Carolina, North Carolina, New Hampshire, New York, Virginia, and Rhode Island. These States first constituted the United States. Vermont was admitted to the Union in 1791, Kentucky admitted in 1792, Tennessee in 1796, and Ohio in 1802. From the territory west of the Mississippi, purchased by the United States from France in 1803, the following States have been admitted to the Union: Louisiana in 1812, Missouri in 1821, Arkansas in 1836, Iowa in 1846, Minnesota in 1858, Kansas in 1861, Nebraska in 1867, North and South Dakotas, Montana and Wyoming in 1890, and Oklahoma and Indian Territory in 1906.

DECADE VI.

1810—1820.

War clouds are forming. Soon the call to arms will be heard. The county's representative in the Senate is not changed until 1818, when Gen. Boone Felton succeeds General Wynns, and the former is succeeded in 1819 by his cousin, John H. Frazier, and the latter is supplanted by the old Sheriff, Thomas Deanes. There are some changes in the county's representatives in the House. Hertford was prolific in her able men. General Felton is again seen in the House in 1811, 1813, 1814 and 1817. Capt. Jethro Darden defeats William Jones and returns to his old place in 1812. General Felton is defeated in 1812 by the scholarly, chivalrous and able lawyer, William H. Murfree, of Murfreesboro. This was a strong team. No county in the State was better represented. Mr. Murfree was one of the ablest lawyers in the State. In the spring of 1813 he was elected to Congress from the Edenton district over Gen. Joseph Riddick, of Gates, Lemuel Sawyer, of Pasquotank, and Hinton, of Chowan, by a majority of 603 votes over his strongest competitor. This we get from the issue of May 13, 1813, of the *Hornet's Nest*. Sawyer was then a member of Congress. Murfree was again elected in 1815, serving four years, 1813-1817. He declined a third nomination. In Congress he was an able and strong defender of the dignity of the United States in its war with Great Britain. He married Elizabeth Meredith Maney, daughter of James Maney IV., of Murfreesboro, and they had a son, William Law Murfree, who was born in Murfreesboro, N. C. In 1823, Hon. William H. Murfree moved, with his family, to Tennessee to look after his large interests there which he inherited from his father, Col. Hardy Murfree, and died in 1827. His son, Wm. Law Murfree, was afforded the best advantages for the highest education. Naturally very bright, he became a profound scholar and lawyer. He graduated at the head of his class at the University of

Nashville, Tennessee. He also inherited a large estate from his father and owned large cotton plantations in Mississippi and Tennessee. He married Fannie Priscilla Dickinson, daughter of David Dickinson, and reared three children. Miss Fanny N. D. Murfree, who is the authoress of a successful novel entitled "Felicia"; and Miss Mary Noailles Murfree, who is also an authoress of nineteen volumes of fiction, published under the *non de plume* of "Charles Egbert Craddock." She now resides in Murfreesboro, Tennessee, a city established by her great-grandfather, Col. Hardy Murfree; and William Law Murfree, Jr., who married Miss Louise Knostman. William Law Murfree, Sr., was himself an able writer. In 1881 he moved from Murfreesboro, Tennessee, to St. Louis, where he edited the *Central Law Journal* for three years, 1886, 1887 and 1888. Many of the legal profession in this State remember well the able articles from his pen, which were freely copied from in the law periodicals of London and Dublin, and in Canada and Australia. While in St. Louis he wrote three law books, viz., "On Sheriffs," on "Official Bonds," and "The Justice of the Peace." He was also an able contributor to the literary magazines, the *Century, Scribner,* and others. He returned to Murfreesboro, Tennessee, in 1890, and died in August, 1892. The Hardy Murfree who graduated at Chapel Hill, N. C., in 1848, was a son of Matthias B. Murfree. There is a town by the name of Murfreesboro in Pike County, Arkansas. The Murfrees and Maneys intermarried. Hon. John Bell, of Tennessee, who was one of the candidates for President of the United States in 1860, married Louisa, the elder daughter of David Dickinson and sister to the wife of Wm. Law Murfree.

In 1811, Col. William Jones first appears as one of the county's representatives in the House. He is the younger

---

Note.—Mrs. J. H. Hillman of Pittsburg. Penn., was Miss Sarah Murfree Fraser, the daughter of Henry Fraser of Tennessee and wife Elizabeth Murfree, daughter of Wm. Law Murfree of Murfreesboro, Tenn.

Decade VI.—1810-1820. 105

brother of James Jones, who retired from public life in 1806. He lived and died on the farm later owned by the late Daniel Vanpelt Sessoms. He served in the house for five terms.

In 1812, the United States became involved in war with England. James Madison was President of the United States. George III. was still King of England. His malignant heart had not relented. He cherished malice against the former colonies. England had a strong navy, and they began in many ways to interfere with American commerce, by sending its warships to hover around American ports and prevent free traffic between Americans and other countries, and in that way injure our commerce and humiliate the States. War was declared in June, 1812. Most of the fighting was near the Canadian borders, yet much fighting occurred along the Atlantic coast as far down as Norfolk, Virginia, and in the Virginia waters, and around Charleston, S. C. Joseph F. Dickinson, of Murfreesboro, entered the war from Hertford, as Brigadier-General, and was put in command of the American troops around Norfolk, Va., a position assigned to Col. Benj. Wynns, of Hertford County, in the War of 1776-1782. The war ended in March, 1814, as a result of the capturing of the British *"Penguin"* off the coast of Brazil, by the American *Hornet*. A treaty of peace between the two countries was arranged and ratified to meet in the summer of 1814, at Ghent, in Belgium. The commissioners on the part of the United States were John Adams, James A. Bayard, Henry Clay, Jonathan Russell and Albert Gallatin. The treaty which was agreed upon, was simply to stop the war and both countries behave themselves in the future. It was "much ado about nothing."

Hertford County furnished to this war, in addition to General Dickinson, the following soldiers:

Irwin Jenkins, Capt.; Everett Garrett, Lt.; Benjamin Hill, Ensign; Andrew Oliver, Cadet; James Spiers, Cadet; Wm. Walton, 1st Sergt.; Hardy Banks, 2d Sergt.; Josiah Battle, 3d Sergt.; John Scott, 4th Sergt.; Arthur Booth, 1st Corp.;

Elisha Horton, 2d Corp.; Charles Jenkins, 3d Corp.; J. Witherington, 4th Corp.; John Manning, drummer; Wiley Brown, fifer; James Early, Lemuel Holloman, James Hayes, Thomas Britton, Luke McGlaughon, Nathan Baker, Cornelius H. Godwin, Anthony Brown, Anthony Williams, Noah Evans, Jacob Sewell, Jethro Sewell, Jacob Hare, John Baker, John Scull, Thomas Holland, Henry DeBerry Jenkins, John Curl, John Denton, William Ballester, Thomas Clark, Josiah I. Atkins, Lewis Carter, Jonas Atkins, Henry Brantley, William Williams, Henry Wiggins, Miles Hobbs, John Everett, Alexander Booth, Thomas Thorne, Zachariah Brown, Edward Crump, Anthony B. Lee, John Benthall, Robert Brantley, Thomas Neal, Alexander Smith, Wm. Brown, Isaac Pearce, George Askew, Edward Brantley, Henry Eure, Joseph G. Rea, William Wynns, Thomas Weston, Allen L. Ramsay, Elisha Mints, James Parker, Benj. Ezell, Britton Sikes, William Andrews, Isaac Foster, John C. Montgomery, Reuben Clark, Lewis Boone, Josiah Robbins, Elijah Archer, Ephraim King, Samuel Boone, Mathuel Archer, James Raleigh, John Weaver, James B. Jones, Hardy Davis, Mills Walters, Abram Boone, West Boone, John Bizzett.

Muster roll of the detached militia organized in August, 1814; 1st regiment, composed of Chowan, Currituck, Camden, Pasquotank, Perquimans, Gates, Hertford, Bertie, Northampton, Halifax, Warren and Nash.

HERTFORD'S LIST.

Irvin Jenkins, Captain; Benj. Hill, Lieut.; Henry G. Darden, Ensign; Benj. Brown, Drummer; Silas Shewcroft, Fifer; William Brown, James Johnston, Willie Willoughby, Luke Hare, John Brown, Burwell Eure, Jacob Overton, Elisha Overton, Jeremiah Aikin, William Wynns, Wm. W. Whitfield, Jeremiah D. Aikin, James Rasberry, Jr., Allen Moore, Wm. Downing, James Barnes, Willie Cullon, Jesse Harrison, Wm. Sessoms, Geo. Holloman, Jr., Justin Holloman, Samuel Britton, Jethro Sewell, Aaron Hare, Isaac

Baker, David Welch, Jr., William Sewell, Thomas Elerton, Benj. Hocal, Geo. H. Bond, Isaac Taylor, Wm. Purnell, Wm. Yeates, Samuel Parker, William Teaster, Benj. Wynns, Samuel Ely, Eli Harrell, Boan Driver, John Dickinson, Thomas Early, John P. Hare, Stephen Howell, John A. Anderson, Benj. Blare, Sterling Francis, Arthur Vick, George Whitley, Jno. Seall, David Williams, James Skinner, Henry Brantley, Daniel Williams, James Worrell, Thomas Faircloth, Benj. Williams, Lemuel Sanders, Gray Mahone, John Vinson, John Vaughan, Jonas Clifton, William Rogers, Nelson Joyner, Wm. Andrews, Robert Montgomery, William Parker, Mathias Cook, Hilary Vaughan, Joel Grizzard, Hardy M. Banks, Wm. A. Payne. Walter B. Myrick was in the war from Southampton County, Virginia.

Below we will give a few names of some of the brave and patriotic sons of other counties in North Carolina, who faced the British on the field of battle, when she was attempting to defeat the American independence and government, viz.:

Capt. Sampson Glenn and Mark Glenn, of Person County; Benj. Glenn, of Surry County, and Benj. H. Wortham, of Granville; John I. Cunningham, Cunningham Sharp, Lancaster Cunningham, and Samuel Wellborne, of Mecklenburg; Duncan Cunningham and Alex. Cunningham, of Richmond, and Benj. Scarborough, of Greene, and Jesse Scarborough, of New Hanover; Peter Wynns, of Tyrrell; David Wynns, Henry Wynns, and George Wynns, of Martin County.

NORTHAMPTON COUNTY.

Capt. James C. Harrison, Stephen Winborne, Lemuel Winborne, Winborne Futrell, David Boone, William Boone, Arthur Tyner, Micajah Futrell, Lemuel Vaughan, Goodwin Daniel, James Vaughan, Benj. Vaughan, Nehemiah Vinson, Jiles Lewter, Benj. Griffin, Gilbert Griffin, James Griffin, Brittain Lassiter, John Jenkins, Benj. Jenkins, Benj. Lawrence, Nathan Pope, Samuel Warren, Edwin Liles.

BERTIE COUNTY.

Benj. Winborne, Lodswick Pruden, Thomas Hoggard, Tristram Capehart, Thos. S. West, Wm. Castellow.

HALIFAX COUNTY.

Lt. John Peebles, Wm. R. Daniel.

GATES COUNTY.

Hardy Williams, Robert Parker, Wm. Pyland, Lt. Isaac K. Hunter.

HORNETS NEST.

On September 3, 1812, the publication of the *Hornets Nest,* a newspaper, in Murfreesboro, was begun. The editor was Bryant Bramble, Esq., and published by Rea & Huntington, of Murfreesboro. Mr. L. J. Lawrence, the law-partner of the author, has several copies of it, and we have had access to its newsy columns. It was spirited and spicy, and a newsy paper. It was correctly named. It contains news not only throughout North Carolina, but throughout Europe, New England, and all the States of the Union. It was thoroughly American in sentiment, and for war.

We culled from these issues of this noted paper some information about the town of Murfreesboro and its people. The "Hertford Academy" was located here, and the General Assembly of the State passed a law authorizing George Gordon, William P. Morgan (who lived on the lot where the author now resides), Patrick Brown and Ephraim Wheeler, of Murfreesboro, to conduct a lottery for the benefit of the Academy. Tickets were regularly sold for prizes, which amounted to $8,000.00.

From this paper we find the names of Alexander Banks, John Wheeler, William Rea and Joseph Rea, John Dawley, Abner Williams, and others of Murfreesboro's business men. We learn of Jabez Wheeler, of Winton. And of Elisha Felton, Lewis Walters, Jno. Vann and Joseph F. Dickinson, commissioners appointed by the County Court to have the county

Decade VI.—1810-1820.

court-house and jail repaired. We also learn from it that Joseph F. Dickinson, in February, 1813, owned the hotel lot and the other lots between that and the Chowan River, now owned by Jordan and Parker, and also the Winton Ferry, and the swamp land across the river in Gates County, and he offers the whole for sale, as he intends to move to Murfreesboro to live. He was then Clerk of the Court. He entered the army in the War of 1812-1814. He was promoted to the rank of Brigadier-General. His deputy performed the duties of the office until his return.

Thomas Deanes made his *debut* as a legislator in 1815. He had served for a number of years as Sheriff of the county, and was well known and belonged to a large and influential family. He was the son of Daniel Deanes, who lived near where Oris Parker, Esq., now resides. Our Clerk of Court, Thomas Deanes Boone, is a descendant of him; so was Gen. William Deanes Barnes, of Florida.

The elegant Thomas Maney, another of Hertfords' gifted lawyers, enters the House in 1817. He was a descendant of Maj. James Maney, who died in Maney's Neck in 1754. He won honors in his profession before leaving the county and State. In 1825 he moved with his family to Tennessee, and became a great judge in that State.

The Maneys were among Hertford's most prominent people during the first fifty years of the Republic. James Maney, the first, a French Huguenot, when he first came to America, early in the 18th century, settled on Long Island. Afterwards he moved to Virginia, and thence to North Carolina, and located on the Chowan River in Hertford County, near the present Maney's Ferry. He soon became the owner of a large body of land bounded by Chowan River, Buckhorn Swamp, and reaching up as high as Como, taking in the land of the late Abram Riddick, Capt. J. H. Picot, Capt. Samuel Moore, and the lands in the Bartonville section. He established Maney's Ferry, which is mentioned in Colonial Records as one of the King's places for landing his army stores. Prior to the formation of Hertford County these lands were in Northampton. He was Major in His Majesty's militia in Northampton County, and also a justice of the peace as far back as 1744, and died in the year 1754. William Short was made major to succeed him. Col. Rec., vol. 5, p. 163. He left a son, James, who married Miss Susanna Ballard. James Maney, the second, was a vestryman in Northwest Parish in Northampton County in 1758, and one of Hertford's representatives in the General Assembly in 1778. He left only one son, James III., who married Elizabeth Baker, the daughter of Gen. Lawrence Baker. They left four children—James, Henry, Susanna, and Priscilla. Susanna married Gen. Thomas Wynns. Henry died while young.

Priscilla married a Mr. Burgess, and James married Miss Mary Roberts, of Murfreesboro. James alone left children. Mrs. Mary Maney, the wife of James, the fourth, died February 13, 1815, aged 46 years and 26 days, and Mrs. Susanna Wynns, wife of General Wynns, died January 5, 1822, aged 56 years and 5 months. Both are buried with their husbands on the Abram Riddick farm, which was the old Maney homestead.

James IV. left six children—James, Elizabeth Meredith, Thomas, Mary, Henry, and William. James Maney, the fifth, was a distinguished doctor in Murfreesboro. He married Miss Sallie H. Murfree, and William married Miss Martha Murfree, daughters of Col. Hardy Murfree, of Murfreesboro, N. C., in this county. Elizabeth M. married Hon. Wm. H. Murfree. Henry married Miss Mary Brown, of Murfreesboro, N. C., daughter of Samuel Brown. Thomas, who was a prominent and leading lawyer in Hertford County and Eastern North Carolina, lived in Murfreesboro, and married Miss Annie R. Southall of that town, sister of the late John W. Southall.

In 1790, as appears from the U. S. Census, James Maney and Mrs. Peggy Maney resided in Hertford. Thomas Ma-

Judge THOMAS MANEY.

ney represented Hertford County in the General Assembly in 1817. The name is spelt in the State histories "Manney." But on investigation of the old records of Northampton and the old Colonial Records of the State, I found that the oldest as well as the younger members, spelt the name Maney, which is correct. I foolishly spelt it Manney in the history of "The Winborne Family" for the first time in all my professional life. I fell in the error by seeing it spelt in the old histories of the State, Manney.

The four Maney brothers—James, Henry, Thomas, and William—emigrated from Hertford County, N. C., to Tennessee about the year 1825. Dr. James and Henry Maney settled near Murfreesboro, Tenn., and Thomas and William at Franklin in that State.

Henry Maney and family left Tennessee early in the fifties and moved to Texas, where his children now reside.

None of these brothers were in public life except Thomas Maney, who was elected Circuit Court Judge about 1839 or 1840, and was re-elected for some sixteen or eighteen years, and before his last term expired he resigned and enjoyed private life until his death, April 10, 1864. After his election to the judgeship he moved from Franklin to Nashville, so as to be in the center of his circuit, which was composed of Williamson, Davidson, and Sumner counties.

None of the Maneys entered political life in Tennessee except David Maney, son of Dr. James Maney, who represented his county in the legislature some few years before his death, some five or six years since. Henry Maney, the third living son of Judge Thomas Maney, was in early manhood editor of the *Nashville Gazette,* and was also elected to the legislature, as floater, of his flotorial district, and who died soon after in 1859. Gen. George Maney, the oldest living son of Judge Maney, was a lieutenant in the First Tennessee Regiment in the Mexican War, and entered political life soon after the close of that war and was elected to the legislature. When our Civil War commenced, he was made Colonel of the First Tennessee Regiment, C. S. A., and was soon made Brigadier-General, and so served throughout the war, but during the latter part was incapacitated for much active service on account of wounds.

Returning home after the war, he was made president of the Tennessee and Pacific Railroad, and became a Republican in politics, and was elected to the Senate in the Tennessee legislature. He had unlimited influence over Governor Senter during the carpet-bag period, and it was greatly to that influence that the government was restored to the Confederates, and the Negro and carpet-bag regime was overthrown, and the State was then governed by the Confederate Democrats. He represented the United States as minister to Columbia for four years and afterwards as minister to Uragua and Paragua for four more.

General Maney died in Washington City on February 9, 1901. James D. Maney, second living son of Thomas Maney, was living in Petersburg, Va., at the beginning of our war, and was captain of a Virginia company; was later promoted to major and transferred to the Army of Tennessee. After the war he returned to Nashville and entered the railroad business and was for many years comptroller of the N. C. and St. Louis Railroad. His health giving away he resigned and is now living a very private life.

Frank Maney, the youngest son of Judge Maney, was at West Point Military Academy when the Italian revolution, under Garibaldi, commenced. He left West Point and joined the revolutionists, serving on the staff of General Avenzaza. At the close of the Italian revolution he returned to the United States and entered the Confederate Army as captain of a battery of artillery, and was captured when Fort Donelson fell. On his way to prison he escaped in Ohio, and made his way through Maryland to Richmond, then back to the Army of Tennessee, when he was made major of a battalion of sharp-shooters. He was killed soon after the war, in New Orleans.

Thomas Maney had two daughters. The oldest, Bettie Maney, married John Kimberly, Professor of Chemistry in the University of North Carolina, and after the Civil War was a resident of Asheville, N. C. They both have been dead many years, and most of their children are residents of Asheville.

The youngest, Annie, married Major John L. Sehon, a prominent young lawyer of Nashville, just at the beginning of the Civil War. On the retreat of our army she accompanied her husband South, and died in Augusta, Ga., in 1864. Major Sehon died a few years after the close of the war.

Dr. James Maney, the oldest of the four brothers, had four children, three sons and one daughter, all of whom are now dead. Henry Maney, who moved to Texas in the fifties, had two sons and three daughters; the eldest son, Henry Maney, became a judge of one of the courts of Western Texas. William Maney raised a large family of five sons and seven daughters, all of whom made good and substantial citizens, but none entered public life. Maney's Ferry, and that beautiful section of the county, "Maney's Neck," took its name from this family, though it is often spelled "Manney's Neck."

"FUDGE."

A REMARKABLE CRIMINAL TRIAL.

About the year 1818 Joseph T. Liles, Thomas Faircloth, James Spiers and William Rogers, four citizens of Murfreesboro of good standing, were arrested and brought before a justice of the peace for a hearing, upon the charge of having, the night before, forcibly entered the dwelling-house of Jethro Pender, who lived at the old Weaver place, on the hill between Murfreesboro and Maple Fork Branch, and beat Pender until he was nearly dead, and robbed his house of a trunk, which was carried out, and $300 and other valuables, taken and carried off.

Liles, Faircloth and Rogers were soldiers in the War of 1812. At the trial the granddaughter of Pender, who alone lived with him, testified that she was in the house with her grandfather when three of the men broke into the house, and one remained on the outside. They were disguised. She begged them not to kill her grandfather; they beat him badly and took out the trunk. That she heard them talking to each other, and she heard them call the names of Jo. Liles, Jim Spiers, Bill Rogers, and Tom Faircloth. Upon this evidence these men were put in jail to await a trial in the Superior Court for their lives. They knew they were not guilty, but their lives were in great jeopardy. Under the law at that time they were not allowed to testify. The friends of each tried to get him to turn State's witness against the other three and receive amnesty from the State. Liles, Spiers and Faircloth declared their innocence, and said they would die before they would swear to a lie to take the lives of their neighbors. Rogers yielded to the pressure and confessed his guilt, and testified, implicating the others. They were convicted, and Liles, Spiers and Faircloth were sentenced to be hanged.

A few days before they were to be executed a message came to the sheriff of the county from a negro in jail in Suffolk, Va., under sentence of death. The sheriff went to Suffolk and saw the negro. He told the sheriff that the men in Winton jail under sentence of death for robbing Jethro Pender, were innocent. That they knew nothing of the robbery. He confessed his guilt and stated to the sheriff all the circumstances of the crime and the names of the other three negroes who were with him. That they disguised themselves, and that they called themselves Jo. Liles, Jim Spiers, Bill Rogers and Tom Faircloth to mislead Pender and his granddaughter. His companions were Willis Fudge, Harvey Fudge and Aaron Wynns. He informed the sheriff how they divided the money, and where he could find the hair trunk. That they took from the trunk, besides $300 in money, a piece of black velvet goods, and Aaron Wynns

DECADE VI.—1810-1820. 115

had a jacket made of the goods. That Harvey Fudge bought a white horse with his part of the money. The sheriff returned and found the trunk in the place where he was told to look, and other facts just as related to him by the Suffolk criminal.

Steps were promptly taken to secure the pardon and release of Liles, Spiers and Faircloth. Spiers survived the ordeal but a short time. Liles and Faircloth lived several years and when the end came their bodies were placed to rest by kind, sympathetic and appreciative friends, in the burial ground on the river hill.

Thomas Faircloth was an old ancestor of the late Chief Justice W. T. Faircloth, of Goldsboro, N. C.

No person charged with crime could testify in his own behalf in North Carolina, as in many other States, until 1881, nor could one testify in his own interest in civil suits until March 12, 1866. There is no doubt but that unnumbered wrongs have been inflicted under the laws as handed down to us by our English ancestors.

The facts of the above trial were published in a pamphlet entitled "Fudge."

During this decade the county received many valuable additions to her population. Among them were Seth Southall and Rev. Daniel Southall, who immigrated from Amelia County, Va., and settled in Murfreesboro in 1815.

Daniel was born August 9, 1768. Prior thereto, in 1806, Rev. Samuel Wells became a citizen of the town, and by his zealous efforts the first Methodist church was established in the town. He lived at the Willis Warren place, and was the grandfather of the wife of the late James W. Hill, of Murfreesboro. Rev. Southall was a man of great energy and success in both spiritual and temporal things. He was a Methodist and preached with great power and pathos. Dr. O'Dwyer often speaks of his powerful and persuasive sermons. By his wonderful discourses on the Gospel he soon established a large membership for the Methodist church and gave it the ascendency in the town. He was twice married.

His first wife was a niece of Gen. Joseph Riddick, of Gates; his second wife was the sister of Gov. John Branch, of North Carolina. Rev. Southall was also a large and successful merchant. He died in Washington City while there on a visit, and was buried in that city about 1835. He lived in the house formerly occupied by Dr. R. H. Worthington, the first compounder and patentee of the famous "Worthington Cholera Compound."

JOHN W. SOUTHALL.

Rev. Southall's eldest son, John W. Southall, was born July 28, 1797, and resided in Murfreesboro up to his death, July 3, 1873. Like his father, he was married twice. He first married Julia, daughter of Richard and Martha Johnson, of New York, at Buckhorn Chapel, November 1, 1825. Their daughter, Julia, married Thomas N. Myrick, December 19, 1847. After the death of his Johnson wife he married, March 4, 1842, Mrs. Mary Wynns, widow of the late Wm. B. Wynns, and acquired by this marriage a large estate. By this marriage he had two daughters, the present Mrs. Capt. L. C. Lawrence and Mary W., who died young.

John W. Southall was a great Methodist, and spent his money freely to advance the cause of his church, and was a devoted friend to the upbuilding of the Wesleyan Female College of his town. He took an active interest in the affairs of the county, and served as a magistrate for a number of years prior to the Civil War. His fine horses were often commented upon and he took great pride in showing them. His last wife died March 22, 1900, in her 89th year.

His brother, James H. Southall, married June 7, 1837, Sarah C., the daughter of John and Sarah Wheeler, and later moved to Columbus, Miss.

Decade VI.—1810-1820.

Rev. Southall had two daughters. His elder daughter, Annie R., married Judge Thomas Maney prior to his removal to Tennessee in 1825. His second daughter married Tristram Capehart, who lived where the late Col. J. N. Harrell resided. Mr. Capehart's daughter, Caroline, married Prof. John Kimberly, the old school-teacher at Buckhorn, and later professor in the University at Chapel Hill. Prof. Kimberly moved to the county from the North when he was a young man, and bought the Titus Darden place at Buckhorn and settled there. His daughter, Miss Rebecca Kimberly, now lives in Asheville, N. C.

Another valuable addition was Robert Warren, of Virginia, who in 1818 settled in Maney's Neck. He was the great-uncle of the writer. While he never married, he was a model citizen, and his example as a noble man and charitable neighbor was of untold value. He was the son of Col. Etheldred Warren, an officer in the Revolutionary War, from Virginia, and a grandson of Samuel Warren, of Virginia.

Dr. Richard B. Baker, of Hickory, N. C., brother of Mrs. Sue J. Myrick, of Murfreesboro, and a former citizen of this county, and a grandson of General Baker, writes that he knew Robert and his brother Etheldred Warren well, and that no nobler men ever lived. This grand old man died in 1846.

ROBERT WARREN.

The writers grandmother, Martha Winborne, often told him that her brother, Robert Warren, was said to resemble George Washington. He was aristocratic in his dress and bearing, and was fond of the music of the chase, and placed great value on his well-trained pack of fox hounds. He persistently declined to accept any office, preferring the liberties of private life. His home was known as "Cedar Hill." Dr. Baker speaks in his letter of December, 1905, of Robert's brother, Etheldred Warren, as the "old Saxon." The latter was a soldier in the War of 1812 from his native State Virginia; and their father was Col. Etheldred Warren, of revolutionary fame, from Virginia. He was born January 16, 1749, and married Margaret R. Darden, October 15, 1775. Colonel Warren was the son of Samuel Warren, of Virginia.

Titus Darden, on December 10, 1819, purchased from Wm. H. Murfree the tract of land where Capt. J. H. Picot now resides at Buckhorn, it being lot No. 3 in the division of the lands of James Maney III. Titus Darden was the brother of Jethro Darden, and died in 1834, leaving a will in which he mentioned his children, William H., Harriet T., James C., and Elizabeth J. Darden. He made Thomas P. Little and John Waddill his executors. William H. Darden married Elizabeth Brett, sister of William and Mills Brett, and lived near Union. They were the parents of our James H. Darden, the leading merchant at Union. (See Decade 8).

Maj. John W. Moore, in his History of the State, speaks of a fashionable wedding in Hertford County in 1803, which was witnessed by many of the celebrities of the county, and the handsome beaux and the gay and beautiful belles of the county made brilliant the occasion; and when under the strains of the eloquent music of the negro fiddlers, the venerable Gen. Thomas Wynns and Robert Montgomery participated enthusiastically in the dancing.

We will present you with the likeness of a bride of Murfreesboro about fifteen years later—Mrs. Frank Jeggitts.

DECADE VI.—1810-1820.

MRS. FRANK JEGGITTS.

The Jeggitts family was one of the old and fashionable families of the Borough. They were of French-Huguenot descent. The name was originally spelled Jegitts. Dr. Lewis M. Jeggitts was in the House from the county in 1822. His brother David moved to Mecklenburg County, Va. They were the sons of William Jeggitts. John Jeggitts married widow Barshaba Hill, and left two daughters, Barshaba and Sallie, who are remembered by many of our people of to-day. Edw. K. Jeggitts, the old sheriff who died in 1846, has a daughter living in town now—Miss Maggie Jeggitts, a faithful friend and companion of Mrs. Susan J. Myrick, the granddaughter of General Baker.

Sheriff Jeggitts first lived near Mt. Tabor Church, but later at the old William Rea place, now owned by H. T. Lassiter. Frank Jeggitts was the son of Edw. R. Jeggitts, and they lived in town where the Rev. C. W. Scarborough now resides. Frank was extremely fond of dress, and always looked like he was dressed for a wedding occasion. Mrs. Jeggitts, whose likeness is seen above, was his second wife. She was regarded as one of the most beautiful women of her day. They moved to Tennessee.

The spirit of education continues. In 1820, Samuel Nicholson, of Maney's Neck, established a high school near the present site of Buckhorn Academy, and for years conducted a successful school at that place. Many of our old ancestors in the Neck received their early education at this ancient seat of learning. Nicholson married the wealthy widow, Sallie Hill, and died in the 8th decade in New York City. After his marriage to the rich widow he gave up the school and was succeeded by a Mr. Durbar, and the latter by a Mr. Warner, of Connecticut, and Warner was succeeded by Mr. Bogart, the father of the late John H. Bogart, of Franklin, Va.

Mr. Bogart was a Northern gentleman and a fine instructor, but he did not remain long, when he was succeeded by Prof. John Kimberly, of Brooklyn, N. Y., a gentleman of culture and refinement, a ripe scholar and a splendid instructor. A few of his students at Buckhorn are still living and they enjoy relating their experiences at this ancient and classic school. Our father was one of the Kimberly boys, and before his death he delighted his family in recalling the fate of some of the boys. Professor Kimberly gave the school a State reputation as a first-class academy, for the thorough training and instruction of young men. Professor Kimberly while teaching this school married Caroline, the daughter of Tristram Capehart, of Murfreesboro, by his first wife Emma, the daughter of Rev. Daniel Southall. His second wife was Bettie, the daughter of Judge Thomas Maney and wife, Rebecca Southall. Miss Rebecca Maney Kimberly, of Asheville, N. C., is the daughter of Professor Kimberly by his last wife. In the early part of the Ninth Decade, Professor Kimberly was elected a professor in the University at Chapel Hill and moved to that place. He owned and lived, while in the county, at the present home of Prof. J. H. Picot at Buckhorn. Buckhorn Academy was incorporated by the General Assembly on January 9, 1847. Under the act the land cannot be sold and can be used only for school purposes. The trustees cannot in any way dispose of it.

Prof. Geo. W. Neal, of Murfreesboro, who married the daughter of John Hart and wife, Betsy, of the same town, succeeded Prof. Kimberly at the Buckhorn Academy. Professor Neal was a scholarly and able teacher. Our Judge

---

NOTE.—Prof. Neal was a member of the faculty of the Wesleyan Female College in Murfreesboro for several years after leaving Buckhorn. At the beginning of the Civil War he was the Principal of the Male Academy in the same town. From here he moved to Franklinton, N. C., where he conducted a high school for boys. From there he moved to New Bern, N. C., where he resided up to his death.

Decade VI.—1810-1820. 121

Walter H. Neal, of Scotland County, N. C., is the learned son of the professor. After several years of successful teaching at the Academy he was succeeded by that elegant, scholarly and Christian gentleman, George A. Brett, of that section of the county. Mr. Brett was a graduate of Chapel Hill, and was one of Professor Kimberly's Buckhorn boys. He first taught at Williamston, Martin County, where he married Miss Slade of that county. About 1857 he was succeeded by our venerable Julian H. Picot, another of the Kimberly boys, and who delights to-day to talk of those memorable days. Professor Picot has presided over the destinies of that classic school with splendid success and commensurate ability from 1857 to the present time, excepting the period he was serving in the Civil War, training and educating the minds and hearts of the young men, and is still, in his old age, its principal, teaching the young idea how to shoot. He has prepared for college over 2,000 young men, and they can be found in all the busy walks of life.

CAPT. J. H. PICOT.

Professor Picot was born May 20, 1832, in Plymouth, N. C., and was the son of Peter O. Picot and his wife Marietta, the daughter of Edmond Blount of that town. Professor Picot was a Confederate captain in the late Civil War, and served throughout the struggle. He was prepared for college at Buckhorn by Professor Kimberly. His father graduated at Chapel Hill in 1818 in the class with James K. Polk. Professor Picot's grandfather was an eminent surgeon in France and a close friend of Louis XVI. He came to this country and settled in Plymouth, N. C., where he died in advanced age in 1847, where he and his nephew, Louis Picot, who came to this country in 1836, are buried side by side. His tomb has the following inscription: "Here lies the exiles of France." Captain Picot married Antoinette, the eldest daughter of T. D. Vann, who lived near Buckhorn, in 1852, and moved to the county in 1855 and bought the home of Professor Kimberly, which was the third lot in the division of James Maney's lands, and where he still lives, enjoying a happy old age. His children will be mentioned later.

Captain Picot, after being prepared for college under the tutorship of Professor Kimberly, and then after two years at William Bingham's Military Academy, entered Columbian College, in the District of Columbia, where he prosecuted his studies with marked success, always ranking among the first in his classes. He completed his collegiate studies at Union University, N. Y., where he received his degree of A.M. in 1852. He is one of the finest and most polished linguists in the State.

France cedes to the United States, as the result of Gen. Andrew Jackson's great victory at the Battle of New Orleans, the territory of Florida in 1819, which was in that year admitted as a State in the Union.

DECADE VII.

1820—1830.

This decade in the history of the county shows many changes. Gen. Joseph F. Dickinson, who had served the county for about twenty years as Clerk of the County Court, and as Brigadier-General in the War of 1812-1814, passes away on the 6th day of June, 1822, in his 47th year. He was the son of Joseph Dickinson, Jr., who was born in England, December 7, 1740, and arrived in America in 1762 and died in Winton in 1784. General Dickinson's grandfather, Joseph Dickinson, Sr., was born in England, February 25, 1712, arrived in America in July, 1774, and died in Winton, July 23, 1776. The General married the beautiful and charming Peggy Gregory, and lived in Winton until 1813, when he moved to Murfreesboro and resided where Col. J. M. Wynns now resides. Mrs. Dickinson's brother, Thomas Gregory, has descendants to-day in Salisbury, N. C. The General was very wealthy. He left no children. In his will he devised most of his large estate to his wife, who some years after his death married Dr. Isaac Pipkin, of Murfreesboro. He made Gen. Thomas Wynns and John Wheeler his executors. Dr. Pipkin by his marriage with the widow Dickinson reared two daughters, Anne Maria and Mary Ellenor. The former died shortly after reaching womanhood, and the latter married Capt. Wm. B. Muse, of the U. S. Navy.

George Gordon succeeded him as clerk. Gordon's first wife was Patsy Sharp, daughter of the first Starkey Sharp, by his second wife Jemima Hare. John Hare Gordon was the son of this marriage. He succeeded his father as Public Register for a short while. Father and son soon died. George Gordon's daughter, Barsha Gordon, by his marriage with the widow Harrell, married Dr. Lawrence O'Bryan, of Murfreesboro.

James Wright Moore has passed away, and in 1825 his widow, Ester Cotton, married Capt. John Jones, of Virginia. Rev. Daniel Southall on June 5, 1825, preached the funeral sermon of Gen. Thomas Wynns.

Andrew V. Duer begins a term of usefulness as Public Register. Lewis M. Cowper throws on the toga of Clerk of the County Court, which he wears for about forty years. He married Miss Collins, daughter of William Collins, of Portsmouth, Va., and reared two sons, the late Pulaski Cowper, of Raleigh, and Dr. R. L. Cowper, of Murfreesboro. R. G. Cowper, the brother of the clerk, takes charge of the office of High Sheriff for twenty years, excepting one term secured by Edw. K. Jeggitts. The office had just been vacated by the death of Jesse Deanes.

W. H. Murfree and Thomas Maney leave for Tennessee. Capt. James Frazier succumbs to the ravages of ripe old age. Rev. Daniel Southall continues to preach the gospel truths to the people with great power and pathos, and increases the membership of the Methodist society, and Jacob Hare and William Morgan are among the number to join. Rev. James Douglas thunders away at the Presbyterian church, and young Rev. William H. Jordan eloquently pleads for Higher Liberty and close communion, and Mrs. John Wheeler, Mrs. W. B. Wise, Miss Darden and Mrs. Perry Carter enroll their names as members of Parker's Baptist church, near Murfreesboro, and Elisha Winborne and wife and Mrs. H. D. Jenkins joined at Mt. Tabor.

In the summer of 1824 Jesse Deanes and Jacob Hare are candidates before the County Court for the office of High Sheriff of the county. Deanes received 18 votes and Hare 2. Peter Butts succeeds John H. Gordon as Public Register, but who is overthrown by Andrew V. Duer in 1825.

On the night of March 19, 1824, Dr. Thomas O'Dwyer, in his diary, states that Prince Murat arrived in Murfreesboro on the stage and puts up at the Indian Queen Hotel, and placed himself under the care of good old Moses Clements, the clever and genial proprietor. He remained in town a

DECADE VII.—1820-1830.   125

day or so, and then continued his journey to Florida, where he afterwards died. The Prince was the son of Joachim Murat, King of Naples, and a celebrated French cavalry leader, who was court-martialed and shot in 1815. It seems that a man had better shoot himself than to be a brave officer in the army of some countries. The Prince was banished from his country on account of his claims to the throne of Naples. He died an exile in Florida in 1847. His mother was the sister of Napoleon Bonaparte.

James Copeland, who represented the county in the House in 1821 and 1823, and in the Senate in 1824 and 1825, was the son of John Copeland and lived in Winton and kept the hotel formerly owned by Gen. Jos. F. Dickinson, located on the lot on which now stands the hotel of Jordan & Parker. He was not a man of collegiate education, but he possessed a strong native intellect, which he had so improved that he became one of the leading men of his county. He died July 11, 1826, at his home in Winton, and the *Raleigh Register* of July 25, 1826, speaks in high terms of this useful citizen. He left a wife and seven young children to battle with the world. His wife was a Miss Kilbus.

JAMES D. WYNNS.

James D. Wynns, who served with Copeland in the House in 1821, was the youngest son of Benjamin Wynns, of revolutionary history, and the uncle of our present Col. James Wynns. Mr. Wynns served long as one of leading justices of the peace, and as one of the Special Court of the county for several years prior to his removal to Bertie County. He married Sallie Johnson, daughter of Col. John Johnson, of Bertie, a nephew of Gov. Samuel Johnson, of Edenton.

Mr. Wynns, after his marriage, moved to his wife's plantation below Coleraine, in Bertie, and later moved to Edenton, where he resided until his death during the Civil War. He was a gentleman of refinement and education, polished in his manners and generous and kind to his neighbors. When young he was a favorite with his uncle, Gen. Thomas Wynns.

John Hamilton Frazier, one of the county's representatives in the House in 1818, and her Senator in 1819, was of an aristocratic Tory family in the county. His father was Capt. James Frazier, who owned a large body of land around Frazier's Cross Roads, from whom the name of the place is taken. Captain Frazier was a man of great wealth and when the colonies seceded from the British government he declined to take sides with the sons of liberty, and commanded a company of Tories and fought on the side of the British in the War of 1776-'82. He was a man of polished and attractive manners and had many strong friends in the county who deplored his stand in the mighty struggle for freedom. His large estate was confiscated. After the war he returned to the county, acknowledged his defeat and began to ingratiate himself in the esteem of his former friends. He was an honest man. He was loyal to the old country—the home of his ancestors. He now agrees to pay fealty to the American cause. His friends forgive him and he is restored in the confidence of his old friends.

Through the efforts of that great man, Hardy Murfree, he succeeds in purchasing his former estate which had been confiscated. His young son, John H., as he grew to manhood became a great favorite with the people of his county. Like his father, he was polished in manners, brilliant and highly educated, and he soon won a place in the hearts of the people. Unfortunately, however, he and his cousin, Gen. Boon Felton, became engaged in some trouble which soon ended the useful lives of these two men. The name is spelled by some Fraser, but the better authority seems to be that it is Frazier. The old magistrate of St. John's, John Bembury, married Jane, daughter of Captain Frazier.

Decade VII.—1820-1830. 127

Gen. Bridger J. Montgomery represented the county in the House and Senate frequently from 1818 to 1832, and served as Clerk and Master in Equity a short time between the terms of office of Howell Jones and William M. Montgomery. He was a militia general and a gentleman of splendid physique, popular with the people, and possessed many of the strong intellectual traits of his father, Robert Montgomery. He married Mary Cowper and died about 1835. His father Robert Montgomery was born February 23, 1757, married Mary Jones, and died October 31, 1808, leaving surviving him four sons—Bridger J., Dr. John C. Montgomery, Col. Kerr Montgomery, and George W. Montgomery. The latter married Martha Pipkin, sister of Dr. Isaac Pipkin, and represented the county in the Senate in 1834 and 1836, and died in Raleigh while a member of the Senate, leaving surviving him his wife and two daughters, the late Mrs. Isaac Pipkin and Mrs. Sue Frank, of Murfreesboro. His widow married the late John W. Harrell, of Murfreesboro. Kerr Montgomery never held any office except the military office of colonel in the militia.

William Meredith Montgomery, the old Clerk and Master in Equity from 1833 to his death about 1864, was the son of Gen. Bridger J. Montgomery. He married Amanda C. Harrell, sister of the late John W. Harrell and Col. Jarrett N. Harrell, of Murfreesboro. He lived at Frazier's Cross Roads and left surviving him several sons and daughters, among them were the late William Preston Montgomery and Robert Montgomery, of Norfolk, Va. Mrs. Maggie Matthews, of Winton, Mrs. Kate Blanchard, of the town of Hertford, N. C., and several others of his daughters married in the county.

Nancy C. Montgomery, daughter of Robert Montgomery, Sr., married Bembury Walton, a brother of Wm. Walton, who married Celia, daughter of James Jones III, his first cousin. William Walton died July, 1825. The *Raleigh Register* of July 26, 1825, contained a notice of the death of this leading citizen of Pitch Landing, in Hertford County.

Col. James Brickle and his wife are numbered among the dead during this decade. Colonel Brickle was the last of the illustrious family of that name, which had played such an honorable part in the early history of the county and State.

In February, 1824, Dr. O'Dwyer says in his diary, that Dr. Thomas Borland, Moses Clements and Capt. James M. Yancey qualified as magistrates. Abner Harrell qualified in 1825.

David E. Sumner represented the county in the Senate in 1822 and 1823. He represented Gates County in the House in 1819 and then moved to Hertford. He inherited from his great uncle, Gen. Luke Sumner, of Chowan County, a large estate, and also inherited a large estate from his great uncle, Robert Sumner, of St. John's. He was also the grandnephew of Gen. Jethro Sumner. His wife was Margaret, the daughter of Chief Justice John Lewis Taylor, of this State, and niece of Judge William Gaston. After the death of Chief Justice Taylor in 1829 his widow resided in this county with her son-in-law, David E. Sumner. Sumner was dissipated, and, like a majority of young men who inherit large fortunes, spent it freely. Before many years he had lost the major part of his patrimony. His widow, after his death, decided to emigrate with her slaves to Mississippi. The mode of travel in those days was by private conveyances. Before reaching her new home she died on the way, it is said, in a log cabin, alone with her young children and slave servants.

Some time after the death of Chief Justice Taylor, his son, of the same name of his father, resided in Hertford County and practiced law. He also was very dissipated. This young man fell on the steps of the Winton Hotel while beastly intoxicated and died in that position. W. T. Bynum qualified as his administrator in Hertford County

---

NOTE.—Chief Justice Taylor married Jane Gaston, sister of Judge William Gaston.

about 1854. In 1855 Bynum, as administrator of Taylor, obtained an order from the County Court of Hertford to sell some lots in Raleigh belonging to his estate. The sale was confirmed November 27, 1855, by the Court. In 1849 Taylor was living at the old Jerre D. Askew place, where Dr. W. H. Sears now resides at Union.

HERTFORD COUNTY MAN ASSAULTED IN GATES.

The *Elizabeth City Star* of May, 1824, gives an account of a deadly assault in Gates County by six negro outlaws on a white citizen of Hertford County. The *Western Carolinian*, of Salisbury, N. C., in its issue of May 18, 1824, refers to the occurrence as an "alarming affair!" A slave holder was passing through Gates County on his way home, when a gang of six negro outlaws, armed with guns, rushed from a thicket into the road to assault and rob the white man. Being unarmed he dashed into the woods and made his escape. No names are given. The paper further states that this lawless and desperate gang had for some time been prowling about in the woods and swamps of Gates and other counties, committing acts of violence and plunder. Our old fathers had their troubles and dangers as well as those of the present day.

" Who breathes must suffer; who thinks must mourn;
He alone is blessed who never was born."

DEATHS OF FINNEY AND RAMSAY.

W. H. Finney, the owner of "Finney's High Hills" and "Lover's Leap," on the romantic banks of the Meherrin River, north of the Borough town, on the farm now owned by the sons of Job R. Hall and wife, Sarah M. Hall, *nee* Harrell, died in 1825, and devised his property to his nephew Thomas S. Finney, and Mary, and Elizabeth Banks, daughters of Hardy M. Banks.

Henry Ramsay, the owner of the Indian and Queen Hotel, died in 1827, and devised his property to Henry W. Bell, and granddaughter Elizabeth R. Moore, and her daughter Elizabeth Hare.

We learn from O'Dwyer's diary for 1824 that Professor Peltier, a Frenchman, lived in Murfreesboro and conducted a dancing school, and that the young people patronized him liberally. Also, that the people of the town during those days were not unlike those of the present day. They were fond of going to the gallery of Mr. Charles Winesdale and having their *likeness taken*. He says he went down one day and had his likeness taken, and when it came the ladies said it was not a good likeness of him. On one occasion when he called at Winesdale's he found Mrs Rea having her *likeness taken*.

The society of the town was gay and festive. He tells us of the annual dance at the Indian Queen Hotel on the night of July 4, 1824. He says he went down to the dance and was surprised to see so few there; that there were only about fifty couples on the floor dancing, when at the last annual dance there were 100.

U. S. Senator Branch was a frequent visitor to the town in those days. We have been told by some of the wise people that pictures were not taken in those days. They are mistaken. Art and poetry are as old as nations. Sculpture and painting go back beyond the memory of man. The principles of photography were practiced by Schule, the Swedish chemist, as far back as the middle of the 17th century, and the utilization of Schule's observation on chloride of silver in the production of photographic likenesses in England began in the 18th century and was improved by Joseph Nicephore Niepee in the beginning of the 19th century. The photographers and likeness-takers followed the early emigrants to the Colonies, where the art has reached great perfection. One should not think that because the present process of taking photographs did not exist beyond a certain period, that no other process existed.

Dr. O'Dwyer tells of many amusing characters in the town. There were many Irish families living here, and he was a man who was greatly respected and a prominent citizen.

He was proud that he was an Irishman, and he hated to see his Irish neighbors act ugly. Barney Usher often received a lecture from him. Usher would get drunk in spite of everything. He came one day to O'Dwyer to borrow some money for his wife to visit Norfolk. The doctor loaned it to his wife and recorded in his diary, "B. Usher called to borrow money for his wife to visit Norfolk. He wants to get his wife away that he may enjoy his rum. He should be ashamed of himself. His wife is entirely too good for him." She remained away for two weeks, and Barney could not hear from her and he became very much distressed for fear she would not return. He called to see O'Dwyer and got his severe reprimand, and sobered up. She returned, and the old fellow was happy.

EDUCATION.

There exists a mistaken idea as to the education and intelligence of our early forefathers in America. Some of the present day think that we have reached a degree of learning and intellectuality far superior to our forefathers of 1776 and of the early days of our republic. For vigorous intellect, clearness of judgment, plainness and purity of language, logical arguments, and the study of man, they were certainly our equals, if not our superiors.

Bancroft and Wheeler in their historical works, referring to the days of the Revolution, wrote that "when reading the resolves of the Provincial Congress, the Provincial Councils, the District Committees of Safety, and the addresses which they published to the country, the purity of the language, the simplicity of style, the cogency of argument, are so remarkable that they cannot be surpassed by the most polished productions of the present age. Even in the handwriting of the men of 1775, as exhibited in the Journals, will bear a fair comparison with those of the present day, and perhaps surpass them in ease and plainness."

The same is true of the ages preceding. Such shows that our forefathers had not been inattentive to the objects of practical education. The first Constitution of North Carolina written and adopted by her sons in December, 1776, and the Constitution of the United States, prepared by the immortal Thomas Jefferson, the messages of George Washington to Congress, and his farewell address to the American people, the State papers and speeches of the early patriots, are lasting monuments to the wisdom and intellectuality of the olden times, and they stand out to-day in bold comparison with the productions of modern times.

In the N. C. Constitution of 1776 it is declared that "all useful learning shall be duly encouraged and promoted in one or more universities"; and in 1789 the University of the State at Chapel Hill was established. We find the question of education in the Province of North Carolina considered by the government as far back as 1736. There were, even then, schools in the country where young men were educated, and many were sent to the old countries, where they received the highest university education and returned to the Province to aid in guiding the destinies of the race. And, further, the population was being constantly increased from the earliest day of the country's history by learned and scholarly men and women from the old countries. History repeats itself, and the progress of mankind in the present day in many of the sciences, inventions, discoveries, and the like, have not reached the perfection and grandeur of remote antiquity, as disclosed by the exhumation of the buried cities of the old countries.

In 1825 the county was honored by a visit from Gilbert Montier, Marquis de La Fayette, the young French General in the American Army for freedom. He reached the town of Murfreesboro from Suffolk, Va., February 26, 1825. The news of the coming of General La Fayette was made known throughout the county and the noble sons and daughters of the county were on hand to greet and honor the distinguished guest.

Maj. John W. Moore tells in his history that a meeting was held in the town several days prior to the arrival of the great Revolutionary Hero, to arrange for his reception. "Dr. Thomas Borland presided and William Rea was Secretary. A committee consisting of Col. James Brickle, Dr. O'Bryan, Lewis M. Cowper and John W. Southall was appointed to meet the General at Somerton, Va., and escort him to the town. He stopped at the Indian Queen Hotel, then owned by Henry A. Ramsay. The brilliant young lawyer, Thomas Maney, in a speech of welcome, greeted the distinguished visitor, who graciously replied." The parlors of the grand old hotel were beautifully decorated with the national colors and patriotic banners. The brass band filled the hearts and souls of the assembled multitude with patriotic music, the noble and beautiful women of the town and county on that occasion would have done honor to a presidential inaugural ball at the present day. A most dignified and elite reception was held, when all were given an opportunity to shake hands with the general. At 11 o'clock p. m. they sat down to supper. The people came in from all parts of the surrounding country the next day to see and shake hands with the great general and join in the great rejoicings. On Monday following he was escorted to Jackson, where Chief Justice John Lewis Taylor was holding court.

Leonard Martin, one of Hertford's members in the House in 1826, had only been a resident of the county for two or three years. He was a lawyer and moved here from Pasquotank County, which county he had represented in the House in 1816, and again in 1819 and up to 1822, inclusive. He died shortly after his return from the session. General Montgomery and Martin were conspicuous in that body for their ability and devotion to the duties of their trust. Elisha Hunter Sharp was elected to the Senate to succeed James Copeland, deceased, but only served one term. Senator Sharp was the eldest son of Maj. Jacob Sharp and the grandson of Starkey Sharp and his wife, Sarah Winborne. His mother was a Nancy Hunter, of Gates County. He married Sallie Carter, daughter of Major Isaac Carter, and reared two sons and a daughter. His son, Jacob H. Sharp, was a brave Confederate soldier from Mississippi, and was promoted before the end of the conflict to the rank of Brigadier General, and is now living in Columbus, Mississippi. His second son, Thos. L. Sharp, was also a gallant Confederate soldier from his native county. He entered the army as Captain, and was promoted to the rank of Lieutenant Colonel, and was killed in battle at Atlanta, Ga., in 1864. E. H. Sharp had several brothers and one sister. In 1827 Mr. Sharp was defeated for the Senate by David O. Askew, of Pitch Landing, who was the grandson of Thomas Outlaw, of Stony Creek, in Bertie County, whose farm is mentioned in the boundary of Hertford County, and a nephew of the old legislator and Moderator of the Chowan Baptist Association, George Outlaw, of Bertie. Mr. Askew was in the Senate again in 1828. Shortly after his return from the Senate he emigrated to Mississippi, where he still has a number of descendants. His brother, Dr. George O. Askew, was in the Senate from Bertie in 1827, and remained a member of that body for six years. The eminent physician, Dr. A. J. Askew, of Bertie, who married Miss Ward, of Norfolk, Va., was also a brother of the Senator. David O. Askew married Martha Etheridge. Their cousin, John O. Askew, of Pitch Landing, was the son of George Askew and wife Annie, the daughter of George Outlaw, the old Moderator, and he was the cousin to the old Congressman, David Outlaw. The Askews and Outlaws were people of wealth and prominence in the eastern part of the State. John O. Askew married Sarah A., the daughter of Abner Harrell, of Harrellsville, a descendant of Abner Harrell, who was a freeholder and one

JOHN O. ASKEW.

DECADE VII.—1820-1830.   135

of the jurors drawn for Bertie in 1740. The Harrells played a prominent part in the early history of the county. John O. Askew was a man of wealth and high character, and was born October 11, 1813, and died in 1878, leaving surviving him three sons, Dr. Abner H. Askew, John O. Askew, Jr., W. S. Askew, and two daughters, Mary R., the wife of W. P. Shaw, Esq., and Pattie E., who married her cousin, W. D. Askew, of Mississippi, where he now resides. She died several years ago.

JOHN O. ASKEW, JR.   MRS. PATTIE E. ASKEW,
                         Daughter of J. O. Askew.

David O. Askew had three sons, George, Joseph, and W. D. Askew, who moved to Mississippi with their father when young. Joseph Askew entered the Confederate Army and took a courageous part in behalf of the "Lost Cause." He received a severe wound, which resulted in the amputation of one of his legs. After the war he served his State as a member of the Legislature, and as Railroad Commissioner. He married Willie, the daughter of Gen. Jacob H. Sharp, of Columbus, Miss., and died about 1895. His daughter, Miss Annie Sharp Askew, of Columbus, Miss., and Miss Sarah Gravier, of Chattanooga, Tenn., were the maids of honor at the annual reunion of the Confederate Veterans at New Orleans, in the spring of 1906. The newspapers commenting on these maids of honor, said: "These two young ladies can boast of Confederate ancestry equal to any in the South."

Gen. Jacob H. Sharp is a Hertford County boy. He is the son of E. Hunter Sharp and wife Sally Sharp, *nee* Carter, as before stated. E. H. Sharp and wife had three children, Thomas L., Caroline, and Jacob H. Sharp. Thomas L. was in the Mississippi Senate in 1857 and was a Colonel in the Confederate army, and killed at Atlanta, Ga., in 1864. Caroline married Hunter Walker, of her father's adopted State, and Jacob H. Sharp entered the Confederate army, and was ranked as follows: Major, Lieutenant-Colonel, Colonel, and in 1864 was promoted to Brigadier-General. He married Miss Harris, of Mississippi, the daughter of Judge Harris of that State. Since the war he has served as State Senator and at one time was mentioned in connection with the nomination for the United States Senate. He still lives in Columbus. He is first cousin to our H. C. Sharp, and of Capt. William and Col. Thos. H. Sharp.

The little county of Hertford continued to send her ablest men to the Legislature. While the county was small, her representatives ranked with the ablest. They were not windy and noisy members, for that was not the character of her people. In 1827 she returned Gen. Bridger J. Montgomery and sent with him her gifted young son John Hill Wheeler, of Murfreesboro, who had just graduated with great distinction at Columbian College, in the District of Columbia, in 1826, obtained his law license in 1827. It was soon discovered that the future had in store greater honors for young Wheeler. In 1830 when in his twenty-fourth year he was nominated by the Democrats in the Edenton district for Congress, but he was defeated by the Whig candidate, Hon. William Biddle Shepherd. He served in the House of Commons for four years. In 1831 he was appointed by the President of the United States Clerk of the Board of Commissioners under the Convention with France. In 1837 he was appointed by the President Superintendent of the U. S. Mint at Charlotte, which office he held until 1841. In 1842

Col. JNO. H. WHEELER,
The Historian.

he was tendered the nomination for the House of Commons by the Democrats of Mecklenburg County, but he declined it. In 1842 he was elected Treasurer of the State. He was married twice; his first wife was Mary Brown, daughter of Rev. O. B. Brown, of Washington City, and his second wife was Ellen, the daughter of Thomas Sully, of Philadelphia. The writer remembers well when he made his graduating speech in Lincoln Hall, in Washington City, at the end of his course of study at Columbian University in 1874, this old gentleman was in the audience, and sent the author a congratulatory note on the rostrum and requested him to remain; that he wished to talk with him at the close of the exercises. His kind and gentle words were greatly appreciated. Colonel Wheeler prepared and had published in 1857 a most valuable history of the State of North Carolina. The Wheeler family are able to trace their lineage back to the origin of Charles II. The first one of the name to settle in America was Joseph Wheeler, the son of Sir Francis Wheeler, an admiral in the English navy during the reign of King Charles II. Col. Wheeler's father was John Wheeler, who was born June 23, 1771, in New Jersey, and moved to Murfreesboro about the beginning of the 18th century and resided here until his death, August 7, 1832, leaving surviving him his widow Sarah, who died July 15, 1833, and several sons and daughters—Col. J. H. Wheeler, Dr. Samuel J. Wheeler, the old postmaster of his native town, and Col. Junius B. Wheeler, Professor of Engineering at West Point. His daughter Julia married Dr. Godwin C. Moore. The old merchants at Winton first—later at Murfreesboro—Ephraim Wheeler and Jabez Wheeler—were brothers of John Wheeler.

Elisha A. Chamblee lived near Pitch Landing, and served in the House in 1829 and 1831. He was a man of means, but with little experience in public matters. He was a quiet, but true member. He has representatives in the county to-day.

ELISHA WINBORNE.

On the 20th of July, 1829, Elisha Winborne, who lived near Winton, and one of the county's justices of the peace, and late chairman of the County Court, died in his 37th year. A good man and a useful and honorable citizen. He and his ancestors had been devoted sons of the county for a long while. April 1, 1819, he married one of the noblest women of her day, Martha Warren, of Southampton County, Va., and the daughter of Col. Etheldred Warren, an officer in the Revolutionary War of 1776-'82. He left his widow with five small children, all under ten years of age, to battle with the world. His children were the late Micajah T. Winborne, of Mobile, Ala.; Maj. S. D. Winborne, of this county; Dr. R. H. Winborne, of Chowan; Caroline, wife of the late Britton S. Moore, of Murfreesboro, and Richard Winborne, of Tennessee. After the death of the father, his family was taken to the home of Robert Warren, the bachelor brother of the widow, in Maney's Neck, where they were cared for and the children educated by that noble man. Elisha left a fair estate, which Mr. Warren took charge of and managed for their good. He was the son of Thomas Winborne and wife, Sarah Copeland, and the grandson of Maj. Henry Winborne and wife, Sarah Hare.

DECADE VIII.
1830—1840.

The decade from 1830 to 1840 was one of the most historical epochs in the affairs of the county between the War of 1812-1814, and the stormy times preceding the Civil War of 1861-1865. During the last decade the county had lost by death and removal some of its most distinguished citizens.

Gen. Joseph F. Dickinson, long the Clerk of the County Court, a man of great wealth, a brigadier-general in the War of 1812-'14, a man of decided ability and of great usefulness, had gone to eternal rest. George Gordon, the Public Register of the county for many years and Clerk of the County Court for a short time, as General Dickinson's successor, was taken from the roll. Hon. Wm. H. Murfree, the lawyer, patriot and statesman, emigrated in 1823 to Tennessee. The brilliant Thomas Maney also emigrated to Tennessee in 1825. Many other such losses the county sustained during these ten years.

At the May Term, 1830, of the County Court, the following justices of the peace were present: Thomas Duer, Silas Parker, Abner Harrell, James D. Wynns, William B. Wynns, Elisha H. Sharp, Thomas Daniel, Elisha A. Chamblee, Abraham Thomas, Thomas Borland, John Vann, Lewis M. Jeggitts, Jacob Hare, Jerry D. Askew, John Granbury, Carr Darden, Daniel V. Sessoms, Wm. P. Morgan, Kinsey Jordan, Watson Lewis, Wm. Nowell, Jacob Sharp, John Winborne, Elisha Sessoms, Sipha Smith, Bridger J. Montgomery.

This was a grand occasion in the county, as were all the May terms of court. Now was the time for the election of all county officers. All the grand Moguls of the county were present. It was a grand display of splendid citizenship.

The following officers were elected:

John Vann, Esq., Chairman of the Court.
Louis M. Cowper, re-elected Clerk of the Court.
Richard Green Cowper, re-elected High Sheriff.

James Sidney Jones re-elected County Attorney.
Andrew V. Duer re-elected Public Register.
Walter Myrick made Foreman of Grand Jury.
L. R. Jernigan made Officer of Grand Jury.
John A. Anderson elected County Trustee.
Thomas Griffith elected Coroner.
Riddick Cross, Treasurer of Public Buildings.
Miles H. Jernigan elected Entry Taker.
Perry Carter elected County Ranger.
Abner Langston elected County Processioner.

L. R. Jernigan, David C. Cross, Abner Harrell, Edward K. Jeggitts, Thomas Winborne, Samuel Moore, Starkey Sharp, Wm. N.. Perry, Ebenezer P. Alineman and Edward Moore were elected Constables of the several captains' districts.

THE APPOINTMENT OF INSPECTORS OF CREEKS AND RIVERS.

Isaac Taylor, of Simmons' Mill-race to Bertie line; Hardy M. Banks, at Murfreesboro; Michael Britton, at Pitch Landing; James S. Scull, from Pitch Landing to Sharp's Mill.

Under our State laws for many years past there were oppointed by the County Court one conductor of elections for each election precinct, and two judges or poll-holders for each ballot-box. The Court at this term appointed the following election officers:

Pitch Landing—Abner Harrell, Conductor; John Winborne and E. B. Norfleet, Judges for Senate box; Thomas B. Sharp and W. W. Sessoms, Judges for Commons box; W. R. Doughtie and W. P. Britton, Judges for Congress box.

St. John's—John Granbury, Conductor; D. Carter and R. Burns, Judges of Senate box; M. E. Newsom and Stephen Washington, Judges of House box; E. H. Newson and Geo. Williams, Judges of Congress box.

Murfreesboro—Hardy M. Banks, Conductor; Jas. Banks and Jno. W. Southall, Judges for Senate box; Tristram Capehart and Benjamin B. Camp, Judges for Commons box; J. A. Brown and E. D. Britt, Judges for Congress box.

Winton—James D. Wynns, Conductor; J. A. Anderson and G. W. Montgomery, Judges for Senate box; Edw. Shaw and Pleasant Jordan, Judges for Commons box; R. Cross and James Jordan, Judges for Congress box.

Deeds were proved and ordered registered; wills probated; overseers of roads, overseers of creeks, guardians for orphan children, administrators of deceased persons; committees appointed to examine accounts of executors, administrators, guardians, and report to Court; the poor looked after and patrols were appointed; county finances looked after. In fact, everything of interest to the county was looked after.

John W. Southall, James Banks, Capt. Benjamin B. Camp, Lemuel Valentine, Tristram Capehart, were among the foremen of the grand jury. John Winborne, William Nowell, David O. Askew, Abram Thomas and Watson Lewis were appointed a committee to audit the account of Matthias Baker, administrator of James Banks. And Timothy Ridley, H. L. Williams, Walter B. Myrick and Tilman D. Vann appointed a like committee to audit the account of S. D. Clark, administrator of John Whitey.

The above gives you some idea of the old County Court, its workings, and the dignity of the office of a justice of the peace in the olden times. The best and most competent men were in those days selected to perform all public duties.

This system was kept up until abolished in 1868. All of our honorable fathers served in all the positions mentioned above. It was a great honor to be a justice of the peace and preside in the old county courts of ancient origin. They were the courts of the people, and were of greater advantage and interest to the people than any other courts they had. It was an honor to be selected as foreman of the grand jury, or its officer, or to be elected a constable in a captain's district. The best men were always selected for all these positions. They were grand days.

We may mention a few other terms of this historic old court to show the new men who were brought forward in

142   HISTORY OF HERTFORD COUNTY, N. C.

public life. It was no easy task to be made a justice of the peace in those halcyon yet dignified days. When a man's name appeared on the roll of the justices of the peace in Hertford County it was the strongest evidence that he was a man of character, of influence, and a worthy citizen of his county.

During the next few years we find added to the list of the justices the names of Thomas V. Roberts, John G. Wilson and James Wells, of Murfreesboro; Godwin C. Moore and Edw. H. Newsom, of St. John's; Demsey Vinson and Geo. W. Montgomery, of Winton district; Thomas B. Sharp and Kenneth Rayner, of Harrellsville district; Abraham Riddick and Samuel G. Darden, of Maney's Neck.

In 1831 L. R. Jernigan was appointed Public Register, to succeed Andrew V. Duer, deceased. And in 1836 Edw. K. Jeggitts dislodged the efficient and popular R. G. Cowper from the office of Sheriff for one term, when the old and skilful politician recaptured the much-coveted office of High Sheriff of the county.

SOUTHAMPTON MASSACRE.

Hertford County, on August 22, 1830, sustained an irreparable loss in the destruction of her records for seventy years, by the incendiary act of one Wright Allen, a degenerate citizen of Northampton County, who lived about five miles from Murfreesboro, on the road to Conway.

On the 21st of August, 1831, the "Nat Turner Insurrection." or "Southampton Massacre," began in Southampton County, Virginia, not far from Hertford's northern boundary. Nat Turner, a negro slave preacher, then belonging to Joseph Travis, of Southampton County, was born October 2, 1800, as the property of Benjamin Turner, of that county, and was a black, flat-nosed, thick-lip and heavy-jawed negro.

For months preceding the butchery of the whites Nat had quietly and secretly organized the negroes in his neighborhood to join him, on August 21st, armed with guns, scythes,

Decade VIII.—1830–1840.

axes, knives, clubs and the like, and to proceed to kill all the white people—men, women and children—they could find. They started on their bloody and brutal mission August 21st, and the first victims were his master, Joseph Travis, his wife and three children. They continued rapidly from place to place to add to the number of the victims of their brutish natures, until they slaughtered fifty-five, if not more, whites, before they were checked and captured.

The whole surrounding country was thrown into a great consternation. Women and children were sent to the villages and towns for protection. A large number refugeed for safety to Murfreesboro. John Wheeler, of Murfreesboro, raised a company of troops and marched quickly to the scene of trouble and rendered valuable assistance in quelling the treacherous and bloodthirsty negroes.

Twenty-four of the devils were tried, convicted and executed. One of the *suspects* was shot and killed in the campus of the C. B. F. Institute in Murfreesboro, and there buried. His mission being to organize the negroes there to join in the bloodshed. Nat Turner was captured October 31st and executed November 11, 1831.

A complete and illustrated history of "The Southampton Insurrection," by Wm. S. Drewry, was published by The Neal Company, Washington, D. C., in 1900, and should be read by every person desiring to know of some of the trials and troubles of the Southern people. Southern life had its thorns and thistles as well as its flowers.

<blockquote>
"Pleasures are like poppies spread,
You seize the flower, its bloom is shed."
</blockquote>

Note.—John Wheeler's Company was composed of 100 men, and a Company of 75 went from Winton.

DR. GODWIN C. MOORE.

There are several on the roll of honor who made their debut as legislators from this county during this decade. Dr. Godwin Cotton Moore, of St. John's, a strong Democrat, was for the first time elected, in 1831, over Maj. Isaac Carter, to the House of Commons. Dr. Moore was a highly educated and polished gentleman. He was a direct descendant of the old, the wealthy, and of the leading families—the Cottons, Browns and Moores of the county. His ancestry ranked high and was ancient. He married Julia Wheeler, the daughter of John Wheeler, of Murfreesboro, and the sister of the historian John Hill Wheeler, of the same town. Hertford was a Whig county, although a Democrat sometimes succeeded in being elected. Dr. Moore was a Baptist, and a great favorite with the members of that denomination, as well as with his Democratic friends. He was moderator of the Chowan Baptist Association for 37 years. Having graduated in the collegiate department of one of the leading universities in our country, he then studied medicine at the University of Pennsylvania, where he received his diploma as a graduate in the science of medicine (if you call it a science), and began the practice of medicine in his native county and met with great success and reached the highest standard of a general practitioner in his chosen profession.

His exalted character, his polished manners and his learning well equipped him for any honors in the gift of his people. He was in the Senate in 1842 and again in the House from 1866-1868. He served for a number of years as one of the Special Court in the county, and just before the Civil War was Chairman of the County Court. He was a candidate of the Democratic party several times for Congress and

Presidential Elector, but, belonging to the minority party, was defeated. His daughter Esther married Dr. R. T. Weaver, of Northampton County. He left several sons, among them being William Moore and J. G. Moore, of Washington City; Thomas Moore, of New York, and the historian, Maj. John W. Moore. We have written of his ancestry in the first decade.

In 1830 Jacob Hare, of Maney's Neck, defeated Gen. Bridger J. Montgomery for the Senate. Hare was the nephew of Col. Starkey Sharpe II. He was noted for his amiable temper and good conduct as a citizen. Soon after his retirement from the Legislature he moved South.

In 1830 Maj. Isaac Carter was elected to the House with John H. Wheeler. Carter was said to be a wily politician, but Dr. G. C. Moore defeated him in 1831. He, however, recovered and was re-elected in 1832, 1833 and 1834. He was the son of Maj. Isaac Carter, who died in Hertford County July 8, 1792, and who was a captain in the Revolutionary War of 1776. Isaac Carter, Sr., left a will in which he appointed his son, Lazarus Carter, his executor. His daughter Parthenia married Shadrack Rutland, November 12, 1775. Isaac Carter, Jr., was a major in the militia, and once Sheriff of the county.

Dr. O'Dwyer says in his diary that a judgment was recovered against Carter in 1824 for $1,000, growing out of some act of his while Sheriff. Major Carter had a good estate and owned fifty or more slaves before his death.

John Vann was in the Senate in 1833.

Sipha Smith, who was in the House in 1833 and 1834, was one of the old justices of the county, and for a long time, in the early years of the State, County Surveyor. He lived in Mill Neck.

NOTE.—Thos. E. Hare, a prominent lawyer, in Vanndale, Ark., and his sister Mrs. J. M. Vann, of the same town, are grandchildren of Jacob Hare.

Thomas V. Roberts served in 1832. He was from Murfreesboro, and lived on the same lot where the late Uriah Vaughan resided. He and the Exums were connected. He was the uncle of the wife of the late Gen. Matt. W. Ransom, of Northampton. It is told of him that he could care for and manage successfully the money of others, but could not manage his own. He died in Northampton very poor and almost friendless. He was an old bachelor, which probably accounts for his misfortunes. The love, attention and advice of some good woman would probably have changed his fate. Before losing his estate he was very popular and was active and prominent in county affairs. He was often seen presiding in the old county courts, and was spoken of as being a good man, a kind neighbor and a true citizen.

"When sorrows come, they come not as single spies,
But in battalions."

In 1834 George W. Montgomery succeeded John Vann as Senator, and died in Raleigh in 1834 during the session of the Legislature, and was succeeded by John Vann in 1835.

As we have said, on the night of the 22d day of August, 1830, one Wright Allen set fire to the court-house in Winton and in a few hours the building and all the records and memorials of the county from its origin were reduced to ashes. It was the greatest calamity that ever befell the county. The records contained the proud history of a noble people.

Allen was indicted in court for forging the name of Timothy Ridley to a note, and he thought the note was in the court-house, and his purpose in burning the court-house was to destroy the evidence of his guilt. But he was mistaken. The note was in the possession of Lewis M. Cowper, Clerk of the Court in Murfreesboro. Allen was convicted and whipped at the whipping-post. No punishment, however, of the offender, nor any amount of money could or can ever repair this great public calamity and wrong.

Hon. KENNETH RAYNER.

DECADE VIII.—1830–1840. 147

CONSTITUTIONAL CONVENTION OF 1835.

The growth of the State and increase of its population demanded a change in the organic law of the State. A Constitutional Convention met in Raleigh, June 4, 1835, composed of delegates from the counties of the State.

The aristocratic Dr. Isaac Pipkin, the polished and reserved Dr. Godwin C. Moore, and young Kenneth Rayner were the candidates in Hertford. The contest was warm and energetic. It was Rayner's first appearance as a candidate for political honors. He was young, bright, aggressive, a splendid debater, and quite an orator. He was elected as the delegate to the Convention, and as a member of that body he won laurels that stamped him as one of the foremost young men in the State. He was also elected to the Legislature that same year after returning from the Convention.

This was the beginning of a long, brilliant and useful public life. He soon became the ideal of the Whig party, of which he was a member. He served in the Legislature again in 1836, then a justice of the peace in his county, when in 1839 he was elected from the Edenton District as a member of Congress, where he served continuously until 1845. He declined a further nomination at the hands of his party, and in 1846 again entered the Legislature of his State and was a member of the House from 1846 to 1852, and in the Senate in 1854. The Whig party in 1848 tendered him the nomination for governor, but he declined it. Charles Manly was nominated and elected. The last political service he performed for his county and State was as a member of the Convention of 1861 that passed the Ordinance of Secession. After the war he moved to Mississippi and became a Republican in politics, and was for some years, prior to Cleveland's first administration as President of the United States, Solicitor-General of the U. S. Treasury in Washington, D. C. He was the son of Rev. Amos Rayner, who lived in Harrellsville Township where his son was born, and in his palmy days before the war was one of the national leaders of the Whig party.

Mr. Rayner married Miss Polk, daughter of Col. William Polk, of Mecklenburg County, and sister of Gen. Leonidas Polk. His widow is now living in El Paso, Texas. J. J. Scull's first wife was Mr. Rayner's sister.

The young but gallant and high-strung Roscius C. Borland, of Murfreesboro, appeared at the August Term, 1830, of the Court, as a young lawyer, with his license written on parchment and signed by the great jurists Leonard Henderson, C. J., and John Hall and Thomas Ruffin, Associate Justices, and took the oath of an attorney.

In 1835 Borland had won the confidence and respect of his people and was elected County Attorney to succeed James S. Jones, Esq., who was then preparing to make his home in the State of Georgia. Borland was also during this year elected with Rayner to serve his county in the House of Commons. John Vann was in the Senate. No county in the State was more ably represented in the General Assembly. Borland, on his return from Raleigh, devoted himself strictly to his profession until 1845, when he moved with his family to Mississippi. He married Temperance Ramsay, daughter of Henry Ramsay. He was the father of the late Thomas R. Borland, of Norfolk, Va., who was born in Murfreesboro. Mr. Borland was one of the sons of Dr. Thomas Borland. His health failed and he went South to visit his brothers and was taken sick and died in 1847.

On the death roll during this decade we find the names of Andrew V. Duer, the Public Register for about eight years just prior to 1831; John Benthall, one of the ancient justices; Elisha Lawrence, the father of the late John V. Lawrence; John Wheeler and his wife Sarah; Elizabeth Meredith, relict of the late jolly Capt. Lewis M. Meredith; Titus Darden; the blind Capt. Jethro Darden, the old legislator; Col. Starkey Sharpe II; Gen. Bridger J. Montgomery; Col. Kerr Montgomery; Isaac Taylor, the grandfather of

Decade VIII.—1830–1840. 149

W. P. Taylor, of Winton; George W. Montgomery; Capt. Benjamin B. Camp; Joseph R., Julia E., and Leonidas Camp; Allen Moore; Starkey S. Harrell, Sr., the uncle of the late Chief Justice Smith; Carr Darden; Charles Gay; William H. Finney; John Moore; Stephen Graham; Josiah Bridger, the father of Sheriff John P. Bridger; Jonathan Jordan; Seth Southall; Rev. Daniel Southall; the old Sheriff Thomas Deanes; Godwin Cotton; John Hamilton Frazier and others.

In 1824 Rev. James Delke moved from Surry County, Va., and settled in Murfreesboro, where he entered upon his great mission of preaching the gospel with great power and success. He was an able and eloquent Baptist divine. No town in the east had abler preachers during this period than Murfreesboro. Rev. Southall, a Methodist, and Rev. Delke, the Baptist, turned on the light of true Christianity with wonderful effect. In 1830 Rev. Delke, as the result of one of his protracted meetings at Meherrin Meeting House, baptized one hundred and fifty persons. He was twice married. His first wife, and mother of his children, was widow Susan Bats Kerr, *nee* Holloway, by whom he had and reared one son, James A. Delke, and one daughter, Susan.

His second wife was the wealthy widow of James Ward, who died in 1843—the daughter of James Jones III and sister of the lawyer, James S. Jones, and the mother of Ann J. Ward, the wife of Maj. John W. Moore, and who was the first graduate at the C. B. F. Institute in July, 1853.

Rev. Delke, after his second marriage, drove around in a fine carriage, with his blooded horses, his driver dressed in livery. But this kingly style furnished him by his wealthy wife did not abate his piety or impair his usefulness. He died December 4, 1862. His daughter married Francis Nolley, a tailor in Murfreesboro, and brother of Rev. Geo. W. Nolley, a distinguished Methodist divine in the Virginia Conference. Their children were Marcellus Nolley, the soldier and scholarly salesman of Baltimore; Emmett W. Nolley, who married Miss Julia Tolar, of South Carolina, and now an honored citizen of Fayetteville, N. C. Their daughter Fannie married a Mr. Oatis, of South Carolina, and he died a few years ago. Susan, their youngest child, was a beautiful young lady, and married in 1878 Samuel J. Pearce, of Chowan County. The author and Miss Nellie H. Vaughan, who afterwards became his wife, were among the waiters at the wedding, which took place at the residence of the bride in Murfreesboro. It is now the home of David A. Day and wife, Ruth R. McDowell, the second daughter of Rev. A. McDowell.

Reverend Delke's son, James A., never married, but devoted his life to teaching and became a great educator in Murfreesboro in this State, and in Murfreesboro in Tennessee. Leaving Tennessee he returned to his native town, and for over twenty years was a professor in the C. B. F. Institute. He was a ripe scholar and a most excellent man.

JOHN VANN.

This distinguished personage came to Hertford County about 1800 from Gates County, when about 33 years of age. He appears on the census of Gates County in 1790 as the head of a family of five males and two females, with two slaves. In 1810 he first appears on the census of Hertford as the head of a family of seven, and owner of eight slaves. He was prominent in Hertford County affairs from about 1812 to 1850, when in September of the last-named year he died in his eighty-third year. He served in the county as one of its justices of the peace for about forty years. At the May Term, 1830, he was elected Chairman of the Court of Pleas and Quarter Sessions of the county. He represented his adopted county in the House of Commons in 1823, 1824 and 1825, and in the Senate in 1833 and 1835, and was a man of exalted character and fine ability. He remained Chairman of the Court until his death.

At the November Term, 1850, Thomas Bragg, Esq., afterwards Governor Bragg, who attended the courts of this county, presented to the justices presiding the following resolution:

"*Resolved,* That we have heard with the deepest regret of the death, since the last term of this Court, of John Vann, Esq., the late, and for many years previous, Chairman of the County Court of Hertford—a man venerable for his years, estimable for his private and public virtues, and we take this occasion to pay some tribute to his memory."

The resolution was unanimously adopted by the Court, and ordered spread upon the minutes of the Court. This action of the Justices of the Court and the Bar is a monument to his worth, and shows how he lived in the hearts of his countrymen.

Mr. Vann left several sons to perpetuate the name, and the fame of this grand old citizen—Tilman D., Jesse B., Albert G., John A., Rensselear, and Cordie. The latter died when young. Rensselear moved South and married and reared an interesting family. Jesse B. Vann married the daughter of Luke McGlaughon of his county, and died about the close of the War of 1865. He represented his county in the Legislature from 1862 to 1864. He left two sons— Thomas J. Vann, of Aulander, N. C., and the late J. J. Vann, Esq., a prominent lawyer of Monroe, N. C.

Albert G. Vann married Harriet Boyette, of Gates County, the aunt of Gen. W. P. Roberts, and served his county for a number of years after the late Civil War as a justice of the peace and County Commissioner. The greatest service he ever did for his county was in the noble children he bequeathed to his county. He furnished the county with five sons and several daughters, all of whom any county would feel proud. His sons were William, John, Thaddeus E., Albert C., and Richard T. Vann.

Richard T., who had the misfortune when a boy to have both hands crushed off in a cane-mill on his father's farm, is an eminent Baptist divine and the President of the Baptist University for Ladies, at Raleigh, N. C.

William was also a Baptist preacher. He and John died in the army during the struggle between the States. Thaddeus E. is one of our leading citizens in Maney's Neck, having served, soon after his majority, as County Surveyor, justice of the peace and later as County Commissioner. He is still one of our magistrates. He married Miss Auquilla Brett, daughter of Henry Brett and his wife Amanda, who resided where Mr. Vann and his happy family now reside. She was the granddaughter of Henry L. Williams, one of the old justices.

Albert C. lives at his father's old home, and married first Annie Newsome, the daughter of Joseph Newsome by his first marriage; and after her death he married the half-sister of his first wife. He has often served his county in official positions.

JOHN A. VANN.

John A. Vann, the son of the old chairman, was much loved by his people and was often called to serve them in some capacity. We first find him in the office of Constable in 1840, then Sheriff, next Clerk of the Superior Court, in the Legislature from 1864 to 1866, then Clerk and Master in Equity, next Treasurer of the county, and finally a justice of the peace and County Commissioner. In 1875 he was the Democratic candidate in the county as a delegate to the Constitutional Convention, but was defeated by J. J. Horton, a Republican. The author's first political speeches were made in that campaign, advocating the election of Mr. Vann. He died full of honors, and leaving surviving him three sons and several daughters. His sons are Henry B.,

Decade VIII.—1830-1840.   153

the late Treasurer of the county; Charles Spurgeon Vann, Esq., of Edenton, a lawyer of ability, and who represented the First Senatorial District in the General Assembly of 1901, 1903 and 1905, and John E. Vann, of Winton, who is one of the county's leading lawyers. He has served in his county as Superintendent of Public Schools, Solicitor of the Criminal Court, County Attorney and as member of the Legislature in 1903. He married Miss Graves, of Selma, N. C., and has honored the county with a still younger John Vann.

The wife of John A. Vann was the sister of the late Dr. J. E. Newsome and daughter of Michael E. Newsome.

Tilman D. Vann, the oldest son of John Vann, Esq., the old chairman, lived in Maney's Neck, a section of the county which has been noted for a great number of years for its elegant population. He married Miss Sarah Shepherd, daughter of Solomon Shepherd, who lived first where J. G. Majette now resides, but Capt. J. H. Picot says he was living at the Tilman Vann place when he died. She was a most excellent woman.

MISS ROWENA VANN.

They left no son, but several handsome and attractive daughters. One of his daughters, Rowena, married Rev. R. R. Savage, and they reared several sons and daughters. Antoinette married Prof. J. H. Picot, the veteran schoolteacher at Buckhorn Academy, who are the parents of the eminent physician, Dr. L. J. Picot, of Littleton, N. C., and of our countyman Guy C. Picot.

Homarselle S. Vann married George Little, of Warren County, a direct descendant of Maj. George Little of revolutionary fame from this county, and of William Little of colonial fame. Willie, another daughter, married Capt. Thomas D. Boone, a brave soldier in the Confederate Army, and for years the efficient Clerk of our Superior Court, which office he now holds.

Mr. Tilman D. Vann, unlike his brothers, never held an office except justice of the peace, but he built a monument to the fame of his county in his children. Among his grand children are Dr. Louis J. Picot, of Littleton, N. C.; Rev. Wm. V. Savage, an eloquent Baptist divine of Churchland, Va.; Mrs. James L. Camp, of Franklin, Va.; Toy D. Savage, an attorney at law in Norfolk, Va.; Guy C. Picot, at Como, and others.

The Vann family originally belonged to Chowan County, and John has always been a favorite name in the family. In 1756 we find John Vann of Chowan signing the official bond of Thomas Jones, as Clerk of the Crown's Court in Chowan (Col. Rec., vol. 5, p. 611). In November, 1758, the Committee of Public Claims met at John Vann's house in Edenton and selected John Starkey as chairman of the committee and Andrew Knox as clerk (Vol. 5, p. 975). On page 983 he is again mentioned. It seems that in the formation of Gates County in 1779 from parts of Hertford, Perquimans and Chowan counties, the Vanns were cut off into Gates. In the U. S. Census of 1790 we find mentioned in Gates County John Vann, Rachel Vann, Darius Vann and Thomas Vann. The family has been from its earliest history people of strong character and of fair ability. Several of them have attained to considerable prominence and displayed great ability. The official record of this county discloses how they stand and have stood with the people of Hertford for nearly a hundred years. In 1740 John Vann and William Vann were freeholders in Chowan County and were on the jury list of that county.

Col. Charles Vann of the county was of a different family. He, after the death of his first wife, married Miss Benthall,

---

NOTE.—Jno. Vann, of Chowan, married Feb. 25, 1752, Mrs. Ann Peterson.

Decade VIII.—1830-1840.

sister of our Jack Benthall, and lived near Benthall's Bridge at the home of our Abner A. Carter, and was in his younger manhood a man of considerable wealth and influence, but his great kindness in signing bonds and other money obligations with his friends caused him to spend his latter days poor and dependent upon the charity of his friends. His son Jesse Thomas Vann, by his first marriage, died January 5, 1856, while a bright student at the University of Virginia. Colonel Vann died about 1880. His first wife was Miss Britt, the aunt of Dr. Thomas P. Britt and Geo. P. Britt, of Maney's Neck. His sister married William Britt, who lived near Union, and they were the parents of Union's chief justice, James E. Britt, and of the mother of Union's leading merchant, James H. Darden. John Taylor, of Maney's Neck, married Elizabeth Britt, the sister of William and Mills Britt. They are the parents of Richard J. Taylor and the late William E. Taylor, of Maney's Neck. William and Mills Britt both married sisters of Col. Charles Vann.

John Vann, the Chairman of the County Court, had some true and faithful assistants in the management of the affairs of the county. Abraham Thomas, one of the Special Court, was always at his post of duty. Mr. Thomas was not only a faithful public servant, but a man of unblemished private character, and respected and admired by all who knew him. It is said of him that during the period of twenty-five years he served his church at Bethlehem as clerk, he was only absent on three occasions. Such fidelity to duty characterized the man's whole life. His parents were James Thomas and wife, Elizabeth Pruden. James was a private in the Revolutionary War, entering the army in May, 1781,

ABRAHAM THOMAS.

serving until its close. Mr. Abraham Thomas married Miss Nancy Mitchell, of Bertie, the daughter of John Mitchell and Winnifred Saunders and sister of James S. Mitchell, who represented Bertie in the Senate in 1842. The latter was the father of the Rev. John Mitchell.

Mr. Thomas died April 13, 1879. He had eleven children, but only four arrived at full age. His daughter Mary was the wife of Howell M. Jones, son of Howell Jones, the old Clerk and Master in Equity in the county. Mr. Jones' father once lived in Murfreesboro and built the house now owned by Miss Ella Jester. His daughter Martha married Rev. W. P. Britton. His son John Q. emigrated to Arkansas when young, but returned at the beginning of hostilities in 1861 and entered the war as a private in the 17th N. C. Regiment; was promoted to the rank of lieutenant and surrendered with General Lee at Appomattox. He returned to Arkansas and married Miss Josephine Robertson, of Memphis, Tenn., and is now a wealthy merchant at Vanndale, Ark. The youngest son, Dr. Rascius P. Thomas, is a model citizen of his native county. He is an alumnus of Wake Forest College, University of Virginia, and the Medical University of New York; was moderator of the West Chowan Baptist Association from 1883 to 1896, and has been president of the Board of Trustees of the C. B. F. Institute since 1887. While an eminent and successful physician, he abandoned the practice of medicine several years ago and has energetically, intelligently and successfully applied his attention to the cultivation of the soil. He married Miss Mary Green Mitchell, of Franklin County, in this State.

In 1822 the county gained a valuable citizen in the per-

DR. R. P. THOMAS.

son of Walter B. Myrick, of Virginia, who married Ann O. Neal, of Southampton County, Va. He was a man of sterling character and belonged to that class of men who by their unbending honesty and frankness makes a country rich. He bought and built on the land, where he resided up to his death, February 19, 1871, in Maney's Neck, and where his two sons, James L. and W. B. Myrick, now live, and who are chips of the old block. His first wife died in 1834, leaving five children, Thomas N., John D., Elizabeth, who became the wife of Dr. Wm. Massenburg, of Southampton County, Va. Lucy A., who became the wife of Kader Biggs, late of Norfolk, Va., and McClure Myrick, who died young. In 1835 he married Mary Barrett, of his native county, and by her he left two daughters, Vrginia and Helen, and three sons, David, James L., and Walter B., Jr. The father was often called upon to serve his county in different capacities, as justice of the peace, commissioner in the division of lands, allotting dower, foreman of grand jury. On account of his great honesty his services were frequently demanded. He served bravely in the War of 1812 as a private in a Virginia Company.

CONSTITUTION AMENDED.

Under the Constitution as amended by the Convention of 1835, the State is divided into senatorial districts, and the number of Senators fixed at 50. The number of members of the House of Commons fixed at 120. Senators were required to be possessed in fee of 300 acres of land and only white persons owning 50 acres of land were allowed to vote for Senators, and only white persons were allowed to vote for members of the House.

The Governor is now elected by the people instead of by the General Assembly. Infidels and atheists not allowed to hold office or any place of trust under the laws of the State. There were other minor changes in the Constitution of 1776.

MISS FANNIE SOUTHALL.

Hertford always boasted of her fair and beautiful women, and the chivalry of her sons. Miss Fannie Southall was the daughter of John W. Southall, of Murfreesboro, by his first marriage to Miss Johnson. This picture was taken in 1848. She was regarded as one of the prettiest and most fascinating women in her day. A peerless beauty, exalted and beautiful character, a universal favorite and admired by the noble and chivalric beaux of her day. She died September 30, 1852, and her death threw a pall of sadness over the community. Her beautiful sister, Julia R., married Dr. Thomas N. Myrick in December, 1847. They lived in Murfreesboro until just before the Civil War, when they moved to Florida. Mrs. Myrick died in the State of their adoption in 1859, and her body was brought home and interred in the family graveyard in Murfreesboro by the side of her sister. She left two sons, John S., now of Texas, and Charles E. Myrick, now of New York. Her husband, Dr. Thomas N. Myrick, died July, 1867. In 1860 Dr. Myrick wedded Miss Susan J. Baker, of Murfreesboro, a most accomplished and elegant woman, and for a number of years since his death she had charge, as principal, of the musical department of the C. B. F. Institute. They reared three children, Walter D. Myrick, of Texas; Lawrence Baker Myrick, of Norfolk, Va., and one daughter, Fannie, who died soon after she entered matured womanhood. Miss Baker was the second daughter of Dr. John B. Baker, of Gates, the son of Gen. Lawrence Baker,

Decade VIII.—1830-1840.

PERRY C. GREGORY.

and whose wife was Mary Wynns Gregory. P. C. Gregory of Tillery, N. C., one of the leading merchants in Halifax County, is a direct descendant from this same Gregory family. He is the son of Casper W. Gregory and wife, Mary A. Randolph. Gen. Joseph F. Dickerson's wife, Peggy Gregory, was a great aunt of P. C. Gregory. The Gregorys of Salisbury, N. C., and of Camden are of the same family. The mother of Mary Wynns Gregory was Mary Wynns, a sister of Benjamin, Major George and Gen. Thomas Wynns, and she married a Gregory. William Rea, Sr., married Margaret Wynns, and after her death he married Mary Wynns. They were daughters of Maj. George Wynns.

The United States is still expanding its territorial possessions and increasing the number of States in the Union. In 1845 the "Lone Star," the republic of Texas, joins the United States and becomes a State in the Union, and adds another star on the flag of the Stars and Stripes.

In 1846 England yields her claims to the Astoria settlement and the Oregon Territory, and the following new States have been carved out of that territory: Oregon in 1859, Washington in 1889, and Idaho in 1890.

From the territory ceded by Mexico to the United States in 1848, the following States have been admitted into the Union: California in 1850, Nevada in 1864, Colorado in 1876, and Utah in 1896, and Arizona Territory includes part of the territory ceded by Mexico, and the Gadsden's purchase in 1853. This territory and the Territory of New Mexico, the Indian Territory, and the territory of Oklahoma, are now knocking at the door of Congress, asking to be recognized and admitted into the galaxy of States in the Union, and may be admitted during the year of 1906.

Alaska Territory was ceded to the United States by Russia in 1867. At the present time there are 45 States in the Union.

NOTE.—Since writing the above, Indian Territory and Oklahoma have been admitted as one State named Oklahoma, and the other two territories are admitted as one State, Arizona, if ratified by the voters in the two Territories.

DECADE IX.
1840—1850.

The period between 1840 and 1850 is not marked with any great events in the county. The loss of many of its valuable citizens was a sad chapter in its history. But while she received her losses, at the same time she had her reinforcements to heal her wounds. We find added to the list of Justices of the Peace during these ten years James A. Moore, Abner J. Perry, Wm. N. Perry, W. W. Mitchell, John A. Anderson, John V. Lawrence, Daniel Valentine, John W. Harrell, James Barnes, Jethro R. Darden, Wm. M. Montgomery, Benj. Bryant, Capt. Samuel Moore, Dr. Edward Neal, W. D. Pruden, Henry L. Williams, Dr. George W. Peete, Wm. B. Wise, Thomas P. Little.

This long list of new Justices shows what havoc death and removals had played with the select men of the county, who figured in its affairs during the last decade. For the principal county officers during these years see the list of officers in the back of the book. At the February Term, 1843, John A. Anderson resigned as County Trustee. Elisha D. Brett, of Maney's Neck, was elected for the unexpired term. At the May Term, 1843, L. R. Jernigan resigned the office of Public Register, and defeated Brett for Trustee. Patrick Perry was elected Public Register. James Banks, Tilman D. Vann, Samuel Moore, Edward F. Dunston, and Thomas J. Deanes are among the foremen of the grand jury during this period. The health of the chivalric and high-strung R. C. Borland, failed, and he resigned as County Attorney, and leaves for Mississippi in 1845. W. N. H. Smith was elected at the November Term, 1845, to succeed Borland. Euclid and Solon Borland, Micajah T. and Richard Winborne, William J. and Richard Jordan Gatling, and others, leave the county to make their homes in the far west.

W. B. Wynns, the old High Sheriff of the county, and another of the faithful assistants of Chairman Vann, on February 4, 1840, in the 44th year of his age, passed away, while in Marianna, Fla., looking after his large interests in that State. He left an estate valued at about $200,000. He was the grandson of Benj. Wynns, and nephew of Gen. Thomas Wynns. He married Martha A. Pipkin, sister of Dr. Isaac Pipkin, who survived him with two sons, the late Thomas P. Wynns, son-in-law of R. G. Cowper, and our Col. James Madison Wynns, of Murfreesboro. Sheriff Wynns had three brothers, Benjamin, Thomas, and James Dean Wynns. Their parents died when they were young, and Benjamin and Thomas went to the Island of Bermuda to their Dean relatives, to be cared for, while Wm. B. and James D. were taken by their uncle, Gen. Thomas Wynns. After the boys grew to manhood they engaged in an extensive trade between the United States and foreign ports. Thomas remained on the island, Benjamin was Captain of the *Flotilla,* one of their vessels, and Wm. B. looked after the business at the ports on the Chowan and Meherrin Rivers. They amassed large fortunes. After the English Government abolished slavery in 1838, Thomas left the island and came to Jamaica, where he remained a short time, then settled in Brooklyn, N. Y., where he died. Capt. Benj. Wynns married Miss Baker, a granddaughter of Gen. Lawrence Baker, and in 1824 bought the home of Howell Jones in Murfreesboro, and on February 12, 1824, settled in that town. He continued, for several years thereafter, his voyages on the water. About 1834 he moved to Florida, where he and his brother, William B. Wynns, began to purchase lands in the land of flowers. By his marriage with Miss Baker he had two children, a daughter who died young, and a son, William Baker Wynns, who was in his day one of the most prominent men of his State, filling many places of public trust.

Mr. W. B. Wynn, Jr., was married twice. He had no issue by his first marriage. He had the letter s eliminated from his surname by an act of the Florida Legislature. His second wife was Susan Clarke, of Huntsville, Ala., the daughter

Decade IX.—1840–1850.

COL. JAMES M. WYNNS.

of William Clarke and wife Susan, of Virginia descent. He was a brave Confederate soldier and died in prison in Elmira, New York, in 1864. He left two sons, Judge Calvert Wynn, of Florida, and Wm. B. Wynn, of Marianna, in the same State. Thomas P. Wynns, son of Sheriff Wynns, married the daughter of R. G. Cowper, and died several years ago in this county. The Sheriff's son, James M. Wynns, still resides in Murfreesboro. He has served his people in important positions. In the 10th decade he served as Justice of the Peace, and as a member of the Special Court of the county, entered the Confederate army as Captain, afterwards promoted to the rank of Colonel. While in the army he was elected to serve his county in the Senate in 1864 and 1865, and for years served as a member of the Board of Education in the county. He loaned his county $4,000 in gold to aid in equipping its soldiers for the war of 1861-5, which he lost, as all the counties were forbidden by law to pay any debt contracted in aid of the so-called rebellion. He lost heavily by the war, but is still in comfortable circumstances. In 1865 he married Miss Jennie Brown, daughter of S. J. S. Brown, of King George County, Va. Mr. Brown was the Clerk of the Court of his county for nearly a lifetime.

MISS JENNIE BROWN.

Col. Wynns and his wife still live in Murfreesboro at the beautiful old home of Gen. Jos. F. Dickinson, with their interesting family of three sons and four girls. Col. Wynns is the only living ex-representative from the county in the General Assembly of the State who served prior to 1868.

In 1842 the people of Harrellsville, then known as Bethel, as we are informed by Major Moore, but later named for Abner Harrell, a most estimable citizen of that place, established, in place of the former private schools of that place, the Union Academy, a school of high grade. Edwin Evarts, of Vermont, a well equipped instructor, was called to preside over its destiny, assisted at one time by the late Jesse J. Yeates, and later by Prof. C. F. Lyon. At this school a large number of Hertford's young men received their education, which so well prepared them for useful citizenship.

And in the west end of the county, at Elm Grove, about four miles from the Boro, Alfred W. Darden had conducted, at his beautiful country home, a high school for young ladies, with Rev. A. J. Battle as Principal, and several competent lady teachers as assistants. For years this was a flourishing and well patronized school. Mr. Darden was himself a scholarly man, and his children inherited many of his traits of character. His wife was the daughter of John Moore, the father of Allen, Alfred, and Samuel Moore. Mr. Darden and his brother, William S. Darden, of Hertford, were sons of Rev. Jacob Darden, a Kehukee Baptist preacher in Southampton County, Va., and for a long time the pastor of Old Southquay church in that county. A. W. Darden reared several children. His eldest daughter, Virginia, married William E. Bond, of Edenton, who were the parents of lawyer W. M. Bond, of that town. W. Carey Parker, late of Wake Forest, married his daughter, Sarah Quinton. John D. Gatling, of the county, married Lilly, another of his daughters. His daughter, Miss Indiana Darden, is a highly cultured woman and has devoted her life to teaching. When

DECADE IX.—1840–1850.   165

young she was a frequent contributor to the literary magazines of the South. His son, Alfred M., served as a gallant soldier throughout the Civil War. After his return from the battlefield he married Bettie, the daughter of William J. Holley, of Chowan, and reared several children. He died in the 14th decade. His wife still survives him. His brother, A. C. Darden, also served in the latter part of the war. He resides in Murfreesboro Township, on a tract of land owned by his grandfather, and which has been in his family 100 years. He has married twice. His first wife was Bettie Dunford, and his second was Maggie, the daughter of Thomas Overby, the loyal pilot of the blockade at Maney's Ferry during the Civil War. His brother Paul died while a soldier in the army.

In 1840 B. T. Spiers, of Maney's Neck, was elected to the Senate.

The amended Constitution of 1835 reduced Hertford's representation in the House to one member, and the young lawyer, W. N. H. Smith, who in 1834 returned to the county as a graduate of Yale College, was elected to the House. He came to the bar in 1839 after elaborate preparation. He was studious and possessed a great discriminating and admirably balanced mind; he soon became recognized as one of North Carolina's greatest men. After the adjournment of the Legislature he returned and devoted himself strictly to his profession. In 1845 he was elected attorney of the County Court, and remained in office until August, 1848, when he resigned. Elected to the State Senate in 1848, and by the General Assembly in 1848 elected Solicitor of the First Judicial District, which office he held for nine years. Elias C. Hines, of Edenton, defeated him for Solicitor in 1857. Hines received 76 votes and Smith 35. Elected to the House in 1858. Elected to Congress in 1859, where he served until the Civil War. In the long and memorable contest for Speaker in the 36th Congress he was placed in nomination, and on one ballot received a majority of the votes cast for Speaker, but before the result was announced several members changed their votes, and he was defeated on the next ballot. Served as a member of the Confederate Congress from the beginning to the downfall of that government. Appointed by Governor Vance Chief Justice, January 10, 1878, which office he held until his death, November 14, 1889. He was a great and good man. No greater eulogy can be written of any man. His opinions, written while Chief Justice, will be compared throughout time with those of the ablest judges in this country. He was born in Murfreesboro September 24, 1812, and resided here until 1869. He, however, never lost his love for his native county and made his annual visits to his old home throughout life. He lived in the hearts of his people. His father was Dr. Wm. L. Smith, who came to the county from Connecticut and married Nancy Harrell, the daughter of Nathan Harrell and granddaughter of the first Starey Sharp, 1741-1791, and wife Sarah Winborne. Chief Justice Smith married Olivia O. Wise, the daughter of Wm. Bartelle Wise, a wealthy merchant and leader of Murfreesboro. Thomas Blount Sharp, who was in the House in 1838, Starkey Sharp III., 1809-1867, who was in the House in 1842, and Jacob Sharp, 1814-1882, who was a member of the House in 1844, were sons of Jacob Sharp, Sr., and wife Nancy Hunter, and grandsons of Starkey Sharp I. and wife Sarah. Col. Starkey Sharp II, 1785-1833, was the son of Starkey Sharp I by his second marriage with Jamima Hare. He was the uncle of Starkey III, Elisha H., Thos. B., J. B., and Jacob Sharp. He was Colonel in the militia, and never married. In his will he gave $1,000 to the poor of the county and provided for its distribution. Col. S. Sharp III was thrice married. His first wife was Mrs. Sallie Simons, widow of John Simons and daughter of Watson Lewis, Sr. His second wife was Eleanor Hardy, daughter of Humphrey Hardy, of Bertie. His third

Chief Justice W. N. H. SMITH.

wife was Jane Lewis, sister of his first wife. His daughter Nannie, by his second marriage, first married James Walton. The latter died leaving his wife and two daughters surviving. E. D. Scull later married the widow Walton and left children. Col. Sharp by his last marriage left two sons, Starkey IV. and Hunter, and two daughters, the present Mrs. Dr. John T. Shubrick, of Rocky Mount, N. C., and grandson of Commodore Wm. B. Shubrick (1790-1874), of U. S. Navy, and who performed distinguished service in the War of 1812, and also in the Mexican War. Fannie, who became the wife of Hon. Thomas R. Jernigan. Starkey Sharp IV. married Annie, the very attractive daughter of the late eminent physician, Andrew J. Askew, of Bertie. J. Bembury Sharp also married a Miss Simons, and they were the parents of the late John, James and Charles L. Sharp. John Sharp was Public Register of the county from 1857-1866, and was Sheriff from 1878-1880.

Jacob Sharp, another brother, married Elizabeth Simons, and they were the parents of Capt. Wm. Sharp, of Confederate fame; Col. Thos. H. Sharpe, of the 17th N. C. Regiment in the late Civil War, and of our H. C. Sharp, the ex-Register of Deeds of the county. The Sharps have been prominent and influential people and of wealth in the county for a long while, and most of them had military titles, acquired either in the militia or in the war of 1861-5. The original Col. Starkey Sharp was the son of William Sharp, who married a Miss Starkey, of the same family as Edward and John Starkey, the old colonial legislators from Onslow County, in this State, and by that marriage the name of *"Starkey Sharp,"* which has been persisted in so long, was acquired.

In 1844 Richard G. Cowper resigned the office of Sheriff to accept the Whig nomination for the Senate against Dr. G. C. Moore, the Democratic candidate. Moore had defeated the Whig candidate, B. T. Spiers, at the preceding election, but the old Sheriff was too well drilled in the art and wiles of politics to be defeated, and he was triumphantly elected, to the joy of his party friends. He and Lewis M. Cowper were brothers and were sons of William Cowper, whose second wife was the daughter of Capt. Lewis Meredith, of Murfreesboro. They had a brother, William, who lived in Gates County. Wm. Cowper's first wife was the daughter of Wm. Rea. The Sheriff married the only daughter of Harry W. Long, of Murfreesboro. Long was a lawyer who lived on his lands in Maney's Neck, until about 1824, when he moved to Murfreesboro to live. George Cowper, the son of the old Sheriff, is very much like his father in favor.

GEORGE COWPER.

B. T. Spiers, the Senator in 1840, was a lawyer by profession, but never practiced. He resided on his valuable plantation near Buckhorn, and enjoyed the frequent visits of friends. He took life easy. He married Miss Margaret L. Rea, the daughter of Sampson Rea, and sister of Sampson Rea III.

B. T. SPIERS.

Mr. Spiers was a high-toned and honorable man, a kind neighbor, and a splendid citizen. He also had a large landed

---

NOTE.—On July 17, 1714, William Rush and wife Martha conveyed to William Sharp 200 acres of land on Wiccacon Creek in Hertford County.

estate in Florida, and when the Civil War ended in 1865 he had in Florida over two hundred bales of cotton. Cotton in 1865 and 1866 sold as high as 60 cents per pound. This was a fine fortune, but the burdens of the war were so great he was not permitted to enjoy his fortune long. But few could carry the burdens caused by the Revolution and the destruction of property. Money and property were gone, and debts and suretyship liabilities remained. He reared several children to reflect honor upon his name. His two most excellent, refined and intellectual daughters were Lucy and Margaret L. The former married Dr. Davis Bryant, of Brooklyn, N. Y., and the latter married E. L. Hill, Esq., of New York City. Hill died a few years ago, leaving surviving him his handsome widow, whose likeness, taken in 1904, is here seen.

MRS. MARGARET L. HILL.
nee SPIERS.

Mrs. Bryant as a young woman was a most remarkable woman. She was a splendid looking woman, lofty and beautiful in character and strong in intellect. She and her husband, with their beautiful daughter, still reside in Brooklyn. Mr. Spiers has two sons, Douglas and William, living in Florida, and one son, Tyrone, in California, and another son, H. McD. Spiers, who lives at the old homestead, near Buckhorn. This noble old citizen died in the 13th decade.

MEXICAN WAR.

The trouble between Mexico and the United States about the boundary line between the two countries culminated in 1846 in a war, during President Polk's administration. A call was made on the States for troops. Hertford County was asked for eighteen soldiers. About fifty volunteered their services, but only a very limited number was wanted.

When they met in Winton W. N. H. Smith made them a patriotic speech and explained the nature and cause of the conflict. Finally twenty-four were accepted. Among them were: Drewry W. Beal, William W. Willoughby, Richard Langston, Tixon Hoggard, and Junius B. Wheeler, who was a graduate at West Point and an officer in the U. S. army. We have been unable to get all the names. This little excitement caused the State to demand a reorganization of her militia in 1847. In Hertford, Starkey Sharp, of Harrellsville, was chosen Colonel, and S. D. Winborne, of Maney's Neck, who was in his 27th year, was elected Major. WinBorne had been a student a few years prior at the U. S. Military Academy at West Point.

COL. STARKEY SHARP.

In 1845 W. N. H. Smith, Elisha D. Brett, Lawrence Eley, Harrison C. Lassiter and William Hays were elected as members of the Board of Superintendents of Public Schools, and in 1846 J. A. Anderson, Capt. Samuel Moore, W. D. Pruden and W. W. Mitchell were elected to serve with Mr. Smith. The people of this county have always taken great interest in public education.

Mr. Smith, in August, 1848, resigned as County Attorney, and his half brother, Antonio P. Yancey, was elected, which position he held until he resigned at August Term, 1851. He was succeeded by W. D. Valentine, of Winton, an attorney of fair ability, and a man of unstained character. He had served as Clerk of the Superior Court. His diary was a most valuable book, but the writer has been unable to get a copy.

The death roll during this period contains the names of Timothy Ridley, son of Day Ridley, of Revolutionary fame,

Maj. S. D. WINBORNE,
1847.

Decade IX.—1840–1850. 171

and once Chairman of the County Court. Miles H. Jernigan, Rev. Amos Rayner, James Worrell, the father of James A., and Cyrus E. Worrell, Jordan Gatling, Silas Parker, W. W. Sessoms, Thomas B. Sharp, Leander Tayloe, father of the late W. S., James, David, and Capt. Langley Tayloe, Mrs. James M. Yancey, the mother of W. N. H. Smith, and Antonio Yancey, passes over the river. Capt. Leander Tayloe was of the same family as Rev. Jonathan Tayloe, a distinguished citizen of Bertie, and a great Baptist. The first Jonathan Tayloe was a freeholder in Bertie as far back as 1711. The second Jonathan Tayloe was in the war of 1812-14.

Henry L. Williams, one of the new Justices of the Peace during this decade, lived in Maney's Neck, where Blount Ferguson now resides, and was engaged largely in the mercantile business, and, also, a large planter. He married the widow, Mary Chamblee, who had three children by her first marriage, Elizabeth, William, and John Chamblee. She had several children by her second marriage to Mr. Williams. Their daughter, Martha E., married Adolphus Jones, of Nansemond County, Va., and another daughter, Amanda, married Henry C. Brett. The latter were the parents of Mrs. T. E. Vann and the late George Culbret Brett. Their son, Eldridge, married Harriet Darden, daughter of Titus Darden. He died leaving his widow and two daughters surviving him. Their daughter, Aromitta, married Capt. Thos. Burbage, of Franklin, Va.

James Worrell was twice married. His first wife was Miss Williams, and they had several children, Richard, James A., and two daughters, who died young. His second wife was Mrs. Martha Johnson, *nee* Wheeler, sister of John Wheeler, of Murfreesboro. By this marriage he reared two sons, the late Dr. Cyrus E. Worrell and John Wesley Worrell. The late Richard Johnson, of this county, was the son of Martha Wheeler, by her first husband, Richard W. Johnson. Miss Wheeler was born in New Jersey in 1749, and died in Hertford County, May 15, 1827. James Worrell died in 1846. James A. Worrell, like his father, was twice married. His first wife was Titus Darden's daughter, Harriet, who first married Eldridge Williams, son of Henry L. Williams. Her daughter by her marriage with Williams was the first wife of L. F. Lee, the busy magistrate of the Neck. The widow Williams was the mother of James A. Worrell's children. They are the grand-parents of lawyer J. A. Worrell, of Jackson, N. C. Elisha Worrell, a brother of James Worrell, died March 3, 1824. Their sister married Francis Williamson. Richard, the brother of James A. Worrell, married first Betsy Camp, of Murfreesboro, and they were the parents of Edward and Richard Worrell, Jr. After the death of his Camp wife, he married Rebecca Hardy, the widow of Charles Hardy, of Norfolk. Dr. Cyrus E. Worrell was born March 10, 1826. He was educated at Buckhorn, Chapel Hill, and the University of Pennsylvania with distinction. He married, in the 11th decade, Miss Beal, of Southampton County, Va. He died January 6, 1875, leaving his widow and two sons, Julian and Cyrus E. Worrell, Jr. His widow later married George A. Brett. John Wesley Worrell married a Miss Eason, of Northampton County. He died a few years ago leaving his widow and several children surviving. They live at the old James Worrell homestead. Charles W. Worrell, the son of James A. Worrell, married Miss Rountree, daughter of Capt. A. J. Rountree, of Rich Square, N. C. Joseph E. Carter, of Maney's Neck, married his daughter, Ida, and his youngest son, Walter Worrell, married Miss Lilly Vick, of Murfreesboro. All of these people were prominent people in Maney's Neck. Miss Vick was a cousin of Mary Vick, the great belle in the fifties in the Neck, who married Mr. McKenny and moved to Marianna, Fla., where she died about four years ago.

DECADE IX.—1840-1850.

RICHARD JORDAN GATLING.

In 1822 James Gatling, an unlettered but an honorable man, who years before married Mary Cowper, sister of Wm. Cowper, died in Hertford County, leaving surviving him two daughters and two sons, Elizabeth, wife of Charles Gay, Polly, Wm. Cowper, and Jordan Gatling. His son, Jordan, married Mary Barnes. From this marriage there were born six sons, the third son being Richard Jordan Gatling, who became a distinguished American inventor, and was born in Hertford County September 12, 1818. His celebrated revolving battery gun, which bears his name, has given him a world-wide fame. His inventive genius began to show itself in his young days. At the age of 19 he began to teach school, but soon abandoned that occupation and engaged in merchandising in his native county at Frazier's X Roads. During that time and shortly after his majority he invented the screw-propeller, now so extensively used in steam vessels. He applied for a patent for his invention, but, much to his disappointment and sorrow, he discovered that a patent had already been granted for such an invention. Not being discouraged, shortly thereafter, about the year 1839, he invented and had patented a seed sowing machine, designed for sowing rice, which he afterwards used for sowing wheat in drills. In 1844 he left his native county and settled in St. Louis. There he had his seed-sowing machine manufactured and placed upon the market, which found ready sale. In 1850 he graduated in medicine at the Ohio Medical College in Cincinnati, and settled in Indianapolis, but did not practice, but engaged in the manufacture and sale of his machines. He was the first to introduce this class of farm implements into the Northwestern States, and probably did more than any other man to secure the adoption of drill culture in the West. His skill as an inventor received recognition from several distinguished sources, including a medal and diploma from the Crystal Palace, London, in 1851, and a gold medal from the American Institute, New York.

He made many other inventions, one of them being the method of using compressed air in working drills in mining operations and in the construction of tunnels, the invention of a steam plow. But the invention that gave him a worldwide fame was the invention of the Gatling Gun.

The idea of the machine gun was conceived by him in 1861, and was first constructed and fired by the inventor at Indianapolis in 1862. In 1865 he had twelve of his guns made by the Cooper Fire Arms Manufacturing Company in Philadelphia. They were subjected to a severe test under direction of the United States War Department. In 1866 the United States Government gave an order for 100 of these guns, which were made at Colts Armory in Hartford, Connecticut, and delivered in 1867.

Dr. Gatling then made his home in Hartford and continued to advertise his guns to the world. It has now been adopted by all the governments of Europe except Belgium, and nearly all the South American governments.

Technically described, the Gatling gun is a group of rifle barrels arranged longitudinally around a central shaft and revolving with it. These barrels are loaded at breech with metallic cartridges while the barrels revolve. The gun is operated by two men, one turning the crank, and the other supplying the breech with cartridges, and when in operation it insures a continuous fire. Dr. Gatling devoted nearly thirty years of his life to the task of perfecting this wonderful invention and has personally supervised and conducted the numerous tests of its efficiency before nearly all the crowned heads of Europe. Everywhere he was received with distinguished consideration, but the honors heaped upon him never changed him. He remained the same well-bred gentleman, gentle in speech and manner, always preserving that republican simplicity which so well befits the American citizen, and is the surest passport to kindly recognition.

He received many honors from the associations of Inventors and Manufacturers, and from scientific bodies, both at

Dr. R. J. GATLING.
The Inventor of the Gatling Gun.

home and abroad. The State of North Carolina may well be proud of this modest and industrious son. His eminent personal merit and high scientific achievements reflect honor upon his American name. He was married at Indianapolis in 1854 to Miss Jemima Sanders, daughter of Dr. John H. Sanders, of that city.

Dr. Gatling died February 26, 1903, in New York City, and was buried at Indianapolis, Ind. His widow and one daughter and one son survive him. Mrs. Gatling resides with her daughter, Mrs. Hugh O. Pentecost, in New York City, and his son, Richard H. Gatling, is a speculator in real estate in the same city.

Dr. Gatling's mother was a woman of strong and sublime Christian character. After the death of her husband in 1848, she was often seen riding about the neighborhood, visiting friends, going to church, and looking after her business alone, in her top gig drawn by her old gentle gray horse. The Doctor's brother, Wm. J. Gatling, was a lawyer by profession, but after going West became a large operator in the gold mines of Canada, while his brother James H. Gatling lived at the old homestead in Maney's Neck, until he was brutally murdered in the morning of September 2, 1879, while feeding his hogs, by a crazy man by the name of Vann. James H. left an estate worth about $25,000, and during the settlement of the estate by the writer, as administrator, Dr. Gatling made frequent visits to Murfreesboro. The sad fate of his brother greatly bereaved him. His eldest brother was Thomas Barnes Gatling, who married and left two children, Isaac and Rebecca; the latter married Jno. T. Peebles, of Northampton County, where they now have descendants living. William and James H. never married, but were men of great industry and ingenuity and both were inventors, as was their noble old father. Mrs. Mary Gatling had three brothers—Thomas, Jesse and Richard Barnes.

Sarah Purdie, of old, who lived across William street from H. T. Lassiter's lot in the Boro Town, was a Miss Sarah

Maget, the aunt of the late John E. Maget and James H. Maget. Miss Maget first married one of the Hills. After his death she married a widower Blount. She was a prim little woman and fond of show and the ball-room, where she delighted the lookers-on by her active and fantastic movements on the well-waxed floor. She was possessed of much of the world's riches, and dressed in the tip of fashion. After the death of her second husband, she married Samuel Nicholson, of Maney's Neck. He died in the eighth decade, while in New York City on a business visit. Sometime after Nicholson's death she was courted by Dr. John H. Purdie, of Enfield, N. C., and she married him. The Doctor was a high-flyer in society, a hard drinker, and was heavily in debt. This was unknown to the rich little widow. Soon after their marriage the Doctor's creditors bounced down on him, and levied on the personal property of his new wife to collect their debts. This horrified his little bride, who had thrice before been a bride, and at the end of about six weeks they separated and the Doctor was persuaded to convey all property rights in her property to Dr. Thos. J. Harper, in trust for the woman he fooled, and she returned to her old home in Murfreesboro and lived the remainder of her days alone with her well-trained colored nurses, who were devoted to her. Their descendants now often speak affectionately of old Mistress Purdie. Her will was written July 22, 1840, and probated at May Term, 1850. Dr. Purdie was a descendant of Alexander Purdie, who was appointed Public Printer of the Province of North Carolina in 1762. Col. Uriah Vaughan administered and settled her estate.

Some of the fashionable marriages in the lower end of the county in 1848 were: Richard Blount, of Memphis, to Miss Bartha Sanders, the lovely and admired step-daughter of Watson Lewis; Watson S. Winborne to the gentle Isabella Lassiter. In the midst of these festive occasions the death of Elleanor Hardy, the young and beautiful wife of Col.

Starkey Sharp III, brings sadness in the gay and festive neighborhood of Mill Neck. Miss Saunders had been a great belle in the lower end of the county, as were Misses Mary Vick and Annie Waddill, in Maney' Neck, and many a stout heart of our young men was pained at her decision to make her home in the far West.

W. D. PRUDEN.

William Dossey Pruden was born in Gates County, February 22, 1812, and died in Hertford County, N. C., January 15, 1874. He was the son of Rev. Nathaniel Pruden and Marcella Newsom, his wife. His parents on both sides were of English extraction, his grandfather James Pruden having come to this country in the latter part of the seventeenth century, or early in the eighteenth, and the Newsom family before that time. Rev. Nathaniel Pruden was one of the pioneer Baptist preachers of Eastern North Carolina, whose career commenced at the beginning of the eighteenth century and continued to his death, about 1818. He was one of the founders of the North Carolina State Baptist Convention. His son was named for the Rev. William Dossey, a prominent Baptist preacher of that day. He was very young at the time of his father's death and, his mother having died before his father, he was taken to Hertford County, N. C., where he became an inmate of the family of his uncle, Capt. Michael B. Newsom. Having very little estate, he was deprived of early educational advantages, but availed himself of such as he had and acquired knowledge rapidly. When he was about twenty years of age he became a school-teacher, among his pupils being the famous Richard J. Gatling, the inventor of the Gatling Gun, and many others, who became prominent in the county. In 1835 he married Martha G.

Riddick, the daughter of James Riddick, of Hertford County. He was always deeply interested in agriculture, as his ancestors had been before him for generations, and shortly after reaching full age he became a farmer and devoted his entire life to that vocation. He pursued it with unusual energy and intelligence, and was always successful. About 1835 he bought valuable lands in what is known as the Mill Neck district of Hertford County, remarkable for the productiveness of its soil, for which he gave his notes. These notes he paid promptly when they came due, and at the time of his death he owned the farm which he first bought, with other valuable lands in that community, which lands are still owned by his children.

Of his marriage eight children were born, three of whom died in infancy, and two sons, when they were approaching manhood, one of them at the University of Virginia, where he was pursuing his education; three survived him, of whom one died shortly thereafter, and his only representatives now are Mrs. Horatio Hayes, who lives at the old home, and W. D. Pruden, a lawyer of Edenton.

He was a man of great independence of thought and action. Early in life he joined the Methodist church, the first one of his family in this country who belonged to any other church but the Baptist. He always, however, had great respect and attachment for the Baptist church, in which his father and his ancestors had worshipped. For more than forty years he was an active member of the Methodist church, and one of its official body. He frequently represented his church in its annual and quarterly conferences, and took great interest in everything which pertained to it. He died in its faith.

In politics he was a Whig, until the Whig party ceased to exist, and was a good representative of that class of worthy citizens who largely composed the Whig party in North Carolina. After that he became a Democrat, and remained one until his death. He neevr sought or desired office. Frequently he presided at the county conventions of his party, and was for many years one of the justices of the peace of the county and a member of the Special County Court. He was an earnest Union man up to the time President Lincoln issued his proclamation calling for troops to coerce the States. He believed in the right of secession, but did not believe that it was at the time practicable or necessary. He clung earnestly to the old flag, and to the history and traditions of his country. The discussions between him and some of his neighbors, who took a different view, at the neighborhood gatherings, were frequent and earnest. He believed that the allegiance of the citizen was due first to the State in which he lived, and could not tolerate the thought that the general government could or would coerce the States to remain in the Union, and when that proclamation was issued he said to one of his nearest neighbors, who was an earnest secessionist, "From this time on I am as strong as you in favor of the Southern Confederacy." No man was more loyal thereafter to the South; no man gave more liberally and willingly of his means and his talents to the support of the Southern cause. His sons, except one, were too young to go into the army. That one did go, with his approval and encouragement, and was in the army at the close of the war. When the war closed, like others he found his estate reduced, labor demoralized, and conditions generally unsatisfactory and gloomy, but he took up arms vigorously against these troubles and overcame them, and prospered until his death in 1874, leading all the time the quiet life of a farmer. His wife died in 1867, and he never married again, but devoted himself to the care and comfort of his children. He was a believer in education, and spent a large part of his income in educating his children. All of them who reached maturity were given every advantage that the schools of the day afforded. His oldest daughter, Mrs. Horatio Hayes, now approaching seventy, a well-educated woman, lives at the ancestral home, and his eldest son, W. D. Pruden, of Edenton, has been a lawyer in active practice in the First Judicial District for more than thirty years.

The record of the courts and the history of Hertford County bear testimony to the active and faithful labor of this man, and his children and friends are justly proud of the record.

In 1703, in the second year of the reign of Queen Anne of England, and during the government of the Lords Proprietors of Carolina, at Edenton, in the county of Albemarle, John Pruden was a vestryman of St. Paul's Church, the established church of England. It may be he was the forerunner of the Prudens in this country.

GEN. W. D. BARNES.

Judge William Deanes Barnes, of Florida, was a native of Hertford County. His parents were Thomas Barnes and wife, Sarah Barnes, *nee* Deanes. They lived about five miles back of Murfreesboro, at the home of the late W. T. Brown. Mrs. Sarah Barnes was the daughter of the old Sheriff Thos. Deanes. Thomas Barnes and Mrs. Jordan Gatling were brother and sister. They moved to Jackson County, Fla., in 1847 while their son W. D. was at the University of the State. After he graduated he studied law and located in Marianna, Fla. He was in the Confederate Army and was promoted to the rank of brigadier-general in the army. After the war he devoted himself to his profession. The writer visited him in 1877 and again in 1879 on professional business. He was a most delightful gentleman and had a lovely family. His wife was a Miss Cotton, of Raleigh, and sister of the wife of Col. W. L. Saunders, the late Secretary of State of North Carolina. In 1854 he was elected Solicitor of the Western District of Florida. In 1879 he was President of the State Senate. From 1880 to 1890 he was Comptroller of the State. In May, 1890, he was appointed Judge of the First Judicial District of his State, which office he was holding when he died in 1896. He was born in 1830.

CHOWAN BAPTIST FEMALE INSTITUTE.

DECADE X.
1850--1860.

During the 8th and 9th decades of the county the Baptist and Methodist denominations had grown strong. The Methodists were in the lead in Murfreesboro, and had established themselves strongly in Winton, Harrellsville, Union (formerly Blue Water), and other places in the county. A rivalry between these two denominations for mastership began, and their ministers in Eastern Carolina instigated a most unwise custom of discussing their creeds and doctrines in public debate. To the writer such vanity seems strange and unaccountable. Why people striving to glorify the one great common Lord and Master should permit their differences as to the mode of worship and the like, to so excite their passions and prejudices to that extent that will cover up their love of Christ and of their neighbors, which is the essence of Christianity, is incomprehensible to the writer.

We were intended to differ, and our differences should not breed intolerance. Who is to be the judge? We cannot expect perfection on earth.

Plato of old dreamed of a perfect and happy republic, when every officer would be guided in his conduct by the most rigid rules of moral ethics. But he never realized the millenium of his dream, nor will we who differ in our notions of religious creeds and modes of worship, ever settle the question as to who is right. Love of Christ and of our neighbors is the only test of true Christianity. But sometimes these controversies, which seem on the surface to be productive of so much unhappy strife, produce the most happy results. This honorable rivalry between these two strong Christian denominations caused the Baptists of the Chowan Association, which received its origin at the Meherrin church (Parker's) near the town of Murfreesboro, to establish the Chowan Baptist Female Institute in Murfreesboro in 1848. It supplanted the Banks' school, and during its primeval days was conducted in the Banks' School building under the auspices of the Baptist denomination of the Albemarle section. The Baptists kept at the head of this institution of learning from its origin to the present time, the foremost teachers of their times.

The first president was Rev. Martin Rudolph Forey, a native of New York, and a graduate of Madison University of that State. Mr. Forey was a Christlike man, of great literary culture, and of wonderful energy and business sagacity. He gave the school a high standard, and its reputation was quickly heralded throughout the States. Dr. Forey was succeeded as head of the institution by that great scholar and Baptist divine, Dr. William Hooper, the grandson of the illustrious William Hooper, one of the signers of the immortal Declaration of Independence in 1776, and whose picture now hangs on the wall in Independence Hall in Philadelphia, reflecting the intellectuality of that wonderful man.

The distinguished Dr. William Hooper was succeeded by Rev. Archibald McDowell, of South Carolina, who was a sublime Christian gentleman and a ripe scholar. Dr. McDowell died in 1881, and Prof. John B. Brewer, of Wilson, N. C., a graduate of Wake Forest and a grandson of President Wait of that college, was put in charge of this famous institution of learning and shaped its onward course for a number of years, when he was succeeded for a short period by Prof. W. O. Petty, of South Carolina. The present chief officer of the institution and successor of Professor Petty, is Hon. John C. Scarborough, who for sixteen years held the office of Superintendent of Public Instruction in North Carolina, and who so ably guided the educational interests of the State.

There are now about 100 or more young ladies whose hearts and minds are being trained at this institution of learning. Its first commencement was held in 1849.

That same honorable rivalry caused the Methodists in Eastern North Carolina and Virginia to establish in the

WESLEYAN FEMALE COLLEGE.

Decade X.—1850–1860.

same town the Wesleyan Female College, and, like the Baptists, they kept at the head of their institution of learning the ablest teachers in the Virginia Conference of the M. E. Church, with a most capable faculty. Rev. Joseph H. Davis, a man of great learning and a devout Christian, was their first president. He was succeeded by Rev. D. P. Wills, a gentleman who kept the college up to the high standard fixed by his predecessors. Then came the eloquent and gifted Rev. Cornelius B. Riddick at its head, who presided with great success for several years when he was succeeded for a brief period by Rev. James D. Coullings. The latter was succeeded by that great scholar and divine of the Virginia Conference, Rev. Paul Whitehead, who is the Chief Justice of that distinguished body. Then followed as its chief officer the eloquent, scholarly and chivalrous Rev. William G. Star, who was at the helm when the magnificent building of the famous college was destroyed by fire in 1877. The college was rebuilt in 1881. In the meantime the dividing line between the Virginia and North Carolina Conferences had been changed by throwing Eastern Carolina into the North Carolina Conference. After the rebuilding of the college it was presided over first by Prof. E. E. Parham, of Warren County, N. C., and secondly by Rev. R. P. Troy, of the N. C. Conference, when it was again destroyed by fire in 1893. It has never been rebuilt since the last fire.

The incalculable benefits received by North Carolina and Virginia from the above two female colleges in sending out within their borders educated Christian mothers are lasting monuments to the founders and friends of those two fountains of knowledge and of wisdom. If denominational controversies and rivalry will always produce such wonderful and happy results, let them continue.

John A. Anderson for a number of years had filled places of important trusts. He had served for years as County Trustee, as a member of the Governor's Council during Governor Manly's administration, and on the death of John

Vann, Esq., in 1850, he was elected Chairman of the County Court, and served with marked ability for several years, when he resigned in 1857, and was succeeded by Dr. G. C. Moore. In 1861 he was again elected Chairman of the Court and held the position to his death, in June of the same year.

Mr. Anderson had a large circle of friends, and was especially a favorite with the members of the bar, who greatly enjoyed his hospitality during the sessions of the Court. He was the owner of a large estate, which was settled by his personal friends John A. Vann and W. D. Holloman. He was a descendant of Maj. John Brown, the old Tory of St. John's.

John A. Anderson was married twice. His first wife, Elizabeth, died February 10, 1825, and he afterwards married the young widow of Dr. John C. Montgomery, who was Harriet, the daughter of Leven Duer and his wife Margaret, and sister to Andrew V. Duer, the Public Register, who died April 17, 1831. At the Spring Term, 1824, of Hertford Court, the suit of Miss Harriet Duer against Dr. Lawrence O'Bryan for breach of promise of marriage was tried in Winton. The jury rendered a verdict in favor of the plaintiff for $218. The costs was said to be about $400. This would indicate that quite a number of witnesses were examined. The old bachelors, Patrick Brown and Dr. Thomas O'Dwyer, had taken considerable interest in the trial and thought their friend O'Bryan got out very easy. O'Bryan afterwards married Barsha Gordon and moved South. Brown said to O'Dwyer on his return from court on the day of the trial:

"A pretty girl who gets a kiss and runs and tells her mother,
Does what she should not do, and doesn't deserve another."

Miss Duer shortly thereafter married Dr. John C. Montgomery, brother of Bridger J. and G. W. Montgomery. He only lived about six months after his marriage.

Decade X.—1850–1860.

Nancy, the widow of Howell Jones, Esq., died January, 1808, and was buried in the Duer graveyard. Howell Jones was Clerk and Master in Equity for a number of years, and was the father of Howell Morgan Jones.

John A. Anderson died in 1861 in his sixty-fourth year, and his wife in 1866. His son, James L. Anderson, who represented the county in the House in 1889 and 1891, died in 1896, aged 57 years. Mr. Anderson had two daughters— Mrs. J. W. Faison, of Winton, and Mrs. H. B. Knox, of New Orleans. The latter was regarded as a great beauty in her younger days.

Lemuel R. Jernigan was one of the most substantial and influential men of his day in the county. He descended from a long line of influential and honorable ancestors. In 1831, when a young man, he was elected Public Register to succeed Andrew V. Duer, deceased, which office he filled until 1843, when he resigned to accept the office of County Trustee (which was the same as Treasurer), to which he was elected in February, 1844, over E. D. Britt by a vote of 19 to 10. J. A. Anderson, John Vann, James L. Grimes and Dr. Edw. S. Neal voted for John L. Jenkins, the father of our bank cashier, Paul E. Jenkins. This office he held until 1854. His official position did not occupy the whole of his time, as we find him during the whole period of his official life engaged in the mercantile pursuits with William B. Wynns at Barfields, and later with his brother-in-law, Starkey S. Harrell, Jr. He lived a busy and active life and accumulated a considerable estate. He kept well posted on all public questions, and those seeking official position courted his influence and aid. He was too old to enter the Confederate Army, but he served his county and his State in various ways in providing for and looking

L. R. JERNIGAN.

after the families of the soldiers in his county. He married Mary, the daughter of Starkey S. Harrell, Sr., and granddaughter of Nathan Harrell. His wife was first cousin to Chief Justice Smith. His father was Miles H. Jernigan, whose will was probated in February, 1843, and his grandfather was Mills Jernigan, who was Public Register in the county from 1800 to 1813, and was Entry Taker shortly after the War of 1776-1782. Hon. Spencer Jarnagan's father was a relative of Mills Jernigan, of Hertford County, and emigrated to Tennesse before it became a State and while it was a part of North Carolina. He graduated at Greenville College in 1813, studied law and was elected to the U. S. Senate from Tennessee as a Whig in 1843 and served from December 4, 1843, to March 3, 1847. He spelt his name different from those in North Carolina, but we have found the name *Jarnagan* in the old State records and also in old papers in this county. It is pronounced in that way even now by the unlettered.

L. R. Jernigan died December 8, 1866, at Barfields, leaving his widow surviving him and two sons and one daughter—John H., Mary H., and Thos. R. Jernigan.

Mr. Jernigan was succeeded in 1854 as County Trustee by Elisha D. Britt, of Maney's Neck, who held the office until 1861. Jethro W. Barnes, the neighbor and friend of Britt, was County Surveyor from about 1834 to 1858. John P. Bridger was elected Sheriff at the November Term, 1848, and remained in office until August Term, 1856, when he was succeeded by John A. Vann, son of the old chairman. Bridger succeeded Abner J. Perry, who succeeded Preston Perry.

Decade X.—1850–1860.

Among the foremen of the grand jury during this decade we find John W. Southall, Uriah Vaughan, L. R. Jernigan, Elisha D. Britt, S. D. Winborne, Jethro W. Barnes. The jolly W. B. Day is frequently on hand as the special officer of the grand jury, a position which had been frequently held by Edw. F. Dunston and Constable Thomas Winborne III.

J. B. Slaughter served for a short time as Clerk of Superior Court just prior to G. W. Beverly. He resigned to be a candidate for the House in 1856 against W. L. Daniel, and was elected.

Among the new justices of the peace found presiding in the county courts during this decade are Samuel Moore, Jno. V. Lawrence, Drewry Vinson, James Barnes, William Darden, W. M. Montgomery, Howell M. Jones, John W. Southall, Jacob Sharp, A. G. Vann, Daniel Valentine, J. B. Sharp, James A. Riddick, T. D. Vann. In 1857 the following new justices of the peace qualified: John P. Lee, S. D. Winborne, L. R. Jernigan, Watson Lewis, Jr., W. L. Daniel, James M. Wynns, B. A. Capehart and Jesse C. Powell.

In August, 1851, A. P. Yancey, on account of bad health, retires as County Attorney and W. D. Valentine, the former Clerk of the Superior Court, is elected to succeed Yancey. At February Term, 1855, W. N. H. Smith qualified as administrator of his half brother, A. P. Yancey, and Daniel Velentine, at November Term, 1856, qualified as administrator of his brother, W. D. Valentine. Jesse J. Yates was elected County Attorney at August Term, 1855, and served until 1860.

A notice of the late John V. Lawrence, who was active and prominent in county affairs during this period will be found in the 5th decade, with the Rea's, one of whom he married.

The wealthy and elegant and aristocratic cavallier, John W. Southall, another of the county's dignitaries of these times, is sketched, with the notice of his father, in the 6th decade.

John Winborne, of the east end of the county, who was for a long while one of the county's worthies, died in 1847, and his highly esteemed son, William J. Winborne, of the same section, succumbs to fever in the prime of life during this period. Elisha Vaughan of the west end follows.

Edward F. Dunston, of whom we have mentioned, was one of the old worthies of the Borough town. He married Miss Mary Louise Vaughan, of the upper Southampton Vaughans, of Virginia, and of revolutionary fame. Edward F. Dunston was a descendant of John Dunston, a distinguished Englishman, who came to America in 1723 to fill the office of Commissioner of Customs at Edenton. He was a man of fine ability and great prominence. Edward's children by his marriage were Dr. Henry V. Dunston, of Windsor, N. C.; Josephine J. Dunston, Gussie, and William E. Dunston, now of Elizabeth City. Gussie has never married. Josephine, after the late Civil War, married Capt. John J. Dyer, a brave, daring and handsome Confederate soldier. He was from a long line of a soldiery ancestry. His splendid military bearing was convincing proof of his noble ancestry. They reared a daughter and a son. The daughter was a handsome and stylish woman, but lived but a few months after marrying. Their son, R. O. Dyer, of Richmond, Va., has much of the military bearing of his father and of the intellectuality of his mother. All of the Dunston children were highly intellectual. Mr. Dyer after his marriage bought the large and valuable Henry Jenkins plantation at Joynersville, in Southampton County, where he resided until his death a few years ago, and which is now the home of his widow. Dr. Dunston is Bertie's leading physician, and one of her most intellectual citizens.

MISS JOSEPHINE J. DUNSTON.

Decade X.—1850–1860.

Nearly all of Mrs. Dunston's family were killed in the Nat Turner insurrection in 1831. Her sister was also killed. Her brother of 19 was permitted to fasten the rope around Nat Turner's neck that swung him into eternity. Mr. Dunston died before the conflict of 1861, but his widow was patriotic to the core. She made and unfurled the first Confederate flag in Hertford County and furnished one gallant son to the cause, he being the only one old enough to enlist.

Daniel Van Pelt Sessoms, of Pitch Landing, was sent in 1850 by the county to the Senate, as successor to W. N. H. Smith, who declined a re-election. Mr. Sessoms was an uncompromising Whig in politics, but an amiable and popular gentleman. Although his occupation was that of a planter, yet he found time to read and keep well posted in the current literature of his day, and was familiar with the political issues of the time. He had a strong and vigorous mind, and was a most entertaining conversationalist. Notwithstanding the Democrats were in the majority in both branches of the Legislature, he received good consideration as a member of the minority. He served on some of the most important committees. He served his people as a justice of the peace for many years before and after the Civil War. Mr. Sessoms was born May 9, 1809, and died October 4, 1888. He was the son of William Sessoms, whose will was probated in 1844, and his first wife, Elizabeth, was the daughter of Daniel Van Pelt, of this county, and sister of Henry B. Van Pelt, who was Public Register of the county in 1845 and 1846. Mr. Sessoms was married twice. His second wife was Eliza Freeman, who was a great help to him in the accumulation of his estate. He left children by both of his wives.

DANIEL VANPELT SESSOMS.

He has a son now living in the county bearing his name. Charles C. Sessoms is a child by his second marriage. He had two brothers, W. W. Sessoms and H. B. Sessoms, the latter being the father of Dr. Jos. W. Sessoms, of Bertie, and of Mrs. J. J. Perry, the mother of J. W. Perry, of Norfolk, Va.

Hon. Kenneth Rayner was in the House during the session of 1850, and by his eloquence and public zeal he continued to reflect great honor on the Hertford people, by whom he was greatly admired.

Albert Moore, a Whig, was defeated for the office of Sheriff by John P. Bridger. Mr. Moore lived in Maney's Neck, and was brother to Capt. Samuel Moore, of Buckhorn, Alfred Moore and Henry Moore, the prince of merchants in the Borough. Their father was Allen Moore, the brother of John Moore, who was the father of Mrs. A. W. Darden. The Moores were leading citizens in their day.

Dr. Edw. S. Neal, who resided in town, where E. C. Worrell now resides, passes away with the end of this decade. He married Annie Baker, granddaughter of Gen. Lawrence Baker, who is now living in her ninetieth year in Washington, N. C. The late Thomas N. Neal of the county was his brother, and Maj. John B. Neal, of Scotland Neck, N. C., is his son.

Major Neal is still a gallant and chivalrous son of Halifax County. He entered the Confederate Army April 14, 1861, as a private in Dreux's Battalion of Infantry, in Louisiana, as from Hertford County, N. C. Later, in 1861, he was transferred to Company I, 1st N. C. Cavalry, and elected 2d lieutenant; later made captain of the company, and in August 1, 1863, was promoted to the rank of major, and still later appointed lieutenant-colonel, but the war was ended before he received his commission. He was born February 4, 1839, and after reaching manhood and completing his education married Annie E., daughter of Richard H. Smith and wife, Sallie Hall, the daughter of former Judge

Hall of our Supreme Court. After her death he married, February 22, 1883, Sallie, the oldest daughter of Dr. Archibald McDowell, of Murfreesboro. Major Neal's paternal grandfather was Thomas Neal and his paternal great-grandfather was Francis Neal. His father came to Murfreesboro from Mecklenburg County, Va. His sister, Mary S. Neal, married in 1857, Robert Perkins, of Burke County, N. C. His other sisters, Annie E. and Sarah T. Neal, married, we think, a gentleman living in Pitt County.

Prof. Geo. W. Neal, the old school-teacher, married Fannie, the daughter of John Hart and wife Bettie Hart, *nee* Dillard, of Murfreesboro. Professor Neal's family came from Southampton County, Va. Professor Neal and wife are the parents of our Judge Walter H. Neal.

A FAMOUS LAWSUIT.

In 1854 the *Murfreesboro Gazette*, edited and published by John B. Drinkard and Canozio Fraetor, in the town of Murfreesboro, was the county newspaper, which often involved in trouble those fond of getting their criticisms in print. The "Know-Nothing," a secret political party, whose motto was "America for Americans," and their pass-word was "Sam," was flourishing about this time. It was composed largely of Whigs, but a few Democrats were allowed to join the Winton Lodge. Alfred W. Darden, a Democrat, joined, but withdrew and published in the *Gazette* a very denunciatory article, in which he criticised the order and its members and exposed many of its secrets. A committee, consisting of John A. Anderson, R. G. Cowper and others, acting on behalf of the "Know-Nothing" Lodge at Winton, published in the *Gazette* some resolutions of that body, touching on the conduct of Darden. The latter deeming the resolutions libelous, sued the committee in Hertford County for $10,000 damages, but afterwards he secured the removal of the suit for trial to Washington County, on account of the great popularity and influence of the defendants.

Judge Heath, P. H. Winston, Col. David Outlaw and John P. Jordan appeared for the plaintiff, and W. N. H. Smith, D. A. Barnes, H. A. Gilliam and Thos. M. Garrett represented the defendants.

The case was tried before Judge Caldwell. The very nature of the suit necessarily caused great excitement, interest and feeling in the county. The "Know-Nothing" party existed in several of the States. Many people from this county attended the trial. The speeches of the attorneys were sharp, spicy and able. The jury gave the plaintiff a few dollars damages and that was the end of the great "Know-Nothing Suit."

Mr. Garrett, one of the attorneys, was reared near Coleraine, in Bertie County, and was prepared for college by Prof. John Kimberly at Buckhorn Academy, in Hertford County. He graduated at Chapel Hill in 1851 and was a brilliant lawyer; was colonel in the war of 1861-'65, and one of the bravest of the brave. He was killed in the battle of the Wilderness.

"SOUTHERN STAR."

Maj. J. W. Moore has furnished us with some information showing the great energy and enterprise of some of Murfreesboro's men. In 1856 there seemed to reappear the revival of the ancient commercial spirit once so noticeable among the sons of Hertford. Jesse A. Jackson, who had settled in the town several years prior, was from New Jersey, and was a man of great energy and ingenuity. He is now well remembered by some of our citizens. He for years operated a saw-mill across the river, where the saw-mill of E. C. Worrell is now located, and also made the bricks for the two female colleges in the town, from which he realized a fair profit. He conceived the idea in 1856 of building a large steamship to make regular trips from Murfreesboro to New York, carrying both freight and passengers. He secured financial aid from Glines & Graham, a New York commission firm,

Decade X.—1850–1860.

and several of the wealthy citizens of Murfreesboro. Thirty thousand dollars were consumed in building the steamer in Murfreesboro. Her engines were built at Wilmington, Delaware. Its model was beautiful and a thing of beauty, and Jackson's ship was destined to become famous. The New York firm failed and his home friends became uneasy about their investment and declined to invest any more money in the visionary project of Jackson. This greatly embarrassed poor Jackson and brought about his insolvency. The writer now has some of his unpaid obligations. The great floating palace was soon sold, and John W. Southall and Capt. Thomas Badger became the purchasers. She was christened the "Southern Star." Southall and Badger sold her to the U. S. government. The government had her rechristened "Crusader," and she became famous as one of the swiftest keels in the water and won renown in chasing steamers engaged in the unlawful business, just before the Civil War, of importing wretched Africans into our Gulf States by the enemies of the South, in their efforts to make slavery as odious as possible.

In 1852 R. G. Cowper defeated W. W. Mitchell for the Senate.

Watson L. Daniel represented the county in the House in 1852 and 1854 as a Whig in politics. Captain Perry was his opponent in 1852. In 1852 he voted for Matthew W. Ransom, a Democrat, for Attorney-General of the State, who was then a brilliant young lawyer in Warren County. This vote soon ended Mr. Daniel's career as a legislator, and young attorney Joseph Blount Slaughter defeated him in 1856 for the Whig nomination and was elected. While it defeated Daniel, it made General Ransom his life-long friend. Attorney-General Ransom afterwards became a distinguished general in the Civil War and a United States Senator of national fame. Major Daniel later served his county as major in the militia, justice of the peace, chairman of the County Court and Register of Deeds. He was the son of Capt. Belcher Daniel and his wife, Julia Flower.

Captain Daniel was the son of a sea captain who came from Ireland about 1760 and settled on Roanoke Island. Capt. Belcher Daniel was born in 1776 and moved to Hertford County and settled at Pitch Landing in 1820 and died in 1831. His wife belonged to the same Flower family from which the late Governor Flower of New York descended. They left three children, all of whom were born on Roanoke Island—Watson L., Nancy, and Spencer. The latter became a celebrated physician and died in 1858. Nancy married Samuel M. Aumack, Sr. Major Daniel died in December, 1889, or January, 1890, while holding the office of Register of Deeds in the county. For a long while he and Daniel Valentine were engaged as partners in the mercantile business at Oak Villa, the old home of Col. Matthias Brickle, near Winton. Daniel Valentine married Miss Duer, and they were the parents of the wife of John O. Askew, Jr. Mr. Valentine was the brother of the old Clerk of the Superior Court, the bachelor lawyer, and County Attorney, W. D. Valentine.

John Blount Slaughter, the member of the House in 1856, was the son of Wm. Slaughter, who married a Miss Blount and died in 1844. Young Slaughter read law under W. N. H. Smith. He was not a man of much mental calibre and force, but he secured the confidence of the people and retained it throughout life, as will be seen from the record of the county affairs. He lived to a ripe old age and married shortly before his death, for the first time.

Watson Lewis, Sr., was for a number of years a leading magistrate and a prominent citizen in the Harrellsville section of the county, and his descendants are numerous and are well scattered. He came to the county during the first quarter of the nineteenth century from Baltimore, Maryland, and settled in the section above stated. He was thrice married. His first wife was the sister of John Winborne, who married Nancy Simons, of the east end of the county, and son of William Winborne and grandson of Henry Winborne. By this marriage he had two children—Edward D., and Sallie Lewis. Edward married Levinia Askew, daughter of David Askew, and niece of Dr. A. J. Askew. They had two children—Sallie D. Lewis, who became the wife of John H. Jernigan, son of L. R. Jernigan, and Emma Lewis, who was the second wife of Joseph J. Perry.

Watson Lewis' daughter Sallie married John Simons. He lived but a short time, and later she married Col. Starkey Sharp and they reared one child, Nannie, who first married James Walton and reared two daughters, one of whom married John Nichols, of Bertie, and the other Walton daughter married J. H. Flythe, of Northampton County, but now of Augusta, Ga. After the death of Walton his widow married E. D. Scull, of Harrellsville, and they reared several boys.

The second wife of Watson Lewis was Fannie, the daughter of Capt. Belcher Daniel, and by his marriage he had seven children—Nannie, who became the wife of James B. Chamblee; Watson Lewis, Jr., who married Anna Crutchelow, of Martin County; Fannie Lewis, who married Thomas Riddick, of Gates County, and Dr. John Lewis, who married Mary Sparrow, of Norfolk, Va. His daughter Jane was the third wife of Col. Starkey Sharp. Caroline married Hiram Harrell, of Bertie County, and his youngest son, Dr. Daniel W. Lewis, married Annie Williams, of Martin County, where they now live.

Watson Lewis' third wife was Sarah Saunders, of Gatesville. They left no issue.

Watson Lewis, Jr., died in the 13th decade, leaving his widow and several children surviving him.

Thomas Riddick and wife Fannie are the parents of Sarah Riddick, who was a most accomplished and cultured lady. She married a Mr. White, of New York City; and of Cora Riddick, who was a very attractive young lady when the writer began the practice of his profession. She married W. D. McAnges, of Suffolk, Va., where they now live.

Dr. John Lewis, who lived near Norfolk, left several daughters, one of whom the author has seen. She was large and tall and a handsome and splendid looking woman, with a bright and cheerful disposition. She married Col. Alexander Savage, of Norfolk, Va. Mrs. Chamblee left one daughter, who married William D. Adkins.

Mrs. Hiram P. Harrell died several years ago, leaving several children and her husband surviving her.

Col. Starkey Sharp and his wife Jane are the parents of Mrs. John T. Shubrick, of Rocky Mount, N. C.; of Mrs. Thos. R. Jernigan, and Hunter Sharp and Starkey Sharp IV.

Dr. Daniel W. Lewis was an officer in the Confederate Army. He is still a leading physician in Martin County. He has no issue.

ABNER HARRELL.

Abner Harrell, late of Harrellsville, and for whom the place was named, was a most worthy man and a man of a large estate. He descended from one of the oldest families in the county. He was the son of Maj. Samuel Harrell, who resigned his military office in 1783. Samuel Harrell was a soldier in the War of 1776-1782, a member of the State Convention of 1788, and a son of Abner Harrell, a freeholder in Bertie County in 1740, as appears from the jury list of that county. Major Harrell left the following children: Noah, James, William B., Willis, Isaac, Andrew, and Abner, Mary and Nancy. George T. Harrell, of Gates County, is a grandson of Major Harrell, and the mother of the late Hon. Jesse J. Yeates was the granddaughter of Major Harrell. Abner Harrell, the subject of this sketch, was for a long while a justice of the peace in this county. He was married four times. His first wife was Jennie Yeates, an aunt of Hon. Jesse J. Yeates. They were the parents of the wife of John O. Askew, Sr. His second wife was Miss Norfleet, his third was Miss Nancy Jones, and his fourth was Miss Mary Womble. He died May 10, 1864, leaving surviving him the following children: Mary, who married the late Rev. Joshua Garrett, a distinguished divine of the Virginia Conference of the M. E. Church, South (Rev. Garrett left one daughter, who married Benj. Thach, of Perquimans County), Mrs. John O. Askew, Sr., Mrs. Benj. F. Beverly of Union, Mrs. D. W. Reed, Wm. J. Harrell, and A. B. Harrell.

Abner Harrell's son, A. B. Harrell, married Anna Mansard, a lady of large intellectual endowments and strong character. They were the parents of the late John Abner Harrell; Herbert B. Harrell, the owner of the Harrell's Printing House at Weldon; L. R. Harrell, a planter in Louisiana; Artemus Harrell, a business man in Pittsburg, Penn. Their daughter, Melissa Harrell, married Henry Hughes, of Virginia, and later of Lexington, Ky. She died leaving a large family of children, who are scattered in the States.

In 1853 the Whigs renominated and elected Col. David Outlaw, of Bertie, to Congress. Colonel Outlaw was a lawyer of consummate ability and a regular attendant upon the courts of Hertford, where he had many kin and a large clientage.

Thomas Bragg, of Northampton, another compeer with Outlaw and Smith at the Hertford bar, and a favorite of the people of the patriotic county of Hertford, was elected Governor of the State in 1854 and made Hertford's son, Pulaski Cowper, his private secretary. In 1859 Governor Bragg was elected U. S. Senator to succeed David S. Reid. U. S. Senator Asa Biggs was appointed U. S. Judge for North Carolina, as successor of Judge Henry Potter, who had recently died in the ninety-sixth year of his age. Potter was appointed judge in 1801 to succeed U. S. Judge Sitzgraves. Thomas L. Clingman succeeded Biggs in the Senate. W. N.

H. Smith was elected to Congress over Henry M. Shaw by a majority of 514 votes, and the immortal Zebulon Baird Vance was first elected to Congress in 1859 from the mountain district.

THE ROBERTS FAMILY.

The wife of the late Matthew Whitaker Ransom, a general in the war of 1861-'65 and a United States Senator from North Carolina from January, 1872, to March 3, 1895, was from one of Hertford County's old families. She was Miss Pattie A. Exum, of Northampton County, N. C. Attorney-General Ransom and Miss Exum were married in Petersburg, Va., January 19, 1853.

About the middle of the eighteenth century, Jonathan Roberts moved to and settled in the territory now embraced in the boundaries of Hertford County. On July 8, 1766, William Griffith, the then owner of the tract of land near the present town of Murfreesboro and known as the "Meredith Field," and on which he resided, sold and conveyed the same to Jonathan Roberts. Griffith built the first grist mill on Ganey's Creek where the E. C. Worrell Mill is now located. Roberts and his wife, Elizabeth, had several children. Their son Jonathan Roberts, Jr., married Esther Wilkinson, of Norfolk, Va., and they left several children—Benjamin, Mary, and others. After the death of Jonathan Roberts, Sr., his widow married Capt. Lewis Meredith, by whom she reared quite a family of children. Mary Roberts married James Maney. Benjamin Roberts married Martha Vaughan, of Murfreesboro, and lived in Murfreesboro at the residence of the late Col. Uriah Vaughan. Mr. Roberts died young, leaving his widow and several children surviving. Dr. Thos. O'Dwyer, in his diary of 1824, speaks of visiting the widow Roberts and her maiden sister, Miss Sallie Vaughan, and the Roberts children. Benj. Roberts' children were Mary, Lavinia, Esther Wilkinson, Dr. Thomas Vaughan, and Benjamin, Jr. The latter died while young. Dr. Thomas V. Roberts never married. We have before spoken of him.

Decade X.—1850–1860. 199

Mary disappointed Gen. Boon Felton and married Matthias Brickle Murfree, a son of Col. Hardy Murfree, of Murfreesboro, and they emigrated to Tennessee. Hardy Murfree, who graduated at Chapel Hill in 1848, was their son. Lavinia Esther Wilkinson Roberts married Joseph J. Exum, of Northampton County in 1829. Their daughter, Mary Thomas Exum, married Dr. W. B. Meares, of Wilmington, N. C., and died in 1881. Their daughter Martha A. (Pattie) Exum married Matt. W. Ransom. Mrs. Ransom is still living.

Joseph J. Exum was the son of Capt. James Thomas Exum, whose mother was a Miss Thomas, the aunt of Gen. Geo. H. Thomas, of military fame in the war of 1861-'5. His father was from Sussex County, Va.

Matt. W. Ransom was a descendant of James Ransom, whose will was probated in Surry County, Va., in October, 1740. James Ransom, the second, married Amy Davis, of Virginia. The third James Ransom of Surry County, and the grandfather of Matt. W. Ransom, moved to Warren County, N. C., in 1763, and married Priscilla Jones in Greenville County, Va., daughter of Edward Jones, of Warren County, and widow of Gideon Macon, the father of Nathaniel Macon, of North Carolina.

John Waddill, of Maney's Neck, was one of the county's foremost citizens for many years prior to the Civil War. He came to the county from Virginia during the first quarter of the nineteenth century. He married the daughter of Solomon Shepherd, of Maney's Neck, and built the house where our Joseph G. Majette, chairman of the County Board of Commissioners, now resides, and lived there.

Mr. Waddill was a man of great wealth and culture, and while he was aristocratic in his bearings, he was a warm friend of worthy young men and often showed his appreciation in various ways. His two daughters, Margaret and Annie, were great belles, and many a poor fellow was made sad by the laconic answer, "No." They were noble women.

Finally they married. Margaret became the wife of Edward Chambers, of Boydton, Va., and Annie became the bride of the celebrated Dr. William Howard, of Baltimore. His son, John Waddill, Jr., entered the Confederate Army as lieutenant in Company F, 31st Regiment N. C. State Troops, but was taken ill and died before entering active service. John Waddill, like many of our wealthy people, became in the forties the owner of valuable cotton plantations in Florida, where he spent much of his time, and where he died in 1854.

The decision of the U. S. Supreme Court in the ever famous Dred Scott case in 1858 greatly angered the Republican party. The Democratic party was still boastful in the United States. The other parties were in a chaotic condition, and the followers of the tottering political organizations united and fought under name of Opposition. R. G. Cowper for the Senate and W. N. H. Smith for the House were the nominees of the Opposition. The Democrats nominated John W. Moore for the Senate against Cowper. The latter was elected by 17 majority. Dr. R. H. Worthington, who was defeated for the House before as the Democratic nominee, declined to again become a candidate and Smith was elected. The Whigs and the Americans or Know-Nothings were becoming disheartened. The Democrats were boastful, warlike and defiant. On July 14, 1858, was issued the first issue of the new Murfreesboro paper, "The Citizen," owned and edited by Dr. Samuel J. Wheeler, a Democrat, and a strong and spicy Democratic organ. In 1859 Wheeler sold "The Citizen" to Charles H. Foster, late of Norfolk, Va., but a native of Maine, and C. C. Nicholson. Mr. Foster became a citizen of the town and soon married the gentle Susan E. Carter, daughter of Perry Carter, of Murfreesboro, a woman of great musical gifts and sunny disposition. Mr. Foster was educated at Bowdoin College and was noted for his scholarship, and grace as a writer. When the struggle came in 1861, on account of his offensive political views, he found it

Decade X.—1850–1860.

wise to make his escape between the suns and seek shelter in a more congenial clime in the North. Before leaving he sold "The Citizen" to S. R. Olmsted. He returned to the county after the cessation of hostilities and joined the "Carpet-Baggers" in their nefarious work against the Southern whites. At the next election R. G. Cowper and Kenneth Rayner became so displeased with the platform of their dying party that they sulked. Cowper refused to again run for the Senate, and Slaughter was elected, and Yeates elected to the House. The Whigs, although their flag did not float as triumphantly as in former days, the brave adherents in Hertford were determined to die in a fearless charge. So to offset "The Citizen," they secured the brave and brilliant Thos. J. Garner, of Northampton County, to come to Murfreesboro and edit the new Whig paper, "The Southron," which with vehemence shelled the camp of the fire-eaters and warlike Democrats. The war destroyed all of the old political parties in the South. New parties were formed after reconstruction in the next Decade.

At the commencement of the Chowan Baptist Female Institute in Murfreesboro, July 1, 1857, the beautiful Susan Deanes graduated, and to complete the grandeur of the occasion, just at the close of the concert, and before the melody of the sweet strains of music ceased to please and charm, Rev. Reuben Jones, of Virginia, who later became Moderator of the Portsmouth Baptist Association, came forward with Miss Susan Deanes and in the midst of her sister graduates were united in the holy estate of matrimony by Dr. Wm. Hooper. Their youngest daughter, Jessie, is now the most interesting wife of the author's brother, Samuel Pretlow Winborne, who reigns at the old Winborne Homestead.

MISS BETTIE PRETLOW.

Miss Bettie Pretlow, whose likeness here appears, is the maternal aunt of the author. She is the daughter of Joseph Pretlow and wife, Mary Pretlow, *nee* Hare, of Virginia. She and her ancestors were Quakers. She was thoroughly educated in the schools of her sect, and was a most gentle, refined and accomplished woman. She never married, but was greatly admired and beloved. She was born February 12, 1835, and died July 10, 1863, at the home of Major Winborne in Maney's Neck, who married her sister, Mary H. Pretlow. This Pretlow family was one of the purest and finest families in the old Commonwealth. "The Winborne Family" gives the genealogy and history of this Pretlow family. The Winbornes are religiously crossed with believers of nearly all the Protestant churches. The Winbornes have been for ages Baptist. But they did not believe in marrying in their own church. Henry Winborne, who came to this State in 1742, married a Quaker lady; his son, Thomas, married a Quakeress; his grandson, Elisha, married a Baptist; his great-grandson, Samuel D. Winborne, married a Quakeress, and the younger ones have married Episcopalians, Methodists, Presbyterians, Christians, and S. P. Winborne, alone, married a Baptist. Is there anything more sublime and attractive than the modest and pure-looking Quaker girl?

SLAVERY.

This institution was as old as the country. The first slaves imported to the Colonies was as early as 1619, if not earlier. A company was incorporated in England, known as the Royal African Company, to carry on the business of importing savage negroes to England and its possessions for sale as slaves. Queen Anne of England held a large block of the stock in this company. At the beginning of the Revolution of 1776 slavery existed in all the Colonies. But in the North it was not as profitable as in the South, and after the Revolution those States began to import their slaves to the South for sale. After disposing of their slave property to the Southern States they became active in their opposition to the institution of slavery. Such a change of front necessarily engendered resentment. Thus began the strife which ended in bloodshed between the two sections of our common country.

"Let fate do her worst; there are relics of joy,
Bright dreams of the past, which she cannot destroy."

THE OLD SLAVE "MAMMY."

This sublime old character in the Southern home is a relic of the past. Hardly any refined Southern home, blessed with children, was without her. She was a well-trained nurse; she was polite, respectful, gentle, and loving in her nature. She was the devoted maid of Mistress and Old Mistress, and generally the "wet nurse" of the young child of Mistress and the true and devoted friend of the family. Their separation always brought tears on the cheeks of "mammy" and the children. She was never neglected by Master and Mistress, and frequently the recipient of bounties from "little Mistress and young Master." Nothing but kindness was her share in life. They are a noble part of the history of the Old South.

This brings us up to the stormy days just preceding the volcanic days of the next decade.

JOHN BROWN'S RAID.

The occasional outbreaks of the Southern slaves were greatly due to Northern fanatics and their teachings. In 1859 John Brown, a white man of Connecticut, formed a diabolical plot to bring about the emancipation of slavery in the Southern States by inciting the slaves to rise in insurrection and kill out the whites. Brown was born May 9,

1800, and grew up to be a sore-eyed fanatic. He engaged in many enterprises in various parts of the country, but failed in all. He then conceived his fanatical plan for emancipating the slaves, so he got him up a company of twenty armed men, and on the night of October 16, 1859, seized the U. S. Arsenal at Harper's Ferry, Va., to secure arms and ammunition with which to arm the negroes, whom he expected to join him. The negroes failed, however, to meet him. He was captured October 17, 1859, by Col. Robert E. Lee with a few U. S. troops, tried for treason October 27, 1859, at Charlestown, Va., and hanged December 2, 1859, "to a sour apple tree." This raid of Brown, while it was insignificant in itself, he had just made himself odious to the South by his fanatical partisan teachings in the admission of Kansas into the Union as a State, and his acts were taken by the Southern people to be the result of the Northern literature on slavery and the speeches of the abolitionists in Congress. The whole Southern country became aroused, indignant, and excited. No doubt but such acts and teachings on the part of these half-crazed fanatics hastened the war and prevented the settlement of the troublesome questions between the two sections of our country.

About this same time an insurrection was threatened in the neighborhood of Murfreesboro, in Hertford County, and the men were armed and placed on guard to protect the town and the homes. The "Norfolk Blues" were dispatched for, and upon their arrival things quieted down. The "Blues" remained in Murfreesboro until things became quieted and the fears of the people were dispelled. The late Gen. Lawrence D. Groner, of Norfolk, Va., was one of the officers in command of the Norfolk company. Such things were constantly happening throughout the slave-holding States. Several of our citizens remember distinctly this exciting occurrence. With such re-occurring events resulting in the South from Northern teachings, war was inevitable. Conservatism and pleas for peace found no place in the minds of men.

Decade X.—1850-1860.

Such acts and the fanatical teachings of the abolitionists checked the growth of the sentiment in the South to gradually abandon slavery.

Now as we look back in the kaleidoscope of the past one hundred years, and take a view of the struggles and victories of the American people and watch the rise and progress of its magnificent civilization and growth in the arts and sciences and in Chrstianity, and see the noble part the sons and daughters of Hertford County have taken in this mighty drama, and the splendid citizenship she has exhibited to the world, it makes us feel proud that we have lived, and that our noble ancestors were among its heroic dead and figured in making a glorious history for a Christian and liberty-loving people. The war with Mexico had settled the troubles between that country and our country, and peace reigned.

The older Wynnses, Brickles, Joneses, Sumners, Hares, Maneys, Murfrees, Winbornes, Ridleys, Bakers, Hills, Sharps, Cottons, Harrells, Moores, Dickinsons, Jeggitts, Montgomerys, Littles, Perrys, Walkers, Colemans, Dardens, Feltons, Carters, Vanns, Askews, Wheelers, Borlands, Southalls, and many others of the old worthies have long since crossed the river of life and are sleeping in the valley of death. But as we look around and about us at this, the closing decade of the first century of the county's existence, we find still living within her confines splendid representative sons and daughters of her wealthy, proud and influential old families—Wynns, Jones, Baker, Ridley, Hill, Sharpe, Cotton, Moore, Harrell, Winborne, Montgomery, Darden, Jernigan, Vann, Capehart, Lewis, Askew, Wheeler, Southall, Smith, Rayner, Yeates, Slaughter, Cowper, Riddick, Spiers, Myrick, Barnes, Waddill, Brett, Perry, Rea, Hutchings, Lawrence, Vaughan, Sessoms, Pruden and Beverly—and many others ready and capable to maintain the old standard and continue the proud record of the fathers and to add new and additional laurels to the crown of the county they so much loved. Yonder in its beautiful campus, shaded by lovely shade-trees of almost every variety, stood, on the southern border of the Borough town, the grand and magnificent building of the Chowan Baptist Female Institute; and just a little north of that stood in the same town the classic and beautiful building of the Wesleyan Female College, erected for the higher and nobler education of the noble daughters of North Carolina, Virginia and other States, presided over by faculties composed of the best and most efficient educators. But this magnificent civilization, and this happy, chivalric, lofty and Christian people, were unconsciously standing over the foaming billows of an angry revolution which was soon to follow and did follow in the next decade.

Hertford County was simply a representative county in its civilization and people in the Southland, which country was the wonder and admiration of the civilized and intellectual world. The history of the Southern States and of the Southern people will always be read with pride by all true lovers of lofty and chivalric manhood and of noble and beautiful womanhood.

DECADE XI.

1860—1870.

The black and angry clouds of war are again casting their gloomy shadows over our fair land. Around every fireside our troubles are discussed; in the Houses of Congress stormy debates are heard; crimination and recrimination are echoed throughout the land; patriotism seemed mad, reason dethroned. Newspapers are filled with exciting appeals, supplications for peace are unheeded, and the American people stand trembling on the brink of a gigantic war between the two powerful sections of our common country, which means a mighty revolution. The Constitution is bleeding and the Union weeping. Our calm, placid and peace-loving Smith is in Congress pleading for the Union. Slaughter in the State Senate and Yeates in the House of Commons, trying to calm the waters of discord, but of no avail. Some of the States secede, and North Carolina is asked to follow. The question of holding a convention to consider what action to take was submitted to the people and at the same time to vote for delegates. John H. Jernigan, a brilliant young lawyer in the county, who had graduated with high honors at the University of Virginia in 1859, and who was orator at the annual celebration of the Columbian Club of that University on April 12, 1859, was nominated by the people of Hertford as a delegate to the convention. The election took place February 7, 1861, and the convention was to meet eleven days thereafter, if a majority of the voters in the State were in favor of it. Jernigan was elected, but the call for the convention received but a few votes in Hertford and was defeated in the State, showing that the "secessionists" were in the minority in the State. Hertford's organ, *The Citizen*, edited by S. R. Olmstead, and published in Murfreesboro, then eloquently pleaded for the Union. We clip from the issue of January 17, 1861, of *The Citizen*, a short poem written by one of our fair Hertford ladies, showing the true feeling of our people. She had just returned from church on the solemn day set apart by our Chief Magistrate of the State as a day for humiliation and prayer, that our Great Father might subdue the rebellious spirit of man, restore order and peace again to our country and save our beloved Union from dissolution:

"LORD, TEACH US HOW TO PRAY."

BY ANNIE.

" Within this earthly court to-day,
  Dear Lord we meet to fast and pray
  That all discord and strife should cease,
  That thou might grant our Nation peace.

We know no other power can bless,
No other hand can give us rest,
And now we come, Dear Lord, to thee,
Bowed down in deep humility.

On thee alone for help we call;
Thy word can make us stand or fall.
And now with humble hearts we plead
That our loved country may be freed.

Oh! drive away the gloomy cloud,
That hangs around us like a shroud,
With strife and discords on its folds,
Sending dismay to human souls.

Now stay the mighty torrent, Lord!
If 'tis consistent with thy word,
And change the hearts of sinful men,
And bid them live in peace again.

Lord, save our dear loved Union, save!
Let it not sink beneath the wave!
Let not the din of battle's roar
Be heard upon our country's shore.

Lord, teach thy children how to pray!
And let them pray from day to day,
Till North and South together meet,
And sisterly—each other greet.

Decade XI.—1860–1870.

> But oh! my Lord, if war must come,
> Help us say, "Thy will be done!"
> On Thee, alone, our hopes are staid;
> To Thee, alone, we look for aid.
>
> To Thee, dear Lord, to Thee we cling;
> Order out of confusion bring!
> Control man's vile, rebellious mind
> And peace around our Union bind."
>
> "ELM COTTAGE, January 4, 1861."

Such were our dear women. Such was our patriotism and love of the Union. Such was the sublimity, beauty and loveliness of the fair women of the South. Where else in the wide world, could such sweet and noble women be found?

It was about this time the author's first distinct recollection of his father begins. Around the fireside at night, after returning to the bosom of his family from the busy walks of life, we nestled around his lap in the presence of mother and grandmother, and listened to his description of the horrors of war, and his love for the Union.

The chivalrous Southern soldiers are willing to fight for "Dixie Land," the home of heroic and lovely women of the South.

THE WAR OF 1861-'65.

North Carolina was slow to withdraw from the Union. She wanted union and peace. She was slow to enter the Union, being next to the last of the original thirteen States to enter, which was November 21, 1789. And she did not withdraw until she was forced to decide either with the North or the South. But when this important hour came she did not hesitate longer. She, in the Spring of 1861, called her convention to meet in May, 1861, in Raleigh, and on the 20th day of that month her delegates passed the resolution of secession and joined the Confederate States. On June 18, 1861, the convention elected Hons. W. W. Avery and George Davis as Senators to the Confederate Congress, and W. N. H. Smith, of Hertford County; Thomas Ruffin, T.

D. McDowell, A. W. Venable, J. M. Morehead, R. C. Puryear, Burton Craig, and A. F. Davidson, as Representatives in the House. Hertford County was represented in this Convention by her brilliant son, Hon. Kenneth Rayner. The Convention adjourned over, from time to time, until about the last of 1862.

Hon. W. N. H. Smith was a member of the U. S. Congress when his State withdrew from the Union, and he was re-elected as a member of the Confederate Congress, and remained a member until the government ended. In 1859 there was a protracted contest over the election of a Speaker of the House of Representatives in the U. S. Congress on account of the divisions in party lines. Hon. W. N. H. Smith was placed in nomination and received a majority of the votes, but before the result was announced several Northern members, who had voted for him, changed their votes and defeated him by one vote on next ballot.

This sanguinary war between a highly-civilized and Christianized people seems to have been the inevitable result of the puritanic, selfish and money-loving spirit of the North on the one side, and the unyielding chivalry and honorable spirit of the cavaliers of the South on the other part. Slavery was at the bottom of this great struggle. For half a century this sectional fire had been smouldering and the flames were increasing with the years, until the final conflict came.

Slavery first existed in the New England States. On account of the coldness of the climate and the nature of the negro, who came from the warm climate of Africa, this class of labor was found unprofitable in the North. So the slaves of the North were brought South and sold to the planters of the South, where the climate was better suited to the negro nature. After disposing of their slaves to Southern citizens, the New Englanders at once became fanatically opposed to the institution of slavery in any of the United States. Organized societies were formed in the North to disseminate

Decade XI.—1860–1870.

MISS SALLIE LEWIS.

COL. THOS. H. SHARP.

MAJ. JNO. W. MOORE.

CAPT. L. C. LAWRENCE.

Hertford's sons go to war in defence of her noble women, and Southern homes.

poisonous and slanderous literature throughout the Northern and Western States against the South, and the institution of slavery. This strife continued, and ended in the unhappy and bloody war of 1861-'65. The South regarded the election of Abraham Lincoln as President of the United States as the culmination of a wicked and vicious assault upon its constitutional rights and its sacred institutions. The debates in Congress for years had been extremely bitter, sectional and stormy between the members from the two sections. The temper of the two contending sections made it plain that they could no longer live together under the Constitution adopted in 1787 to 1789 by the States. The country was wild and mad with excitement. South Carolina, Georgia, Florida, Alabama, Mississippi and Louisiana claimed the sacred compact was broken; that the final clash had come. They at once seceded from the Union, withdrew their members from the United States Congress, and, by their delegates in convention assembled in Montgomery, Alabama, on February 4, 1861, declared their independence. On February 8, 1861, they formed a union between themselves as the Confederate States of America, and adopted a constitution for their mutual protection and government, and invited the other Southern States to join them. The Constitution adopted was fashioned after the United States Constitution. Section 7 provides that the importation of African negroes from any foreign country other than slave-holding States of the United States is hereby prohibited. And that Congress shall have power to prohibit the importation of slaves from any State not a member of this Confederacy.

Jefferson Davis, of Mississippi, was chosen President, and Alexander H. Stephens Vice-President. On the same day a peace conference of delegates from twenty-one States met in Washington to try to avert the great pending calamity, but the United States Congress turned a deaf ear to all messages of peace and compromise. The cry was war and hate. In December, 1860, South Carolina passed her resolution of secession and withdrew from the Union. In January, 1861, President Buchanan ordered a re-enforcement of the garrison at Fort Sumter, in South Carolina. This State claimed to be an independent State, and that no other government had the right to invade her domain without her consent. And when the United States steamer "Star of the West" was approaching the harbor of Charleston on April 13, 1861, with provisions and re-enforcements for the port, it was fired on and driven back by a Confederate battery. The war was now begun. The sad news was flashed over the country, and preparations for a great conflict rapidly progressed. Lincoln gets to Washington and takes the reins of government. A call is made on the non-seceding States for troops. This was the test. What will the other Southern States and the Southern soldiers in the United States army do? They joined hands with their kith and kin of the South—joined the Confederate States of America and took up their cause. The bloody struggle continued to April 9, 1865, when Gen. Robert E. Lee, at Appomattox, Va., surrendered to Gen. U. S. Grant the Army of Northern Virginia.

Never was such bravery, endurance and skill in war exhibited by any part of the civilized world as was exhibited by the Southern army and Southern people in this mighty conflict. Success crowned the Confederate army in the early battles of the war. The soldiery of the South was superior to that of the North, and it was not until the Northern army was re-enforced by the multitudes of all Europe, thereby placing in the Northern army, on the fields of battle, almost ten men to one on the Confederate side, that the North was able to drive back its Southern foe. North Carolina furnished a larger number of soldiers than any Southern State, and Hertford County sent her full quota of her fairest and bravest sons. A large per cent of them fell at the altar of the "Lost Cause," and their bodies were left sleeping in distant lands where they surrendered their lives in defence of what they believed to be right. We miss them now.

May the Great God of Nations receive their souls in his wonderful love, and bless them throughout eternity. Noble heroes were they!

> "Soldier, rest! thy warfare is over,
> Dream of fighting fields no more."

O cruel war, what sorrows and pains it entails! At the close of the conflict the survivors of the "noble boys" returned home, with a record that excited the admiration of the world, to see wife, daughter, sister and other dear ones. Some are found. Some are dead and gone. Homes are dilapidated; need and almost poverty in place of plenty; money and property gone; homes burned; briars in place of stalks of cotton, corn and other food plants and money products; teams old and poor; farming implements worn and unfit to reclaim the fallow lands; the old people at home sad and depressed. Mother, wife and sister, who had been accustomed to ease and comfort, now driven to the cook-room and wash-tub; father and uncle, who had always commanded and ordered, now at the plow-handles with their bended shoulders.

Such was the picture presented to the returning Southern soldiers in the Spring of 1865.

SAD, YET SUBLIME.

There was much suffering in the South. The brave mothers and tender children were forced by the condition of the Southland to drink from the cup of sorrow and pain. In 1863 Confederate money had so depreciated that it could hardly be denominated money. It was only worth about five cents on the dollar. Provisions were scarce, fathers were on the battlefields, and feeble mothers and little babes were not able to labor and secure the necessary sustenance for health.

The following incident illustrates much of the sadness of those days in the South:

In 1863 Edward Cooper, a brave and gallant Confederate soldier, was tried before one of the courts-marital of the Army of Northern Virginia upon the charge of desertion.

Decade XI.—1860-1870. 215

Cooper declined to employ counsel. The Judge Advocate opened the case and Cooper's guilt was clearly shown, and he was then asked to produce his evidence, if any he had. He stated to the Court he had no witnesses and his only defence was a letter from his wife, which he handed to the Court. It read as follows:

"My Dear Edward:

I have always been proud of you, and since your connection with the Confederate army, I have been prouder of you than ever before. I would not have you do anything wrong for the world; but before God, Edward, unless you come home, we must die. Last night I was aroused by little Eddie's crying. I called and said, 'What is the matter, Eddie,' And he said, 'O mamma, I am so hungry.' And Lucy, Edward, your darling Lucy; she never complains, but she is growing thinner and thinner every day. And before God, Edward, unless you come home, we must die. Your Mary."

The members of the Court were melted into tears. They asked the brave soldier what he did upon the reception of the letter. He replied that he made three ineffectual attempts to obtain a furlough, and then resolved at the expense of his life he would visit Mary and the children. That upon meeting his wife, she was broken-hearted at learning his absence from his post of duty was without leave. Now, gentlemen, said Cooper, I am here, not brought back by military power, but in obedience to the command of Mary, to abide the sentence of your Court. Under the unbending rules of the military code, Cooper was ordered to be shot. The papers and evidence were sent to that great Christian chieftain, Gen. R. E. Lee, for review before the sentence of the Court was executed. Under military law the general was bound to approve the sentence, but he immediately pardoned Cooper, and ordered him to report for duty to his battery, and dispatched a courier to the home of Cooper to have Mary, Eddie and Lucy provided for. Such was the suffering of many of our women and children, and such was the patriotism of our women in those trying days, and the nobility of the Southern soldier and the humanity of the Confederate generals.

The following persons were exempt from military service by an Act of the Confederate Congress, approved May 1, 1863:

Justices of the Peace, if appointed prior to May 11, 1863; County Trustees; County Solicitors; Public Registers; Tax-collectors; Sheriffs; one Deputy Sheriff in each county; Constables, if bonded prior to said date; Clerks of Courts; one Deputy Clerk; one County Commissioner in each county to distribute provisions amongst soldiers' families; agents appointed by the General Assembly, and Commissioned Officers of the Militia, and some few others.

At a general muster of the county militia on March 11, 1861, at Oak Villa, near Winton, Dr. John T. Lewter, of Murfreesboro, was elected Colonel in place of Col. Starkey Sharp, and Samuel D. Winborne, of Maney's Neck, was elected Major, a position to which he was first elected in 1847.

BRIEF SKETCH OF SOME OF HERTFORD'S SOLDIERS.

The war records are in many respects incomplete, but those accessible will show that Hertford County was not behind her sister counties in her contributions of men and material to the Confederate Army. The first company organized in the county was known as the Hertford Light Infantry, and had for its officers Thomas H. Sharp, Captain; W. B. Wise, Jesse A. Perry and Julian G. Moore, Lieutenants. By the promotion of Captain Sharp to Major and Lieutenant Colonel of the 17th N. C. Regiment, W. B. Wise and L. F. Everett became captains in succession, and William J. Lattomer, John Q. Thomas and William Carey Parker were commissioned as lieutenants. The Hertford Light Infantry became Co. C, of the 17th N. C., Regiment. When the Federal fleet assaulted the weak and incomplete works at Hatteras and effected a landing, this company, with the rest of the garrison of seven companies, was captured and for a time held as prisoners of war. Having been exchanged early in the war, they did good service and sustained the reputation of North Carolina as hard fighters in Eastern North Carolina, and later in the Army of Northern Virginia. There were from first to last ninety-eight (98) rank and file in this company, all of whom, except five (5) enlisted from Hertford County.

Quite a number of the members of this company still survive, among whom the names of the following are recalled: Julian G. Moore, William Carey Parker, Joseph Barnes, R. T. Barnes, P. P. Parker, Epenetus Creel, Arelius Britt, I. W. Worrell, K. R. Maddry, J. E. Jones, J. R. Beal, G. W. Banks, Geo. L. Arps, F. Q. Copeland, J. B. Evans, R. B. Gatling, J. T. Modlin, Joseph Weed, and H. L. Worthington. They are widely scattered now, but wherever they cast their lots they have become good and useful citizens. They were of the best of Hertford's young manhood. The second company, according to the time of organization, was called "The Hertford Grays"—afterwards Co. F, of the 1st N. C. Regiment of Infantry. The name of Hertford Grays was misleading, as there were more men from Northampton County in the company than there were from Hertford. The company, however, was organized at Murfreesboro, and the officers were mainly from Hertford. The officers chosen upon the organization were: J. N. Harrell, Captain; William S. Shepherd, Cicero F. Lyon and James P. Jenkins, Lieutenants. Lieutenant Lyon, a teacher in this county for years, was a native of Pasquotank, and died of wounds received at Ellyson's Mill, August 7, 1862, in Petersburg, Va. Lieutenant William S. Shepherd, a native of Suffolk, Va., the older brother of James E. Shepherd, late Chief Justice of the Supreme Court of North Carolina, was killed in an action at Sharpsburg, Md., September 17, 1862, and left on the field. Lieutenant James P. Jenkins, of Northampton County, was wounded at Sharpsburg, and having returned to active service too soon, contracted pneumonia and died at Strasburg, in the Shenandoah Valley, and was buried there close by the

Lutheran church, in November, 1862. Thomas D. Boone succeeded Lieutenant Lyon, and upon the death of Shepherd and Jenkins and the promotion of Captain Harrell as Major, became Captain of Co. F, a position that he held when he surrendered it at Appomattox Court-house.

Time would fail to tell of the number of battles and the killed in action, from this company. A remnant, growing less and less as the years glide swiftly by, still survive to fight their battles over in memory. Here are the names as they recur to me now: Thomas D. Boone, Lewis C. Lawrence, R. J. Askew, James P. Darden, C. T. Deanes, James H. Griffin, John Jenkins, W. P. Montgomery, H. T. Parker, John Reams, Edwin Ricks, Asa Saunders, Elias R. Vick, Britton C. Vick. At the proper place no mention was made of the fact that L. C. Lawrence and James F. Adkins were made lieutenants to fill vacancies in the company. L. C. Lawrence was promoted to Captain A. C. S. of the 68th N. C. Regiment, and still lives, honored in his old age. The number of Hertford County men in this company was forty-six (46). There were at least ten from Bertie County; the remainder of the original company enlisted from Northampton County.

Company "D" of the 17th N. C., was composed almost entirely of Hertford County men, and was officered as follows: J. M. C. Luke, Captain; Starkey Sharp, Norman L. Shaw, and Dorsey Taylor, Lieutenants. Upon the resignation of Captain Luke, N. L. Shaw became Captain, and some time during the war Richard W. Askew and Isaac Lafayette Taylor were made Lieutenants. Among the surviving members of that company may be mentioned the names of Dorsey Taylor, R. W. Askew, H. H. Overton, and others whose names do not occur to me at this time.

Company "G," of the 31st N. C. Regiment, was also composed entirely of Hertford County men. The captains, from time to time, were Jesse J. Yeates, Julian H. Picot and Isaac Pipkin. The lieutenants who served with the company were

DECADE XI.—1860–1870. 219

John D. Gatling, S. B. Pool, John A. Slaughter and John L. Everett. Jesse J. Yeates was promoted major upon the organization of the regiment, and was succeeded by Julian H. Picot and Isaac Pipkin as captains as above indicated. Captain Picot, at a ripe old age, still survives, and his friends hope that many years will pass away before he crosses the river. Among the members living may be mentioned John D. Gatling, W. P. Taylor, who served as lieutenant in 68th N. C. Regiment, Samuel Barnes, H. D. Harrell, at one time County Surveyor, E. W. Nolley, M. J. Nolley, Charles N. Pruden, W. E. Taylor, Richard J. Taylor, and perhaps others. There were 95 men in the company from Hertford County.

In the 19th N. C. Regiment (2d Cavalry it was called) there was Company C, in which was James M. Wynns, 1st Lieutenant, and afterwards Captain, may be found the names of more than forty (40) as good soldiers as ever drew sabre. Nicholas Harrell, 2d Lieutenant, commissioned in 1864, pronounced by his commanding officer the bravest man he ever knew, was from Hertford County.

In the 3d Battalion of Artillery, commanded by Major John W. Moore—an honored citizen of Hertford County, still living—there was Co. C, of which Juhan G. Moore, of Hertford County, was Captain, and Alfred M. Darden 1st Lieutenant, from the same county. In this company the record shows that at least seventy (70) by actual count were citizens of Hertford County.

The 4th Battalion of Cavalry, S. J. Wheeler, Major, had upon its rolls the names of twenty-two (22) men who were not ashamed to call Hertford their home.

In Company D, 59th N. C. Regiment, known as the 3d Cavalry, William Sharpe was Captain; Thomas Ruffin, of Bertie County, Daniel W. Lewis and W. P. Shaw, of Hertford County, were Lieutenants. Of these commissioned officers W. P. Shaw alone survives. There were forty-six (46) men enlisted in this company from Hertford County, among the survivors we find the names of Luther R. Tyler, R. T. Brett, Richard A. Cook, S. J. Doughtie, Media Evans, J. J. Hoggard, W. D. McGlaghon.

In the 68th N. C. Regiment there were two (2) companies from Hertford County—D and E, according to Moore's Roster; but unfortunately the record does not contain a list of the enlisted men. This ought by all means to be supplied and recorded before it is too late. Company D had Hillory Taylor and Len Askew as Captains, with W. P. Taylor and David A. Parker as Lieutenants. The late Langley Tayloe was Captain of Company E, with Benjamin B. Williams, John Brett and Joseph Holloman, Lieutenants. W. P. Taylor, an enterprising, public-spirited citizen, who has been honored by his native county, survives and is an active business man.

The 15th Battalion of Cavalry, of which James M. Wynns was Lieutenant-Colonel, had at least one Company A in it; M. M. Wise and J. T. Beaman were Captains; H. J. Jenkins and A. J. Cobb, Lieutenants. There are no records to show how many and who were the men that composed the enlisted men of the company. This is an omission that needs to be remedied as soon as possible. It is a pleasure to record that Col. Wynn still lives. There were a large number—how many cannot now be ascertained—who were citizens of Hertford County, and several in companies from other counties, for whom Hertford gets no credit. There are a number of Confederate soldiers now living in Hertford County who served in other commands, both in and out of the State. Geo. W. Grimes, living in Murfreesboro, where he is postmaster, was 1st Lieutenant in Company G of the 17th N. C. Regiment. In one of the battles in which his regiment was engaged he was severely—thought to be mortally—wounded. In the incomplete record of his company no mention is made of this, or of any facts that would assist the future historian in giving credit to whom it is due.

DECADE XI.—1860-1870. 221

The above sketch of Hertford's soldiers was furnished the author by Capt. Thomas D. Boone, who is mentioned in the sketch. The captain is, and has been for years, the Clerk of our Superior Court. He was a brave and gallant soldier and fought in many of the great battles of the war, and nothing delights him more to-day than to discourse to a circle of friends about the scenes and dramas of the war. In addition to the soldiers mentioned by Captain Boone from the county, the author recalls the names of N. J. Battle, James W. Battle, John Battle, James L. Myrick, Walter B. Myrick, Douglas Spiers, George Cowper, Pompey Darden, Samuel A. Riddick, James Maget, James P. Massenburg, Euclid Howell, Watson S. Howell, J. D. Brett, William Brett, J. E. Brett, of Maney's Neck, J. A. Carter, J. B. Parker, J. E. Vaughan, J. N. Lawrence, John N. Vaughan, J. C. Vinson, A. C. Darden, T. K. Warren, W. B. Wise, of Murfreesboro. The county should secure a record of all of her soldiers. She could do no prouder deed. In after days her sons and daughters would thank her on bended knees. Their record is a lasting monument to the county's fame. Brave soldiers! your praises will be sung throughout all after ages. You acted nobly your part in the greatest war in the history of the world.

> You, your country will never forget,
> And may God, your souls protect;
> Your noble deeds of valor we love;
> May you enjoy, with the angels, God's love.

The war was a bloody and devastating strife. It was fought principally on Southern soil, and our people were left almost in poverty. Gen. W. T. Sherman of the Union army, foaming with mad hate, to cap the climax of cruelty, in the closing days of the great struggle, burned Atlanta and made a raid through the South to the sea of 250 miles, with his army, burning homes, towns, cities, insulting the noblest and purest women of our beloved Southland, and destroying everything that came within his reach. Its wickedness has no parallel in the history of civilized warfare, and can only find its approach in the barbaric wars of ancient times. It was a shame and disgrace to the Northern soldiery. He boasted of his shame.

"O shame, where is thy blush?"

He reported: "I have pursued mine enemies and destroyed them; and turned not again until I consumed them." His allies shouted in joy over his barbarism.

The Civil War is ended. The whole Southern country is weeping. But it was "Majestic, though in ruin." Our sorrows continue. Jefferson Davis, the beloved chieftain, is arrested upon the charge of treason and thrown in a dark prison cell at Fortress Monroe, hands and feet fettered with chains.

" Black it stood as night,
Fierce as ten furies, terrible as hell."

Not yet satiated with wicked deeds, our immortal Governor Vance is also imprisoned in Washington City, and General Schofield is made Military Governor of the State to rule over our people, until W. W. Holden, a traitor to his people, was made Provincial Governor.

Our sorrows, sufferings, and calamities are great, but the worst is yet to come.

Why should the secession of 1861 have been considered treason, and why should those who left the United States service have been regarded as traitors? The Federal Constitution did not make allegiance to the Union paramount to that of the State. Secession as a right, had at various times in the history of our country been asserted by Massachusetts, New York, Connecticut, Rhode Island, and other States, long before the secession of the Southern States. The right of secession on the part of the States in the Union was generally recognized and actually taught in the U. S. Military Academy at West Point as late as 1863, and that a citizen's paramount allegiance was to his State. This lesson was taught the men commanding the U. S. Army at the time the Southern States seceded. Virginia, New York and Rhode

Island expressly affirmed the right of secession when they adopted the Federal Constitution. New England was the hot-bed of secession in the early periods of the Republic, and those States were constantly threatening withdrawing from the Union. Their right was not denied. They did not regard it treason when they desired to withdraw. Then why was it treason in the South?

Slavery was an institution as old as the government. It was all right so long as the North found it profitable in that clime, but all wrong when it became unprofitable in the North, but profitable in the South. Had there been no war, slavery would have been gradually abolished in the South. That sentiment had been growing in the South for years. After the battle of Appomattox, if the North had inaugurated gradual emancipation of the slaves, or paid the owners some reasonable price for the slaves, by the General Government, the restoration of the Union would have been speedy, and much hardship, bloodshed, hatred and suffering would have been avoided, and the negro would not have become the hater of the whites, with whom he had to live. But the heart of the North was enthroned in passion. Men who never fired a gun nor faced danger, but remained in safe places during the heroic strife, shaped the policy of the North after the war. Grant and his brave soldiers would have inaugurated a different policy. A brave soldier admires and loves his brave adversary.

The State and counties kept up their governments as best they could during the war. Some times selecting her civil officers from the military ranks. Col. Henry T. Clark, President of the Senate, on the death of Governor Ellis on July 7, 1861, acted as Governor of the State until September 8, 1862. In August, 1862, Col. Zebulon B. Vance was elected Governor of the State, and called from the ranks of the army to serve as Chief Magistrate of the State. He entered his new office September 8, 1862, and became the Great War Governor of North Carolina.

Joseph Blount Slaughter was Hertford's Senator during the war to 1864, when Col. James M. Wynns was elected Senator and called from the ranks to serve during the sessions of the Senate. Jesse B. Vann and John A. Vann were at different times in the House.

The terms of the Superior Courts were occasionally held in the county. After 1862 the terms of Court of Pleas and Quarter Sessions were very irregular, and when held they were at Union and other places in the county.

On February 20, 1862, another awful calamity befel the county. On that day three warships of the Union navy passed up the Chowan River by Winton and were fired upon by Colonel Williams' command. They fell back to Barfield's Ferry, about a mile off, and fired bomb-shells from their heavy guns on the town of Winton for some hours. Then they landed a portion of their armed forces, who moved on the town, and finding the town unguarded and unprotected, and to gratify a most ruthless and malignant spirit, set fire to the town and court-house, and burned every house in the town, except a small house on the lot on which J. S. Mitchell now resides, and owned once by Capt. Hiram Freeman, the grandfather of our present Register of Deeds, and the old Methodist church building. The old Franklin Hotel building, which stood adjoining the residence lot of John A. Anderson, was destroyed in this fire. The court-house with all of the county records, except a few record books of the County Court, since the fire in August, 1830, were again absolutely destroyed. We are satisfied that were it possible for those who committed this terrible calamity, since the passions of war have subsided, to undo this great wrong, they would gladly do so, and ask God to forgive them.

In the midst of the troubles and sadness of our Southland, our people continued to wed. In 1860 Dr. Richard T. Weaver and Esther Cotton, daughter of Dr. G. C. Moore, were united in holy wedlock, a few days thereafter Dr. T. N. Myrick was wedded to the elegant Susan J. Baker. In

1865 Col. J. M. Wynns captured the beautiful Jennie Brown on February 21. On June 6, Dr. Wm. H. Daughtry, of Southampton, steals from Hertford her accomplished daughter, Helen Myrick. On June 29 the gallant Maj. Isaac Pipkin celebrates his marriage with the beautiful Georgie W. Montgomery, and on the same day Capt. Julian G. Moore's marriage to Emily Bland Southall is announced, and November 29 John T. Mebane weds the attractive Julia M., daughter of Col. Samuel J. Wheeler.

While these happy festivities were going on death was claiming her victories. Rev. Wm. A. Vann, of the 53d N. C. Reg. falls asleep April 29, 1864. May 6, 1865, Maj. Benj. Porter, father of the late Epinetus Porter, passes away, and he is followed on the 10th by Capt. Abner Harrell. Wm. Bartelle Wise, on November 7, 1865, enters for good his well-prepared grave, which he had caused to be arranged several years prior. March, 1866, the body of Dr. L. M. Jeggitts is brought home from Mississippi for interment; he is followed March 19th by Perry Carter. In July, 1867, T. N. Myrick succumbs to the fate of all mankind. The Wesleyan Female College loses her President, Rev. J. D. Coulling, on November 28, 1866, and the county hears the farewell words of her faithful son, L. R. Jernigan, on December 8, 1866.

In the sessions of the legislature in 1866-'7 and 1867-'8 the county was represented in the Senate by James C. Barnes, and Godwin C. Moore in the House. Mr. Moore was instrumental in the session of 1866-'7 in having restored in North Carolina the common law right of dower, which was abolished in 1784. The act was ratified March 2, 1867. The whipping post, one of the modes of punishing criminals, was abolished August 22, 1868.

RECONSTRUCTION.

The so-called Reconstruction Period following the ending of the war between the States is the most hellish and blackest page in the history of the United States Government.

General Lee surrendered the army of Northern Virginia April 9, 1865, to General Grant on liberal terms; General Johnson formally surrendered the army under his command April 26, though he sent a proposal to Gen. Sherman April 14, for surrender. Also, on April 26, General Kirby Smith surrendered the Confederate forces west of the Mississippi. That crazy fanatic, John Wilkes Booth, an actor, on the night of April 14, 1865, shot and killed President Abraham Lincoln in Ford's Theatre, in Washington, an. act that greatly added to the sufferings of the Southern people, who sincerely regretted the sad catastrophe. Andrew Johnson, a North Carolinian by birth, and a U. S. Senator from Tennessee, who had been elected Vice-President with President Lincoln in 1864, by the Republicans, was sworn in as President of the United States the next day. Lincoln's death was a great calamity to the South. His idea of reconstruction was, that, all who would take the oath to support the U. S. Constitution should be allowed to vote, if 10 per cent of the voting population of any State, recently among the Confederate States, took the oath, they could reorganize a State government. Under this plan the Southern States would have soon been back in the Union, and much hardship and humiliation that followed would have been averted. The cowardly act of Booth entailed upon the Southern people woes unnumbered. Johnson tried to carry out Lincoln's policy. But not having the great influence with the Republican members of Congress as Lincoln would have had, as Johnson was not a Republican, but a Union Democrat, he had little influence with the members of that party. Congress, which met in 1865, ignored Johnson's actions, and refused to recognize the representatives who had been elected to Congress from the late seceding States, under a proclamation of President Johnson. Congress then inaugurated a policy of reconstruction, the horrors of which have never been realized, except in the South. It was worse than the war. It was hate and humiliation.

Decade XI.—1860-1870.

President Johnson, on May 29, 1865, issued his famous Amnesty Proclamation, in which a general pardon was extended to all persons, except those who had participated in the organization and defense of the Confederacy, upon their taking the oath of allegiance to the United States. Those excepted in the proclamation were required to file with the President a special application for pardon, which was granted or refused at the will of the Great Chief. Our father was one of the excepted class. An election was ordered by the military satrap of North Carolina, under the direction of the President, for delegates to a Constitutional Convention of the State to meet in Raleigh, October 2, 1865. Hertford sent her faithful son, Richard G. Cowper, as her delegate to this convention. E. G. Reade, of Person, was president of the convention. The convention at once repealed the Ordinance of Secession, October 9, 1865. It also passed an ordinance abolishing slavery in the State, and providing for holding an election in the several counties on the second Thursday in November, 1865, for the election of members of the General Assembly, members of Congress, and a Governor. Only those could vote who had been pardoned by the President of the United States. Of course the vote was small. Candidates were required to be from the class who were allowed to vote. This was not regarded, and many were not allowed to enjoy their victory. The time fixed for the meeting of the General Assembly was the fourth Monday of November, 1865. Hertford sent R. G. Cowper to the Senate and W. N. H. Smith to the House. It was an able body, and one of the most important sessions since the days following the Revolution of 1776-'82. Smith of Hertford was a leading member. He introduced and secured its passage an act to permit negroes to testify in the courts in legal proceedings, also the act to permit parties in interest to testify in suits, thereby changing an ancient law that had worked great wrongs.

Holden was still Provincial Governor, and he and Jonathan Worth were candidates at said election for Governor, and Worth was elected. The ordinances repealing the Ordinance of Secession and of abolishing slavery were also submitted to the people for ratification or rejection. There was in Hertford 83 votes cast for repealing the Ordinance of Secession and 21 against. The ordinance abolishing slavery received in Hertford 37 votes for and 29 against. County officers were also elected. The sheriffs of the counties were required to send the returns of the elections to the Provincial Governor, and he was to canvass and declare the result. None of the congressmen elected at this election were allowed to vote. The convention of October, 1865, met on October the 19th and removed from office every officer in the State who had taken the oath to support the constitution of the Confederate States, and disqualified them from holding any office or place of trust and profit which he held when he took the oath, until he was re-appointed or re-elected to the same, and then declared all such offices vacant.*

J. B. Hare was elected Sheriff, Geo. W. Beverly elected Clerk of the Superior Court, L. M. Cowper elected as Clerk of the Court of Pleas and Quarter Sessions, John A. Vann re-appointed Clerk and Master in Equity, W. W. Mitchell made Chairman of the County Court, with S. D. Winborne and W. P. Beaman as members of the special court, S. M. Aumack appointed County Trustee, William Sharp elected County Attorney, Joseph P. Jordan elected Public Register. Terms of the officers elected at the November election began at the end of the terms of the officers of the Provincial Government.

Hare resigned as Sheriff at February term, 1868, of the County Court, and Isaac Pipkin was appointed by the justices as his successor.

---

*NOTE.--Art. 14, Oct. 19, 1865. This was in harmony with the previous action of the General Government at Washington. U. S. Government treated all acts and appointments to office under the C. S. Government as void.

Decade XI.—1860–1870.

The justices of the peace during this period were W. W. Mitchell, W. D. Pruden, W. L. Daniel, A. G. Vann, S. S. Harrell, J. W. Harrell, Oris Parker, Daniel Valentine, W. S. Tayloe, D. V. Sessoms, Miles Mitchell, H. T. Lassiter, W. D. Holloman, S. D. Winborne, Jno. D. Gatling, W. P. Beaman, G. W. Beverly, Seth Nowell, J. M. Wynns, G. C. Moore, Zeph. Askew, Alex. Brett, H. C. Maddry, A. P. Hines, Langley Tayloe, J. M. Trader, Kindred Hollomon, G .A. Brett.

At the November term, 1867, Judge Smith qualified as administrator of Starkey Sharp, deceased, and Jno. W. Harrell qualified on the estate of Wm. M. Montgomery, the old Clerk and Master in Equity, who died several years prior thereto. J. B. Slaughter succeeded Sharp, resigned, as County Attorney. This grand old court of the people held its last session in February, 1868, and was presided over by S. D. Winborne, W. P. Beaman, Oris Parker, and several others. This ancient court, which had been the joy and pride of its people for over one hundred years, was soon to be abolished by the "Carpet-Baggers."

Upon the election of Jonathan Worth as Governor, some hope of peace was entertained by our people, but it was soon dissipated when the U. S. Congress, December 13, 1865, passed an act refusing the admission of Southern Senators and Representatives recently elected to Congress, and repudiated President Johnson's whole policy. These States were not allowed to participate in the making of laws by which they were to be governed. The hatred of the North seemed to boil over and become more malignant than ever. Congress passed the Civil Rights Bill, March 13, 1866, to force social equality between the races in the South, but it was promptly defeated by Johnson's veto.

At the August election in 1866, the work of the convention of October, 1865, amending the State Constitution, was submitted to the voters of the State and rejected by a good majority. This angered Congress, and on February 20, 1867, an act was passed by the *Mad Congress*, over the veto of the President, destroying all civil government in the South. Governor Worth was removed from office and Gen. Edw. S. Canby, of the U. S. Army, was military ruler with unlimited power over North Carolina. This Military King ordered an election to be held in the counties, October 19, 1867, for the election of delegates to a State constitutional convention, to convene in Raleigh, January 14, 1868. In Hertford, Jackson B. Hare, Charles H. Foster, and L. Wash Boone, a colored preacher, were the candidates. Hare was elected to the convention. Over 20,000 of the best citizens of the State were denied the right to vote. The work of this convention is too well known. Its members were mostly "Carpet-Baggers" of the North. The ex-slaves had been given the right to vote, while a large per cent of their former masters were disfranchised and not allowed to vote or hold office, until pardoned by Congress. The Constitution, generally known as the "Canby Constitution," had incorporated in it many objectionable features. It was submitted by General Canby to the recent slaves, the "Carpet-Baggers," and a few of the true native white sons of the State for ratification at an election held April 21, 22 and 23, 1868. The ex-slaves voted three days, under the direction of corrupt "Carpet-Bag" leaders. The returns of the election in each county, like the returns of the preceding election for delegates, were ordered to be sent to General Canby, and his will became the result of the election. The Constitution was declared ratified. Arbitrary power and humiliation of the white people of the South alone gratifies the passion and hate of the North. Love finds no place in their hearts.

The judges appointed by the Provincial Governor and General Canby were allowed to continue in office until July 1, 1868; so were many of the county officers allowed to remain in office until the officers elected under the Canby Constitution should take charge. Among the judges appointed by Holden, in December, 1865, were D. A. Barnes,

Decade XII.—1870-1880.

of Northampton; D. G. Fowle, of Wake, and A. S. Merrimon, of Buncombe. Holden first appointed Jesse J. Yeates Judge of the First District, but Yeates declined it and requested the appointment of D. A. Barnes. Fowle soon resigned, and General Canby appointed in his place Alexander Little, of Anson. Judge Merrimon received a command or order from the Military Ruler which he refused to obey, and resigned, and the Ruler appointed a Northern man by the name of Cilley, who was an officer in the Federal army.

At the April election, the Governor and other State officers, members of the legislature, judges for the courts, and all county officers, were elected. W. W. Holden was elected Governor. E. T. Snipes, of Quaker proclivities and an honest and fair man, was elected in Hertford by the Republicans to the House of Representatives of the State. S. S. Harrell, elected Clerk of the Superior Court (the County Court had been abolished), James M. Trader elected Register of Deeds (the name of the office of Public Register had been changed), Isaac Pipkin elected Sheriff, J. J. Horton elected Treasurer (the name of County Trustee being also changed). The other officers will be found in the list of County Officers.

The reign of dishonor in the State begins. These were sad times among our true native people. Lost all, but their honor, by the war. Humiliated and oppressed by their victorious foe. Life was sad and burdensome, and many of the noblest and bravest fell under the weight of their sorrows and the tyranny of their ignominious rulers.

On goes the reign of plunder.

> "Fate never wounds more deep the generous heart,
> Than when a blackhead's insult points the dart."

DECADE XII.
1870—1880.

The State and most of the counties in the State are still in the hands of "Carpet-Baggers" and corruptionists, and robbery and plunder of the State and county treasuries continue by this horde of vipers. In November, 1870, the Democrats secured control of the Legislature, and Governor Holden was charged with High Crimes and Misdemeanors in Office, tried and impeached, and disfranchised. The Republicans still have the governor and the judges, but the Legislature proceeds to bring order out of chaos as far as it is possible. It was slow work. Most of the eastern counties were still submerged by the negro vote and carpet-bag radicalism. Hertford is represented in the Senate by a Republican, and in the House by W. D. Newsom, colored. Newsom was not a vicious or bad man, but a respectful free-born negro, but thoroughly incompetent. In 1871 the General Assembly passed an act, ratified February 8, 1871, providing for an election to be held in the State on April 13, 1871, at which would be submitted the question of holding a Constitutional Convention, to convene in Raleigh on the 4th Monday in May, 1871, and for the election of delegates to the Convention. The Democrats of Hertford nominated J. J. Yeates, and the Republicans George H. Mitchell. Yeates was elected by a majority of 11, but, however, he did not serve, as the people voted not to hold the Convention. Some needed changes were, however, made by the General Assembly of 1872, which was largely Democratic. Hertford County did not suffer near as much as many of the eastern counties in her local affairs, as she had most of the time some good men on her Board of County Commissioners. From 1868 to 1870 the late John W. Harrell, the late Robert S. Parker, of Murfreesboro, Samuel Holloman, of Union, were members of the board—all good and honest business men and true sons to the best interest of the county. W. D. Newsom and William Reed were both colored. From 1870 to 1872 we had five very efficient and excellent members. The next term there was only one Democrat on the board, S. D. Winborne. He succeeded, however, in checking much reckless management of the affairs of the county. The chairman, E. T. Snipes, was a fairminded, honest man, and in him Winborne found a good right bower. From 1874 to 1876 there were two Democrats, Winborne and Vann, who, with the aid of Snipes, controlled the board. From 1876 to 1878 for the first time in the history of the county it was under the control of five Republicans. After that to the present time her Commissioners have been Democrats except during a short period between 1894 and 1900.

The Canby Constitution was still resting heavily on the people, and they were determined to have a Constitution of their own, framed by her own sons and adapted to the needs of her best citizenship. On August 4, 1875, an election was held for the election of delegates to a Constitutional Convention, to convene in Raleigh on September 6, 1875. The Democrats of Hertford nominated John A. Vann, and the Republicans nominated Jordan J. Horton. The Republican party in the county was composed of a few whites, some of whom were sincere and honest people, and some were exceedingly vicious. They, with the negroes in the county, had about 250 majority of voters, and Horton was elected. He was a planter and a very weighty member, as he weighed between 300 and 400 pounds. Many changes were made in the organic law, but not as many as were needed or desired, as the Democrats had only one majority. One of the changes made enabled the General Assembly to relieve the eastern counties of inefficient and corrupt county officers. The justices of the peace were to be elected by the General Assembly, and they were to elect the County Commissioners. It also authorized the Legislature to provide Inferior Criminal Courts for the counties, which was done by the Legislature at its session of 1876-'77. The Inferior Court, with a limited criminal jurisdiction, was established in Hertford. The presiding officers were to be three, and to be selected from the body of the county by the justices of the peace. The officers can be seen by reference to the "list of officers." Many of the noblest men and women during the last decade succumbed to the troubles wrought by the revolution of 1861-'65, and during this decade they fell rapidly and continued through the succeeding decades to drop off until now there is scarcely any left to tell of the Old South.

The old Public Register, W. J. Perry, had died in 1862, and William Porter, of Maney's Neck, died in 1865. William Bartelle Wise, the father of Mrs. Judge Smith, also died in 1865. Mr. Wise was a man of much wealth and was always ready to assist worthy young men and his neighbors when in trouble. Before settling in Murfreesboro he was engaged in the coast trade on the high seas, and in that business he made most of his large estate. He married twice. His first wife was Christianna Deanes, by whom he left one son, Capt. Marshall M. Wise. His second wife was Sarah Copeland, of Northampton County, N. C., and by her he left one son, Major William Wise, and one daughter, Mary Olivia, who became the wife of W. N. H. Smith. Captain Marshall M. Wise first married a Mississippi woman, and their children were William B. Wise, who went South after the war; W. D. Wise, who married J. W. Hill's daughter, of the Borough, a brave soldier, who carried a leaden ball in his body until death. He died in Durham, N. C., a few years past; George W. Wise was a soldier in the army from this county, but moved to Mississippi after the war and became the private secretary to the governor of that State and married his daughter; Sallie Wise, who became the wife of Walter M. Griffin, near Murfreesboro, died without issue; Annie L. Wise married Robert Parker, formerly of of this town, but later of Norfolk. Marshall's youngest son, June M. Wise, married Miss Sauls, and now lives near his

Decade XII.—1870-1880. 235

fathers's old place. M. M. Wise's second wife was Mollie Ellis, of Northampton; they left one child, Lula.

Early in the year 1870 faces which had been so familiar to our people began to yield to the havoc of time—men too noble to survive the bitter hate and oppression of the North. Dr. William H. Hutchings, a celebrated physician in the County, suddenly passes away in death. He was tall, erect and commanding in appearance, scholarly and chivalrous and aristocratic in bearing, and quick to resent an insult. He was the soul of honor. His parents were Col. William Hutchings, who lived where Rev. H. B. Parker now resides, until he removed to the Borough several years before his death, which took place November 16, 1821, and his wife the widow Skinner, *nee* Little. The doctor lived in town up to his death. A few days prior to Dr. Hutchings' death his friend and a distinguished physician in Winton, Dr. R. H. Shields, fell dead in Hutchings' office, while on a visit to the man he so much admired. Shields came to the county many years before the war from Virginia. Neither of these two old Southern gentlemen ever married, but it was not due to a want of the highest admiration for noble women. They failed to secure the jewels they loved. In their devotion for each other they were like the old bachelors, Patrick Brown and Thomas O'Dwyer, of remote days.

Abram Riddick, who resided on the old Maney plantation on the Chowan River, was in 1871 covered in his grave. He was born in Nansemond County, Va., in 1801, and moved to this county in 1825, and soon became one of Hertford's most worthy and useful citizens. For a long while prior to reconstruction he was one of her faithful magistrates, and successful business men. At the beginning of the war his home was palatial and the buildings for his large plantation, which were kept painted and whitewashed, resembled a town of several hundred inhabitants. He was kind to his neighbors and humane to his slaves. He was married several times. His first wife was the daughter of Benjamin Brett, who lived at the residence of the late W. D. Bryant in Maney's Neck, whom he married October 5, 1824. We think his second wife was a Miss Battle. His third wife was Anne Maria Dillard, daughter of James Dillard, of Nansemond County, Va. By this marriage he had several children, two sons and four daughters—Samuel A., who was in the Confederate Army and died or was killed in Pennsylvania when Lee's army invaded that State. His other son, J. D. Riddick, now resides at his father's old home. His daughter Pattie married Rev. James Murray, a Presbyterian minister in Virginia. His daughter Virginia R. married George Cowper. His last wife was widow Lavinia Whedbee, *nee* Leigh, of Perquimans County. His Dillard wife was the mother of his children. His father was James Riddick, of Virginia, and his mother was a Miss Cross. The old worthies are rapidly departing. John W. Southall, R. G. Cowper, the old Sheriff and legislator; Lewis M. Cowper, the old Clerk of the former County Court, and others are numbered among the dead in 1873. J. A. Worrell, John G. Wilson, the old Presbyterian merchant of our town, who married the daughter of Abner Harrell, followed in 1874. John B. Sharp, Robert S. Parker, of the Borough town, and the old accountant to whom was often referred the statement of complicated accounts by the courts, and a close friend of W. N. H. Smith, followed in 1875. Lewis T. Spiers, the handsome, polite and well-dressed old merchant of the Borough, died in 1879, and his worthy partner, Jas. W. Hill, in 1888, and his friend W. W. Mitchell in 1897. Mr. Mitchell was one of the patriarchs of the county. He was chairman of the County Court from June, 1861 to 1866, and had served the county as one of its leading justices for twenty-five years. He was a man of stern and positive character and a strong member in his church and denomination from early manhood to his death, and a great advocate of education. He was an uncompromising Baptist in his religious faith, and gave liberally of his large means to the

W. W. MITCHELL.

advancement of its cause. He was one of the prime movers in the building and establishment of the Chowan Baptist Female Institute, and contributed largely to the expense, and was chairman of its board of trustees for a number of years until his health became so enfeebled that he declined further election. During his active life he was always ready to respond to its needs, and faithfully attended all meetings of the trustees, and his face was familiar on the rostrum at the annual commencement exercises. He married the sister of the late Rev. Jno. Mitchell, who was so well known throughout North Carolina. She was the daughter of James S. Mitchell, the legislator from Bertie in 1842. He left several children—three sons, James S., John P., and W. J. Mitchell. The first married Miss Owen, whose parents came to the county from Granville, and John P. married Mary, the daughter of Wade H. Garriss, and is the niece of Mrs. A. I. Parker, of Winton. John P. is now the cashier of the bank in Winton. William J. married Sallie, the daughter of the late John A. Vann. James and John, with their families, live in Winton, and William and his family live near Ahoskie. Chairman Mitchell's oldest daughter, Mary, married the late James L. Mitchell, an attorney at Winton for some years before his death about 1878. His second daughter, Sallie, married Lt. W. P. Taylor, of Winton. Pauline, the third daughter, first married W. D. Holloman, and after his death she married C. W. Mitchell, of Aulander, N. C., an influential Baptist, an intelligent legislator and successful merchant and planter. The youngest daughter, Bettie, married Thomas J. Vann, son of Jesse B. Vann, Hertford's representative in the House in 1862.

Jesse was the son of the old chairman, John Vann, of the County Court. Lt. W. P. Taylor was the son of Maj. Hillory Taylor, of Mill Neck.

JUDGE D. A. BARNES.

In 1872 Hon. D. A. Barnes, of Jackson, N. C., the silver-haired bachelor lawyer of Northampton, and *aide-de-camp* to Governor Vance during the Civil War, married the young, fascinating and much-admired Bettie Vaughan, third daughter of Col. Uriah Vaughan, and settled in Murfreesboro with his young bride and became a citizen of Hertford. Judge Barnes had been well and long known to our people, as he had been a regular attendant upon our courts for a number of years. He was the eldest son of Collin W. Barnes, a wealthy planter of Northampton, by his second marriage to his cousin Louisa Barnes. Judge Barnes remained with us until his death in 1892. His widow, three daughters and only son, David Collin Barnes, still live at his beautiful residence erected by him in 1874 in the old town of the many worthies of olden days. His son is one of our promising young lawyers and the president of our town bank. Judge David A. Barnes graduated in 1840 at the University at Chapel Hill and was one of the Representatives in the House of his State in 1844, 1846, 1850 and 1858 from his native county of Northampton.

MISS BETTIE VAUGHAN.

A member of the Secession Convention of 1861. Appointed Provisional Judge of the Superior Court in the First Judicial District by the Provisional Governor, W. W. Holden, in December, 1866, which office he held until July 1, 1868. . Candidate of the Conservative party in 1870 against C. L. Cobb for Congress, but was defeated by a large majority. Judge Barnes was a lawyer of considerable reputation. His jury speeches were unique in style, but very effective. Like most of the older lawyers of the State who were trained under the old practice, he never became reconciled to The Code practice. The judge never married until late in life. He was much the senior of his bride in 1872, she being at the date of her marriage in her 24th year. He had two brothers—the late Joseph B. Barnes, of Northampton, who married Bettie, the daughter of Henry C. Edwards of his native county, and George Badger Barnes, late member of the commission house of Vaughan & Barnes, of Norfolk. George never married and survived his brother David A. Barnes but a few years. He had three sisters—Mrs. William Faison, of Northampton; Mrs. William H. Drewry, of Southampton County, Va., the mother of John C. Drewry, of Raleigh; and Mrs. Jesse Moore, of Northampton County. Judge Barnes' father, Capt. Collin W. Barnes, represented his county in the State Senate in 1829 and 1830. He was a native of Nansemond County, Va., but moved to Northampton County when young and became a large property holder and an influential citizen.

Joseph W. Perry was Clerk of the Superior Court from 1870 until he resigned in 1872. He was appointed by the judge of the district to fill the vacancy caused by the resignation of S. S. Harrell. Mr. Perry was a young and active business man in Winton when he was appointed. He in the latter part of this decade moved to Norfolk and engaged in the cotton commission business, and has been extremely successful. His parents were Joseph J. Perry and wife, who was the daughter of William Wynns Sessoms. His grandfather was Freeman Perry and his great-grandfather was Josiah Perry, who married a lady in Edgecombe County.

On April 11, 1873, Gen. Edw. S. Canby, the former military potentate of North and South Carolina, was killed in the rocky jungles of "The Land of Burnt-out Fires," in the State of Oregon, by Captain Jack, a Modoc Indian Chief. An account of this treacherous act can be found in the September number, 1905, of the *Metropolitan Magazine*. Such was the fate of this man who took part in the humiliation of the proud and good people of the South during the days called reconstruction.

At the August election in 1875 Jesse J. Yeates, of Murfreesboro, was elected by the Democrats to Congress from the Edenton District to succeed Clinton L. Cobb, who had served six years but was defeated in this election by Yeates. Congress had again tried to pass another Civil Rights Bill and force social equality between the races in the South. Cobb, who was a bitter Republican, voted for the measure. Yeates was eloquent in this campaign in denouncing this effort of Congress and this vote of Cobb. White men and white women flocked to the appointments of Yeates to hear him. Men cursed and women wept under his powerful appeals for the wives and daughters and homes of the Southern whites. The women electioneered on the white men who had been voting with the negroes and "carpet-baggers" *to save them*. The result was the triumphant election of Yeates. He was re-elected for the two following terms, serving in Congress from December 6, 1875, to March 3, 1881.

Yeates was a lawyer of great power and eloquence. He had filled many offices. They were: County Attorney, member of House of Commons, Solicitor of First Judicial District for six years, Major in the army, Council of State during the short time Worth was Governor, appointed Judge of the First District by Provincial Governor Holden, but declined it. He was born May 29, 1829, and died about 1893, in Washington City. He was married

HON. JESSE J. YEATES.

Decade XII.—1870–1880. 241

twice. His first wife was Miss Maria Piper, of Virginia. She died August 21, 1854, about two years after their marriage, leaving one daughter, Janie, who after reaching womanhood married her cousin, Dr. Edw. Yeates, of Mississippi. His second wife was Virginia, the daughter of James Scott, of Baltimore, and granddaughter of Gen. John Scott, of Hertford County. She was sister of Mrs. H. T. Lassiter, and cousin to General Scott of Florida. She preceded him several years to the grave. They left four sons and one daughter—Charles M. Yeates, of Washington City; William Scott Yeates, of Georgia; J. J. Yeates, of Birmingham, Ala.; George Yeates, of the U. S. Army. His mother was the sister of Abner Harrell, and his father was James Yeates, of this county, who was the son of Jesse Yeates, whose name appears in the U. S. Census of this county in 1790. His daughter, Jennie, married Daniel L. Smith, a lawyer of New York, and they are now living in Boston, Mass. She was a very handsome and a representative Southern woman. His father died when he was young, leaving several children. Jesse J. Knight, who lived near Union, married his sister. Major Yeates had a hard struggle to secure his education and prepare himself for his profession. Another of his sisters married Hezekiah Revel, of Bertie, and later of Murfreesboro, and still later of the western part of this State.

While the old fathers are falling thick and fast, their worthy sons are coming boldly to the front in defence of the honor of the South, the purity of its noble women, and the sanctity of their homes, and repelling the cowardly attacks of the Republican Congresses with indignation and scorn. The South begins the brave and glorious work of driving from power the "carpet-baggers," the Benedict Arnolds of the South, and the enemies of the virtuous homes of that fair Southland, which had been the honor and glory of America for over a hundred years. It was the land of patriotism and statesmen, the home of the purest and noblest women of the
16

civilized world, without which no people can be great. Many of the Southern States are securing the election of their ablest and truest men to Congress. North Carolina sends the brilliant and gifted Gen. M. W. Ransom and A. S. Merrimon to the U. S. Senate in place of the "carpet-bagger" Joseph C. Abbott, and John Pool, one of the Judases of the South. In 1874 she elects a large majority of both branches of the Legislature, and the act was passed calling the Constitutional Convention of 1875. In the House, Hertford was still represented by a Republican—Solomon Parker—but in the Senate sat two Democrats from the northeastern counties, including Hertford, and comprising the First Senatorial District—W. B. Shaw, the son of the old Congressman, Henry M. Shaw, of Currituck, and Thos. R. Jernigan, of Hertford. Mr. Jernigan was the son of one of Hertford's noblest anti-war gentlemen, Lemuel R. Jernigan, and brother of the brilliant young lawyer of 1861, Jno. H. Jernigan. He was a graduate from the University of Virginia, well versed in general literature, familiar with the political history of the country, a lawyer of ability, chaste in his diction, incisive in his orations, and brave as Julius Cæsar. It was the beginning of a useful public life. He had been defeated in 1870 and 1872 for the House. He made an enviable reputation in the Senate, and was often after that a candidate before the people for Presidential Elector, for the State Senate, and other honors. But like his brother John H., he early became deaf and had to abandon his profession. President Cleveland appointed him Consul to Japan in 1885, which office he held until 1889. Returning home he devoted his attention to journalism, and ably edited for several years in Raleigh *The Intelligencer,* which the editor declared as its head lines, the words "Impartial, not neutral; and devoted to the best interest of North Carolina, inseparable from Democratic principles." In 1895 he was appointed by President Cleveland Consul-General to Shanghai, China. After the expiration of his office he took up his residence in Shang-

Hon. THOS. R. JERNIGAN.

hai, where he now resides. He has written the commercial history of China from 1864. He was born in 1847, and in 1885 married Fannie, the youngest daughter of Col. Starkey Sharpe III. His brother, John H. Jernigan, grew very deaf in his early manhood and was compelled to abandon his profession; was disqualified by his want of hearing from serving in the army, where he would like to have been. He was born in 1836 and died in 1870. In 1861 he married Sallie, the daughter of Watson Lewis, Jr., who was the aunt of his brother Thomas' wife. She was said to be the prettiest woman in the county at that time. He left two sons, one of whom, John Hunter Jernigan, is living. Mrs. Sallie Mitchell, of Winton, the handsome wife of our young lawyer J. R. Mitchell, is his granddaughter.

H. C. Maddry, Democrat, successfully contested the seat of Jordan J. Horton, Republican, in the House in 1876.

The Wesleyan Female College closed its session in June, 1877, with a roll of 177 young ladies, under the presidency of Rev. William G. Star, and the college building was mysteriously burned during the vacation, which caused widespread sorrow and regret among the non-communicants and communicants of all religious denominations. A mighty calamity. It was rebuilt in 1881, and again destroyed by fire in 1893.

The Chowan Baptist Female Institute goes on in her grand work of educating minds and hearts of noble young women for the elevation of mankind.

The brave work of rebuilding the shattered fortunes of the South goes nobly on. In 1877 the justices of the peace are appointed by the Legislature and they elect the County Commissioners from her truest sons, as may be seen by reference to the list of officers. We will make a brief sketch of the retiring county officers and their successors:

Capt. Isaac Pipkin, who left the office of Sheriff in 1876, was a grandson of Gen. Isaac Pipkin, of Gates. He was a Democrat in politics, was a gallant soldier in the Confederate Army, and a very polite and attractable gentleman. He had married Georgie, the daughter of the late George W. Montgomery, of this county. He and his wife are both dead. Their two sons, Isaac and Thomas W. Pipkin, now reside in the old Borough village. Their daughter, Georgie, married Lewis C. Lawrence, Jr.

His successor from 1876 to 1878 was Jackson B. Hare, who had been an officer in the county during the war and during reconstruction. His son, John Hare, survives him. His second wife was the daughter of Lemuel Howell, of Maney's Neck. He was greatly her senior. She and their little child survived him. Subsequently she married John Holloman, and they are living at his late residence.

James M. Trader, who was Register of Deeds in the county from 1868 to 1876, and who was also postmaster at Murfreesboro for a number of years, was a unique yet interesting character. Not industrious, but economical and saving, carless about his dress, yet proud and quick to resent any reflection on his character. Not studious, but possessed of a strong mind well-stored with a wonderful amount of information. He obtained license after 1868 to practice law under a statute allowing any one to obtain license by proving good moral character and paying a tax fee of $20. He never practiced in any of the courts, except probably in the courts of justices of the peace, but wrote deeds, wills and the like for those seeking cheap work. He was the son of William Trader, of Murfreesboro, and his wife, Betsy Darden. Williams' wife Betsy died in 1822, and in 1824 he married Mary Gatling. He died in 1826, leaving surviving him one daughter and five sons by his first marriage—W. H. Trader, who emigrated to Arkansas; John Trader, who died in Washington, D. C., while holding a government office; D. C. Trader, who emigrated to Memphis; Henry G. Trader, who was a prominent merchant like his father, in Murfreesboro for a number of years. Just prior to the Civil War he moved to Mississippi, and James M. Trader, who spent his

Decade XII.—1870–1880.

days in his native town. He married Mary E. Brown, the daughter of Samuel Brown and wife, Nancy, and granddaughter of Maj. John Brown, the old Tory of colonial times. Dr. Godwin C. Moore and John A. Anderson were also grandsons of the old Maj. John Brown. Samuel Brown lived in Murfreesboro, at the home of the late Edw. F. Dunston. William Trader's daughter was the last wife of Ely Carter, of this place. The old Register of Deeds and postmaster died in 1882, leaving one son, John B. Trader, one of our present magistrates and chief justice of the town.

HENRY CLAY SHARP.

Trader's successor in the office of Register of Deeds was Henry C. Sharp, a member of the ancient and prominent Sharp family of this county, and the son of Jacob Sharp II, who married Eliz. Simons. Mr. Sharp was born in 1844, graduated at the University of Virginia, and ranking high in his class. W. D. Pruden, Esq., says Henry C. Sharp is the best mathematician in the world. He is a quiet and unoffending man, economical and saving, accurate and square in his dealings with his fellow-man. He served in the Confederate Army. As a civil officer he was honest and efficient. Col. Thomas H. Sharp and Capt. William Sharp, two of Hertford's brave soldiers, were his brothers. Both of them died in Charleston, S. C.

Henry C. Sharp married the widow of his cousin, Charles L. Sharp, the son of J. Bembery Sharp and wife. She was the sister of James M. Powell, of Harrellsville. He is still a worthy citizen of the county.

Samuel D. Winborne, the chairman of the Board of County Commissioners, had long served his countymen in different positions of honor. He was born March 7, 1821.

He was the son of Elisha Winborne, who died about the end of the 7th decade, and his wife Martha Warren, and grandson of Thomas Winborne, and great-grandson of Maj. Henry Winborne, of colonial times and revolutionary fame in 1776-'82. On his maternal side he was grandson of Col. Etheldred Warren, of the Revolutionary War, from Virginia, and the great-grandson of Samuel Warren, of that State, and who purchased the Warren homestead in 1736 from William Gooch. Young Winborne was appointed a cadet to the Military Academy at West Point in 1839, by Hon. Kenneth Rayner. He entered the Academy in 1840, and in the fall of 1841 his health failed, and after remaining in the hospital four months he resigned and came home. In 1847, when the State militia was reorganized, he was made major in his county, which office he held for some years. March 30, 1850, he married Mrs. Mary Hare Massenburg, nee Pretlow, of Southampton County, Va., who was the mother of his children. About 1854 he was appointed a justice of the peace in the county, a position which he held up to within a few years of his death on April 3, 1895. He was one of the "Special Court" when the Court of Pleas and Quarter Sesssions was abolished in 1868. A strong Whig before the war and a consistent and positive Democrat since reconstruction.

On March 11, 1861, there was a battalion muster of the Hertford militia at Oak Villa, near Winton. Dr. John T. Lewter, of Murfreesboro, succeeded Col. Starkey Sharp in command of the regiment, and Maj. Samuel D. Winborne, of Maney's Neck, was again elected major. The terms of these officers was three years. The above military facts we get from an old county record furnished us by Major Moore. This regiment was composed of several companies in the county.

Most of the time from 1862 to the close of the war, Major Winborne was a purchasing agent of the Confederate Government of supplies for the army, at one time delivering his purchases to Maj. Roger Prior, at Franklin, Va. Major Prior later became Gen. Roger Prior. He was a friend to the families of the Confederate soldiers and the poor. He served his county as County Commissioner from 1872 to 1890, excepting the term from 1876 to 1878, when he was defeated by William Reed, a colored preacher near Murfreesboro. The war stripped him of his comfortable estate, except his land. Before his death, by wise and prudent management he had nearly regained his former estate. He dropped dead at his dining table in the 74th year of his age, from a third stroke of paralysis, in the presence of his family and only sister, who was on a visit to him. Modesty prevents me from saying more of this good man. Let others write his epitaph. His eldest brother, Micajah Thomas Winborne, died in Mobile, Ala., in 1843; his youngest brother, Richard, died in La Grange, Tenn., in 1862. His other brother was Dr. Robert H. Winborne, who graduated at the University of the State at Chapel Hill in 1847, and settled in Chowan County. After graduating in medicine at the University of Virginia and the University of Pennsylvania, he became a distinguished physician. He represented that county in the Constitutional Convention of 1865, and died in October, 1898, aged 72, leaving behind

MAJ. S. D. WINBORNE.

NOTE.—Tilman D. Vann writes, "that Robert Henry Winborne is the finest young man Hertford county has ever produced." Young Winborne graduated at Chapel Hill in the class of 1847, with J. J. Pettigrew, M. W. Ransom, John Pool and others. Pettigrew took the first honor. Gen. M. W. Ransom has told the author often of the long and close struggle between himself and Bob Winborne for the second position in that illustrious class. Ransom finally won, after a protracted contest, on some catch question. He in his latter days loved to talk to the author about this class contest and of his admiration for "Bob Winborne." The latter was made the valedictorian of the class. They were of the warmest friends through life.

him an honored name. His sister Caroline, wife of Britton Moore, of Murfreesboro, died November 1, 1898, in Edenton. Maj. S. D. Winborne left surviving him his widow, three sons and two daughters. Mrs. T. I. Burbage, of Maney's Neck, and Mrs. Leroy J. Savage, of Norfolk, Va., are his daughters; and Samuel P. Winborne, who lives at the old homestead, Robert W. Winborne, of Roanoke, Va., and the author, are his sons. He was a man of strong and stainless character, a devoted husband, a true neighbor, model citizen, and the companion of his children. The author's book, "The Winborne Family," gives a sketch of all the old Winborne families in North Carolina. Several of them in early days emigrated to Tennessee and other Southern States, and the far West. In March, 1906, Harry Winborne, a rich miner of Colorado, was killed by a snow-slide on a mountain side.

S. M. AUMACK.

Samuel M. Aumack, one of the new County Commissioners, has long been a faithful and useful citizen in his county. When a young man he studied law, but never practiced. As County Trustee, County Commissioner, Superintendent of Public Schools, and as justice of the peace, he has honored his county. His father of the same name was born in Edentown, N. J., in 1807, and when a young man, in 1835, he moved to Hertford County and settled at Pitch Landing, then a thrifty little village. In 1838 he married Nancy Daniel, the sister of the late Major Watson L. Daniel, of Hertford County, and the daughter of Capt. Belcher Daniel, who married a Julia Flower. Samuel M. Aumack, Sr., died in 1843, leaving surviving him his son and his widow. The latter died in 1887, aged 75. S.

M. Aumack, Jr., has been married three times. His second wife was the daughter of the late John L. Jenkins, and his present wife was a widow Gillam, and daughter of Dr. Joseph W. Sessoms, of Bertie County. He is still one of the leading justices of the peace in the county.

COL. J. N. HARRELL.

Another of the new Commissioners was one of Hertford's brave Confederate colonels in the War of 1861-'65. He was Jarret Norfleet Harrell, a descendant of her old Harrell families, from which she so often selected her officers. He was born January 24, 1824, and was the youngest of a family of four sons and one daughter—Joseph, John W., Andrew J., Jarret N., and Amanda C. Harrell. Their parents were John Harrell and Winnifred Harrell, nee Bell, of Enfield. The father, John Harrell, was the grandson of Lt. John Harrell, who was Sheriff of Hertford County from 1774 to 1777, when he enlisted in the Continental Army and was ranked as lieutenant. Colonel Harrell's father died when he was very young. After the death of his father, ex-Sheriff William B. Wynns, a friend of the family, took charge of Jarret and his brother John W., and stood *in loco parentis* to them. Mr. Wynns was then living at Barfields, and conducted a large mercantile business as one of his enterprises. John W. Harrell was clerk in Wynns' store, and when he grew to manhood Wynns made him a partner in his business, and Jarret N., who had become qualified by age and education, was made head clerk in the store. After reaching matured manhood he and his brother moved to Murfreesboro and began the mercantile business under the firm name of J. W. Harrell & Bro., and met with fine success. His brother John W. was considered one of the best business men in our county. Colonel Harrell was twice married. On June 17, 1856, he married Susan Ruffin, of Surry Court-house, Va., and sad to relate, she died August 14th of the same year. He entered the Confederate Army at the call for arms, as captain, and soon promoted to the rank of major. On November 5, 1863, Major Harrell married the patriotic and attractive Ellen O., eldest daughter of John V. Lawrence, of Murfreesboro, and the granddaughter of James Rea. Later Major Harrell was promoted to the rank of colonel. Colonel Harrell at the close of hostilities returned to his old home and he and his brother John W. renewed their former mercantile business at the same place, which was continued during the remainder of their lives. The colonel was frank, honest and positive in manner, but very fond of young society and always made himself pleasant and entertaining. He was tall, erect and large, and a splendid-looking man. He had a commanding and military bearing. He served his county as County Commissioner from 1878 to 1890, and always took an active part in politics and county affairs. He died November 4, 1892, leaving surviving him his widow and two daughters, Gertrude and Linda. Gertrude married her cousin, Charles T. Vaughan, son of the late William Vaughan, and they are living with the widow at the beautiful home of the late Colonel Harrell. Linda married Isaac Walke, of Norfolk, Va., where they live.

MRS. C. T. VAUGHAN,
nee GERTRUDE HARRELL.

Amanda C. Harrell married William M. Montgomery, the old Clerk and Master in Equity, of whom we have written. Joseph Harrell lived in Northampton and died many years ago, leaving surviving him his widow and several young children, George and Cola

DECADE XII.—1870–1880.

R. The latter is chairman of the Board of Commissioners of his county, and once served his county in the Legislature. He married his cousin, the youngest daughter of his uncle, Andrew J. Harrell, and is now a prominent merchant at Potecasi, in Northampton County. George was in the commission business with his uncles, John W. and J. N. Harrell, when he died September 30, 1888. The sister of George and Cola married Everet B. Lassiter, of Potecasi. She died two or three years ago, leaving several children. Mr. Lassiter, on June 22, 1905, married Miss Boyette, daughter of Charles Boyette and wife, Tempance O. Godwin, of Murfreesboro. Andrew J. Harrell married Mary Deanes, and for a number of years was a prosperous merchant at Woodland, N. C. Later he moved to Norfolk, Va., and conducted successfully with his brothers, John and Jarret, a commission business. He died in Norfolk in January, 1890. Like his brother Jarret he was a handsome and fine-looking man. He left several children, two sons and two daughters. His elder daughter, Roberta, married Dr. P. C. Jenkins, of Roxobel, N. C., and his younger daughter, Mary, married, as before stated, Cola R. Harrell. His elder son, Cecil W. Harrell, of Woodland, married Bessie, the second daughter of the late John E. Maget, and his younger son, Paul, married Miss Viola Hall, of Nansemond County, Va. John W. Harrell, the eldest of the brothers, and the survivor of all of them, was a leading citizen of Murfreesboro for a great number of years. He was widely known as a most excellent business man and leading Methodist, and a hospitable gentleman. He married the widow of George W. Montgomery, who was Martha Pipkin, the sister of Dr. Isaac Pipkin, and by her he reared two daughters, Sarah M. and Florie. The latter died without ever marrying, and the former married the late Jcb R. Hall, of Ahoskie, but after his marriage he became a citizen of Murfreesboro. Their daughter Florie died young. He reared three sons—John H., Charles E., and

Marvin Hall. The boys are married and doing well. John H. is in Baltimore, Charles is in Norfolk, and Marvin in Pittsburg, Pa.

Another member of the new Board of Commissioners was John A. Vann, of whom we have written in the 8th decade.

James Thomas Wynns, the fifth new Commissioner, lived in Union, and was one of the county's most successful merchants and a faithful officer. He was born January 8, 1823, and received only a limited education at the public and neighborhood schools. He was a good man, a just and correct man, and an energetic citizen. He married Sarah A. Dunn. She was born August 31, 1823, and died December 10, 1891. He always took a deep interest in trying to rescue the county and State from the Republican party. His father was Benjamin Wynns, a son of William Wynns. Benjamin Wynns lived and died near where the town of Union is now located, and married Polly Carter, a sister of Perry and Eley Carter, of Murfreesboro. James Thomas Wynns died July 2, 1900, and left only one child, Annie, who married Dr. W. H. Sears. They live at her father's home. Dr. Sears' mother was the daughter of Thomas Griffith, who was born December, 1780, and died April 19, 1848. His father was John Griffith, who was born March 12, 1754. Thomas Griffith was married three times. His first wife was Temperance Gatling, his second Martha Jenkins, the mother of Mrs. H. C. Maddry and the grandmother of Dr. Sears. His third wife was Mrs. Elizabeth Weston, *nee* Warren. She left no issue. Griffith's daughter married first William H. Sears, of Gates, and they were the parents of Dr. W. H. Sears, the husband of Miss Annie Wynns. Sears, Sr., died and his widow married the late H. Carter Maddry, of Northampton, who after his marriage moved to Hertford, where he became a prominent and leading citizen and office-holder. Mr. Maddry died after a protracted illness in 1893, without issue. His widow still sur-

Decade XII.—1870-1880.   253

vives and lives with her son. Edgar G. Sears, of Maney's Neck, and Mrs. W. J. Boyette, of Mapleton, are first cousins of Dr. W. H. Sears.

The Griffiths and the Wynns are among the oldest families of the county. The author found an old deed which recited the following interesting facts: That George Ganey, in 1713, secured a patent for all the lands in and around where the town of Murfreesboro is located, and sold it off in smaller tracts. The tract now known as the old Meredith Field was sold to William Griffith, and he in 1766 sold it to Jonathan Roberts, who in turn sold it to Captain Meredith. It was willed by Meredith, subject to his wife's life estate, to James, William and Henry Maney; also the gristmill now owned by E. C. Worrell was owned by James Maney, and the creek from the mill to Meherrin River was known as Ganey's Creek. The above-named Maneys sold the Meredith tract to the late John G. Wilson.

George W. Wynns, the Coroner of the county for many years, and the older brother of the Commissioner, was married several times and worked diligently to comply with the Biblical command to "Go forth, multiply and replenish the land." He was the father of eighteen children, most of whom he reared, and they are scattered in every direction, carrying out the Divine injunction. This Biblical injunction, "Be fruitful, and multiply, and replenish the earth, and subdue it," is not obeyed in these days of higher civilization as much as in the honest days of olden times.

The grand work of rebuilding the bleeding South and protecting her noble and dear womanhood still goes on. The basic walls of Northern hate are undermining. The better class of Northern citizenship are showing their admiration for the nobility and brave men of the South, whose efforts have been unrelenting in the defence of their civilization and the honor of their homes and dear ones. But many of her politicians continue to flirt the red shirt and prevent the healing of the wound, that they may retain power. Victory will yet come.

Samuel J. Tilden was elected in 1876 President of the United States by the Southern and Northern Democrats over R. B. Hayes, the Republican nominee. But the Radical politicians of the North refused to permit them to reap the benefit of their great victory. Their greed for power was too great. A great popular upheaval and revolution is threatened, but the cool and patriotic people of America submitted to the mighty wrong. The insult was in time avenged. The immortal Z. B. Vance succeeds Judge A. S. Merrimon in the U. S. Senate from North Carolina March 18, 1879, and locks hands with the gifted and scholarly Ransom. Our State also has in the House, with her Yeates, Scales, Bob Vance, Robbins, Steele, and Waddell, some of her bravest, ablest, most chivalrous sons. Georgia sends her Gordon and her Ben Hill. Mississippi sends her great scholar and philosopher, Lamar, and the other Southern States augment the brave and brainy defenders of Southern honor and Southern womanhood, who by their consummate ability, courage and eloquence dash back, with stunning effect, into the faces of the traducers of the honor and virtue of our dear Southland, their insults and vile efforts to force amalgamation of the races in the South. God never intended such should be, and His curses have always been and will always be visited on those who attempt such an impious deed. The South is still gaining friends among the better people of the North, and the haters are weakening. The horizon grows brighter and brighter as the years roll around.

DECADE XIII.
1880—1890.

As we approach this epoch in our history, we find Thomas J. Jarvis in the governor's chair in our capitol at Raleigh. He is one of the State's truest sons and a descendant of Capt. John Jarvis, one of the State's brave and gallant officers in the mighty struggle of 1776-'82. The Legislature of the State is still in the control of her loyal sons. The last of the judges belched up by the evolution of reconstruction are numbered among the things of the past, stripped of power. The elegant and profound jurist, W. N. H. Smith, is Chief Justice, in place of Richmond M. Pearson, who was learned in the law but who in that awful hour during Governor Holden's reign of terror and lawlessness, when Holden was imprisoning honorable citizens of the State to gratify his venom and passion, application was made to Chief Justice Pearson for the enforcement of the great writ of *habeas corpus,* he quacked out that the writ of liberty was suspended and "the judiciary was exhausted." We had returned to the rule inaugurated by the fathers, of the Superior Court judges rotating, by riding a different district each term. R. B. Hayes is still usurping the seat of Samuel J. Tilden as President of the United States. The Republican politicians are still waiving the bloody shirt and trying to keep open the half-healed wounds of former days. Hot debates in Congress break out at times like young volcanoes. In 1881 James A. Garfield, a Republican, but a great and humane man, was sworn in as President of the United States and called around him as members of his cabinet strong and conservative members of his party. The South breathed easier and was more hopeful. The National Republican party was on the eve of dissolution. Imperialism had been the dream of many of the leaders of that party. Garfield did not belong to that school. The dreamers of absolute power were in the minority, and their hopes were dissipated. The

President quickly began the work of civil service reform. But the American people were soon to be robbed of their victory, for on July 1, 1881, he was cowardly assassinated in Washington by a mad man. Chester A. Arthur was inaugurated September 20, 1881, as President.

In the State House of Representatives Hertford is still represented by a Republican. Col. Geo. H. Mitchell, the member in 1883, lived in Winton. He was a kind and good-hearted man, and his Republicanism was always a surprise to his countrymen. During the days of reconstruction he and two others were arrested and lodged in prison by order of a military *Brevet* in 1865, for whipping a negro girl. In 1867 Governor Holden appointed him colonel of the militia in Hertford, and he allied his fortunes with the followers of Holden. He has been thrice married. His first wife was the eldest daughter of Luke McGloughon, of this county. His second wife was Jesse B. Vann's widow, and sister to his first wife. His third wife was James Northcott's widow, by whom he had no children. He is again a gay widower and looking out for his fourth. He has two sons living in the county by his second marriage—Dr. Jesse H. Mitchell, of Ahoskie, an able physician and strong Democrat, and Arthur Mitchell, of Ahoskie, another Democrat.

For the first time since reconstruction the noble little county of Hertford in 1884 became tired and weary of not being represented in the House of Representatives in her State by one of her brave and gallant Democrats. She put forth a powerful effort and elected by a majority of 65 her able and polished young attorney, Robert W. Winborne, of Murfreesboro. Young Winborne was in his 24th year, but he served in the session of 1885 with marked ability. His ability and well-trained mind soon won for him laurels in that deliberative body. He had graduated with distinction at the University of the State in the Class of 1881, obtained his license to practice law in February, 1883, and settled in Murfreesboro and formed a partnership with his brother,

R. W. WINBORNE, Esq.,
Attorney-at-Law,
Roanoke, Va.

Decade XIII.—1880-1890.

the author, and they practiced law under the firm name of Winborne & Bro. He was very popular, pleasant in his manners, well-versed in the principles of the law, apt in their application, and smooth, attractive and convincing in his arguments before the jury. He married, November 24, 1887, the beautiful Dora M. Merrifield, of Valpariso, Indiana, youngest daughter of Judge Thomas J. Merrifield of that State, and by her had two children—Roger M. and Robert W. Winborne, Jr. In 1891 he moved with his family to Buena Vista, Rockbridge County, Va. In 1897-'98 he was one of the Representatives from that county in the House of Delegates of Virginia. In 1903 he was a candidate for the Democratic nomination as one of the delegates from Rockbridge to the Constitutional Convention of Virginia, Hon. Henry St. George Tucker being his opponent for the nomination. After a protracted balloting, a dark horse was nominated. He was one of the leading attorneys in his adopted county. For a number of years he was Commonwealth Attorney in Buena Vista. His wife, who was a most talented woman, died January 21, 1900. On February 3, 1903, he married the stately and accomplished Rosa Vaughan, of Murfreesboro, N. C., the fifth daughter of the late Col. Uriah Vaughan. They resided in Buena Vista until the year 1904, when he moved with his family to Roanoke, Va., where he is enjoying a very lucrative law practice. He was born October 2, 1861, and was the second son of Maj. S. D. Winborne and his wife, of Hertford County. He was educated at Buckhorn Academy and took his degree of A. B. at the University of the State in 1881. Young Winborne declined a re-nomination and applied himself strictly to his profession. He was succeeded in 1887 by E. T. Snipes, a Republican, of the Menola section. Mr. Snipes was a planter with strong Quaker proclivities. We have spoken of him before. He still lives and is a worthy and reliable citizen. He is not an educated man, but he is utilizing his means in trying to educate his children. He

17

now has two of his sons at the University at Chapel Hill, who are taking a good stand among the best students. They will reflect credit and honor on the old father and mother, who are making the sacrifice and effort to give them such excellent advantages. Would that all the parents would do likewise.

In 1889 the Democrats are again triumphant in the election, and send James L. Anderson, of Winton, to the House. Mr. Anderson was the son of the late John A. Anderson, who figured so prominently in the Whig party in the county before its dissolution. Mr. Anderson was a deformed man, caused by a fall when an infant, but he had a strong and clear intellect. He was educated before the Civil War at the University at Chapel Hill, to which institution he was devoted throughout life. He was re-elected in 1890. The following year his health began to fail, and he died. He was too unwell to serve in the session of 1891.

Lt. W. P. Shaw, of whom we have written, served in the Senate from the First Senatorial District as a Democrat, in the sessions of 1887 and 1889, and was a safe and prudent legislator, serving on some of the most important committees.

In 1880 Maj. John W. Moore, of Pitch Landing, who had been a conspicuous citizen of the county for twenty-five years or more, had published his most excellent History of North Carolina from 1584 to 1876, in two volumes. This history is far superior to any history of the State that has ever been published. He was the son of Dr. Godwin C. Moore and wife, Julia Wheeler. His paternal and maternal ancestry had been for generations people of great refinement and culture. Major Moore graduated at Chapel Hill in June, 1853, and in September of that year he married Miss Anne J. Ward, of this county, who was the first and only graduate at the C. B. F. Institute in July, 1853. She was the daughter of James Ward and wife Anne, who was the daughter of James Jones III, of Pitch Landing. When Mr. Jones moved South he sold the old ancestral home of the

James Joneses to his son-in-law, James Ward, who moved there from Bertie to live. Miss Ward when she married young Moore was very wealthy. The young barrister, who had obtained his law license, bought the tract of land near the Borough, just back of the C. B. F. Institute, where Jefferson Davis Gatling resides, and built a magnificent Southern mansion on that beautiful site overlooking the town, and moved there to live in 1855 and opened his law office in Murfreesboro in the same year. Moore was cultured and literary, handsome and with pleasing manners. He was a Democrat in politics like his father, and this being a Whig county and in a Whig district, he was never elected to office, though often a candidate before the people for Congress and other high and important positions. He was elector on the Breckenridge and Lane ticket in 1860, which was elected in the State. He served in the Confederate Army as Major of the 3d Battalion of Artillery. During the war his beautiful home near Murfreesboro was destroyed by fire, with his valuable furniture and a goodly part of his valuable library. His family lived in a small house in the yard until after the close of the conflict. On his return home he moved with his family to his wife's farm in the lower end of the county, near Powellsville, in Bertie County, where he has since resided. This home was the ancestral home of the James Joneses, and has been in the family for nearly 200 years. Maj. James Wright Moore, his brother, and a gallant soldier of the Confederacy, fell dead in 1862. In 1881 Major Moore had published his most interesting volume, "The Heirs of St. Kilda," a beautiful story of the Southern past. In 1882 he published his school history of North Carolina, and also his Roster of North Carolina Troops in the Civil War of 1861-'65, in four volumes. By his historic writings he has built a monument to the glory of his State more lasting and more beneficial than the deeds of those who have held high offices. When the Inferior Court was established in the county in 1877 he was elected its chairman, which office he filled with ability and great satisfaction to his people. For a likeness of Major Moore, see beginning of Decade XI.

Hertford has always been able to boast of her historians. In 1901, Denny Worthington, the son of Dr. R. H. Worthington, of the Borough, contributed to the literature of his State "The Broken Sword," a pictorial page in reconstruction, which he dedicated to the daughters of the confederacy, whose fathers had followed the Southern Cross. Worthington came to the Hertford bar about 1870, but after a few years moved to Windsor, Bertie County, and married the widow Mebane, daughter of Col. S. J. Wheeler, late of Hertford County, and who won his renown in the *bloody battle* of Mt. Tabor, when in the imagination the earth was covered with the dead bodies of Union soliders, and the waters of the noble Potecasi Creek was running red with their blood, notwithstanding no one was hurt and no damage was done, except a cabbage cart distributed its cargo along the road from Hill's Bridge to Murfreesboro, and the horses of the gallant band were soon windless from the speedy retreat from the ghost of Banquo.

In 1880, Joseph J. Jordan, of Winton, brother of our present William Jordan of that place, succeeded John Sharp as Sheriff of the county. Mr. Jordan had only a limited education, but had been successful in business enterprises. The Republicans still had a safe majority in the county, but the Democrats had made white Republicanism in the South so odious, that many whites who had been affiliating with the negroes and scalawags for office, were becoming ashamed of their associations. They felt the just indignation of the white women and their decent white fellow-citizens, and many were seeking a way to get into the Democratic ranks. Neither of the political parties made any nomination this year for the office of sheriff. The Democratic committee quietly got Jordan to declare himself an independent candidate for sheriff. Soon thereafter James H. Matthews, of Winton, also, declared himself an independent candidate for the same office. Both had been life-long Democrats and true to their race since Reconstruction times. Both were seeking in this fight for Republican votes, and they were timid in declaring their political dogmas. During the campaign the county candidates met in Murfreesboro to address the people. Jordan and Matthews were on hand dodging on the outskirts of the assembled crowd. When the nominees concluded their speeches, the voters vociferously called for Jordan and Matthews. Matthews made his escape and declined to declare his colors. Jordan finally mounted the platform, with the promise of the writer that he would stand behind him and tell him what to say. He was to repeat what the writer uttered from behind, which he did, to the great amusement of his hearers. Here is the speech: "Fellow Citizens: I am a candidate for the office of Sheriff. If I am elected I will fill the office to the best of my ability. *I am a Democrat.* Where is my opponent? What is his politics? Come up here Matthews (in a very loud voice), ding your soul, (a common expression of Jordan) and tell these people what are your politics." Matthews did not show up and Jordan was elected by a handsome majority. The negroes refused to vote for Jordan because he declared himself a Democrat, and refused to vote for Matthews because he would not get up and declare himself a Republican. We Democrats worked every ingenuous plan that our minds could suggest to secure the election of the white man's candidates. The writer led the brave Democratic hosts in the county for many years in their battles against Southern radicalism. He was much criticised as being the king, the ruler, the ring-leader, by those who were ready to accept office at the hands of the negroes, but were deterred from joining that party by the brave and bold stand of that noble and immortal band of loyal Democrats who contested every election as if the life of the Republic depended upon their efforts.

Jordan was re-elected in 1882. He died in the 14th decade, leaving one child, Etta, who now lives with her aunt, Mrs. A. I. Parker, in Winton. In 1884 he was succeeded as Sheriff by James S. Mitchell, a Democrat, and son of our worthy citizen, W. W. Mitchell, of whom we have written. Mitchell made a good and efficient officer.

The old bachelor and Christian gentleman and Democrat, Wm. J. Gatling, of Harrellsville, who entered the Clerk's office in 1872, still holds forth, and Maj. W. L. Daniel, another good Democrat, presides with great efficiency in the office of Register of Deeds from 1882-'90. A kind Providence seemed to be favoring us. The Republicans would almost invariably elect their candidates at the polls, but their blunders often lost them the fruit of their victories. We recall one of their blunders in those trying days that resulted in seating the Democratic candidates. The Republican poll-holders in St. John's precinct, in making out their election returns at that voting precinct, did not write out the number of votes their candidates received, as the law required. To illustrate, they returned as follows, Smith being the Democrat and Jones the Republican:

Smith received one hundred votes.

Jones " " " and ninety votes.

The returning board only allowed Jones ninety votes. It is said that the Republicans who made out that return have never made a ditto mark since, and declare to-day that it is unlawful to make a ditto mark.

The cold hand of death has not failed to touch some of our most worthy citizens. Dr. Godwin C. Moore is taken in 1880. The good and greatly beloved Rev. Archibald McDowell, the President of the C. B. F. Institute, succumbs in 1881, and leaves his grand and noble wife, Mary Owen, surviving him, with several children—Dr. W. O. McDowell,

Decade XIII.—1880–1890.

and Archer McDowell, now of Scotland Neck; Sallie, the late wife of Maj. John B. Neal, of Halifax County; Ruth, the wife of D. A. Day, of Murfreesboro, and Eunice, an highly educated and worthy daughter, who is devoting her life to teaching. Wm. Vaughan, near Murfreesboro, falls in 1884, and he is followed in 1885 by that courteous gentleman of Maney's Neck, Captain William J. Majette, who was Captain in the Home Guard during the late Civil War. Then follows the energetic Joseph Newsome, near Winton, in 1886, and the bright and cheerful D. V. Sessoms, of Pitch Landing, in 1888, and others whom we do not now recall.

In 1884, the closing year of the first quarter of the second century of the county's existence, finds the Southern people rejoicing as in olden times. At the November election the Democrats North and South succeeded in electing that great man, Grover Cleveland, of New York, President of the United States, and on March 4, 1885, he takes the oath of office and enters upon the duties of his great office. Thomas A. Hendricks, of Indiana, is also elected by the Democrats Vice-President. The hearts of the noble women of the South pulsate with indescribable joy and they sing praises to the brave and untiring efforts, for years, of the loyal sons of the beautiful Southland. Honest and fearless Cleveland calls around him in his cabinet some of the country's truest and ablest statesmen, such as Thos. F. Bayard, of Delaware; Daniel Manning, of New York; Lucius Q. C. Lamar, of Mississippi; W. C. Endicott, of Massachusetts; W. C. Whitney, of New York; W. F. Vilas, of Wisconsin, and Augustus H. Garland, of Arkansas. With this band of patriots in charge the country is safe and they move placidly on in the patriotic work of cleansing the political household, reforming the abuses of power, breaking down sectionalism, bringing together the North and the South, and extending the right-

MISS FANNIE SHARP.

hand of fellowship and planting flowers in the South instead of placing crowns of thorns on the heads of its pure and lovely women, and spears through the hearts of its sons. The President honors the South in making his appointments to office. He honors North Carolina in many instances, and honors Hertford County in the appointment of her chivalrous son, Thomas R. Jernigan, as Consul of the United States to Japan. Such was the crowning glory of the long, heroic and bitter struggles of the loyal whites of our Southland for twenty long years. We had won the admiration of a vast number of our Northern fellow citizens. True courage, noble and pure womanhood, and lofty and brave manhood will always in the end receive its wreath of flowers and the love of mankind. The lower House of Congress is, also, Democratic, but the Senate is Republican, and while Democratic principles cannot be enacted into law, yet no harm can be done the South.

Now, as we look back over the pages of the decades since 1860, we grow pale and awe-stricken. Beneath the grandeur and beauty of 1860 we see our fair land painted with the blood of her noblest sons, we see our homes reduced to ashes, our fathers and mothers bending and groaning under the weight of care and hardships, and our beautiful young women opening the sacred trunks where the sacred garments of mother, grandmothers, and other dear ones have been stored away as mementos of the departed dead, to secure clothing for themselves. The greatest war known to the world has been fought on our Southern soil, and after four years of bloodshed and desolation it ended. Slavery an institution as old as the government, has been abolished, and we thank God for that. We see the horrors of Reconstruction, and the unholy effort to force social equality between the white sons and daughters of the South with the ex-slaves. We see county offices in the possession of the untutored negro men. We also find them on the bench, in the legislative halls of the States, and also in both Houses of Congress. We find them also presiding as Governors in some of the Southern States. We hear that the Great Writ of Liberty is suspended and the Chief Justice of our State crying out, "the judiciary is exhausted." We see the Governor impeached for high crimes in office. We witness the gradual overthrow of Carpet Bagism in the State and in the South. We behold the slow re-habilitation of the South and its people. We witness and engage in the mightiest struggles in modern times of a brave and noble people to rise up and shake off the incubus of misrule and shame, and throw around their homes and their pure women the impenetrable shield of honor and brave manhood. And we rejoiced in the grand climax in the election of 1884.

FREEMANS—BEVERLYS.

The diseases of which the human flesh is heir to have been successfully baffled for years by Murfreesboro's senior physician, Dr. William G. Freeman. He was born August 19, 1840, in Bertie County, and was educated at the neighborhood schools and at Wake Forest College. After leaving Wake Forest College he began the study of medicine at the University of Virginia and completed his course of study at the Medical University of Pennsylvania, where he graduated with honors in 1861. His patriotic impulses caused him to enlist in 1862 as a private in the Sussex Light Dragoons of Virginia, which was Company H, 13th Va. Confederate Cavalry. He braved the fate of battle until 1864, when he was seriously wounded. After returning to the ranks he was captured at Apperville and held as a prisoner of war, but was shortly exchanged and allowed to return to his command; he, in the spring of 1864, applied for and obtained from the army medical examining board a commission as Assistant Army Surgeon, which position he held in different hospitals until the end of the conflict. In January, 1866, he located at Union, in Hertford, to practice his profession. In 1868 he removed to Harrellsville, where he practiced his profession with great success. On February 25, 1869, the Doctor married the beautiful and intellectual Miss Lucy T. Boone, of Northampton. In 1874 he moved with his bright and attractive young wife to Murfreesboro to live, where he has since and is still engaged in baffling the ills of the flesh and restoring the sick to health. Doctor is the son of John Freeman, who was Sheriff of Bertie County for about twenty years just prior to 1850, and was a man of a large estate, and one of the largest land-owners in the county. He was twice married. His first wife and the mother of his children was Sarah King, of Bertie. Gates was his native county, where he was born in 1801, but after his marriage he moved to Bertie, where he resided until 1856. His wife died August 26, 1852, leaving surviving two sons and one daughter. The sons were Dr. William George Freeman, and James P. Freeman. Their daughter was Mary E. Freeman. Sheriff Freeman, in 1854, married Annie Smith, of Norfolk, Va., and in 1856 he moved to Norfolk, where he resided until his death in 1865. Sheriff Freeman by his last marriage had two daughters, Sallie and Julia. The former married W. F. Bynum, son of W. T. Bynum and his Stallings wife, of Maney's Neck, but now of Richmond, Va. Julia married W. A. Perry, the faithful Constable and Tax Collector at Harrellsville, and son of the old Public Register, W. J. Perry. Dr. William G. Freeman's wife was the daughter of Mr. William Boone and wife Julith Boone, *nee* Deanes, of Northampton. Mrs. Boone was the daughter of the old Sheriff and legislator of Hertford, Thomas Deanes, of whom we have written. William Boone, and the late Chief Justice William T. Faircloth were kin. John Boone, the father of William Boone and the mother of Judge Faircloth, were half brother and sister. Dr. Freeman's son, George, married Carrie Hart, of Emporia, Va., the granddaughter of Dred Hart, of Southampton County, Va., who married a Suitor, of Northampton. Mrs. Dr. Freeman's paternal grandmother was Lucy Tyner, daughter of Nicholas Tyner, Jr., of Northampton County, by his first marriage. We cannot ascertain his wife's maiden name, but we learn from O'Dwyer's diary of 1824 that Nicholas Tyner's wife died September 29, 1824. Mr. Tyner was the son of William Tyner and grandson of Nicholas Tyner, Sr., of Dobbs County, who took out a patent for a large tract of land on the Meherrin River, from the Lords Proprietors in 1724. He conveyed 640 acres of this land January 12, 1761, to his son, William Tyner, of Northampton County. William Tyner's other children were Drew, Mary, Sarah, Priscilla, Mildred, Arthur, and William. Lucy Tyner's sister, Lucretia, married Etheldred Peebles, an ancestor of Judge R. B. Peebles. O'Dwyer also tells that in September, 1824, Turner Peebles' daughter married a Stancell.

Mrs. Dr. Freeman is the sister of Thomas D. Boone, the Clerk of the Superior Court of Hertford. Dr. Freeman and wife have only one child living. He is George King Freeman, the efficient railroad agent at Conway, N. C. Mrs. Dr. Freeman is regarded as one of the best read and most scholarly women in the State.

Dr. Freeman's brother, James P. Freeman, lives at Union and has for a number of years been one of the county's principal officers. For years after the war he and his brother-inlaw, George W. Beverly, conducted successfully a mercantile business at Union under the firm name of Beverly & Freeman. He was one of the County Commissioners for several years and later served the county as her Register of Deeds, an office which he resigned in 1905.

NOTE.—Nicholas Tyner on April 1, 1707, conveyed to William Williams 300 acres of land on which Sarah Sowells lived.

In 1867 he married Mary E. White, of Bertie, and by this marriage he reared one son, John Freeman, now of Union, and one daughter, Lila, who first married John Eley, of Union. Since his death she married, in 1905, Dr. J. H. Mitchell, of Ahoskie.

Sheriff Freeman's daughter, Mary E., married about 1858 George W. Beverly, of Hertford County, the son of Allen Beverly, and grandson of Benj. Beverly, of St. John's. The Beverly's have been among Hertford's prominent people for over 150 years. They were among the earliest settlers of Ahoskie Ridge. Mr. Geo. W. Beverly served his county in many official positions, as will be seen by a reference to the list of officers in the back of the volume. He died several years ago. Benj. F. Beverly, his brother, resides near Union, and is a substantial planter and worthy citizen. He married Abner Harrell's daughter by his last marriage. A. Bascom Beverly, the younger brother, is a prosperous merchant and planter in Florida. Geo. W. Beverly left no issue.

Rev. Joseph E. Carter, the late eloquent Baptist divine, so well known throughout the State and the other Southern States, was a Murfreesboro boy. Hertford has had no son who reflected more renown and finer character than this man. He was born in Murfreesboro February 6, 1836, and in his early manhood he was attracted to the study of the law. He first read law under the late Chief Justice W. N. H. Smith in his native town, then continued his study of the law at the law school of the late Chief Justice Pearson, and from there he applied for and obtained his license from the Supreme Court about 1857. He only continued on Hertford's roll of attorneys but a few years. On January 30, 1859, he closed his law office and decided to become a minister of the gospel. He was a brilliant young man, but had been a little wild and dissipated in his habits, and his sudden change from the legal profession to the pulpit was somewhat a surprise. But it was one of those irresistable changes in one's life that was brought about by divine power. He at once entered the

Theological Department of the Union University of Murfreesboro, Tenn., and from that institution he received his degree of graduation June 16, 1861, and on June 30 was formally ordained to the ministry in his native town. He administered the ordinance for the first time in Meherrin River at his native town on the following 15th of September. During this month he moved to West Tennessee and began his great career as an eloquent, able, forcible and profound expounder of the teachings of our Lord, the great Saviour of human souls. On May 14, 1862, he married Miss Priscilla Burton, of Murfreesboro, Tenn., a granddaughter of Col. Hardy Murfree, and settled there to live in August, 1862, serving as pastor of one of the Baptist churches of that place. In 1863 he was called to the pastorate of the church in Rome, Ga. At various times he served the principal churches in Tennessee, Georgia, Kentucky and Alabama as pastor, up to January, 1880, when he was called to Wilson, N. C., where he remained two years and accepted a call at Hendersonville, N. C., and was pastor of the Baptist church at that place until 1885, when he became the editor of the *Western N. C. Baptist,* and when this paper became consolidated with the *Biblical Recorder,* in 1888, he remained the western editor of the *Recorder* until his death, February 24, 1889, at his mountain home, in his 53d year. His remains were brought to his native town and interred by the side of his parents and sisters, March 1, 1889, in the presence of a large concourse of people, friends, kindred, old schoolmates, who knew his life, his renown, all of whom loved and cherished him. Several of his old friends and classmates spoke eloquently of this good and

MISS PRISCILLA BURTON.

gifted and saintly man at the grave. He was not only a true Christian man and a powerful and effective pulpit orator, but a fluent and forcible writer. He was a great contributor to the Baptist church literature. In 1875, while as pastor in Lebanon, Ky., he wrote and had published a brief but valuable treatise on "Baptists and Higher Liberty," showing the leading part the Baptists took in all the struggles for religious and civil liberty. And again, in October, 1883, he wrote and had published another book, titled "Distinctive Baptist Principles." His writings are of the clearest style, and logical, strong and convincing. He left his impress in the hearts of many people. He was tall and thin, energetic and untiring. He put his whole soul and strength in his work. His motto seemed to be—

" Live while you live; Life calls for all your powers;
This instant day your utmost strength demands.
He who wastes himself, who stops to watch the sands
And, miser-like, hoard up the golden hours."

His parents were Perry Carter and Priscilla Carter, *nee* Warren, of Southampton County, Va., daughter of Col. Etheldred Warren. His mother was the sister of Martha, the wife of Elisha Winborne. Mr. Perry Carter was a man of great energy and a thrifty business man and large property holder. The beautiful old ancestral home still stands on the corner of Main street and Seminary Ave., well preserved, and is now the home of Rev. Carter's only living sister, Miss Ellen V. Carter, and his niece, Miss Priscilla W. Williamson. His parents died a few years after the close of the Civil War. His wife, who survived him, died a few years ago. His daughter married Prof. John E. Ray, of Raleigh, N. C. His sons are living in the Northwest. His cousin, Edw. J. Carter, to whom he was so much attached in his younger days, was killed in battle in 1863, while a soldier in the Confederate army. Edward was the son of his uncle, Eley Carter, of his native town, and his wife Mary the

Decade XIII.—1880-1890. 271

daughter of Edw. Murphy, of the same town. They were married April 20, 1824. Mrs. Wm. J. Echols, widow of the late Wm. J. Echols, a wealthy merchant and banker in Fort Smith, Ark., was also his cousin. Mr. Eley Carter, after the death of his first wife, married Miss Martha Trader, of his town, and she is the mother of Mrs. Echols, Mrs. E. F. Rice and J. A. Carter, of Murfreesboro, of John Carter of Newport News, Va., and of Dodge and Tom Bragg Carter, of Memphis, Tenn. T. Jefferson Deanes, the old coach maker and the father of our W. D. Deanes, was married twice, and each time married the sister of Eley and Perry Carter. W. D. Deanes, our housebuilder and contractor, married Norma I., the daughter of the late Benj. Spiers, of the Boro, who was for a long time the steward of the Chowan Baptist Female Institute.

A. B. Adkins, of Bethlehem, near old Pitch Landing, deserves to be noticed as one of the untiring and zealous friends of the Chowan Baptist Female Institute, and of education. While he has no issue of his own, he takes the place of a father of several needy and worthy young girls, and has them educated at the above institution of learning. He was very active in raising by voluntary contribution, money to aid in the construction of the recent additions to the main building of that institution. He is the son of Thomas Adkins and wife, who was the daughter of Maj. W. P. Britton. The late Wade H. Adkins, of Murfreesboro, was his uncle, and Thomas and Wade were sons of David Adkins and his wife, who was a Miss Bullock, of Edgecombe County.

Note—Boro and Borough refer to Murfreesboro.

DECADE XIV.

1890—1900.

The beginning of this decade finds the country tranquil and in peace. Daniel G. Fowle, of Wake, is still the Chief Executive of the State. Hon. A. S. Merrimon had succeeded Chief Justice Smith in that high office. At the head of the United States Government sat Benjamin Harrison, of Indiana, as President. Hon. Thomas G. Skinner is in Congress from the First District, and in the U. S. Senate from North Carolina sit the great statesman M. W. Ransom and the matchless commoner Z. B. Vance. No State was represented in Congress by abler men. In the State Senate from the First District are P. H. Morgan, of Currituck, and James Parker, of Gates, both Democrats. In the House was the wide-awake little James L. Anderson. The legislature and all the State offices were under the control of the Democrats. But these quiet days were soon to be followed by a little gale in the United States, and a storm in the State. Such disturbances generally follow a calm. In 1891 our Governor Fowle dies, and Thomas M. Holt takes the oath of Governor. The U. S. Government gets in trouble with the Italian Government, on account of mob violence in New Orleans, where the Italians of that city had become so extremely obnoxious to the Americans, by their secret organization, the Mafia Society, where doctrines wholly unamerican were taught. Some of its lawless members were suspected of committing great outrages in the city, and of killing the Chief of Police of that city. Sufficient evidence could not be obtained to convict, and the people were so exasperated that a mob broke open the jail, and eleven of the Italians were put to death. The Italians in America and the Italian Government took serious offense at such treatment of their fellow countrymen, and that war between the Italian and the United States governments was barely avoided. The United States and the

Decade XIV.—1890-1900.

Republic of Chili, also, became involved in trouble. The Republic of Chili was having some domestic trouble. Those opposing the existing government were known as the Congressionalists. They needed arms and ammunition for carrying on the insurrection against their government. They secured a steamer belonging to the South American Steamship Company, to take on a load of arms and other ammunition of war at one of the Pacific ports of the United States, to take over to Chili for the insurgents. The U. S. Government ordered that the ship be not allowed to leave her waters with the cargo, and an officer was placed on the steamer to guard same. One night the crew on the steamer put the officer off in a small boat and sent him ashore, and sailed at once for her destination. This affair came near causing the United States to enter the domestic troubles of the little Republic of Chili and force both contending factions to behave themselves and cease their unjust and barbaric strife.

In 1891, the people of Hertford became desirous of a change in her courts. The Inferior Court had become unpopular in the county, for the reason that to make a court efficient it should be presided over by a judge trained in the law. So the legislature of 1891 abolished the Inferior Court of Hertford and established in its stead a Criminal Court of Record, and required that the presiding officer should possess the same qualifications as a judge of the Superior Court. The act creating the court gave it full criminal jurisdiction except over capital cases. The author was induced by his people to surrender a lucrative criminal practice to accept the judgeship of the new court at a small salary, but was allowed to keep up his civil practice, and to practice in other courts. In 1893 the General Assembly gave the Criminal Court of Hertford full and complete criminal jurisdiction, with the right of appeal to the Supreme Court from the rulings of the judge on questions of law; and required that the judge should be commissioned by the Governor of the State as other judges of courts of record.

Blount Ferguson, the member of the Board of County Commissioners from Maney's Neck from 1890-'92, is a sober and thoughtful citizen. He had before and since then served his people in local offices and has the respect and confidence of those who know him. He is a farmer. He was born July 27, 1850, and received a business education at the Buckhorn Academy in his native county. His father, Joshua Ferguson, married in 1842 Catherine Gatling, of the Buckhorn section, a cousin of Dr. Richard J. Gatling. Joshua Ferguson was a substantial and highly respected citizen. He was murdered about 1861 by one of his slaves, and his body burned in a pile of logs. The writer remembers the shocking news of his death and the several days search for the absent man. The negro was caught and hanged. His son Blount married Julia Gilliam, of Mississippi, in 1872. He lives at the home of his father and previously the home of Henry L. Williams, the old merchant and magistrate, and grandfather of Mrs. T. E. Vann.

W. T. Brown, the chairman of the Board of County Commissioners from 1890 to 1896, was a farmer, and lived near Murfreesboro at the home of Wm. Dunning, who purchased it from Thomas Barnes before he moved to Florida in 1847. Mr. Brown moved to this county from Bertie and married Jennie, the daughter of Mr. Dunning, by whom he reared one son, Wm. D. Brown, of this county, and one daughter, Grace, who married J. P. Holloman, of Rich Square. After her death he married Ida, daughter of John E. Maget, of Northampton. By this marriage he reared two sons, Thos. E. and Archer Brown, and one daughter, Bettie. Mr. Brown died June 5, 1904. His widow, her two sons, and daughter, reside at the homestead. Thos. E. Brown graduated at Wake Forest College in 1902, and taught school in Elizabeth City one year, and is now the Superintendent of Public Instruction in the county. He was born March 17, 1881, and married, January 10, 1906, Miss Martha Broadus Farrar, of Culpepper County, Va.

Decade XIV.—1890–1900. 275

J. T. Williams was a member of the Board of Commissioners from Harrellsville from 1894 to 1896. He was born February, 1851, his father being Rev. B. B. Williams, a Baptist divine, and his wife Elizabeth, the daughter of —— Harrell. Mr. Williams has followed the mercantile pursuits since manhood and is an energetic business man. In October, 1892, he married Addie C., the daughter of P. H. McDade and wife, who was a Miss O'Donal. He is a Democrat in politics. Rev. Williams was the son of Capt. Jack Williams and wife, Mary Ward, of Bertie, and grandson of Francis Williams and his wife, who was the daughter of Benj. Brown, a Welchman. Francis was the son of Jno. Williams, Esq., born March 1, 1776, and died March 30, 1816. The ex-commissioner has a very promising nephew, now in the University at Chapel Hill studying medicine. The Commissioner B. F. Williams, from 1900 to 1904, is a younger brother of J. T. Williams. He and his brother Tom have been engaged in the mercantile business for a number of years under the firm name of Williams Bros. Frank is a great wit and enjoys a good joke. He is an old bachelor, a successful merchant, and a favorite in his county. Their father, Rev. Williams, was born August 28, 1824, and died January 17, 1900. John, the brother of the Divine, was born May 4, 1799, and died April, 1875.

In 1892, the Farmers' Alliance began to disturb the calm waters of politics in the State. It was an organization organized several years prior ostensibly for the mutual protection of the farmers and growers of the State. The farmers and those interested in securing better prices for their products were in great need of organized action. All other interests were organized, except the farmer. He was left an easy prey to his foes, who were fixing the prices of the farmer's produce at which he must sell, and also fixing the prices of those articles that the farmer had to buy from them. The original idea and purpose of the Alliance was good, and a great number of them in the State joined, with no idea of aiding unscrupulous office seekers to bring shame on the State, and returning to power the devils of 1868, and again painting the banner of white supremacy with all the horrors of Carpet-Bagism in those shameful days that followed Reconstruction. Their meetings were held in secrecy, and its members were sworn not to reveal the doings of the Alliance. Soon unscrupulous politicians and office seekers obtained control of the Alliance and began their devilish work of destruction and shame. Many of their members were delegates to the State Convention in 1892. Among these members were some of the men who were trying to convert this noble society, composed principally of many of our truest citizens, into a secret political organization, upon which to elevate themselves to power. The idea of their leaders was to secure enough of their men as delegates to this convention to control it, take charge of the Democratic party, and build their ignoble government on the ruins of this party of the people. In this they failed. Many of the Alliance men were honest believers in the tenets of their society as first organized, which were for their mutual protection in the markets of the world, but were unwilling to sell themselves to corrupt and designing men, who were simply after power and spoils. Failing to control the convention, Marion Butler, the leader, and a number of his like, left the convention and called a convention of Alliance men and organized "The People's Party," in a convention held in Raleigh, and nominated a full ticket in the State and counties. The Democrats nominted for Governor Elias Carr, of Edgecombe County, one of the largest farmers in the State, and an ex-president of the Alliance, and then a member of that organization. The Democrats elected their State ticket and had control of the General Assembly of 1893, but the party was greatly weakened and its majority in the legislature was much reduced. It was evident by the action of the Alliance members, in that body, that the Alliance had become a secret political organization, and had drifted from its noble prin-

Judge B. B. WINBORNE,
1895.

ciples. Their leaders were of the most *unscrupulous office seekers*. There was a money crisis in the country during this period, and the great political head of the Alliance, Col. L. L. Polk, who was ambitious to be Governor of the State, and his successor, Marion Butler, an arch enemy of the people of his State, succeeded in making many of the Alliance people believe that the Democratic party was the cause of their ills and woes, and taught them, in "those hard times," to look upon the members of the Democratic party, who were not members of the Alliance and who did not agree with their extreme and passionate views, expounded by these leaders, as their worst enemies. So many of our good people blindly followed them. Strange power of influence! We could not understand the magic power of these corrupt leaders. Their charms and fascinations seemed to be more wonderful, even, than Aladdin's Wonderful Lamp. Lifelong friendships were sundered. Men who once had our confidence and respect, now look upon us with suspicion and hatred. Men who had trusted us, and who had always found us true to our trust, now regarded us worse than criminals.

In the Democratic County Convention in 1892, when the author, who had been a lifelong Democrat and the chairman of the party in the county for many years, appeared as a delegate to the convention from his township, the question was being asked in every direction by the Alliance men, What right has Judge Winborne to enter this convention? as if they constituted the Democratic party, and that I and all of our kind had been expelled from the party. Such was the result of the corrupt teachings of our plain, honest, and inexperienced farmers in the wiles of the corrupt and unscrupulous demagogues, political hypocrits, and enemies of personal liberty and individual happiness.

We elected in Hertford, in 1892, William P. Taylor, of Winton, to represent the county in the House in the session of 1893. Mr. Taylor was a staunch Democrat, and was a valuable member of that body, which had to deal with many

W. P. TAYLOR.

delicate questions in the effort of the true patriots of the State to avert a most horrible disaster to our people. Mr. Taylor was an old Confederate soldier and had some experience in dealing with men who were controlled by passion. He was a native-born of Hertford, and had been one of the author's right-bowers in the county for years, in fighting radicalism. He was the son of Maj. Hilory Taylor and grandson of Isaac Taylor, of the east end of the county. He married the daughter of W. W. Mitchell.

James S. Mitchell, who was put in the office of Sheriff in 1884, and who had continuously served in that office since 1884, allied his fortunes with that of the People's or Populist party and left his old friends and supporters.

In the election of 1894 the State was all excitement; the Republican and Populist parties had "fused." The Republicans, the old enemies of the State and of good government, and who had written the blackest pages of its history, said to the leaders of the Populist Party, let us join hands, divide offices, and whip out our common enemy, the Democratic party. They wear clean linen and look with scorn upon us. Break aloose from them and join with us and we will give you great power and make you the lords of the State. It was another case of the spider and the fly.

" Walk into my parlor said the spider to the fly,
It is the prettiest parlor you ever did spy."

All remember the fate of the *fly*.

Harry Skinner, a former Democrat, had joined the Populist party and was elected by the fusionists to Congress from the First District, defeating the Democratic candidate, W. A. B. Branch, of Beaufort County; E. T. Snipes, Republican, of Hertford, and Theo. White, of Perquimans, a former Democrat, but a devotee of the Populist party, were elected in the First District to the State Senate. And the author was nominated by the Democrats in Hertford against John F. Newsom, the fusion candidate. B. B. Winborne received the certificate of election and was sworn in as Hertford's member in the House in the memorable session of 1895 of the General Assembly. The result of the election in about three-fourths of the counties of the State conveyed sad news to the Democrats. The Republicans and Populists had elected a large majority of the members of each house. The Democrats had elected four Senators out of 50, and 39 out of 120 in the House. It was a thunderbolt of surprise to all political parties.

Sheriff Mitchell, while his parties were so successful in the State, was defeated and dislodged from his office by the young and quiet W. E. Cullen, of Harrellsville, the boy County Commissioner. Hertford elected at this election all of her county officers. The author, a few days before the election, resigned as judge of the Criminal Court, in order to make himself eligible for election. The General Assembly met in January, 1895. All were wild with excitement. The seats of all the eastern Democrats had been, under the advice of the Populist leaders, contested. We appeared in Raleigh, and so mad were the political victors that we were told that we would not be allowed to be sworn in, but our seats would be given to our contestants without any hearing. The victors were drunk with the idea of power. It was a sad time for the State. Its political horizon began quickly to grow black and gloomy. The little band of the unterrified Democratic members, like Spartan soldiers, stood firmly at our post of duty. No soldiers, no patriots, and no courageous men, ever stood firmer and braver, and guarded the State's interests and welfare with more courage and devotion than did this little squad of intrepid Democrats in the session of 1895. This mad passion grew wilder as the session progressed.

280 HISTORY OF HERTFORD COUNTY, N. C.

The cunning and foxy Marion Butler succeeded in perfecting complete "fusion" of the Republicans and Populists. It was an incongruous combine, and could not survive long. The team did not work smoothly. They see-sawed and balked, but Dr. Butler knew how to talk to them and charm them and make them pull. Again the new harness galded and they would fret and threaten to kick, but Dr. Butler knew how to relieve against the pinching of the new harness and heal the galded places, and thus they moved on. Dr. Marion Butler, of Sampson County, editor of the "Caucasian," and president of the Farmers' Alliance, succeeded in having himself elected United States Senator to succeed the scholarly statesman, Hon. Matt. W. Ransom. He promised the Republicans, so they claimed, that if they would elect the Doctor, the patentee of the healing oil and a tonic for sulky men, to the U. S. Senate, then in 1897 the combine would elect Jeter C. Pritchard, the chairman of the Republican party in the State, to succeed Thos. J. Jarvis, who was filling the expired term in the U. S. Senate of Z. B. Vance. During this great storm of political hatred and madness, many amusing scenes happened which were much enjoyed by the patriotic Democrats. The two elements of the "combine" often gave exhibitions of a want of confidence in each other. There was not much love between these two allied forces. Many of the Populists were not Republicans, and they would often revolt and storm out in rage when their eyes were being opened to the designs and selfish purposes of their leaders to carry them into the Republican party, and forswear further allegiance to the hellish combine. Dr. Butler would at once appear on the scene with his wonderful tonic. Then probably, on the next day we would hear the Republicans using all manner of vile and opprobrious epithets towards the Populist leaders. Dr. Butler would get behind one of the large columns and, like the hissing snake, whisper to them, Democrat! Democrat!! Democrat!!! At once the trouble and angry waters of passion would subside, and the warring elements embrace each other like twin sisters. Then the little fat Ewart would cease firing his scorching denunciation of Dr. Butler and pace up to the thin Casius-looking Butler behind the Speaker's desk and fall in the arms of the hungry Casius and look sweetly in the face of the dangerous man and plead for forgiveness.

When the combine was in a volcanic condition and destruction threatened, the patriots quietly looked on and enjoyed the belching and the rise and fall of the thermometer. But as soon as the volcanic disturbances subsided in the camp of the combine and they fell asleep to recover from their riotous revelry, then the patriots began to storm them with powerful shells from Democratic guns and create awe and dismay in the camp of the combine. They had contested about 18 of the patriots' seats—one-half. The combine could not get time to consider the contests. They only found time to consider four of them. Three of the patriots they arbitrarily turned out. The committee reported unanimously that L. L. Smith, of Gates, was entitled to his seat. The report was unanimously adopted. Up to this time the member from Gates sat under the clock waiting for his sentence. After the vote was announced by the Speaker that Mr. Smith was entitled to his seat, the irrepressible little member from Gates immediately arose and addressed the Speaker and began to argue the evidence in the contest for his seat, and desired to prove to the House that he was honestly elected, when the hairless-head member from Northampton, another of the patriots, arose to interrupt the member from Gates. Permission was given, and Capt. R. B. Peebles, addressing the Speaker, stated that as the member from Gates seemed not to be satisfied with the action of the House, he moved that the vote by which the gentleman from Gates was declared entitled to his seat be reconsidered. Smith threw up his hands and exclaimed, No! No!! No!!! and fell in his seat like a lead ball. This ended the scene.

Later on in the session the Republicans demanded of the

Populists that the negroes should share in the offices. They were dependent upon the negro votes for success, and there were negro members in the House for the first time in many years. This was distasteful to the Populists, and they again raged and threatened destruction to the combine. The Republicans then threatened that if their demand was not granted they would vote for the candidates of the patriots. Dr. Butler was summoned at once. He arrived and administered his tonic and the political waters were calmed. When the session of 1895 went into history the people of the State gave a sigh of relief.

In all of this political madness we formed friendships that will linger with time.

There is *good* in all men.

There is *bad* in all men.

All of us love for the *good* in us to be noticed.

All of us love for the *bad* in us to be unnoticed.

So it behooved the patriots to look for the good in our enemies, and make the best use of it in behalf of our State. The author adopted that rule of action in this *mad hour,* and thereby did much good and kept off much harm. In matters not political he secured the passage of many bills for his political friends, and defeated several malicious and wicked non-political bills. He introduced the first bill to prevent a greater rate of interest than six per cent, but he was not allowed to get the credit as being the father of that law. No Democrat was allowed to receive credit for such legislation. The author served on the Committees on Judiciary, on Education, the Joint Committee for Selecting Trustees for the University, and other committees. W. T. Lee, the patriot member from Haywood, and the author, were the only Democrats on the above joint committee, and we succeeded in getting six staunch Democrats on the board of trustees. It was marvelous. The author prepared, introduced and secured the enactment of chapter 14, Public Laws 1895, for the protection of the estates of minors, which is the latter part of section 2768 of the Revisal of 1905.

Let us perpetuate the names of the patriot members of the General Assembly of 1895:

HOUSE.

R. C. Higgins, Alleghany County.
*L. D. Robinson, Anson County.
*A. S. Rascoe, Bertie County.
J. L. Nelson, Caldwell County.
H. M. Harrelson, Columbus County.
W. C. Gallop, Currituck County.
J. B. Etheridge, Dare County.
*J. H. Baker, Jr., Edgecombe County.
*W. O. Howard, Edgecombe County.
*L. L. Smith, Gates County.
*J. N. Grizzard, Halifax County.
*J. A. House, Halifax County.
W. T. Lee, Haywood County.
*B. B. Winborne, Hertford County.
J. F. Reinhardt, Lincoln County.
*Lee Crawford, McDowell County.
J. Frank Ray, Macon County.
M. T. Lawrence, Martin County.
E. J. Harrington, Moore County.
J. D. McCall, Mecklenburg County.
J. T. Kell, Mecklenburg County.
John G. Alexander, Mecklenburg County.
Herbert McClammy, New Hanover County.
*R. B. Peebles, Northampton County.
Rudolph Duffy, Onslow County.
D. R. Julian, Rowan County.
J. W. McKenzie, Rowan County.
R. L. Smith, Stanly County.
J. S. Woodard, Swain County.

R. L. Stevens, Union County.
*W. C. Monroe, Wayne County.
*J. H. Edwards, Wayne County.
*J. Tomlinson, Wilson County.
J. H. Higgins, Yancey County.
*T. B. Hooker, Pamlico County.
*R. L. Payne, Robeson County.
*S. G. Mewborne, Greene County.
*A. A. Lyon, Granville County.
*A. C. Ward, Pender County.
*D. D. Carlyle, Robeson County.
Those marked * their seats were contested.

We entered the House with 40 Democrats. The "combine," by the use of the political guillotine, beheaded six of the patriot members.

In the Senate sat four powerless but brave Democrats— A. S. Abell, of Johnston; W. J. Adams, of Moore; W. C. Dowd, of Mecklenburg, and C. W. Mitchell, of Bertie. The latter's seat was contested, but the axe was not applied.

After this notable session of the General Assembly adjourned, the author resigned his seat and Gov. Elias Carr re-appointed him Judge of the Criminal Court of Hertford. He returned home in March in time to see for the last time his old father, Major Winborne, who was so proud of the record of his son. On April 3, 1895, this grand old citizen fell dead in his dining-room. The sad news was wired to the author, who was then in Norfolk, Va., with his family.

In 1896 the Fusionists again captured the State and elected Daniel Russell, an old 1868 Republican, Governor of the State, and elected a large majority of the members of the Legislature. This year Hertford elected to the House a Republican, Starkey Lowe, a young man who had just acquired his law license. He was adopted by Jackson B. Hare a few years prior thereto, and he then adopted the name of Hare.

The Fusionists of the session of 1897 repealed nearly every law that had been enacted by a Democratic Legislature which had not been repealed by them in 1895, and enacted most offensive laws to the white people of the State. They flooded the State and eastern counties with negro officers. In their madness they abolished about all non-constitutional officers, and created others and filled them from their ranks. They abolished Hertford's Criminal Court and took off the judicial head of the author, and painted the political canopy of the State black as the darkness of Egypt. The Republicans gloated in the wickedness of their shame and abuse of power. The true Populist and Alliance men, now saw plainly the evil desires of their leaders and forswore further allegiance to the unholy combine, and returned to the party of their first love, where the olive branch was extended, and they kindly and lovingly received in the homes of their fathers, and former political friends.

The election of 1898 approaches, and the white people of the State rise up in their mighty indignation and proclaim in a voice that thunders throughout the State, that their patience is exhausted, and that this is the white man's State, and white man's government, that they will no longer submit to the indignities and insults and misrule of the unworthy leaders, whose ambition for power and spoil has no limit, but that they will drive from power the hater of Anglo-Saxon blood and forever consign them to graves of dishonor and shame. The Alliance men who had been deceived and misled, joined in this mighty cry of the Anglo-Saxon race. The Democrats triumphantly redeemed the State from negro thraldom and placed it in the control of her noble and loyal sons. The Democrats had a large majority in both Houses of the Legislature, and they prepared and passed an Amendment to the Constitution to be submitted to the voters of the State for ratification, at the election in 1900. Hertford was again represented by a Republican, in the person of a young man, Isaac F. Snipes, the son of E. T. Snipes, who was conservative and fair minded like his father, Hon. T. G. Skinner, of Perquimans, and George Cowper, of Hertford, Democrats, were in the Senate from the First District. Mr. Skinner was an ex-member of Congress, and Mr. Cowper was an able attorney at Winton and son of the old legislator from Hertford, R. G. Cowper.

This Legislature was composed of some of the State's ablest men, and they entered nobly upon the grand work of bringing order out of chaos, and making it impossible for a return of negro rule. We mean by negro rule the rule of men who were willing to ride into power by misleading the negro voter, that they might plunder and disgrace the State.

In 1896 and in 1898 the Fusionists elected all of the county officers in Hertford. In 1896 they elected as County Commissioners Geo. W. Mitchell, of Winton; J. B. Vaughan, of Maney's Neck, and E. T. Snipes, of St. John's. In 1898 they elected as commissioners Geo. W. Mitchell, J. B. Vaughan and J. M. Eley. The General Assembly on January 19, 1899, increased the number of Commissioners for Hertford to eight and appointed A. I. Parker, J. C. Vinson, Jesse H. Mitchell, Joseph G. Majette and B. F. Williams, all of whom were Democrats. They were sworn in and became members of the board and controlled it. In 1900, under the "Fusion law," Hertford was only allowed to elect three Commissioners. The Democrats elected Majette, of Maney's Neck, A. I. Parker, of Winton, and B. F. Williams, of Harrellsville. In order to give each township a member, the Legislature on January 31, 1901, appointed J. C. Vinson, of Murfreesboro, and Jesse H. Mitchell, of St. John's, members of said board.

James S. Mitchell in 1896 was returned by the Fusionists to the office of Sheriff, which he held until 1900. He was a graduate of Wake Forest College, and made a good officer, but his political somersaults for the past few years brought upon him much criticism by his former friends.

Col. URIAH VAUGHAN.

Decade XIV.—1890–1900.   287

At the election in 1900 the Constitutional Amendment was to be voted upon, which, if ratified, the horrors of 1895 to 1898 could never again occur in North Carolina. It threw around the right of suffrage such safeguards that would eliminate the ignorant negro voters from the ballot box and thereby disarm the vicious Republicans and consign them to a place of long rest, where they might repent of their shameful revelries in the past. The campaign was the most exciting one in the history of the State. The amendment was ratified by a tremendous majority, and the Democrats elected a great majority of the members of both Houses of the General Assembly. Hertford redeemed herself and elected to the House Lloyd J. Lawrence, the law partner of the author, over James S. Mitchell, the strongest man in the opposition party. Lawrence was defeated in 1898 by E. F. Snipes, of St. John's. The State is now safe and the troubles of the past forty years are settled. Peace now reigns throughout our beloved State. The young and brilliant Charles B. Aycock is called to the chair of the Chief Executive of the State. The future historian will write impassionate history of these mysterious years. Let charity and forgiveness and justice guide our every step. Let the curtain fall and hide from view the strife that so divided and embittered our honorable people.

During this decade we feel the loss of several of the majestic men who had for so long graced the annals of Hertford's fair name. In 1892, Rev. R. R. Savage, of Buckhorn, who had so long labored with us and whose name is indelibly written in the religious and educational history of Hertford, sleeps the sleep of death; then in 1893 the untiring and loyal H. C. Maddry shakes our hand and bids us farewell. For years and years we had labored together in the great battles of democracy. Judge David A. Barnes had preceded him on June 24, 1892. Col. Uriah Vaughan, after a long, honorable and successful life, on January 19, 1890, succumbed to the will of his Master. Colonel Vaughan was one of

Hertford's most remarkable men. In his young life at the age of 15, in the year 1828, he became restless to embark in the mercantile business, so he left school and came to Murfreesboro and hired himself to William Rea, a leading merchant in town, as a clerk. He soon developed such remarkable talent for the mercantile business that he became the wonder of all who knew him. Within a few years he launched out in his own boat to fight the fight of a busy life. Success crowned his efforts on every hand. With great energy, clear perception, great foresight, and with a quick and discriminating mind, he walked easily up the ladder of fortune. Always bright and cheerful, until when it became necessary to become serious and courageous, then he was ready for the occasion. A master of politeness, inborn chivalry, pure in thought and God-loving in his life, he stamped his impress on the lives of those who knew him best. He had made a large estate before the Civil War, but most of it was swept from him by the war. After that sad tragedy in our history he renewed his energies, and when he died January 19, 1900, he was the wealthiest man in his county. His father was John Vaughan, of Hertford, who was a soldier in the War of 1812. His mother was Sarah Rogers, daughter of Jonathan Rogers, of this county. His paternal grandfather was William Vaughan, a continental soldier in the War of 1776. Colonel Vaughan when a young man married Sarah A., the daughter of Henry DeBerry Jenkins, of this county, and a soldier in the War of 1812. Mr. Jenkins died September 8, 1856. A fuller history of these people can be found in "The Winborne Family." The sons and daughters of Colonel Vaughan and his wife Sarah are the late Mrs. George L. Arps, of Norfolk, Va.; Mrs. David A. Barnes, Mrs. R. H. Stancell, Mrs. B. B. Winborne, Mrs. R. W. Winborne and Mrs. T. W. Hawkins. He left two sons, Thomas J. and Uriah, who are prominent merchants in the town of their father. The Vaughan family is an old family in this county and have in all ages been noted for their business qualifications. Col. Vaughan was a natural-born merchant and trader. The traits of character that had been dormant in his family for one or two generations were produced prominently in him. The oldest male member of this Vaughan family, that we have any information of, is William Vaughan, who in 1709 purchased from Thomas Bayfield the sloop "Roanoke" for £184. On March 31, 1713, William Vaughan & Co., merchants, recovered judgment in the court in Edenton against Roland Buckley on an account for goods sold. And in 1714 William Vaughan is a witness in court at Edenton to prove a power of attorney witnessed by him in Boston, Mass. The next William Vaughan, supposed to be his son, we notice was some years later put under bond to keep the peace for fighting, and later he filed his petition asking to be released from his bond, as he had kept good the order of the Court. In 1714 Capt. William Vaughan of the militia under the government of the Lords Proprietors, is ordered to command a squadron of militiamen and visit the Indians at Poteskey Toune and complete some negotiations with them on the part of the Lords Proprietors.

J. B. Slaughter, who had for many years been a public servant in the county, and who was always faithful to his trusts, died in 1893. That grand woman, Mary A. Southall, in her 89th year goes to her Master.

DECADE XV IN PART.
1900—1906.

As we approach the closing years of our work we look out and see that peace and good will reigns throughout our State. The political waters are calm. The young men of the State are coming to the front to relieve their aged fathers who had stood faithfully by the ship of State. The young and gifted Charles B. Aycock, of Goldsboro, a graduate of the State University, who was elected governor by the Democrats, takes the oath of office, and enters upon a grand campaign of education in the State and soon attracts the notice of the leaders of thought throughout the States. He is now spoken of in many of the newspapers, North and South, as the next Democratic candidate for Vice-President of the United States. He has a bright future before him.

L. J. Lawrence, Hertford's young attorney, and partner of the author, enters the House of Representatives in Raleigh in 1901 as the member from Hertford, takes the oath of a law-maker, and beholds the beautiful forms and faces in the gallery, and pleads for the upbuilding of the State, and for its moral and educational advancement. It is now evident everywhere that the sons of the fathers must come to the front. The old guard is fast passing away. The schools, colleges, and University are fast preparing our young men for the responsibilities of a high citizenship.

Our colleges and schools for young women are training the hearts and minds of our young women for the higher elevation of man. The Chowan Baptist Female Institute in our own county is still doing a grand and noble work along this line. The ancient and classic academy at Buckhorn, under the tutorship of the aged pedagogue, Prof. Julian H. Picot, has prepared at this academy for the battle of life over 2,000 young men, and who is still carrying on the noble work, and not only adding to his own fame, but building a lasting monument to its founders.

Decade XV.—1900-1906.

In July, 1900, the town of Murfreesboro sustained a great loss in the death of her distinguished physician, Dr. John Turner Eldridge. Dr. Eldridge moved to Murfreesboro in 1885 to succeed Dr. John C. Lawrence, deceased. He was intelligent, highly educated in his profession, and a successful physician. Doctor Eldridge was born in 1834, and well educated in the best schools of the country before he studied medicine. His mind developed young. He graduated in medicine at Jefferson Medical College in 1851, when very young. He served as physician and surgeon in the U. S. Army prior to the Civil War. His parents were John Eldridge, of Halifax County, Va., and wife, Miss Turner, of Southampton County, Va. His father was a merchant in Halifax County until he moved to Texas prior to the war and became a large planter. The doctor married Alberta, the daughter of Capt. J. M. S. Rogers, of Northampton County, N. C., who was frequently in the Legislature from Northampton between 1828 and 1850. Doctor Eldridge had by his marriage several daughters. L. J. Lawrence married Eva, his youngest daughter. She lived only about a year after their marriage. His third daughter, Rydie, soon followed her sister Eva, then soon followed their mother. The death of his daughters and wife rendered the doctor very unhappy, and he never recovered entirely from his bereavement. Dr. Roderick H. Gary, of Northampton, married his daughter Cora, and Rev. C. W. Scarborough married his eldest daughter, Anna. After the death of Doctor Eldridge his son-in-law, Dr. R. H. Gary, moved to Murfreesboro in August, 1900, and became the owner of the beautiful home of the late doctor and succeeded him in his practice. Dr. Gary is a very successful physician and a natural-born doctor. He was born December 10, 1856, and graduated in medicine in 1881 at the College of Physicians and Surgeons of Baltimore. Doctor Gary comes from an honorable ancestry. His father was Richard Henry Gary, of Halifax County, N. C., who married a Bailey, of Sussex County, Va. His great-uncle was Roderick B. Gary, of Northampton, who represented that county as one of its members in the House of Commons from 1821 to 1831 continuously, then again in 1832, 1835 and 1836. The late Gen. Thomas J. Person, of Northampton, was his great-uncle. He was named Roderick Henry for his father and great-uncle.

The State still moves on in the grand work of education and development and opening up her mighty possibilities. She is in the lead of many of her sister States in education, in manufacturing, in development of her hidden resources and mines of unlimited wealth. Her white population is increasing with surprising rapidity. Her towns are growing marvelously in wealth, in factories, in population and in everything that tends to make progress and advancement. The most perplexing question with us is the labor question. The negroes are becoming tired of work, and they cannot be depended on as reliable workmen. The solution of this question will command our best thought and philosophy. In 1893 Hertford sends her true son, John E. Vann, of Winton, to the House, where he reflects honor on his county, as well as on the name of his prominent ancestors.

In the county her affairs are honestly and faithfully looked after by a board of commissioners noted for their loyalty to duty. They are (1) J. G. Majette, chairman; (2) John C. Vinson, (3) C. W. Parker, (4) A. I. Parker, and (5) William E. Cullens.

Majette is the son of Capt. William J. Majette, of Maney's Neck, and the grandson of Capt. James Majette and Capt. Jethro Darden, the old legislator from Maney's Neck. His mother was Virginia, daughter of George H. Barnes and wife, Priscilla Parker, who after the death of Mr. Barnes married Alexander Brett. He was educated in the schools of his county, and is an energetic and thrifty business man. He married Blanche, the daughter of W. T. Bynum by his

2   5   1   3   4

COUNTY COMMISSIONERS.

1. J. G. MAJETTE, Como, Chairman.
2. J. C. VINSON, Murfreesboro.
3. C. W. PARKER, Menola.
4. A. I. PARKER, Winton.
5. W. E. CULLENS, Harrellsville.

last marriage, who was the eldest daughter of the late Jethro W. Barnes and wife, Miss Brett, the sister of Elisha D. Brett, of the same section of the county. Mr. Majette is a planter and successful lumberman.

J. C. Vinson, of Murfreesboro, was a soldier in the last year of the Civil War. He entered the army under the call for young men as low down as 17 years of age. He joined Captain Holloday's cavalry company. These young soldiers did mostly picket duty in the counties where the Buffaloes were committing their robberies and plundering. He is the son of J. Henry Vinson, of Northampton, and wife, Martha Vinson, *nee* Wells. His mother was the daughter of honest Brooks Wells and wife Mary, of Maney's Neck, who was Mary Gilliam, of Southampton, Va. Brooks Wells died prior to 1830, and his widow appears on the Census of 1830 as the owner of 13 slaves. Vinson married, April 8, 1869, Mary W., the daughter of John Deloatch and wife Kezia, of Northampton, who was the mother of his children. Mr. Deloatch and Mr. Vinson's father were men of large estates and men of high character. After the death of his wife, which happened August 3, 1885, he in December, 1889, married widow Lewis, of Washington County, N. C. She did not live long, and since her death he has remained single. After his removal to the county he took an active interest in the politics of the county, and did most valuable work for his party. He is a planter, and operates several large farms. Mr. K. S. Deloatch of our town is brother to the first Mrs. J. C. Vinson.

C. W. Parker is a planter and successful merchant at Menola. He was born May 29, 1857. His parents are Joseph Parker, a prosperous farmer near Menola, who married Mary C., the daughter of the late William Vaughan and wife Betsey, the daughter of Elisha Lawrence. Mr. Vaughan was the older brother of Col. Uriah Vaughan and the father of John N. Vaughan, of Norfolk, Va., and C. T. Vaughan, of Murfreesboro. He was named for his grandfather, who bore the name of his ancestors. His daughter Sarah married Peter Garriss; Martha married J. G. Edwards, of Northampton, and Hester married A. J. Allen, of Northampton. Commissioner Parker, on January 31, 1883, married the handsome Janie J., the only daughter of the late Jordan J. Horton, of St. John's. He has inherited much of the business sagacity of his uncle John N. Vaughan. He is an advocate of education and is giving his children such educational advantages as will give them excellent social positions.

Alfred Isley Parker, familiarly known as "Ike Parker," lives in Winton and dispenses wholesome food at the Winton Hotel, which stands in front of the court-house on the lot where stood the hotel owned by General Dickinson early in the 19th century, and afterwards presided over by James Copeland, W. T. Bynum, Col. Pleasant Jordan and others. Mr. Parker was born in Nansemond County, Va., in 1839. He was the son of Willis Parker and wife Elizabeth Parker, nee Benton. He entered the Civil War as a Confederate soldier at the beginning of hostilities and served through the entire war in Co. I, Nansemond Cavalry, under Captain P. H. Lee, and experienced much of the hardships of those days. He was taken a prisoner of war in 1865 a short time before the fatal battle of Appomattox and imprisoned at Newport News, Va. He was released July 3, 1865, and reached home the next day. In 1866 he removed to Gates County. On February 22, 1872, he married Pattie, the eldest daughter of James Jordan, of Hertford, and settled in Winton and began his life work, and is now one of our most substantial citizens. In addition to his hotel he is engaged in farming, merchandizing, and is president of the bank in his town. His brother-in-law, William Jordan, of Winton, is his partner in his hotel and mercantile business, their firm name being Jordan & Parker.

William E. Cullens lives in Harrellsville. He was born February 16, 1861, and is the son of Nathaniel L. Cullens and wife Sarah, the daughter of William Lassiter and wife, Parthenia Scull, of that part of the county. Watson S. Winborne, who lived in the east end of the county, married Arabella, another daughter of Mr. Lassiter. Mr. Cullens was first elected a Commissioner when quite young. He resigned in 1894, and was that year the successful Democratic candidate for Sheriff. His pursuits have been in the mercantile line. On December 19, 1889, he married Willie Pauline, daughter of William Powell and wife, Augustine Parker. Re-elected Commissioner in 1904.

A. E. Garrett, of Ahoskie, the present Sheriff of the county, was born in 1864 and is interested in farming and merchandizing. He is not a native of the county, but has been with us for a number of years and is a most efficient officer and a gentleman of unsullied character. In 1900 he did some brave work for the cause of white supremacy. He is a brave and fearless man in the discharge of his duty. In April, 1889, he married Minnie, the daughter of T. C. Hayes and wife, Fannie Hayes, nee Montgomery, daughter of William M. Montgomery, who lived near the present town of Ahoskie.

John Northcott, who was one of the first justices of the peace appointed in 1778 for this county, and a relative of James Northcott, the great portrait painter in London, is still represented in the county in the person of our present Register of Deeds, John A. Northcott. The latter was the son of Andrew J. Northcott and wife Bertie, the daughter of Capt. Hiram Freeman and wife, Louisa Freeman, nee Knight, of Hertford County. Mr. Freeman was a Northern man who came to our waters before the war and made his home in Winton. He was noted for his courtly manner and he quickly made friends wherever he went. Andrew J. Northcott was the son of James Northcott and his wife, Nancy Northcott, nee Stephenson. Andrew J. was for a long while postmaster in Winton, and at one time the entrytaker in the county. He was a very competent business man. Much of the time while the author lived in Winton, from 1875 to 1880, Andrew J. was the efficient and polite agent at Winton of the Albemarle Steam Navigation Company. Both he and his father, James, were magistrates in the county during their day. Widow Elizabeth Northcott, the mother of James, died in 1834. Andrew J. Northcott died about 1882, and the author was his administrator and the guardian of his son and daughter. Young John A. Northcott was for years, before he was appointed to his present office by the County Commissioners, the efficient agent of the Atlantic Coast Line at Tunis. He, on April 27, 1902, married Mamie, the daughter of W. J. Lassiter and wife Imogen, of Rich Square, in Northampton. Without intending any disparagement of the efficiency of his predecessors, James P. Freeman, Geo. A. Brown, W. L. Daniel, S. E. Marsh, it is a fact that he is one of the most competent officers in the State. George A. Brown, now of Winton, filled the office with great satisfaction from 1890 to December, 1896, and was one of the working Democrats. He married in 1872, Mary E., the daughter of Alfred Riddick, the son of the older James Riddick, an honorable man, and a member of a family of the county long respected for its high character. By this marriage Mr. Brown reared several daughters, of whom our county is proud. Miss Janie Brown, a member of the faculty of the C. B. F. Institute, is one of these worthy daughters. So are Mrs. E. B. Vaughan and Mrs. David Parker, of Mapleton. His second wife was Miss Rosa Story, of Gates, the daughter of J. B. Story and niece of Parker Story, of Southampton County, Va., whom he married in 1902.

Capt. Thos. D. Boone, the intelligent and capable Clerk of our Superior Court, is one of the heroes of 1861-'65. We have before written of this worthy man and his charming wife, Willie Vann, daughter of Tilman D. Vann, of Maney's Neck. Captain Boone's father was William Boone, of Northampton, and his wife, Judith Boone, nee Deanes, the daughter of the old Sheriff, Thomas Deanes, of Hertford. His grandmother on his paternal side was Lucy Tyner, the daugh-

Decade XV.—1900–1906.

ter of Nicholas Tyner II, of Northampton. Sheriff Thomas Deanes' daughter Susan married Rev. Reuben Jones, and his daughter Malissa Anne married John E. Maget, of Northampton. The old Sheriff was married twice. By his first marriage he reared two sons, Mike and Thomas Deanes, Jr. The mother of his daughters was Susan Perry, a daughter of Capt. Abner Perry, of revolutionary fame, and who died in 1810.

Dr. Jesse H. Mitchell, of Ahoskie, is the present chairman of our County Board of Education. He is the son of Col. Geo. H. Mitchell, of Winton, and grandson of Luke McGlaughon, of Ahoskie. He has married twice. His first wife was the daughter of William M. Montgomery by his first marriage, and is the mother of his children. He married in 1905 the widow of the late John Eley, of Union, the daughter of J. P. Freeman. He was educated at Wake Forest College, and the Medical University in Baltimore, Md.

Samuel P. Winborne, another member of the Board of Education, lives in Maney's Neck, at the home of his father, Maj. S. D. Winborne and of his great-uncle, Robert Warren. Of him we have written. He is a direct descendant of Henry Winborne, who figured in early history of the county. He married Jesse, the daughter of Rev. Reuben Jones and wife, Susan Jones, and the granddaughter of Sheriff Thomas Deanes, who lived at the home of Tulley M. Forbes, Jr., near Murfreesboro.

The other member of the Education Board is Elisha Hunter Joyner, of old St. John's. He has been all through life an uncompromising and unforgiving Democrat. He is about 52 years of age, and failed to marry until a few years ago, when he married Miss Baker, of his neighborhood, a lady of respectable parentage.

The author a few days ago was reflecting, and the sad fact appeared that in the county he could only recall four persons living in the county who held a civil office prior to 1868. They were our venerable and Christian townsmen,

Henry Thomas Lassiter, who was one of the magistrates and was on the bench at the last session of the Court of Pleas and Quarter Sessions in February, 1868. The second was Oris Parker, who still lives near the Borough, who was a magistrate and sat on the bench at the same time with Mr. Lassiter. Mr. Parker is the son of Silas Parker II, a justice in his day, and brother of Carey W. Parker, Peter P. Parker and the late David Parker, of Mapleton. His grandfather was Peter Parker and his great-uncle was Silas Parker, both of whom were magistrates in their day. Mr. Parker is still a justice of the peace, and his son, Oler S. Parker, is also one of our young justices. The third old officer is Samuel M. Aumack, who was County Trustee from 1866 to 1868. The fourth is Col. James M. Wynns, of the Borough. He was a justice in the 10th decade and a member of the Special Court, and he is the only living ex-representative from the county in the General Assembly of the State who served prior to 1868. While he has been in poor health for the last few years, we hope he will be with us for many years to come. His mother lived to reach the ripe old age of 89 years. He lives at the beautiful old Southern residence purchased by Gen. Joseph F. Dickinson in 1812 from William H. Murfree, surrounded by an affectionate wife and his beautiful daughters and noble sons.

Among the old worthies yet living in addition to those four named, who figured in the ante-bellum days in the county, are Maj. John W. Moore and Prof. Julian H. Picot. It makes us sad, sad indeed. For thirty-one years we have been intimately thrown with the business people of this county, and had been with many of them for years prior thereto. We now feel lonely and deserted.

Albert B. Adkins, of Bethlehem, near old Pitch Landing, deserves to be noticed as one of the untiring and zealous friends of the C. B. F. Institute and of education. He married, but was not blessed with issue to train and educate. He, however, assumed the place of a father of several needy and worthy young girls and had them educated at the above

Decade XV.—1900-1906.

institution of learning. He was very active in raising, by voluntary contributions, money to aid in constructing the recent additions to the main building of the Institute. He is the son of Thomas Adkins and wife, who was the daughter of Maj. W. P. Britton, of the Pitch Landing section. The late Wade H. Adkins, of Murfreesboro, was his uncle. Thomas and Wade were the sons of David Adkins and wife, who was a Miss Bullock, of Edgecombe County.

Winton, the old colonial town of the county, is awaking from its slumbers and putting on new life and marching onward and upward in the glorious work of educating and refining its citizenship. Churches and academies of high grade are seen in place of the old bar-room. The young little town of Ahoskie, on the Atlantic Coast Line, which traverses the county, is increasing her population, erecting homes for its citizens, and, with her churches and academy, standing out in bold contrast with former days is moving on to take her place in the young and enterprising towns of the 20th century. Harrellsville, the town of the Sharps, the Harrells, the Prudens, the Rayners, the Jernigans, the Sculls, of John and Watson Winborne, and many others of the old landmarks and heroes, is still the pride of the east end of the county, while the ancient village of Pitch Landing, the home of the James Joneses, the Watsons, the Askews, the Daniels, the Wards, the Sessoms, has long since folded her flag and surrendered her streets and gardens to the plowman, and the ancient and colonial court green and colossal oaks of old St. John's, around which clustered the Sumners, the Granburys, the Perrys, the Cottons, the Moores, the Browns, the Beverleys, the Tayloes, the Everetts, and others, has long ago existed only in name, and the famous Ahoskie Ridge is now one of the most fertile farming sections in the eastern part of the State. The little town of Union sits quietly and serenely in the central part of the county and chants her beau-

---

NOTE.—Maj. W. P. Britton was the father of Rev. W. P. Britton who married the daughter of Abraham Thomas.

tiful music in praise of the older Winbornes, her Hares, her Wynns, her Beverleys, her Bretts, her Browns, her Dunns, her Dukes, her Tayloes, her Montgomerys, her Askews, her Knights, her Vanns, and her other sons, who did so much in building a monument to their county's fame. Maney's Neck, the home of the old James Maneys, the Hills, the Warrens, the Colemans, of Edward, Jacob and Thomas Hare, the Ridleys, the Littles, the Worrells, the Gays, the Barneses, the Gatlings, the Myricks, the Riddicks, the younger Winbornes, the Cowpers, the Spiers, the Vanns, the Peetes, the Bakers, the Whitleys, and many others who were bright stars in the galaxy of Hertford's sons and daughters, is still the home of many of the county's most prosperous, refined, and cultured people, nestling around their beautiful embryotic little capital, Como, which is destined to become as famous as the Neck and its people.

Murfreesboro, the beautiful and healthy town of 1787, on the Meherrin, the home of many of Hertford's wealthy and fashionable and patriotic citizens—Murfrees, Reas, Dickinsons, Gordons, Deanses, Carters, Smiths, Yanceys, Vaughans, Jenkinses, Parkers, Wells, Hills, Longs, Mannings, Hutchings, Morgans, Murphys, Wheelers, Moores, Merediths, Wilsons, Southalls, Capeharts, Browns, Traders, Banks, Finneys, Foreys, Spiers, Jeggitts, Maneys, Pipkins, Neals, Harts, Borlands, O'Briens, O'Dwyers, Wynnses, Cowpers, Lawrences, Ramseys, Clementses, and many others of the old worthies, is still the town of refinement and beauty in the west end of the county. The old fathers of 1787 made no mistake when they petitioned the legislature to establish a town on the elevated plateau of land at Murfree's Landing, on the south side of the Meherrin. It is eighty feet above the water of the river, which is drained by nature's waterways. Its beauty, its healthfulness, and the pure and health-giving quality of its water makes it an ideal home. The late Civil War greatly marred the beauty of the town, impoverished many of its noblest citizens, and brought sorrow and pain in many of its homes, where once existed wealth, true manhood, noble womanhood, happiness and joy. While she has not been able to recover her former glory and renown, she has retained her air of refinement and culture, and the beauty and loveliness of her homes. As we look out through our window this beautiful May morning, we behold the town of our aristocratic and Christian fathers, guarded by their descendants and successors and clothed in her lovely spring costume, quietly resting beneath the covering of her classic and spreading shade trees, with the air around us reverberating with the sweet strains of perfect music, as its waves spread out through the parlor windows of her fair daughters, reminding us that the joyous days of old and the happy gatherings of the fair daughters and noble sons of bygone days, in the beautiful parlors of the Indian Queen Hotel, and in the hospitable homes of her honored sons, still have their equals to-day.

On May 17, 1906, the celebration of the fifty-eighth anniversary of the Chowan Baptist Female Institute took place, and we give below the reported account of this occasion, written by F. B. Arendell, of Raleigh, and published in the *News and Observer*, of Raleigh, of May 19, 1906:

"Murfreesboro, N. C., May 18.—I sat yesterday under the shade of the towering oaks and majestic elms of Murfreesboro, and witnessed the coming together of a conclave of the best type of folks that live in this or any other land. They came with attire akin to the prevailing bloom of springtime—nothing gorgeous—merely bright and beautiful. They came from homes ripe in history, rich in tradition, and complete in the development of the purest and best civilization and citizenship.

"The day's attraction at Murfreesboro was two-fold in its importance. For the fifty-eighth time that grand old headlight of learning, the Chowan Baptist Female Institute, was to hold its commencement, and on the programme was a literary address by Eastern North Carolina's distinguished orator, statesman, jurist and scholar, Lieutenant-Governor Francis D. Winston.

"The people came from Hertford, Chowan, Bertie, Northampton and Gates until the hospitable old town almost overflowed. The venerable college, planted by Forey and his compeers, watered by Hooper of blessed memory, and nourished by the immortal McDowell, guided later on by Brewer and Petty, and at present so well directed by that strenuous genius of teaching, John C. Scarborough, threw open its broad gates, its broad doors, and its broader hearts. Even the hundreds of spreading elms that shade the broad and beautiful campus seemed to whisper a generous welcome.

"The Institute—fifty-eight years old to-day—has never yet had its doors closed in war times or in peace. Grand old nursery of mental and moral training, it has retransplantd its tender, blooming plants, equipped for beautiful and useful womanhood, into hundreds of the homes of Eastern North Carolina.

"Its annual commencements have for more than half a century constituted important epochs in the history of this great tide-water country. The exercises on this occasion were delightfully pleasing. The concert on Tuesday evening was charming, enchanting.

"The salutatory, the valedictory, and the other essays by the ten graduates were particularly classical and scholarly. And then came the masterly address by Governor Winston. In touch, it was, with the chaste, refined environment, in line with the classics of the graduates, and the beautiful thought embraced in their essays. In harmony, too, with the budding womanhood all about him and the beautiful, blooming woodland and winding rivers that encircle the good old town.

"He spoke of woman, not the new woman—not the old woman—but woman. The woman changed because of changed conditions, the woman with a mission greater than of old—the woman with prerogatives broader and greater than of yore, the woman with opportunities transcending any enjoyed in by-gone days. He spoke with feeling and power, with force and logic, with unmatched eloquence, his characteristic humor, his pathos, his sweeping flights of eloquence played over the vast audience, and left it now enrapt in smiles, now in tears, and then in bursts of vociferous applause.

"His subject—a fruitful one—his power as an orator almost unmatched—his audience sympathetic—appreciative—his friends, his neighbors, his kinfolks. It was a real, royal, literary feast, a glorious finale of a brilliant occasion.

"And I rode over and about old Murfreesboro, set up on a beautiful plateau some eighty feet above the winding Meherrin River, a hundred years old and more. The chief town of old Hertford County—itself more than a century and a half old. In the heart of the fertile Chowan section, dedicated before the Revolution to culture, refinement, virtue and bravery, inhabited then and now with brave men and braver women, they have written history, thrilling, interesting history, on every foot of this sacred soil, and written their own names on the fabric of Carolina to remain there forever.

"Down yonder are the ruins of the old home of Hardy Murfree, one of the blazers of this forest and a hero of the Revolution. Near by stood the old Indian Queen Hotel, where LaFayette was royally entertained some years after the Revolution had ended. Over yonder lived and still live the Bakers—the Vaughans, the Winbornes, the Wynnses, the Harrells—and clustered about them were the Carters, the Cowpers, the Freemans, the Smiths, the Moores, the Wheelers, the Myricks, the Worthingtons, and others. Independence winners, history makers, civilization builders.

"Murfreesboro is both old and new; but there is nothing old here—that is, too old—not even the well-preserved vine-clad colonial homes. There is nothing new that is too new, not even the artesian well. There is a blending—a beautiful blending—a blending of tradition and trade—a blending of history and hustle—a blending of colonial coronets and caromels—a blending of slavery days and sulky plows—a blending of the old and the new all along the line in this beautiful Chowan country, rich and fertile, venerable, honorable, healthful, and happy."

In 1904 your humble servant engaged in a quadrangular contest in the county primary for the Democratic nomination for the House. He was nominated, and elected in November of that year. At the opening of the session of the General Assembly in January, 1905, he entered another quadrangular contest for the Speakership, but did not meet with the same success as in the first. O. H. Guion, of Craven, was nominated, and Hertford's member was made chairman of the Judiciary Committee of the House, and appointed on the following other committees: Claims, Constitutional Amendments, Courts and Judicial Districts, Election Laws, Rules, Regulation of the Liquor Traffic, and the Joint Committee on the Revision of the Laws. In January, 1906, Governor R. B. Glenn appointed the author one of the delegates from North Carolina to a congress composed of delegates from all the States, to meet in Washington City, February 19, 1906, to draft a uniform divorce code, to be submitted to the several State legislatures for ratification.

The writer was educated at Buckhorn Academy, in his native county, at Wake Forest College, and at Columbian University in the District of Columbia. He studied law at the law school of that University in addition to taking a collegiate course of studies, and received his degree of B.L. in June, 1874, in the 20th year of his age. In September, 1874, he entered the law office of Smith & Strong, in Raleigh, as clerk, and in February, 1875, he applied for and obtained his license to practice law, but not then being of full age his license was held by Judge Smith, under direction of the Court, until his majority, April 14, 1875. In June, 1875, he located in Winton to practice his profession. He at once identified himself with the Democratic party and

NELLIE H. VAUGHAN.
Became Mrs. B. B. Winborne Dec. 23, 1879.

took an active part in all county affairs. In 1876, while waiting for clients, he wrote a Historical Brief of Political Economy, which was published in sections in the *Albemarle Times,* a newspaper edited in Windsor, N. C., by the late P. H. Winston, Jr. This Brief has since been published in book form. In 1877 he was made chairman of his party, which position he held, except two short intervals, until 1901. On December 23, 1879, he married Miss Nellie H. Vaughan, the fourth daughter of Col. Uriah Vaughan, of Murfreesboro. In January, 1880, he moved to the town of his bride, where they have since lived. In 1895, he was elected to the House from Hertford, and served on several important committees. In 1896 he was elected a delegate from the First Congressional District to the National Democratic Convention, in Chicago, and voted for Wm. J. Bryan, as the Democratic nominee for President. Later, in 1896, his friends wanted to nominate him for Congress, but he declined to receive the nomination. He has often served on the district and State committees of his party. In the State Convention of 1904, which met in Greensboro, he was appointed on the Platform Committee. Judge of Criminal Court from 1891 to 1897, except the period from October, 1894, to March 14, 1895, while he served as a member of the legislature. In 1905 he wrote and published a history of "The Winborne Family," for which he has been much complimented. By his marriage he has had born unto him four sons—Uriah V., Stanley, Micajah, and Benj. B., Jr. The first and third died young. Stanley is now closing his junior examinations at the University of North Carolina, and Benjamin is with his parents.

The author was born April 14, 1854, and reared on a farm, and inherited a fondness for stock raising and of farming. He in his young days cheerfully and energetically performed all kind of plantation work. From the age of seven years he has been watching the struggles of men. He never buckled down to the hard study of books, until he went to the Columbian University in September, 1872. His father was always a busy and active man. His mother was a bright, cheerful and energetic Christian woman, and a valuable aid to her husband in his long struggle. The writer took much notice of the events of war times and the melancholy days succeeding the civil strife and became familiar with the public affairs by his intimate associations with his father and other public men. After he came to the Bar, he continued his study of the law, and has been a busy lawyer for about twenty-eight years. It seems that we have lived more than a generation. On February 26, 1902, his health suddenly gave way, and he was taken ill in his office and became unconscious within thirty minutes, and remained so for several weeks, suffering with pneumonia and pleurisy. He was finally resurrected from the Valley of the Shadow of Death. For two and one-half years he lingered in wretched health, and his recovery was miraculous. The writing of "The Winborne Family" and of this book would have probably never been undertaken had he not met this great sickness.

The author, in 1887, joined others in organizing an agricultural fair, to be held annually in Murfreesboro. He was made President of the organization, and for several years it was one of the best fairs in the State. Among the distinguished speakers at its annual meetings were Hon. Kemp. P. Battle, as President of the University of North Carolina, U. S. Senator Hon. M. W. Ransom, the peerless statesman, the ripe scholar, and the magnetic orator; Governor Thomas M. Holt, and U. S. Senator Hon. Z. B. Vance, the great commoner and patriot. The fair went down about 1892, and was revived in 1905. The writer was again made its President, and in October of that year the Great Fair was again opened. Col. John S. Cunningham, of Person County, made the opening speech, and on Thursday, October 12, Gov. R. B. Glenn, the able, eloquent and Christian Governor of North Carolina, delivered to an audience of several thousand people one of the finest addresses that

Mrs. MARY H. WINBORNE,
Nee PRETLOW.
Wife of Maj. S. D. Winborne.
Died August 24, 1900, aged 72 years and 7 months.

DECADE XV.—1900-1906.   307

has ever been delivered to an argricultural people. At the end of his great speech he held a reception, when thousands of people gladly grasped his hand. In July preceding, the Confederate veterans of the county held their annual reunion in Murfreesboro, when they were addressed by that brave old soldier and ornate orator, B. F. Dixon, the Auditor of the State. This was a gala day in the old town.

In 1901, the writer obtained from the General Assembly a charter for a telephone company, and began the work of connecting the towns of the county by telephone lines. In 1904 the company was re-organized, and now, under the efficient management of President L. J. Lawrence and General Manager A. E. Garrett, we have a complete system of 'phone service. We can now sit at our desk and talk to people at any village or town in Hertford, Northampton and Bertie counties, and at the towns along the line of the Seaboard Air Line from Boykins, Va., to Norfolk.

Among the sons of Hertford who have reached prominence in their adopted home in Norfolk, Va., and who have not been heretofore mentioned, are J. W. Perry, the successful commission merchant and Vice-President of the Citizens' Bank of Norfolk, Va.; John N. Vaughan, Charles A. Lawrence, Wallace E. Lawrence, Robert Montgomery, Hugh Pete and George A. Williams, sons of the highly respected Peter Williams, one of the old merchants of the Borough; Nathaniel Beaman, President of the National Bank of Commerce of Norfolk, Va. Beaman is a native of Murfreesboro and the son of the late W. P. Beaman and wife, Annie Beaman, of Sleepy Hollow, Va. His father died in the 12th decade, and a few years thereafter his mother, with her three children, moved to Norfolk. Young Beaman, when young, was a bright and thoughtful boy, and his wonderful success in life is positive proof that he is no ordinary man.

Among our young men who are off at school this year are Stanley Winborne and Edgar Thomas Snipes, at the University at Chapel Hill. The latter is soon to become a full-fledged lawyer. A. M. Brown, G. V. Brown, H. J. Brown, K. R. Curtis, W. L. Curtis, L. Hale, Herbert Jenkins and L. A. Parker at Wake Forest College. Jesse Powell at the College of Physicians and Surgeons in Baltimore. Paul Jernigan at Randolph-Macon College. Robert Jernigan, Landon Burbage and Benj. Sears at Randolph-Macon Academy, Bedford City, Va. J. O. Askew, Jr., at Franklin, Va. Pembroke Baker at Norfolk Business College. At the A. and M. College, Raleigh, N. C., are W. W. Taylor and M. R. Herring, of Winton, and J. E. Overton, of Ahoskie.

At the end of 146 years of the county's existence, we look back and view the struggles, the triumphs, the defeats, and the victories, of our ancestors and our beloved country, its progress and advancement, and as we look upon this panorama of the past, it fills our souls with greater hopes for the victories and triumphs of the future. Our State has passed through a war in each quarter of a century since 1759. The war with Great Britain 1776-'82, the Rebellion in the State in 1784-'5, and the attempted establishment of the State of Frankland. The war of 1812-'14 with England, the Seminole war of 1818-'19, the Mexican war of 1846-'48, the Civil war of 1861-'65, and the Spanish war of 1898. In the war of the United States with Spain the patriots who wore the blue, and those who wore the gray in the civil strife in 1861-'65, and their sons, fought side by side under the glorious old flag of the Union and rejoiced together over the victories of the defenders of the American Union. The Angel of Peace had returned to remain with the brave foes of the 60's and with their sons and daughters. We here quote from the recent speech of Cardinal Gibbons on the "Triumphs of Peace," delivered in New York. He is too pacific in his reference to the warfare of 1861-'65.

Cardinal Gibbons said in part:

"Nearly two thousand years have rolled by since the birth of the Prince of Peace, whose advent was announced by the angellic host singing 'Glory to God in the Highest, and on Earth Peace, Good Will to Men.'

"Christ's mission on earth was, above all, to break down the wall of partition that divided nation from nation, that alienated tribe from tribe, and people from people, and to make them all of one family acknowledging the Fatherhood of God and the Brotherhood of Christ.

"When looking back and contemplating the wars that have ravaged the Christian world during the last twenty centuries, some persons might be tempted at first sight to exclaim in anguish of heart that the mission of Christ was a failure.

MISSION HAS NOT FAILED.

"My purpose, in the brief remarks which I shall make, is to disabuse the faint hearted of this discouraging impression and to show that Christ's mission has not failed, but that the cause of peace has made decisive and reassuring progress.

"It is by comparisons and contrasts that we can most effectually gauge the results of Christian civilization.

"Compare the military history of the Roman Empire from its foundation to the time of Augustus Cæsar, with the military record of our American Republic from the close of the Revolution to the present time.

"In pagan Rome war was the rule, peace was the exception. The Temple of Janus in Rome was always open in time of war, and was closed in time of peace. From the reign of Romulus to the time of Cæsar, embracing 700 years, the Temple of Janus was always open, except twice, when it was closed for only six years. It was subsequently closed at the birth of Christ, as if to symbolize the pacific mission of the Redeemer of mankind.

AMERICA'S FOUR WARS.

"The United States has existed as a sovereign nation for about one hundred and twenty years, since the close of the

Revolution. During that period we have had four wars: the war with England, from 1812 to 1815; the war with Mexico, from 1845 to 1848; the Civil war, from 1861 to 1865, and the recent Spanish war. The combined length of these campaigns was about ten years. Hence we see that the United States has enjoyed twelve years of peace for one year of war, while the Roman Empire enjoyed less than one year of tranquility for every century of military engagements.

"But the blessed influence of our Christian civilization has been experienced not only in reducing the numbers of wars, but still more in mitigating the horrors of military strife.

"Prior to the dawn of Christianity the motto of the conqueror was 'Va victis'—'Woe to the vanquished.' The captured cities were pillaged and laid waste. The wives and daughters of the defeated nation became the prey of the ruthless soldiery. The conquered generals and army were obliged to grace the triumphs of the victors, before they were condemned to death or ignominious bondage.

ALEXANDER AND SCOTT.

"Alexander the Great, after the capture of the city of Tyre, ordered 2,000 of the inhabitants to be crucified, and the remainder of the population were put to death or sold into slavery.

"How different was the conduct of General Scott after his successful siege of the City of Mexico. As soon as the enemy surrendered, not a single soldier or citizen was sacrificed to the vengeance of the victorious army, and not a single family was exiled from their native land.

"During the siege of Jerusalem in the year 70 of the Christian era, under Titus, the Roman general, more than a million of Jews perished by the sword and famine. Nearly 100,000 Jews were carried into captivity. The sacred vessels of the Temple of Jerusalem were borne away by the blood-stained hands of the Roman army. Simon, the Jewish chieftain, with the flower of the Jewish troops, was conducted to Rome, where he graced the triumph of the Roman general, and then a rope was thrown around his neck and he was dragged around the forum, where he was cruelly tormented and put to death. And yet Titus was not accused by his contemporaries of exceptional cruelty. On the contrary, he was regarded as a benevolent ruler and was called the 'delight of the human race.'

TREATMENT OF CONFEDERATES.

"Let us contrast the conduct of Titus toward the Jews with General Grant's treatment of the defeated Confederate forces. When General Lee surrendered his sword at Appomattox Court-house, he and his brave army were permitted to return without molestation to their respective homes.

"Imagine General Lee and his veterans led in chains to Washington, followed by the spoils and treasures of Southern homes and Southern sanctuaries. Imagine the same Confederate soldiers compelled to erect a monument to commemorate their own defeat. Would not the whole nation rise up in its might and denounce a degradation so revolting to their humanity?

"A hundred years ago disputes between individuals were commonly decided by a duel. Thanks to the humanizing influence of a Christian public opinion, these disagreements are now usually adjusted by legislation or conciliation. Have we not reason to hope that the same pacific agencies which have checked the duel between individuals, will in God's own time, check the duel between nations?

BULLY NATIONS.

"In our school-boy days the most odious and contemptible creature we used to encounter was the bully who played the tyrant towards the weak, but cringed before his stronger companions. But still more intolerable is a bullying nation that picks a quarrel with a feeble nation with the base intent of seizing her possessions.

"I can recall at least four instances in the last twenty years in which international conflicts have been amicably settled by arbitration.

"The dispute between Germany and Spain regarding the Caroline Islands was adjusted by Pope Leo XIII. in 1886.

"The Samoan difficulty between Germany and the United States was settled by a conference held in Berlin in 1889. A treaty of peace between the United States and Mexico was signed in Washington at the close of Cleveland's administration. And a few weeks ago a war between France and Germany, perhaps a general European conflict, was averted by the Algeciras conference in Morrocco."

While we may not exactly agree with the Cardinal in all he says, we can but admit that in the main he pictures forceably the progress of the United States of North America. While it is true we are having our troubles with the trust, which is the evil of great aggregation of capital in the hands of a few, and which cause many to have fears of the speedy downfall of the Republic, yet we have hopes in the wisdom and patriotism of the American people, that they will in due time strike down this would-be assassin of our Republic. And we strongly believed that the conservatism and patriotism of the South will be appealed to by all true Americans to perform this great mission. History repeats itself, and the sons of those who did most to create the Republic will be the ones called upon in the crucible hour to save it from destruction.

WAR IS CRUEL AND EXPENSIVE.

It has been the custom of nations for all ages to resort to arms and bloodshed in order to settle civil differences. This is, and always has been, wrong. Wars are the result of the ambition of selfish men. Such men are willing to crucify the people at the cross, to gratify their ambition and selfishness. These men have existed in all ages and in all countries. It is time that the civilization and Christianity of the present day to put an end to such cruelty and barbarity. The United States have paid out for war, to say nothing of the Indian wars, the following astounding sums of money, in addition to the numberless lives that were sacrificed:

The Revolutionary War, 1776-'82.. $135,193,703.00
The War of 1812 .... 107,159,003.00
The Mexican War 66,000.000.00
The Civil War 6,500,000,000.00
The Spanish-American War 150,000,000.00

What becomes of the advocates of war and strife? Here presents a great moral question.

CONCLUSION.

After much hard and the most fatiguing labor, I have succeeded in getting together much of the hidden information about the history of Hertford County and its people. The flames had consumed the records of these people for the first 132 years of the county's existence. To get the facts found in this volume I resorted to the Colonial and State Records of North Carolina, Wheeler's and Moore's histories of the State, Dr. Thos. O'Dwyer's diary for 1824, and old deeds, wills, and copies of old court records, found among the papers of many of the old families of the county. My letters reached many points in several of the States seeking information. I have compiled the result of my labors. I know it is not perfect, and I, also, know my effort to save from oblivion some information of our people will be severely criticised by many. Some who possessed some information declined to put me in possession of it, while most others were glad to render what aid they could. To Maj. John W. Moore, of Hertford, and Miss Mary Murfree, of Tennessee, and others in that State, and friends in New Jersey, and H. C. Sharp, of Harrellsville, and all others who gave me facts, I return my thanks for the valuable aid rendered me. I am glad I have done this work. It has given me information about the county, the

State, and country at large, that otherwise I would not have obtained. In my writing, I often felt like wandering off into the realms of metaphysics and moral science and general history, and discoursing on the mysteries of life and of death and of resurrection, and paint, in a feeble way, the picture of eternity—the end of measured time—as it appears to me; but such thoughts would have been out of place in such a book as this, which was only intended to gather the facts for the future historian of the State, that the noble people of Hertford County, whose records have been destroyed, may not be overlooked and forgotten. Untrue history is the curse of a people. True history is the glory of a people.

> " The book is completed,
> And closed like the day;
> And the hand that has written it
> Lays it away.
>
> Dim grow its fancies;
> Forgotten they lie;
> Like coals in the ashes,
> They darken and die."

BENJ. B. WINBORNE.

Murfreesboro, N. C., May 24, 1906.

HERTFORD COUNTY'S LIST OF OFFICERS.

Lawyers of Hertford County, 1906, and the times of their respective admissions to the Bar:

Winborne & Lawrence, Murfreesboro, N. C. Benj. B. Winborne—February term, 1875; Lloyd J. Lawrence, February term, 1892.

George V. Cowper, Winton, N. C.—June term, 1878.

Jno. E. Vann, Winton, N. C.—September term, 1887.

David Collin Barnes, Murfreesboro, N. C.—September term, 1896.

Roswell C. Bridger, Winton, N. C.—September term, 1899.

Jas. R. Mitchell, Winton, N. C.—August term, 1901.

Wm. W. Rogers, Winton, N. C.—February term, 1903.

HERTFORD'S CONGRESSMEN.

1802-'07—Gen. Thomas Wynns, near Winton.
1813-'17—William Hardy Murfree, Murfreesboro.
1839-'45—Kenneth Rayner, near Harrellsville.
1859-'61—W. N. H. Smith, Murfreesboro.
1875-'81—Jesse J. Yeates, Murfreesboro.

CONFEDERATE CONGRESS.

January, 1862-April, 1864—W. N. H. Smith.

PRESIDENTIAL ELECTORS.

1801—Gen. Thomas Wynns.
1809—Gen. Thomas Wynns.
1848—Kenneth Rayner.
1860—John W. Moore.

MEMBERS OF GOVERNOR'S COUNCIL.

Col. James Jones, Col. Matthias Brickle, Gen. Thomas Wynns, John A. Anderson, Maj. Jesse J. Yeates.

CONSULS AND MINISTERS.

1855—John H. Wheeler, Minister to Nicaragua.
1885-'89—Thos. R. Jernigan, Consul to Japan.
1895—Hunter Sharp, Consul to Japan.
1893-'97—Thos. R. Jernigan, Consul to Shanghai, China.

1831—Clerk of the Board of Commissioners under the Convention with France: John H. Wheeler.

1837—Superintendent of U. S. Mint at Charlotte: John H. Wheeler.

1842-'44—Treasurer of the State: John H. Wheeler.

U. S. Senate from Arkansas: April, 1848-'53—Solon Borland, a Murfreesboro boy.

Solicitor of First District: 1849-'58—W. N. H. Smith; 1860-'66—Jesse J. Yeates.

Chief Justice of the State: January, 1878-November, 1889—W. N. H. Smith.

Judge of Criminal Court: 1891-'97—B. B. Winborne.

Chairman of Judiciary Committee in House of Assembly: 1800—Robert Montgomery; 1905—B. B. Winborne.

First Constitutional Convention of November 12, 1776: Delegates—Lawrence Baker, William Murfree, Robert Sumner, Day Ridley, and James Wright.

Hillsboro Convention of 1788, to consider the adoption of U. S. Constitution: Delegates—Maj. Geo. Wynns, Gen. Thomas Wynns, Rev. Lemuel Burkitt, Maj. Wm. Little, and Maj. Samuel Harrell.

Fayetteville Convention of 1789, which adopted the U. S. Constitution: Delegates—Gen. Thomas Wynns, Robert Montgomery, Col. Hardy Murfree, Henry Hill, and Henry Baker.

Constitutional Convention 1835: Kenneth Rayner.
Secession Convention of 1861: Kenneth Rayner.
Constitutional Convention of 1865: R. G. Cowper.
Constitutional Convention of 1868: Jackson B. Hare.
Constitutional Convention of 1875: Jordan J. Horton.

Hertford County was represented in the Colonial Assembly and in the Senate and House of the General Assembly of North Carolina from the time it became a sovereign State in December, 1776, up to the present time, as appears below.

Its Colonial representatives were as follows:
1762-'63—Henry Winborne and William Murfree.
1764-'65—Benj. Wynns and Robert Sumner.
1766-'68—Benj. Wynns and Matthias Brickle.
1769-'70—Peter Wynns and Edward Hare.
1771-'72—Benj. Wynns and Edward Hare.
1773-'74—Benj. Wynns, Sr., and Benj. Wynns, Jr.
1775-'76—William Murfree and George Wynns.

After North Carolina declared her independence of the British Government and adopted its first constitution, Hertford's representatives in the General Assembly of the State have been as follows:

1777—Senate, Robert Sumner; House, Jos. Dickinson, James Garrett.
1778—Robert Sumner; Wm. Baker, James Maney.
1779—Robert Sumner; William Wynns, Nathan Cotton.
1780—Pleasant Jordan; William Wynns, John Baker.
1781—John Baker; Lewis Brown, Thos. Brickle.
1782—John Brickle; William Wynns, Thos. Brickle.
1783—John Baker; Lewis Brown, Thos. Brickle.
1784—John Baker; William Hill, Thos. Brickle.
1785—Robert Sumner; James Maney, Robt. Montgomery.
1786—Robert Sumner; William Hill, Thos. Brickle.
1787—Robert Sumner; Thos. Wynns, Robt. Montgomery.
1788—Robt. Montgomery; Henry Baker, Henry Hill.
1789—Robt. Montgomery; Henry Hill, Henry Baker.
1790—Thos. Wynns; Robt. Montgomery, Henry Hill.
1791—Thos. Wynns; Robt. Montgomery, Henry Hill.
1792—Thos. Wynns; Henry Hill, James Jones.
1793—Thos. Wynns; Jethro Darden, Henry Hill.
1794—Thos. Wynns; Jethro Darden, Robt. Montgomery.

1795—Thos. Wynns; Henry Hill, Robt. Montgomery.
1796—Thos. Wynns; Jethro Darden, James Jones.
1797—Thos. Wynns; Jethro Darden, James Jones.
1798—Thos. Wynns; Robt. Montgomery, James Jones.
1799—Thos. Wynns; Robt. Montgomery, James Jones.
1800—Thos. Wynns; Robt. Montgomery, James Jones.
1801—Robt. Montgomery; James Jones, Abner Perry.
1802—Robt. Montgomery; James Jones, Abner Perry.
1803—Robt. Montgomery; James Jones, Abner Perry.
1804—Robt. Montgomery; James Jones, Abner Perry.
1805—Robt. Montgomery; Jas. Jones, Wm. H. Murfree.
1806—Robt. Montgomery; James Jones, Abner Perry.
1807—Robt. Montgomery; Lewis Walters, Abner Perry.
1808—Thos. Wynns; Lewis Walters, Abner Perry.
1809—Thos. Wynns; Boone Felton, Abner Perry.
1810—Thos. Wynns; Boone Felton, Lewis Walters.
1811—Thos. Wynns; Boone Felton, William Jones.
1812—Thos. Wynns; Wm. H. Murfree, Jethro Darden.
1813—Thos. Wynns; Boone Felton, William Jones.
1814—Thos. Wynns; Boone Felton, William Jones.
1815—Thos. Wynns; Thomas Deans, William Jones.
1816—Thos. Wynns; Thomas Deans, William Jones.
1817—Thos. Wynns; Boone Felton, Thomas Maney.
1818—Boone Felton; Jno. Hamilton Frazier, B. J. Montgomery.
1819—Jno. H. Frazier; B. J. Montgomery, Isaac Carter.
1821—Thomas Deans; Jas. Copeland, Jas. D. Wynns.
1822—David E. Sumner; Isaac Carter, Lewis M. Jeggitts.
1823—David E. Sumner; James Copeland, John Vann.
1824—James Copeland; John Vann, Isaac Carter.
1825—James Copeland; John Vann, Isaac Carter.
1826—Elisha H. Sharpe; B. J. Montgomery, Leonard Martin.
1827—David O. Askew; B. J. Montgomery, John H. Wheeler.

1828—David O. Askew; B. J. Montgomery, John H. Wheeler.
1829—B. J. Montgomery; Elisha A. Chamblee, John H. Wheeler.
1830—Jacob Hare; Isaac Carter, John H. Wheeler.
1831—B. J. Montgomery; Elisha A. Chamblee, Godwin C. Moore.
1832—B. J. Montgomery; Isaac Carter, Thos. V. Roberts.
1833—John Vann; Isaac Carter, Sipha Smith.
1834—Geo. W. Montgomery; Isaac Carter, Sipha Smith.
1835—John Vann; R. C. Borland, Kenneth Rayner.

The amendments to the Constitution in 1835 reduced Hertford's representation in the House to one member and made the sessions biennial.

1836—Geo. W. Montgomery; Kenneth Rayner.
1838—Thomas B. Sharpe; Kenneth Rayner.
1840—B. T. Spiers; Wm. N. H. Smith.
1842—Godwin C. Moore; Starkey Sharpe.
1844—Richard G. Cowper; Jacob Sharpe.
1846—Richard G. Cowper; Kenneth Rayner.
1848—William N. H. Smith; Kenneth Rayner.
1850—D. V. Sessoms; Kenneth Rayner.
1852—Richard G. Cowper; W. L. Daniel.
1854—Kenneth Rayner; W. L. Daniel.
1856—Richard G. Cowper; Joseph B. Slaughter.
1858—Richard G. Cowper; W. N. H. Smith.
1860-'61—J. B. Slaughter; Jesse J. Yeates.
1861-'62—J. B. Slaughter; Jesse J. Yeates.
1862-'63—J. B. Slaughter; Jesse B. Vann.
1863-'64—J. B. Slaughter; Jesse B. Vann.
1864-'65—James M. Wynns; John A. Vann.
1865-'66—R. G. Cowper; W. N. H. Smith.
1866-'67—James C. Barnes; Godwin C. Moore.
1867-'68—James C. Barnes; Godwin C. Moore.

In 1868 a Constitutional Convention was held in North Carolina to alter the fundamental law of the State. The delegates to the convention were composed chiefly of "Carpet-Baggers" from the most vicious element of the Northern army and its sympathizers, who, after the cessation of hostilities, remained in the South, to rob and plunder the Southern States. But few of the true and loyal sons of the State were allowed to participate in the deliberations of the political bodies of those times. Jackson B. Hare was the delegate from Hertford County. The Constitution prepared by this posthumous or illegitimate convention was submitted to a portion of the people of the State for ratification, at an election held on the 21st, 22d and 23d days of April, 1868. The ex-slaves voted three days. A large per centum of the best and truest citizens of the State were disfranchised and not allowed to vote, and in their place the recent slave negro men were armed with the ballot and allowed to vote at the election as directed by these "Carpet Baggers" and the native traitors to our State. General Canby, the military potentate of North and South Carolina, sitting in Charleston, S. C., declared the Constitution ratified by the voters of the State. The chivalrous and proud people of the State had no alternative but to submit to the indignities heaped upon them by such cowards as Thad. Stevens and W. H. Stewart, the haters of the South, and its own Benedict Arnolds.

Under the Constitution of 1868, Bertie and Hertford counties formed the Fifth Senatorial District, and given one senator in the General Assembly. The terms of office of the members of the Assembly began with their election and continued for two years. The General Assembly met annually on the third Monday in November. The Fifth Senatorial District was represented as follows:

1868-'69—J. W. Beasley, R., Bertie County.
1869-'70—J. W. Beasley, R., Bertie County.
1870-'71—J. W. Beasley, R., Bertie County.
1871-'72—J. W. Beasley, R., Bertie County.

The legislation and corruption of the above sessions of the General Assembly form the blackest pages of North Carolina's history. It is a lasting shame and disgrace to the Republican party of the State. It will never be forgotten by the true and honorable people of the State and their descendants. In the summer of 1872 the white people of the State succeeded in electing a large majority of the members of the General Assembly, and that body, by an act ratified January 19, 1872, by a three-fifths vote of all the members, amended the Constitution of 1868 in several particulars. One of the amendments was in changing the sessions from "annual" to "biennial." That same body, by an act ratified February 2, 1872, re-appointed the representation of the State, and put Hertford County in the First Senatorial District, with the six other counties east of Chowan River, and they were given two members. The members from the First Senatorial District, thereafter, were as follows:

1872-'74—John L. Chamberlain, R., Camden County;
C. W. Grandy, R., Pasquotank County.
1874-'76—Wm. B. Shaw, D., Currituck County;
Thomas R. Jernigan, D., Hertford County.
1876-'78—Octavius Coke, D., Chowan County.
W. C. Mercer, D., Currituck County.

In 1875 another Constitutional Convention was held in North Carolina, and presided over by Edmond Ransom, of Tyrrell County, who was elected as an independent to said convention. The members of the Republican and Democratic parties were about evenly divided. The Democrats secured the co-operation of Mr. Ransom by electing him President of the convention. This gave the Democrats one majority on the floor. Many important amendments were made in the organic law of the State by this body. Much of the sting of the Canby Constitution of 1868 was eradicated. No man of the majority could afford to be absent from his seat during this all-important session. The devotion of the

Democratic members of this convention was never better shown than during the days of this momentous session of this exciting convention. Hertford County was represented in this convention by Jordan J. Horton, a Republican.

The time for the biennial meetings of the General Assembly was changed from the third Monday in November next after the election of its members, to the first Monday after the first Monday in January next after the election of its members. The General Assembly of 1876-'77, by an act ratified March 12, 1877, provided that the general election in the State should be held in the year 1880, on the Tuesday after the first Monday in November, and every two years thereafter. The members from the First Senatorial District continued:

1878-'79—Geo. H. Mitchell, R., Hertford County;
          Rufus White, R., Perquimans County.
1880-'81—W. H. Manning, D., Gates County;
          J. M. Woodhouse, D., Currituck County.
1882-'83—W. W. Speight, R., Gates County;
          J. M. Woodhouse, D., Currituck County.
1884-'85—Wm. M. Bond, D., Chowan County;
          James Parker, D., Gates County.
1886-'87—W. P. Shaw, D., Hertford County;
          W. J. Griffin, D., Pasquotank County.
1888-'89—J. K. Abbott, D., Camden County;
          W. P. Shaw, D., Hertford County.
1890-'91—P. H. Morgan, D., Currituck County;
          James Parker, D., Gates County.
1892-'93—J. K. Abbott, Camden County;
          J. J. Gatling, D., Gates County.
1894-'95—E. T. Snipes, R., Hertford County;
          Theo. White, P., Perquimans County.
1896-'97—J. L. Whedbee, R., Perquimans County;
          Jno. F. Newsome, P., Hertford County.
1898-'99—T. G. Skinner, D., Perquimans County;
          George Cowper, D., Hertford County.

1900-'01—C. S. Vann, D., Chowan County;
    W. H. Bray, D., Currituck County.
1902-'03—C. S. Vann, D., Chowan County;
    P. H. McMullen, D., Perquimans County.
1904-'05—C. S. Vann, D., Chowan County;
    S. M. Beasley, D., Currituck County.

HOUSE OF REPRESENTATIVES.

1868-'69—E. T. Snipes, R.
1869-'70—E. T. Snipes, R.
1870-'71—W. D. Newsom, Col., R.
1871-'72—W. D. Newsom, Col., R.
1872-'73—James Sharp, R.
1873-'74—James Sharp, R.
1874-'75—Soloman Parker, R.

1876-'77—J. J. Horton, R., was given certificate of election, but his seat was contested by H. C. Maddrey, D., and Maddrey was seated.

1879—J. J. Horton, R.
1881—E. T. Snipes, R.
1883—George H. Mitchell, R.
1885—Robert W. Winborne, D.
1887—E. T. Snipes, R.
1889—James L. Anderson, D.
1891—James L. Anderson, D.
1893—W. P. Taylor, D.
1895—Benj. B. Winborne, D.
1897—Starkey Hare, R.
1899—Isaac F. Snipes, R.
1901—Lloyd J. Lawrence, D.
1903—John E. Vann, D.
1905—Benj. B. Winborne, D.

THE INFERIOR COURT.

At the election of 1876 the Democrats elected the Governor, all the State officers and a large majority of the General Assembly. The Constitution had been amended in 1875 in many respects and the amendments had been ratified by the people at the August election in 1876. The negro population had so crowded the criminal dockets of our courts in the East that there was a demand for additional court facilities to relieve the Superior Courts of the criminal work, that the civil cases might be tried. The Legislature of 1876-'77 appointed the justices of the peace for the several counties, and empowered them to establish *Inferior Criminal Courts* for their respective counties, which courts were given a limited criminal jurisdiction. They were to be presided over, where established, by three suitable persons to be selected by the justices of the peace from the body of the county. This court was established in Hertford in August, 1877. The officers at different times were as follows:

1877-'79.

Maj. J. W. Moore, Chairman; G. V. Cowper and W. P. Shaw. Cowper resigned in August, 1878, and H. C. Maddry was elected to fill the vacancy.

1879-'81.

W. P. Shaw, Chairman; H. C. Maddry and J. B. Slaughter. Slaughter resigned in August, 1880, and S. M. Aumack elected to fill the vacancy.

1881-'83.

W. P. Shaw, H. C. Maddry and J. B. Slaughter. Slaughter resigned in February, 1884, and George W. Beverly elected to fill vacancy. They continued in office until August, 1887.

1887-'89.

David A. Barnes, H. C. Maddry and George W. Beverly.

1889-1891.

George W. Beverly, H. C. Maddry and S. M. Aumack.

SOLICITORS.

1877 to August, 1883—B. B. Winborne.
1883 to October, 1884—R. W. Winborne.
1884 to August, 1889—B. B. Winborne.
1889 to February, 1891—R. W. Winborne.

THE CRIMINAL COURT.

Here the Inferior Court ended, and there was a popular demand throughout the county for the abolition of this court and for the establishment of a *Criminal Court,* with full criminal jurisdiction, to be presided over by a judge with all the qualifications of a Superior Court Judge. This was done by the Legislature of 1891. By the almost unanimous demand of the county the author was elected Judge of the new Criminal Court. He accepted the office at a great sacrifice to himself. He remained Judge of the Court until 1897, except for the short period from October, 1894, to March, 1905, when he resigned to serve in the Legislature of the State. After the adjournment of the Legislature of 1905 he was re-appointed Judge of said Court by Governor Carr. He served as Judge until the Court was abolished in 1897 by the Fusion Legislature. About 600 cases were tried before him, covering all grades of criminal offences, statutory and common-law crimes. And only one appeal to the Supreme Court was taken from his rulings, and he was affirmed in that—State v. Harrison, 115-706.

SOLICITORS AT DIFFERENT TIMES.

Peter B. Picot, Esq.
John E. Vann, Esq.
George Cowper, Esq.

CLERKS.

The Clerks of the Superior Court were ex-officio Clerks of the Inferior and the Criminal Courts.

COUNTY OFFICERS.

It may be of interest to some to know the names of the officers of the county from its formation to the present time:

SHERIFFS.

1760-'62—John Baker.
1762-'66—Matthias Brickle.
1766-'71—William Murfree.
1771-'74—Nathan Harrell.
1774-'77—John Harrell.
1777-'82—Starkey Sharp I.
1782-'84—James Boon.
1784-'86—Josiah Sumner.
1786-'88—Moses Sumner.
1788-'90—Starkey Sharp I.
1790-'94—William Wynns.
1794-'98—Matthias Brickle, Jr.
1798-'1800—James Cherry.
1800-'12—Thomas Deanes.
1812-'17—Isaac Carter.
1817-'24—William B. Wynns.
1824-'25—Jesse Deanes.
1825-'36—Richard Greene Cowper.
1836-'38—Edw. K. Jeggitts.
1838 to May, 1844—R. G. Cowper.
May, 1844, to August, 1844—Preston Perry.
1844 to November, 1848—Abner J. Perry.
1848 to August, 1856—John P. Bridger.
1856-'60—John A. Vann.
1861-'67—Jackson B. Hare.
1867-'76—Isaac Pipkin, D.
1876-'78—Jackson B. Hare, R.

HERTFORD COUNTY'S OFFICERS. 327

1878-'80—John Sharp.
1880—A. C. Vann, Tax Collector.
1880-'84—Joseph J. Jordan.
1884 to December, 1894—James S. Mitchell.
1894-'96—William E. Cullen.
1896-1900—James S. Mitchell.
1900-'03—William H. Tayloe.
1903-'06—A. E. Garrett.

CHAIRMEN OF THE OLD COUNTY COURT PRIOR TO WAR OF 1776.

Robert Sumner.
Henry Winborne.

AFTER THE WAR.

Col. Matthias Brickle.
Thomas Winborne.
Thomas N. Brickle.
Timothy Ridley.
Thomas P. Little.
1829—Elisha Winborne.
1830-'51—John Vann.
1851-'57—John A. Anderson.
1857-'61—Dr. Godwin C. Moore.
1861, to June 18, 1861—John A. Anderson.
June, 1861-'66—William W. Mitchell.
1866-'68—Watson L. Daniel.

CLERKS OF THE COURT OF PLEAS AND QUARTER SESSIONS.

1760-'64—Benjamin Wynns.
1764-'72—Benjamin Wynns, Jr.
1772-'78—George Wynns.
1778-'80—Benjamin Wynns.
1780-'90—Samuel Harrell.
1790-'94—Nathan Harrell.
1794-'97—William Wynns.
1797-1802—Nathan Harrell.

1802-'03—Benjamin Wynns, Jr.
1803-'22—Joseph F. Dickinson.
1822-'23—George Gordon.
1823-'58—Lewis M. Cowper.
1858 to August, 1861—Starkey S. Harrell.
1861 to May, 1868—Lewis M. Cowper.

CLERK AND MASTER IN EQUITY.

1806-'33—Howell Jones.
1833-'35—Bridger J. Montgomery.
1835-'63—William M. Montgomery.
1863-'68—John A. Vann.

COUNTY ATTORNEYS DURING THE DAYS OF THE OLD COUNTY COURTS.

1777-'90—Henry Hill.
1790-1800—Robert Montgomery.
1800-'05—Sharp Blount.
1805-'12—William H. Murfree.
1812-'20—Thomas Maney.
1820-'35—James S. Jones.
1835 to November, 1845—Roscius C. Borland.
1845 to May, 1849—W. N. H. Smith.
1849 to August, 1851—A. Poma Yancey.
1857 to August, 1855—W. D. Valentine.
1855-'60—Jesse J. Yeates.
1860-'62—John H. Jernigan.
1862-'65—Joseph B. Slaughter.
1865-'66—William Sharp.
1866-'68—J. B. Slaughter.

CLERKS OF SUPERIOR COURTS.

1848-'51—William D. Valentine; resigned August, 1851.
1851-'54—John A. Vann.
1854-'58—Starkey S. Harrell, Jr.
1858-'68—George W. Beverly.

HERTFORD COUNTY'S OFFICERS. 329

1868 to October 5, 1870—Starkey S. Harrell.
1870 to January 2, 1872—Joseph W. Perry.
1872 to December, 1886—William J. Gatling.
1886 to April, 1889—Thomas D. Boone.
1889 to December, 1890—William J. Gatling.
1890 to December, 1898—Thomas D. Boone.
1898 to March, 1901—John F. Newsome.
1901 to December, 1906—Thomas D. Boone.

NATIVE-BORN LAWYERS OF THE COUNTY, AND WHO PRACTICED IN THE COUNTY.

Henry Hill ....Murfreesboro.
Robert Montgomery ....Murfreesboro.
Sharp Blount ....Winton.
William Hardy Murfree.................Musfreesboro.
Harry W. Long........................Murfreesboro.
Thomas Maney ....Murfreesboro.
James Sydney Jones...................Pitch Landing.
Roscius Cicero Borland................Murfreesboro.
John Hill Wheeler ....Murfreesboro.
William Nathan Harrell Smith............Murfreesboro.
Antonio Poma Yancey...................Murfreesboro.
Jesse Johnson Yeates...................Murfreesboro.
William Darden Valentine....................Winton.
John Wheeler Moore....................Murfreesboro.
Joseph Blount Slaughter................Pitch Landing.
John Hunter Jernigan...................Harrellsville.
William Sharp ....Harrellsville.
Pulaski Cowper ....Murfreesboro.
Joseph E. Carter ....Murfreesboro.
James Lawrence Mitchell....................Winton.
Denny Worthington ....Murfreesboro.
Thomas Robert Jernigan..................Harrellsville.
William Dorsey Pruden..................Harrellsville.
Benjamin Brodie Winborne..............Murfreesboro.
John Jesse Vann............................Winton.

George Cowper ....Winton.
Robert Warren Winborne.................Murfreesboro.
Charles Spurgeon Vann........................Winton.
Willis C. Warren ....Murfreesboro.
Lloyd Jennings Lawrence.................Murfreesboro.
John Eley Vann ....Winton.
Peter Blount Picot............................Winton.
David Collin Barnes.....................Murfreesboro.
Roswell C. Bridger............................Winton.
James R. Mitchell............................Winton.
William W. Rogers...........................Winton.

Judge David Alexander Barnes moved to the county from Northampton County in 1875 and resided in Murfreesboro until his death in 1892. Hon. Kenneth Rayner and Brackney T. Spiers studied law and obtained license, but did not practice. Charles H. Foster and James M. Trader obtained license to practice law under a strange statute enacted by the "carpet-bag" Legislature of 1868-'69, which permitted any one to secure license by paying a license tax of $20 (Laws 1868-'69, ch. 46).

PUBLIC REGISTERS.

1760-'64—Benjamin Wynns, Jr.
1770-'74—Joseph Worth.
1780-1890—Nathan Harrell.
1790—'91—Starkey Sharp.
1791-'97—Nathan Harrell.
1797-'98—Jacob Sharp.
1798-1800—Jacob Sharp.
1800-'13—Mills Jernigan.
1813-'20—George Gordon.
1820-'24—John H. Gordon.
1824-'25—Peter Butts.
1825-'31—Andrew V. Duer.
1831-'43—L. R. Jernigan.

1843-'45—Patrick Perry.
1845 to August, 1846—Henry B. Vanpelt.
1846 to February, 1857—William J. Perry.
1857-'66—John Sharp.
1866-'68—Joseph P. Jordan.

REGISTER OF DEEDS.

1868-'76—James M. Trader.
1876-'82—Henry Clay Sharp.
1882 to January, 1890—Watson Lewis Daniel.
1890 to December, 1896—George A. Brown.
1896 to December, 1900—S. E. Marsh.
1900 to October, 1905—James P. Freeman.
1905-'06—John A. Northcott.

COUNTY TRUSTEES PRIOR TO 1790.

Samuel Harrell.
Nathan Harrell.
George Wynns.
Starkey Sharp I.

AFTER 1790.

1830-'43—John A. Anderson.
1843 to May, 1844—Elisha D. Brett.
1844-'54—Lemuel R. Jernigan.
1854-'61—Elisha D. Brett.
1861-'62—James Barnes.
1862-'66—Starkey S. Harrell, Jr.
1866-'68—Samuel M. Aumack.

COUNTY TREASURERS.

1868-'70—Jordan J. Horton, R.
1870-'76—John A. Vann, D.
1876-'78—Joseph J. Brown, R.

Since 1878 the Sheriff of the county has been ex-officio Treasurer of the county.

ENTRY-TAKERS PRIOR TO THE WAR OF 1776.

Matthias Brickle.
Henry Winborne.
William Wynns.

AFTER THE WAR.

Mills Jernigan.
Andrew J. Northcott.
The Register of Deeds is now ex-officio entry-taker.

COUNTY SURVEYORS PRIOR TO WAR OF 1776.

1762-'66—John Baker.
1766-'70—Godwin Cotton.

SINCE THE WAR.

Pleasant Jordan.
John A. Wynns.
1800-'10—Samuel Bell.
1810-'33—Sipha Smith.
1833-'54—Jethro W. Barnes.
1854-'68—Zepheniah Askew.

SINCE 1868.

Thadeus E. Vann.
J. W. Jessups.
John F. Newsom.
H. D. Harrell.
J. D. Parker.

COUNTY COMMISSIONERS.

1868 to 1870—John W. Harrel, Chairman; R. S. Parker, William D. Newsome, William Reed, Samuel Holloman.

1870 to 1872—J. W. Harrell, Chairman; G. A. Britt, Langley Tayloe, Jackson B. Hare, W. J. Gatling.

1872 to 1874—E. T. Snipes, Chairman; W. B. Alexander, William Reed, S. D. Winborne, L. S. Davis.

1874 to 1876—S. D. Winborne, Chairman; A. C. Vann, William Reed, W. B. Alexander, E. T. Snipes.

MISCELLANEOUS INFORMATION. 333

1876 to 1878—E. T. Snipes, Chairman; W. B. Alexander, William Reed, James I. Elliott, A. D. Godwin.

1878 to 1880—S. D. Winborne, Chairman; S. M. Aumack, J. Norfleet Harrell, John A. Vann, J. T. Wynns.

County Attorney—B. B. Winborne.

1880 to 1882—S. M. Aumack, Chairman; J. N. Harrell, John A. Vann, S. D. Winborne, J. T. Wynns.

County Attorney—B. B. Winborne.

1882 to 1886—J. N. Harrell, Chairman; S. M. Aumack, J. L. Anderson, J. P. Freeman, S. D. Winborne.

County Attorney—B. B. Winborne.

1886 to 1888—J. N. Harrell, Chairman; S. M. Aumack, A. I. Parker, J. P. Freeman, S. D. Winborne.

County Attorney—B. B. Winborne.

1888 to 1890—J. N. Harrell, Chairman; J. P. Freeman, J. F. Newsome, J. D. Riddick, W. E. Cullens.

County Attorney—B. B. Winborne.

1890 to 1892—W. T. Brown, Chairman; W. E. Cullens, Blount Ferguson, John F. Newsome, C. W. Mitchell.

County Attorney—B. B. Winborne.

1892 to 1894—W. T. Brown, Chairman; W. E. Cullens, George W. Beverly, John F. Newsome, J. B. Vaughan.

County Attorney—J. J. Yeates.

1894 to 1896—W. T. Brown, Chairman; A. I. Parker, T. E. Vann, J N. Holloman, J. T. Williams.

County Attorney—J. J. Yeates.

1896 to 1898—G. W. Mitchell, Chairman, J. B. Vaughan, E. T. Snipes.

County Attorney—George Cowper.

1898 to 1900—J. H. Mitchell, Chairman; G. W. Mitchell, J. B. Vaughan, J. M. Eley, A. I. Parker, J. C. Vinson, J. G. Majette, B. F. Williams.

County Attorney—George Cowper.

1900 to 1902—J. G. Majette, Chairman; A. I. Parker, B. F. Williams, J. C. Vinson, J. H. Mitchell.

County Attorney—John E. Vann.

1902 to 1904—J. G. Majette, Chairman; J. C. Vinson, A. I. Parker, C. W. Parker, B. F. Williams.

County Attorney—L. J. Lawrence.

1904 to 1906—J. G. Majette, Chairman; J. C. Vinson, A. I. Parker, C. W. Parker, W. E. Cullens.

County Attorneys—Winborne & Lawrence.

U. S. CENSUS OF 1900.

Population of United States 84,907,156
Population of North Carolina................ 1,893,810
Population of Virginia...................... 1,854,184
Population of Hertford County, N. C......... 14,294

TOWNS IN THE COUNTY.

Murfreesboro—Incorporated 1787. Population in 1906 about 900.

Average Temperature for	Degrees.
January	45 11-14
February	42
March	50½
April	60 23-30
May	67½
June	72½
July	77
August	76 5-28
September	72
October	59 2-3
November	49 3-5
December	45 1-3

This average temperature of Murfreesboro was ascertained by an accurate diary of the thermometer kept for each day throughout the year.

Winton—Incorporated in 1768. Population in 1906 about 800.

Union—Incorporated in 1889. Population in 1906 about 150.

Miscellaneous Information.

Harrellsville—Incorporated in 1883. Population in 1906 about 400.

Ahoskie—Incorporated in 1893. Population in 1906 about 300.

Mapleton—Incorporated in 1901. Population in 1906 about 40.

In addition to the newspapers mentioned in text, which have been published in the county, are the *Murfreesboro Enquirer,* from about 1876 to 1883; edited by E. L. C. Ward. That was followed by the *Murfreesboro Index,* which still lives, and edited by John W. Hicks. The *Hertford Herald* is also published by A. J. Conner, of Rich Square, Northampton, and it hails from Ahoskie, N. C.

COUNTIES IN NORTH CAROLINA.

Name.	County-seat.	When created.
Alamance	Graham	1848.
Alexander	Taylorsville	1846.
Alleghany	Sparta	1859.
Anson	Wadesboro	1749.
Ashe	Jefferson	1799.
Beaufort	Washington	1741.
Bertie	Windsor	1722.
Bladen	Elizabethtown	1734.
Brunswick	Smithville	1764.
Buncombe	Asheville	1791.
Burke	Morganton	1777.
Cabarrus	Concord	1792.
Caldwell	Lenoir	1841.
Camden	Camden C. H.	1777.
*Carteret	Beaufort	1777.
Caswell	Yanceyville	1777.
Catawba	Newton	1842.
Chatham	Pittsboro	1770.
Cherokee	Murphy	1839.
Chowan	Edenton	1716.
Clay	Hayesville	1861.
Cleveland	Shelby	1841.
Columbus	Whiteville	1808.
Craven	New Bern	1710.
Cumberland	Fayetteville	1754.
Currituck	Currituck C. H.	1729.
Dare	Manteo	1870.
Davidson	Lexington	1822.
Davie	Mocksville	1836.
Duplin	Kenansville	1749.
Durham	Durham	1881.

* This territory was allotted to Lord Carteret, who refused to sell to the Crown in 1729, and became a county in 1777.

Miscellaneous Information. 337

Name.	County-seat.	When created.
Edgecombe	Tarboro	1733.
Forsyth	Winston	1848.
Franklin	Louisburg	1779.
Gaston	Dallas	1846.
Gates	Gatesville	1779.
Graham	Robbinsville	1871.
Granville	Oxford	1746.
Greene	Snow Hill	1791.
Guilford	Greensboro	1770.
Halifax	Halifax	1758.
Harnett	Lillington	1855.
Haywood	Waynesville	1808.
Henderson	Hendersonville	1838.
Hertford	Winton	1759.
Hyde	Swan Quarter	Prior to 1729.
Iredell	Statesville	1788.
Jackson	Webster	1850.
Johnston	Smithfield	1746.
Jones	Trenton	1779.
Lenoir	Kinston	1791.
Lincoln	Lincolnton	1779.
Macon	Franklin	1828.
Madison	Marshall	1850.
Martin	Williamston	1774.
McDowell	Marion	1842.
Mecklenburg	Charlotte	1762.
Mitchell	Bakersville	1861.
Montgomery	Troy	1779.
Moore	Carthage	1784.
Nash	Nashville	1777.
New Hanover	Wilmington	1728.
Northampton	Jackson	1741.
Onslow	Jacksonville	1734.

22

Name.	County-seat.	When created.
Orange	Hillsboro	1751.
Pamlico	Bayboro	1872.
Pasquotank	Elizabeth City	1729.
Pender	Burgaw	1875.
Person	Roxboro	1791.
Perquimans	Hertford	Prior to 1729.
Pitt	Greenville	1760.
Polk	Columbus	1855.
Randolph	Ashboro	1779.
Richmond	Rockingham	1779.
Robeson	Lumberton	1786.
Rockingham	Wentworth	1785.
Rowan	Salisbury	1753.
Rutherford	Rutherfordton	1779.
Sampson	Clinton	1784.
Scotland	Laurinburg	1901.
Stanly	Albemarle	1841.
Stokes	Danbury	1789.
Surry	Mt. Airy	1770.
Swain	Bryson City	1871.
Transylvania	Brevard	1860.
Tyrrell	Columbia	Prior to 1729.
Union	Monroe	1842.
Vance	Henderson	1881.
Wake	Raleigh	1770.
Warren	Warrenton	1779.
Washington	Plymouth	1799.
Watauga	Boone	1849.
Wayne	Goldsboro	1779.
Wilkes	Wilkesboro	1777.
Wilson	Wilson	1855.
Yadkin	Yadkinville	1850.
Yancey	Burnsville	1833.

MISCELLANEOUS INFORMATION. 339

LORDS PROPRIETORS.

The times of the Lords Proprietors and their government dates from the settlement of Carolina up to 1729, when all the Lords Proprietors except Lord Carteret sold their rights to the soil of Carolina and franchises acquired under the charter of King Charles II., to the King of England for $45,000.

The oldest of the Lords Proprietors was made the Palatine or President of the Lords who claimed rights under the Great Grant of Carolina.

COLONIAL TIMES.

The Colonial days of North Carolina were from 1729 to November, 1776.

STATEHOOD DAYS.

The days of Statehood of North Carolina date from November, 1776.

COLONIAL GOVERNORS.

Date when sworn in—
- 1730—George Burrington.
- 1734—Gabriel Johnson.
- 1753—Matthew Rowan.
- 1754—Arthur Dobbs.
- 1765—William Tryon.
- 1771—Josiah Martin.

STATE GOVERNORS OF NORTH CAROLINA.
ELECTED BY THE GENERAL ASSEMBLY.

Dates when sworn in.	Names.	Counties.
1776	Richard Caswell	Lenoir.
1779	Abner Nash	Craven.
1781	Thomas Burke	Orange.
1782	Alexander Martin	Guilford.
1784	Richard Caswell	Lenoir.
1787	Samuel Johnson	Chowan.

340   HISTORY OF HERTFORD COUNTY, N. C.

Dates when sworn in.   *Names.*   *Counties.*

1789—Alexander Martin ....Guilford.
1792—Richard Dobbs Speight, Sr. ....Craven.
1795—Samuel Ashe ....New Hanover.
1798—William R. Davie ....Halifax.
1799—Benjamin Williams ....Moore.
1802—James Turner ....Warren.
1805—Nathaniel Alexander ....Mecklenburg.
1807—Benjamin Williams ....Moore.
1808—David Stone ....Bertie.
1810—Benjamin Smith ....Brunswick.
1811—William Hawkins ....Warren.
1814—William Miller ....Warren.
1817—John Branch ....Halifax.
1820—Jesse Franklin ....Surry.
1821—Gabriel Holmes ....Sampson.
1824—Hutchings G. Burton ....Halifax.
1827—James Iredell ....Chowan.
1828—John Owen ....Bladen.
1830—Montford Stokes ....Wilkes.
1832—David L. Swain ....Buncombe.
1835—Richard Dobbs Speight, Jr. ....Craven.

The Constitutional Convention of 1835 amended the Constitution of 1776, and since then the Governors have been elected by the people at the ballot-box.

1837—Edward B. Dudley ....New Hanover.
1841—John M. Morehead ....Guilford.
1845—William A. Graham ....Orange.
1849—Charles Manly ....Wake.
1851—David S. Reid.....................Rockingham.
1854—Warren Winslow, *ex officio* ....Cumberland.
1855—Thomas Bragg ....Northampton.
1858—John W. Ellis ....Rowan.
1861—Henry T. Clark, *ex officio* ....Edgecombe.

MISCELLANEOUS INFORMATION. 341

1863—Z. B. Vance ....Buncombe.
1866—W. W. Holden (provisional) ....Wake.
1866—Jonathan Worth ....Randolph.
1868—W. W. Holden ....Wake.
1870—Tod R. Caldwell ....Burke.
1874—Curtis H. Brogden ....Wayne.
1876—Z. B. Vance ....Buncombe.
1879—Thos. J. Jarvis ....Pitt.
1885—Alfred M. Scales ....Guilford.
1889—Daniel G. Fowle ....Wake.
1891—Thomas M. Holt ....Alamance.
1893—Elias Carr ....Edgecombe.
1897—Daniel L. Russell ....New Hanover.
1901—Charles B. Aycock ....Wayne.
1905—Robert B. Glenn ....Forsyth.

STATES IN THE UNION.

THIRTEEN ORIGINAL STATES.

The dates given show when they entered the Union by ratifying the Federal Constitution.

Delaware ....Dec. 7, 1787.
Pennsylvania ....Dec. 12, 1787.
New Jersey ....Dec. 18, 1787.
Georgia ....Jan. 2, 1788.
Connecticut ....Jan. 9, 1788.
Massachusetts ....Feb. 6, 1788.
Maryland ....April 28, 1788.
South Carolina ....May 23, 1788.
New Hampshire ....June 21, 1788.
Virginia ....June 25, 1788.
New York ....July 26, 1788.
North Carolina ....Nov. 21, 1789.
Rhode Island ....May 29, 1789.

The following States were admitted into the Union by a vote of Congress:

Vermont	Mar. 4, 1791.
Kentucky	June 1, 1792.
Tennessee	June 1, 1796.
Ohio	Nov. 29, 1802.
Louisiana	April 30, 1812.
Indiana	Dec. 11, 1816.
Mississippi	Dec. 10, 1817.
Illinois	Dec. 3, 1818.
Alabama	Dec. 14, 1819.
Maine	Mar. 15, 1820.
Missouri	Aug. 10, 1821.
Arkansas	June 15, 1836.
Michigan	Jan. 26, 1837.
Florida	Mar. 3, 1845.
Texas	Dec. 29, 1845.
Iowa	Dec. 28, 1846.
Wisconsin	May 29, 1848.
California	Sept. 9, 1850.
Minnesota	May 11, 1858.
Oregon	Feb. 14, 1859.
Kansas	Jan. 29, 1861.
West Virginia	June 19, 1863.
Nevada	Oct. 31, 1864.
Nebraska	Mar. 1, 1867.
Colorado	Aug. 1, 1876.
North Dakota	Nov. 2, 1889.
South Dakota	Nov. 2, 1889.
Montana	Nov. 8, 1889.
Washington	Nov. 11, 1889.
Idaho	July 3, 1890.
Wyoming	July 10, 1890.
Utah	Jan. 4, 1896.

Arizona, New Mexico, Oklahoma and Indian Territory will probably be admitted within the next year. The two former territories will be admitted as one State, and the latter two as one State.

Note.—Since writing the above, Oklahoma and Indian Territories have been admitted in the Union as one State named Oklahoma, and the other two were admitted upon the condition that their admission as one State, Arizona, is ratified by the voters.

PRESIDENTS OF THE UNITED STATES.

Elected for the following terms—
1789-1796—George Washington.
1796-1800—John Adams.
1800-1808—Thomas Jefferson.
1808-1816—James Madison.
1816-1824—James Monroe.
1824-1828—John Q. Adams.
1828-1836—Andrew Jackson.
1836-1840—Martin Van Buren.
1840-1844—William H. Harrison.
1844-1848—James K. Polk.
1848-1852—Zachary Taylor. He died, and Vice-President Millard Fillmore was sworn July 9, 1850.
1852-1856—Franklin Pierce.
1856-1860—James Buchanan.
1860-1864—Abraham Lincoln.
1864-1868—Abraham Lincoln. He was elected, but assassinated April 14, 1865, and Andrew Johnson, Vice-President, on April 15, 1865, was sworn in as President, and impeached and acquitted May 26, 1868.
1868-1876—U. S. Grant.
1876-1880—R. B. Hayes.
1880-1884—J. A. Garfield was elected, but was assassinated September 19, 1881, and Vice-President Chester A. Arthur sworn in as President, September 20, 1881.
1884-1888—Grover Cleveland.
1888-1892—Benjamin Harrison.

1892-1896—Grover Cleveland.

1896-1900—William McKinley.

1900-1904—William McKinley. He was assassinated September 6, 1901, and Theodore Roosevelt, Vice-President, was sworn in as President, September 15, 1901.

1904-1908—Theodore Roosevelt.

Henry Clay was defeated for President three times. Daniel Webster defeated once. John C. Calhoun was never a nominee for President. James G. Blaine defeated once, and William J. Bryan defeated twice. Thomas Jefferson was defeated once before he was elected. The eloquent John C. Breckenridge could never be elected President. It is no criterion that an officer is the greatest man and better qualified than others to fill the office. It very often happens that very inferior men are elected to fill the most important offices.

SOME USEFUL RULES FOR THE FARMER AND BUSINESS MAN.

HOW TO KEEP HAMS.

Rule 1.—After smoking them, take them down and thoroughly rub the flesh part with molasses, then immediately apply ground black pepper, as much as will stick to the molasses, then hang them up to dry. They will keep perfectly sweet, and insects will not appear on them.

Rule 2.—After your hams have taken salt, smoke them well, then take them down and dip them for a few seconds in boiling water. This will kill all eggs of insects, if any, then roll them in dry ashes while wet and rehang them. Resmoke them if you choose. The shoulders and sides may be treated in the same way. With this treatment bugs and skippers will never appear.

REMEDY FOR PEAR-TREE BLIGHT.

Mix one pint of common salt with four times its bulk of ashes. Spread around the roots a foot or more from trunk of tree, but do not let the mixture come in contact with tree.

MISCELLANEOUS INFORMATION.

HEALTH.

Avoid hog-pens near your residence. They breed fevers, sickness and death.

A DURABLE WHITEWASH.

The U. S. Government formula. The author has tried it and found it almost equal to oil paint.

To ten parts of good slack lime add one quart best hydraulic cement, or any other good quality of cement. (The Portland is the best cement.) Mix well with salt water and apply quite thin. There is no other whitewash equal to this.

HOW TO LOOK AFTER YOUNG CHICKENS.

Chicken lice go to the head of the chicken at night. When the young chicken is four or five days old, grease its head with lard. You may mix a little coal-oil with the lard if you choose.

YOUNG PIGS.

The summer is the time to look after your pigs and keep them healthy and in a thrifty condition. Never feed them with the larger hogs. Always have a pen with a slip for the pigs to get in, and feed them separate. You can teach the sow and pigs quickly to govern themselves to fit your rules.

HOW TO KILL IRISH POTATO BUGS.

Mix an ounce of London purple with three gallons of water, and by the use of a watering pot sprinkle the vines of the potatoes. The London purple is better than the Paris green.

HOW TO KEEP POTATOES.

Dust the floor of your bin with lime. Then lay the potatoes over six or seven inches deep, then dust well with lime again, and repeat the layer of potatoes, and so on. One bushel of lime will do for forty bushels of potatoes. The lime will improve the flavor of the potatoes, and is harmless.

HOW TO MEASURE CORN IN BULK.

Level the corn so as to get an even depth throughout the pile, then measure the length and breadth of the pile, and multiply the length by the breadth, which will give the number of cubic feet of the bulk of corn. Divide the product of the multiplication by 12, and the quotient will be the number of barrels of shelled corn in the bulk. Should there be a remainder, it will be so many twelfths of a barrel of shelled corn over.

LAND MEASUREMENT TABLE.

625 sq. links...................... 1 pole.
16 poles .... 1 sq. chain.
10 sq. chains .... 1 acre.
640 acres .... 1 sq. mile.

An acre is the unit of land measure, and is 10 sq. chains. A rood is a quarter of an acre, and contains 25,000 sq. links. A perch, or pole, or rod, is the 160th of an acre, and contains $30\frac{1}{4}$ sq. yards, or 625 sq. links. The Gunter's chain used by surveyors is 22 yards long, and divided into 100 links of 7 92-100 inches each. An acre embraces 10 sq. chains, or 100,000 sq. links. The outside measurements of land is estimated by running chains and links, and the contents by sq. chains and links.

HOW TO MEASURE LAND.

Multiply the length by the width (in rods) and divide the product by 160, and this will give the number of acres and hundredths of an acre. When the sides of the land are irregular and of unequal length, add them together and take one-half for the main length or width. Multiply this by the depth and divide by $31\frac{1}{2}$. This will give the number of acres in the piece of land. 21,500 cubic inches will contain ten bushels of shelled corn, but the same space filled with corn in the ear will shell out rather more than five bushels. These 21,500 cubic inches contain 12 cubic feet and 764 cubic

MISCELLANEOUS INFORMATION.   347

inches over. Two barrels or ten bushels of corn in the ear will generally in shelling overrun these 764 cubic inches.

HOW TO RID YOUR LAND OF STUMPS.

In the autumn bore a hole one or two inches in diameter, according to the size of the stump, about 18 inches deep. Fill this hole with one or two ounces of saltpetre, then fill the hole with water and plug it up close. Next spring take out the plug and fill it with kerosene oil and ignite it. The fire will soon burn the stump down to and throughout its roots.

HOW TO LAY OFF LOTS OF LAND.

In laying off small lots the following measurements will be found accurate and correct:

52½ feet square, or 2,722½ square feet, is 1-16 of an acre.
74 2-3 feet square, or 5,415 square feet, is ⅛ of an acre.
104⅛ feet square, or 10,590 square feet, is ¼ of an acre.
147½ feet square, or 21,780 square feet, is ½ of an acre.
208 2-3 feet square, or 43,560 square feet, is 1 acre.

HOW TO ASCERTAIN THE NUMBER OF FEET IN SCANTLING, JOISTS, PLANKS, SILLS, ETC

For scantlings, sills, joists, etc., multiply the width by the thickness and then multiply the result by the length, then divide the product by 12. This will give the number of square feet in the piece of timber. To measure boards multiply the length (in feet) by the width (in inches) and divide the product by 12. The result will be the number of square feet the board contains.

HANDY RULES TO CALCULATE INTEREST.

Rule 1.—For finding the interest on any principal for any number of days, multiply in each case the dollars by the number of days, and for ascertaining at the rate of
4 per cent, divide the amount by 90.
5 per cent, divide the amount by 72.

6 per cent, divide the amount by 60.
8 per cent, divide the amount by 45.
9 per cent, divide the amount by 40.

I hope interest will never get higher, so I will annex the table.

Rule 2.—Multiply the principal by the number of days; separate the right hand figure from the product and divide by 9, if the rate of interest is 4 per cent. If 5 per cent, multiply by number of days and divide by 72. If 6 per cent, multiply by number of days, separate the right hand figure and divide it by 6. If 8 per cent, multiply by the number of days and divide by 45.

The author never calculates interest according to the above rules, but follows the old established rules given in the academic arithmetics.

Rule 3.—For finding the interest on any principal for any number of days, the answer in each case being in cents, separate the two right hand figures to express it in dollars and cents. Four per cent, multiply the principal by the number of days to run; separate the right hand figure from the product and divide by 9. Five per cent, multiply by number of days and divide by 72. Six per cent, divide by 60. Seven per cent, divide by 57. Eight per cent, divide by 45.

FOR CHOLERA INFANTUM.

Two whites of two eggs well beaten; mix with pure water and one tablespoonful of orange-flower water and a little sugar, and give a tablespoonful every hour. It is said to cure the worst cases of cholera infanutm. The eggs cool and heal the bowels.

FOR CROUP.

Dip a flannel cloth in a mixture of sweet oil and kerosene oil and tie it around the child's throat at night, and he will be well by morning. The sweet oil prevents the kerosene oil from burning and taking the skin off.

Fullname Index

ABBOTT, J K 322 Joseph C 242
ABELL, A S 284
ACKERMAN, A T 87
ADAMS, John 88 105 343 John Q 343 W J 284
ADKINS, A B 271 Albert B 298 David 271 299 James F 218 Thomas 271 299 Wade H 271 299 Willam D 196
AGATHA, Sarah 93
AIKIN, Jeremiah 106 Jeremiah D 106
ALEXANDER, John 36 John G 283 Nathaniel 340 Tibbs 70 W B 332-333
ALINEMAN, Ebenezer P 140
ALLEN, A J 294 Hester 294 William 20 Wright 142 146
ANDERSON, Elizabeth 184 J A 141 170 185 J L 333 James 18 James L 185 258 272 323 John A 31 107 140 161 183-185 191 224 245 258 315 327 331 Jos 49 Mr 184
ANDREWS, Richard 70 William 106 Wm 107
ANNE, Queen Of England 180 202

ANTHONY, Lord Ashley 10
ARCHDALE, John 13
ARCHER, Armstrong 69 Caleb 69 Elijah 106 Evans 69 Jacob 69 Mathuel 106 Peggy 69 Thomas 70 Wm 69
ARENDELL, F B 301
ARNOLD, Benedict 54
ARPS, Geo L 217 Mrs George L 288
ARTHUR, Chester A 256 343
ASHE, Samuel 340
ASKEW, 205 299-300 A J 32 134 195 Aaron 69 Abner H 135 Andrew J 167 Annie 134 167 Annie Sharp 135 Charnady 70 Cullen 69 David 195 David O 134-135 141 318-319 Edward 195 George 106 134-135 George O 134 J O Jr 308 James 69-70 Jerre D 129 Jerry D 139 John O 32 61 134-135 John O Jr 135 194 John O Sr 197 Joseph 135 Len 220 Levinia 195 Mary 69 Mary A 32 Mary R 61 135 Pattie E 135 Priscilla 70 R J 218 R W 218 Richard W 218 Sarah A 61 Shadrack 70

ASKEW (cont.)
  W D 135 W S 135 Willie 135
  Wm 69 Zack 70 Zeph 229
  Zephaniah 332
ATKINS, Jonas 106 Josiah I 106
AUMACK, Nancy 194 S M 228
  324-325 333 S M Jr 248-249
  Samuel M 248 298 331 Samuel
  M Sr 194 248
AVENZAZA, Gen 112
AVERY, W W 209
AYCOCK, Charles B 287 290 341
BABB, James D 93
BACON, James 70
BADGER, Thomas 193
BAILEY, 292 Wm 70
BAKER, 205 300 303 Agatha 52
  Anne 52 Annie 190 Benj 42 70
  Blake 72 Bray 51 Dr 118
  Elizabeth 52 110 Gen 52 117
  119 Henry 18 36 51 57 59
  316-317 Isaac 106-107 J H Jr
  283 John 26 34 36-37 42 59
  106 317 332 John B 49 53 158
  John Burgess 52 Judith 52
  Katharine 51 Lawrence 37 39-
  40 47-49 51-52 59 65 110 158
  162 190 316 Lawrence S 53
  Maj 39 Maria 52 Martha
  Susanna 52 Mary Wynns 53
  159 Matthias 141 Miss 162
  297 Nathan 106 Pembroke 308
  Richard 53 Richard B 117
  Simmons J 52-53 Susan J 158
  224 William 47 51 59 William
  J 53 Wm 317 Zadoc 71
BALEY, Wm 71
BALLARD, Susanna 110
BALLESTER, William 106
BANCROFT, 9 11 131
BANK, 300
BANKS, Alexander 71 98 108 Benj
  71 Elizabeth 129 G W 217
  Hardy 105 Hardy M 107 129
  140 Hardy Murfree 41 James

BANKS (cont.)
  141 161 Jas 140 Mary 129 Mrs
  James 87 Sally 98 Thomas 36
BANN, Jesse B 151
BANNER, William 70
BARDEN, James 71 Wm 71
BARFIELD, James 36 Richard 36
  Thomas 36 William 36
BARKER, Thomas 18 Thos 16-17
BARNES, 205 300 Bettie 238-239
  Collin W 238-239 D A 192
  230-231 238 David A 238-239
  287 324 David Alexander 330
  David Collin 238 315 330
  George Badger 239 George H
  292 J W 32 James 106 161 187
  331 James C 225 319 Jesse 175
  Jethro W 101 186-187 293 332
  Joseph 217 Joseph B 239 Judge
  238-239 Louisa 238 Mary 173
  Mrs David A 288 Priscilla 292
  R T 217 Randolph 71 Richard
  175 Samuel 219 Sarah 180
  Thomas 175 180 274 W D 180
  William Deanes 109 180
BARRETT, Mary 157 Thomas 20
BARROW, John 71
BASS, Willis 71
BASSET, Eliz 71
BATTLE, A J 164 James W 221
  John 70 221 Josiah 105 Kemp
  P 306 Martha 70 Miss 236 N J
  221 William 19-20 37
BATTON, John 70
BAYARD, James A 105 Thos F 263
BAYER, John 71
BAYFIELD, Thomas 289
BEAL, Drewry W 170 J R 217 Miss
  172
BEAMAN, Annie 307 Cullin 70 J
  T 220 John 70 Manning 70
  Nathaniel 307 W P 228-229
  307
BEASLEY, J W 320 S M 323
BELCH, Elisha 71

BELL, Francis 70 Henry W 129
  James 70 John 104 Louisa 104
  Martha A 94 Samuel 94 332
  Winnifred 249
BEMBURY, 66 Jane 126 John 126
BENBERRY, Bryan 70
BENBURY, John 18
BENSON, Exekel 71
BENTHALL, Daniel 71 Jack 155
  John 106 148 Joseph 70 Miss
  154
BENTON, Elizabeth 294 John 37
BERKLEY, William 10-11
BERRY, Geo 49
BEST, David R 71 Henry 71 Mary
  71 Thomas 71 Wm 70
BEVERLEY, 299-300
BEVERLY, 205 A Bascom 268
  Allen 268 Benj 268 Benj F 197
  268 G W 187 229 Geo W 228
  268 George W 267-268 324-
  325 328 333 John 36 Mary E
  268
BIGGS, Asa 197 Kader 157 Lucy A
  157
BIRD, Edward 36 John 36 Mary 70
  Robert 72
BISHOP, Jesse 70 John 70
BIZELL, Solo 71
BIZZETT, John 106
BLACKSTONE, 34
BLACKWELL, Julia 98
BLAINE, James G 344
BLAKE, Eliz 72 Ellis Gray 71
  Joseph 13
BLANCHARD, Kate 127 Miles 71
  Zilpha 47
BLARE, Benj 107
BLOUNT, Bartha 176 Edmond
  121 Jacob 17 Joseph 18
  Marietta 121 Miss 194
  Penelope 97 Richard 176 Sarah
  176 Sharp 97 328-329
BOGART, John H 120 Mr 120
BOLTON, Jane 70 Thomas 70
BONAPARTE, Napoleon 125

BOND, G H 86 Geo H 107 Sally
  86 Virginia 164 W M 164
  William E 164 Wm M 322
BOON, David 42 James 36 326
  William 36
BOONE, Abram 106 Allen 71
  Arthur 70 Capt 221 296 David
  107 James 48 John 266 Judith
  296 Julith 266 L Wash 230
  Lewis 106 Lucy T 266 Mary 71
  Nicholas 71 Samuel 106
  Thomas D 154 218 221 267
  329 Thomas Deanes 109 Thos
  D 296 West 106 William 107
  266-267 296 Willie 154 296
BOOTH, Alexander 106 Arthur
  105 John Wilkes 226 Katharine
  51
BORLAND, 205 300 Armstead 95
  Dr 93 Elizabeth R 93-94 Euclid
  93-95 161 Harriott Godwin 95
  Phogian A 95 R C 161 319
  Roscius C 95 148 328 Roscius
  Cicero 93-94 329 Solon 93-94
  161 316 Thomas 93 128 133
  139 148 Thomas R 148
  Thomas Roscius 95
BOROUGHS, Hardy 70 Sam 70
  Sarah 70
BOUTWELL, Adam 70
BOWSER, Thomas 71
BOYETTE, Charles 251 Harriet
  151 Miss 251 Tempance O 251
  W J 253
BRAGG, Gov 151 197 Thomas
  150 197 340
BRAMBLE, Bryant 108
BRANCH, Geo R 60 John 116 340
  W A B 278
BRANTLEY, Benj 72 Edward 106
  Henry 106-107 Robert 106
BRAY, Angelico 51 W H 323
BRECKENRIDGE, 259
BRECKINRIDGE, John C 344
BRETT, 205 300 Alex 229
  Alexander 292 Amanda 152

BRETT (cont.)
  171 Auquilla 152 Benjamin
  235 Elisha D 95 161 170 293
  331 Elizabeth 118 G A 229
  George A 121 172 George
  Culbret 171 Henry 152 Henry
  C 171 J D 221 J E 221 John
  220 Mills 118 Miss 95 Priscilla
  292 R T 220 William 118 221
BREWER, 302 Jesse 71 John B 182
BRICKLE, 64 66 205 Aaron 70
  Col 31 128 James 128 133
  John 30 34 63 70 317 Jonathan
  72 Levinia Bembury 31
  Matthias 24 26 29 31 36-37 39-
  40 42 45 48 72 194 315 317
  326-327 332 Matthias Jr 326
  Sarah 45 Thomas 41 63
  Thomas N 327 Thos 317 Thos
  N 71 Wm 72
BRICKLES, Mathias 68
BRIDGER, John P 149 186 190
  326 Joseph 71 Josiah 149
  Roswell C 315 330
BRIDGERS, Joseph 36
BRIDGES, Benj 36
BRITT, Abram 71 Arelius 217
  Arthur 71 Benj 71 E D 140
  185 Elisha D 186-187 Elizabeth
  155 G A 332 Geo P 155 James
  71 James E 155 Joseph 71
  Martin 71 Mills 155 Miss 155
  Silas 71 Thomas 71 Thomas P
  155 William 155
BRITTON, Benj 71 D R 61
  Martha 156 Michael 140
  Samuel 106 Thomas 106 W P
  140 156 271 299
BROGDEN, Curtis H 341
BROWN, 66 144 299-300 A M
  308 Anthony 106 Archer 274
  Benj 36-37 48 71 106 275 Benj
  Jr 37 Bettie 274 Eliza 71
  Elizabeth 71 Francis 70 Fred 72
  G V 308 Geo A 296 George A
  296 331 Grace 274 H J 308

BROWN (cont.)
  Ida 274 J A 140 James 70 Janie
  296 Jennie 163 225 274
  Jeremiah 37 70 Jno 31 John 17
  31 34 36 45 70 106 184 203
  245 John Jr 45 Joseph J 331
  Lewis 70 72 317 Martha
  Broadus 274 Mary 110 137
  Mary E 245 296 Nancy 100
  245 O B 137 Patrick 65 71 92
  108 184 235 Rhoderick 71
  Richard 72 S J S 163 Samuel 70
  110 245 Sarah 31 72 Sophia 71
  Stephen 71 Susan 32 Thomas
  70 Thos E 274 W T 180 274
  333 Wiley 106 William 106
  Wm 106 Wm D 274 Zachariah
  106
BROWNE, John 16
BRUSE, Abram 71 Bennet 71
BRYAN, Edward 17 Needham 17
  Thos 17 William J 344 Wm J
  305
BRYANT, Benj 161 Davis 169 Lucy
  169 Needham 17 Thomas 16
  W D 236
BUCHANAN, James 343 Pres 213
BUCKLEY, Roland 289
BULLOCK, Miss 271 299
BURBAGE, Aromitta 171 Landon
  308 T I 248 Thos 171
BURGESS, Maria 52 Mr 110
  Priscilla 110 Thomas 52
BURKE, Thomas 41 339
BURKITT, John Jr 57 John Sr 57
  Lemuel 56-57 101-102 316
BURNS, R 140
BURR, Aaron 88
BURRINGTON, George 14 339
BURTON, Hutchings G 340 John
  42 71 Mr 45 Priscilla 269
BUTLER, Dr 280-282 Marion 276
  280 William 42
BUTTS, Peter 124 330
BYNUM, Annie 100 Blanche 292
  Mary 100 W F 60 266

BYNUM (cont.)
   W T 128-129 266 292 294
   William T 100
BYRAM, Jno 70 Thos 70
CAIL, Jeremiah 72
CALDWELL, Judge 192 Tod R 341
CALF, James 72
CALHOUN, John C 344
CAMP, Benj B 100 Benjamin B
   140-141 149 Betsy 172 Col 100
   James L 154 Joseph R 149 Julia
   E 149 Leonidas 149 Mary Ann
   100 William 100
CAMPBELL, Col 54 John 17 20
CANBY, Edw S 230 240 Gen 230-231 320
CANIDY, John 72
CANLESS, Nancy 98
CAPEHART, 205 300 B A 187
   Caroline 117 120 Mrs Tristram
   117 Tristram 108 117 120 140-141
CAREY, Thos 14
CARLYLE, D D 284
CARR, Elias 276 284 341 Gov 325
   Lawrence 72 Matthew 72
   Robert 37 72
CARTER, 205 300 303 Abner A
   155 D 140 Dodge 271 Edw J
   270 Eley 252 270-271 Ellen V
   270 Ely 245 Giles 42 Ida 172
   Isaac 41 72 133 144-145 318-319 326 Isaac Jr 145 Isaac Sr
   145 J A 221 271 James 73 John
   271 Joseph E 172 268 329
   Lazarus 145 Lewis 72 106 Maj
   145 Martha 73 271 Mrs Perry
   124 Parthenia 145 Patrick 36
   Perry 140 200 225 252 270-271
   Polly 252 Priscilla 270 Rev 270
   Sallie 133 Sally 136 Susan E
   200 Tom Bragg 271
CARTERET, George 10 Lord 336 339
CARTWRIGHT, Geo 12

CASTELLOW, James 16-17 Wm 108
CASWELL, Gov 63 Richard 39 41 47 92 339
CATHCART, William 19-20 Wm 17
CHAMBERLAIN, John L 321
CHAMBERS, Edward 200 Margaret 200
CHAMBLEE, Elisha A 137 139 319 Elizabeth 171 James B 195 John 171 Mary 171 Mrs 196 Nannie 195 William 171
CHARLES, II King Of ? 11 15 29 137 339
CHARLES, II King Of England 10 14
CHATHAM, Lord 38
CHAVIS, Caesar 42
CHERRY, James 72 326
CHILD, Thomas 18
CHRISTIA, David 72 James 72
CHRITENTON, Eliz 72
CILLEY, 231
CLARK, Henry T 223 340 Reuben 106 S D 141 Stephen 72 Thomas 106
CLARKE, Kerney 72 Susan 162-163 William 163 Wm 72
CLAY, Henry 105 344
CLEMENT, 300
CLEMENTS, Moses 124 128
CLEVELAND, 147 Grover 263 343-344 Pres 242
CLIFTON, Jonas 107
CLINGMAN, Thomas L 197
CLINTON, Henry 54
COBB, A J 220 C L 239 Clinton L 240
COKE, Octavius 321
COKELEY, Benjamin 67
COLEMAN, 205 300 Thomas 41 72
COLLETON, John 10
COLLINS, Annis 98 Josiah 65

COLLINS (cont.)
  Miss 124 William 124
CONNER, A J 335
CONNOR, Demsey 65
COOK, Charles 72 Daniel 73
  Mathias 107 Richard A 220
COOKE, Benj 72
COOPER, 215 Ashley 11 Edward
  214-215 Lucy 215 Mary 215
COPELAND, Eli 72 F Q 217
  Hollowell 72 James 25 60 73
  125 133 294 318 Jas 318 John
  72 125 Mary 72 Sarah 25 138
  234 Stephen 73 Thomas 72
  Thos 72
CORBIN, Francis 18
CORNELIUS, Martha 72
CORNWALLIS, 46 55 Gen 54-55
COSTER, Langdon 63
COTTON, 144 205 299 Arthur 31
  Betsey 31 Ester 124 Esther 224
  Godwin 26 31 41 72 149 332
  James 72 John 31 Miss 180
  Nathan 47 68 317 Noah 72
  Sam 72 Thomas 72 Wm 72
COULLING, J D 225
COULLINGS, James D 183
COWPER, 205 300 303 G V 324
  George 59 168 221 236 286
  322 325 330 333 George V
  315 L M 98 228 Lewis M 98
  124 133 146 168 236 328
  Lewis Meredith 91 Louis M 139
  Mary 127 173 Mrs William 91
  Pulaski 124 197 329 R G 124
  142 162-163 191 193 200-201
  227 236 286 316 319 326 R L
  124 Rebecca 93 Richard G 167
  227 319 Richard Green 139
  Richard Greene 91 326 Virginia
  R 236 William 91 168 Wm 93
  168 173
CRADDOCK, Charles Egbert 104
CRAIG, Burton 210
CRAWFORD, Lee 283
CREEL, Epenetus 217

CRETCHILOR, Providence 72
CROSS, David C 140 Miss 236
  Nancy 100 R 141 Riddick 140
  Stephens 72
CROW, Eliz 73
CRUGER, James 72
CRUMP, Edward 106
CRUTCHELOW, Anna 195
CRYER, Samuel 36
CULLEN, W E 279 William E 327
  Willie Pauline 295
CULLENS, Mr 295 Nathaniel L
  294 Sarah 294 W E 333-334
  William E 292 294
CULLON, Willie 106
CULPEPPER, 12-13
CUNNINGHAM, Alex 107
  Duncan 107 John I 107 John S
  306 Lancaster 107
CURL, John 106
CURTIS, K R 308 W L 308
DANEY, James 20
DANIEL, 299 Belcher 193-195 248
  Capt 194 Goodwin Daniel 107
  Joseph 73 Julia 193 Maj 193-
  194 Nancy 194 Nannie 195
  Robert 14 Spencer 194 Thomas
  139 W L 187 229 262 296 319
  Watson L 193-194 248 327
  Watson Lewis 331 Wm R 108
DARDEN, 205 A C 165 221 A W
  164 Alfred M 165 219 Alfred
  W 164 191 Betsy 244 Bettie
  165 Carr 139 149 David 73
  Edward R 85 Elisha 73
  Elizabeth 118 Elizabeth J 118
  Harriet 171-172 Harriet T 118
  Henry 73 Henry G 106 Indiana
  164 Jacob 164 James C 118
  James H 118 155 James P 218
  Jet 73 85 Jethro 73 85 103 118
  148 292 317-318 Jethro R 85
  161 John 73 John A 85 Maggie
  165 Margaret R 118 Miss 124
  Mrs A W 190 Penelope 85
  Pompey 221 Sam 73

DARDEN (cont.)
  Samuel A 85 Samuel G 142
  Sarah E 85 Titus 117-118 148
  171-172 Virginia 164 William
  187 William H 118 William S
  164 Willis 73
DARE, Virginia 10
DAUGHTIE, James 73 Jethro 73
  Wm 73
DAUGHTRY, Eliz 73 Helen 225
  Wm H 225
DAVIDSON, A F 210 Thomas 42
DAVIE, William R 340
DAVIS, Amy 199 Blake 73 George
  209 Hardy 106 Jefferson 212
  222 Joseph H 183 L S 332
  Luke 73 Mary 73 Sam 73
DAWLEY, John 108
DAWSON, John 16-19
DAY, D A 263 David A 150 Eunice
  263 Ruth 263 Ruth R 150 W B
  187
DEANES, C T 218 Christianna
  234 Daniel 73 109 James 73
  Jesse 124 326 Judith 296 Julith
  266 Malissa Anne 297 Mary
  251 Mike 297 Norma I 271
  Sarah 180 Susan 201 297 T
  Jefferson 271 Thomas 73 91
  103 109 149 266 296-297 326
  Thomas J 161 Thomas Jr 297
  Thos 180 W D 271 Wm 73
DEANS, Thomas 318
DEANSE, 300
DEBERRY, Benj 20 Henry 67 John
  19
DELKE, James 149 James A 149-
  150 Rev 149-150 Susan 149
  Susan Bats 149
DELOATCH, Etta P 60 John 293
  K S 293 Kezia 293 Mary W
  293 Susan R 60
DEMING, Emelius 36
DENNIS, Littleton 73
DENTON, James 73 John 106
  Polly 73

DICKERSON, John 73 Joseph F
  159 Peggy 159
DICKINSON, 66 205 300 Daniel
  35 David 104 Fannie Priscilla
  104 Gen 86 105 123 139 294
  John 91 107 Jos 317 Jos F 125
  164 Joseph 26 42 47 Joseph F
  47 60 91 105 108-109 123 139
  298 328 Joseph Jr 123 Joseph
  Sr 123 Louisa 104 Patsy 91
  Peggy 123
DILDAY, Joseph 73
DILLARD, Anne Maria 236 Bettie
  191 James 236
DIXON, B F 307
DOBBS, Arthur 14 22 339 Gov 22
DOSSEY, William 177
DOUGHTIE, S J 220 W R 140
DOUGLAS, 87 James 86 124 Rev
  86-87
DOWD, W C 284
DOWNING, Wm 73 106
DREW, John 19 Richard 73
DREWRY, John C 239 William H
  239 Wm S 143
DRINKARD, John B 191
DRIVER, Boan 107 John 73
  Martha 73 Sam 73
DRUMMOND, Geo 12 George 11
DUDLEY, Edward B 340
DUER, 185 Andrew V 124 140
  142 148 184-185 330 Ann 73
  Harriet 184 Leven 184
  Margaret 184 Miss 194
  Thomas 139
DUFFY, Rudolph 283
DUKE, 300 John 19 42
DUKES, James 36 John 20
DUNFORD, Bettie 165
DUNMORE, Gov 46
DUNN, 300 George 73 Sarah A
  252
DUNNING, Jennie 274 Sam 73
  Wm 274
DUNSTON, Dr 188 Edw F 187
  245 Edward F 161 188

DUNSTON (cont.)
  Gussie 188 Henry V 188 John 188 Josephine J 188 Mr 189 Mrs 189 William E 188
DURBAR, Mr 119
DYER, John J 188 Josephine 188 R O 188
EARLY, James 106 John 27 Thomas 107
EASON, Miss 172
EASTCHURCH, Geo 12-13
ECHOLS, Mrs Wm J 271 Wm J 271
EDEN, Charles 14
EDES, Stephen 74
EDMONDS, Nicholas 67
EDMUNDS, Howell 67
EDWARD, Earl Of Clarendon 10
EDWARDS, Henry C 239 J G 294 J H 284 John 17 19 Martha 294
ELDRIDGE, Alberta 291 Anna 291 Cora 291 Dr 291 Eva 291 John 291 John Turner 291 Rydie 291
ELERTON, Thomas 107
ELEY, Edward 73 Ely 37 J M 286 333 John 268 297 Lawrence 170 Lila 268 Michael 73
ELIZABETH, Queen Of England 10
ELLIOTT, James I 333
ELLIS, Gov 223 John W 340 Mollie 235
ELY, Samuel 107
ENDICOTT, W C 263
ETHERIDGE, J B 283 Martha 134
EURE, Burwell 106 Henry 106 Mills L 50
EVANS, Benj 73 Cornelius 73 Francis 74 J B 217 Media 220 Noah 106 Peter 74 Robert 74 Thomas 74 Wm 73-74
EVARTS, Edwin 164
EVERARD, Gov 14 Richard 14

EVERETT, 299 James 74 John 106 John L 219 L F 216 Polly 31
EVERTS, Edwin 61
EWART, 281
EXUM, James Thomas 199 Joseph J 199 Lavinia Esther Wilkinson 199 Martha A 199 Mary Thomas 199 Pattie A 198
EZELL, Benj 74 106
FAIRCLOTH, 114-115 Judge 267 Thomas 107 113 115 Tom 114 W T 115 William T 266
FAIRLEN, Zadoc 74
FAIRLESS, Robert 74 Wm 74
FAISON, Mrs J W 185 Mrs William 239
FARRAR, Martha Broadus 274
FAUNEY, Wm 74
FAWN, Ann 74
FELLS, Edw 74
FELTON, 205 Boon 126 199 Boone 91 103 318 Elisha 74 108 Gen 92
FERGUSON, Blount 171 274 Joshua 274
FIELD, Meredith 253
FIGURES, Bartholomew 67 John 20 Matthew 67 Nathaniel 67 Thomas 67 74 William 67 Wm 74
FILLMORE, Millard 343
FINNEY, 300 Thomas S 129 W H 129 William H 149
FLOWER, Gov 194 Julia 193 248 Rand 74
FLYTHE, J H 195
FORBES, Tulley M Jr 297
FOREY, 300 302 Dr 182 Martin Rudolph 182
FOSTER, Charles H 200 230 330 Isaac 106 James 74 Robert 19
FOWLE, D G 231 Daniel G 272 341 Gov 272
FRAETOR, Canozio 191
FRANCIS, Sterling 107

FRANKLIN, Jesse 340
FRASER, 126 Elizabeth 104 Henry 104 Sarah Murfree 104
FRAZIER, Capt 126 James 60 124 126 Jane 126 Jno H 318 Jno Hamilton 318 John H 103 John Hamilton 60 126 149 Mrs James 60
FREEMAN, 303 Annie 266 Bertie 295 Carrie 267 Dr 267 Edmond B 86 Eliza 189 George 267 George King 267 Hiram 224 295 J O 86 J P 297 333 James P 266-267 296 331 John 266 268 Jonathan Otis 86 Josiah 74 Julia 266 Lila 268 Louisa 295 Lucy T 266 Mary E 266 268 Mrs Dr 267 Rev 86 Sallie 266 Sarah 266 Sheriff 266 268 William G 265-266 William George 266
FUDGE, Harvey 114-115 Willis 114
FUTRELL, Micajah 107 Winborne 107
GALE, Chief Justice 96
GALLATIN, Albert 105
GALLOP, W C 283
GANES, Anthony 74
GANEY, George 68 253
GARFIELD, J A 343 James A 255
GARIBALDI, 112
GARLAND, Augustus H 263
GARNER, Thos J 201
GARRETT, A E 295 307 327 Everett 105 James 49 317 Joseph 47 Joshua 197 Mary 197 Minnie 295 Mr 192 Rev 197 Thomas 18 Thos M 192
GARRISS, Mary 237 Peter 294 Sarah 294 Wade H 60 237
GARVEY, Patrick 74
GARY, Cora 291 Dr 291 R H 291 Richard Henry 291 Roderick B 292 Roderick H 291
GASTON, William 128

GATES, Gen 54
GATLING, 300 Arthur 74 Catherine 274 David 74 Dr 174-175 Edw 74 Elizabeth 173 Hardy 74 Isaac 175 J J 322 James 74 173 James H 175 Jefferson Davis 259 Jemima 175 Jethro 74 Jno D 229 John D 164 219 Jordan 171 173 Lilly 164 Mary 173 175 244 Mrs Jordan 180 Polly 173 R B 217 Rachel 74 Rebecca 175 Richard H 175 Richard J 177 274 Richard Jordan 161 173 Temperance 252 Thomas Barnes 175 W J 332 William J 161 329 Wm 74 Wm Cowper 173 Wm J 175 262
GAY, 300 Boble 42 Charles 149 173 Elizabeth 173 James 74 John 74
GEORGE, Duke Of Albemarle 10
GEORGE, II King Of ? 16 36
GEORGE, III King Of ? 16
GEORGE, III King Of England 38 105
GIBBES, Robert 13
GIBBONS, Cardinal 308
GILLAM, 249
GILLIAM, H A 192 John 19 Julia 274 Mary 293
GLENN, Benj 107 Mark 107 R B 304 306 Robert B 341 Sampson 107
GLISTON, Daniel 74
GLOVER, William 14 Wm 74
GODWIN, A D 333 Barney 74 Cornelius H 106 Harriet 93 John 74 Kerney 74 Tempance O 251
GOOCH, William 246
GOODMAN, David 74
GORDON, 254 300 Barsha 86 123 184 George 86 108 123 139 328 330 Jemima 123 John H 124 330 John Hare 123

GORDON (cont.)
  Patsy 123
GOULD, George 17
GRAHAM, Chancey 74 Stephen 149 William A 340
GRANBURY, 299 John 139-140
GRANDY, C W 321
GRANT, 223 Gen 226 310-311 U S 87 213 343
GRANTHAM, James 74
GRAVES, Miss 153
GRAVIER, Sarah 135
GREEN, Joseph 74 Thomas 42
GREENE, Gen 54
GREGORY, Casper W 159 Isaac 65 Mary A 159 Mary Wynns 53 158 P C 159 Peggy 123 Thomas 123
GRIFFIN, Benj 107 Gilbert 107 James 107 James H 218 John 36 Sallie 234 W J 322 Walter M 234
GRIFFITH, 253 Bunnell 74 Hartwell 74 Jno 74 John 252 Martha 252 Temperance 252 Thomas 140 252 William 198 253
GRIMES, Geo W 220 James L 185
GRIZZARD, J N 283 Joel 107
GRONER, Lawrence D 204
GUION, O H 304
GUNDY, Felix 59
GURLEY, 66 John 25 93 Sarah 25 Sarah A 93 Wm 36
HACKETT, Redmond 65
HAINE, Benj 75 Jesse 76
HALE, Fereby 76 L 308
HALL, C J 148 James 42 Job R 129 John 148 Judge 190-191 Mary 76 Sallie 190 Sarah M 129 Viola 251
HALSEY, William 18
HAMILTON, Alexander 88
HANCE, Judge 99 Tibbie 99
HANDCOCK, Nehemiah 75
HANDSFORD, Thos 17

HARDY, Charles 172 Eleanor 166 Elleanor 176 Humphrey 166 Rebecca 172 Robert 17 34
HARE, 205 300 Aaron 106 Bryan 24 32 Charity 32-33 Edw 36 Edward 24 32 48 68 300 317 Eliza E 32 Elizabeth 129 Elizabeth R 32 Emma 32 Francis 32 J B 228 Jackson B 83 230 244 284 316 320 326 332 Jacob 32 106 124 139 145 300 319 Jamima 32 166 Jemima 123 Jesse 32 34 John 32 75 244 John P 107 Luke 106 Mary 32 202 Mary A 32 Moses 32 36 Moses Jr 32 Moses Sr 32 Sarah 25 138 Starkey 323 Starkey S 32 Starkey S Jr 32 Thomas 32 300 Thomas E 32 Thos E 25 32 145
HARPER, Thos J 176
HARREL, John W 332 Marvin 252
HARRELL, 123 135 205 299 303 — - 275 A B 197 Abner 35 128 134 139-140 164 196-197 225 236 241 268 Amanda C 127 249-250 Andrew 196 Andrew J 249 251 Anna 197 Artemus 197 Bessie 251 Capt 218 Caroline 195 Cecil W 251 Charles 252 Charles E 251 Col 249-250 Cola R 251 Edw 35 Edw Jr 36 Eli 107 Elijah 75 Elizabeth 25 85-86 275 Ellen O 100 250 Florie 251 George 250-251 George T 196 Gertrude 250 H D 219 332 Herbert B 197 Hiram 195 Hiram P 196 Isaac 196 J N 100 117 217 251 333 J Norfleet 333 J W 229 332 James 196 Jarret 251 Jarret N 249 Jarret Norfleet 249 Jarrett N 127 Jesse 37 75 Jethro 37 Jno W 229 John 16-17 36 42 48 249 251 326

HARRELL (cont.)
 John Abner 197 John H 251-252 John Jr 17 36 John Sr 17 36 John W 127 161 232 249-251 Joseph 249-250 L R 197 Linda 250 Maj 196 250 Marvin Hall 252 Mary 75 86 186 196-197 251 Melissa 197 Nancy 86 166 196 Nathan 25 76 85-86 93 166 186 326-327 330-331 Nicholas 219 Noah 196 Paul 251 Roberta 251 S S 229 231 239 Sally 86 Samuel 36 56-58 86 196 316 327 331 Sarah M 129 251 Starkey S 86 328-329 Starkey S Jr 86 185 328 331 Starkey S Sr 149 186 Starkey Sharp 86 Viola 251 William B 196 Willis 196 Winnifred 249 Wm 75 Wm J 197
HARRELSON, H M 283
HARRINGTON, E J 283
HARRIS, Arthur 19 Judge 136 Miss 136
HARRISON, 325 Benjamin 272 343 James 75 James C 107 Jesse 106 Thos 75 William H 343 Wm 76
HART, 300 Betsy 120 Bettie 191 Carrie 267 Dred 267 Fannie 191 John 75 120 191
HARVEY, John 13 38 Thomas 13
HASSEL, James 14
HAWKINS, Ann 97 Mrs T W 288 Philemon Jr 97 William 340
HAYES, Ezekel 75 Fannie 295 James 106 Joseph 75 Marmaduke 75 Minnie 295 Mrs Horatio 178-179 R B 254-255 343 T C 295 Thomas 36 Wm 76
HAYS, William 170
HAYWOOD, John 33 Sherwood 33 Stephen 33 William 33 Wm 32 Wm H 33 Wm H Jr 33
HEATH, Judge 192

HENDERSON, Leonard 148 Richard 49 W H 96
HENDRICKS, Thomas A 263
HENRY, Patrick 42 Roderick 292
HERON, Joseph 18
HERRING, M R 308
HEWES, Joseph 39
HICHBORN, Emily M 93
HICKS, John W 335
HIGGINS, J H 284 R C 283
HILL, 205 300 Barshaba 119 Ben 254 Benj 16-18 35 106 Benjamin 105 Charles 75 E L 169 Green 20 Hardy 75 Harry 41 59 64 84 Henry 26 34 36 57 59 75 84 96 316-318 328-329 Henry Jr 85 Isaac 16 J W 234 James W 115 Jas W 236 John 17 75 Joseph 76 Margaret L 169 Michael 75 Sallie 119 Sarah 176 Whitmel 65 Whitmell 75 William 64 317
HILLMAN, J H 104
HINES, A P 229 Elias C 50 165 William 35
HINTON, 103
HIPTON, Wm 75
HITCHBORNE, John 75
HOBBS, Abram 75 Elisha 75 Jacob 75 Miles 106 Sarah 76 Wm 75
HOCAL, Benj 107
HOGGARD, J J 220 Thomas 108 Tixon 170
HOLDEN, 228 230-231 Gov 232 240 255-256 W W 222 231 239 341
HOLLAND, Hezekiah 76 Thomas 106 Thos 75
HOLLEY, Bettie 165 William J 165
HOLLODAY, Capt 293
HOLLOMAN, Aaron 75 Christopher 75 Cornelius 75 David 75 Geo Jr 106 Grace 274 Hanche 75 J P 274 John 75 244 Joseph 220 Justin 106 Lemuel 106 Malichi 75

HOLLOMAN (cont.)
  Pauline 237 Samuel 75 332
  Silvia 75 W D 184 229 237
HOLLOMON, Kinchen 42 Kindred 229
HOLLOWAY, Susan Bats 149
HOLMES, Gabriel 340
HOLT, Thomas M 272 306 341
HOOKER, James 36 John 19 T B 284
HOOPER, 302 William 39 182 Wm 201
HORTON, Elisha 106 Eliz 75 Hugh 75 J J 152 231 323 Janie J 294 Jordan J 233 243 294 316 322 331 Matthew 75 Williford 75 Wm 76
HOUGH, Daniel 24
HOUSE, J A 283
HOWARD, Annie 200 Elisha 75 James 69 Luke 75 Martin 49 Moses 75 W O 283 William 200
HOWE, Col 41 Robert 39
HOWELL, Euclid 221 John 76 Lemuel 244 Stephen 107 Watson S 221
HUGHES, Henry 197
HUMPHRY, Wm 75
HUNTER, Isaac K 108 Miss 25 Nancy 133 166 Robert 17 William 18
HUTCHING, 300
HUTCHINGS, 205 Dr 235 William 97 235 William H 235 Wm H 97
HUTCHINS, — 75 Aaron 75 Wm 75
HYDE, Edward 14
IREDELL, James 340 Judge 64-65
IRELAND, Grofton 76
IVES, Sam 76
JACK, Capt 240
JACKSON, 193 Andrew 122 343 Isaac 76 Jesse A 192 Lon 76
JARNAGAN, Spencer 186

JARVIS, John 255 Thomas J 255 Thos J 280 341
JAY, John 44
JEFFERSON, Thomas 83 88 132 343-344
JEFFRIES, Osborn 19
JEGGITT, 205
JEGGITTS, 300 Barshaba 119 Edw K 119 124 142 326 Edw R 119 Edward K 140 Frank 119 John 119 L M 225 Lewis M 119 139 318 Maggie 119 Mrs Frank 118-119 Sallie 119 Sheriff 119 William 119
JEGITTS, 119
JENKINS, 218 300 Benj 76 107 Charles 76 106 Dempsey 76 H J 220 Henry 76 188 Henry Deberry 106 288 Herbert 308 Irvin 106 Irwin 105 James P 217 John 13 69 107 218 John L 185 249 Martha 252 Mrs H D 124 P C 251 Paul E 185 Roberta 251 Samuel 76 Sarah A 288 Thomas 35 Webb 76 Winborne 76 Wm 76
JERNIGAN, 205 299 Fannie 167 243 Jno H 242 John 76 John H 186 195 207 242-243 328 John Hunter 243 329 L R 140 142 161 186-187 195 225 330 Lemuel R 86 185 242 331 Mary 86 186 Mary H 186 Miles H 140 171 186 Mills 91 186 330 332 Mrs Thos R 196 Needham 76 Paul 308 Robert 308 Sallie 243 Sallie D 195 Thomas 243 Thomas R 167 264 321 Thomas Robert 329 Thos R 186 242 316
JESSUPS, J W 332
JESTER, Ella 156
JIGGETTS, Lewis Meredith 91
JIGGITTS, Edw 76 Wm 76
JOACHIM, King Of Naples 125
JOHN, Lord Berkley 10

JOHN (cont.)
   Lord Carteret 14
JOHNSON, Andrew 226 343 Anna
   76 Barnaby 42 Betsey 31
   Charles 65 83 Gabriel 14-16 19
   27 339 Gen 226 Gov 65 John
   31 125 Julia 116 Martha 116
   171 Miss 158 Nath'l 13 Pres
   227 229 Rachel 98 Richard 42
   116 171 Richard W 171 Sallie
   125 Sally 31 Samuel 57 125
   339 Samuel Iredell 31
JOHNSTON, James 106 Samuel 18
JONES, 205 262 Abram 37
   Adolphus 171 Albrighton 52
   Amilescent 76 Anne 52 85 258
   Capt 52 Celia 127 Edward 199
   Harwood 20 Henry 36 Howell
   85 127 156 162 185 328
   Howell M 156 187 Howell
   Morgan 185 J E 217 James 22-
   23 36 41 76 85 90 105 259
   299 315 317-318 James B 106
   James III 127 149 258 James S
   148-149 328 James Sidney 140
   James Sydney 85 329 Jas 318
   Jesse 297 Jessie 201 John 19-20
   124 Martha E 171 Mary 127
   156 Nancy 185 197 Priscilla
   199 Reuben 201 297 Robert Jr
   19 Samuel 41 Sarah 76 Susan
   297 Thomas 41 154 William
   85 103-104 318 Wm 76
JORDAN, 125 261-262 Abner 60
   David 60 Eliz 76 Etta 262
   James 47 60 141 294 John 60
   John P 192 Jonathan 149
   Joseph J 60 260 327 Joseph P
   228 331 Joseph Perry 60 Kinsey
   60 139 Mary 60 Matilda 60
   Mrs David 60 Mrs Pleasant 60
   Pattie 294 Pleasant 60 91 141
   294 317 332 Richard 60
   William 36 60 260 294
   William H 124 Wm 76

JOYNER, Charles 76 Elisha Hunter
   297 Nathan 36 Nelson 107
JOYNES, Tibbie 99
JULIAN, D R 283
KEELE, Jacob 76
KEENE, Jacob 76
KELL, J T 283
KELLEY, Delphia 76
KERR, Susan Bats Kerr 149
KILBUS, Miss 125
KIMBERLY, Bettie 113 120 Emma
   120 John 113 117 120 192
   Prof 117 120-122 Rebecca 117
   Rebecca Maney 120
KINCHEN, William 16-17 19
KING, Ephraim 106 Henry 26 34
   36 Jesse 76 Sarah 266
KINSEY, Miss 60
KNIGHT, 300 Dempsey 76 Jesse
   42 Jesse J 241 Louisa 295
KNOSTMAN, Louise 104
KNOTT, William 42
KNOX, Andrew 154 James 76 Mrs
   H B 185
LAFAYETTE, 303 Gen 45 132
   Marquis De 132
LAMAR, 254 Lucius Q C 263
LAMON, John 19
LAND, Bird 77
LANE, 259 Joel 68
LANGSTON, Abner 140 John 77
   Luke 77 Martha 77 Richard
   170
LASSITER, Arabella 295 Brittain
   107 Everet B 251 H T 98 119
   175 229 241 Harrison C 170
   Henry Thomas 298 Imogen
   296 Isabella 176 Jacob 42 Jason
   77 Mamie 296 Mr 295 Mrs H
   T 96 Parthenia 294 Sarah 294
   Thomas 42 W J 296 William
   294 Wm 77 Zadoc 77
LATTOMER, William J 216
LAWED, Margaret 77
LAWRENCE, 205 300 Anna 99

LAWRENCE (cont.)
  Annie 100 Benj 107 Betsey 293
  Bettie 99 Charles A 99 307
  Elisha 148 293 Ellen O 100
  250 Emily B 100 Eva 291
  Exum 77 Hannah Peck 99 J N
  221 James N 99 Jno V 99 187
  John C 99 291 John V 148 161
  187 250 L C 99 218 L J 108
  290-291 307 334 Lewis C 218
  Lewis C Jr 244 Lloyd J 98-99
  287 315 323 Lloyd Jennings
  330 M T 283 Mattie A 99 Mrs
  L C 116 Robert 36 Sue E 99
  Wallace E 307
LAWSON, John 16
LEE, Anthony B 106 Gen 156 226
  236 311 James 76 John P 187 L
  F 172 Mrs L F 172 P H 294 R
  E 61 215 Robert E 204 213 W
  T 282-283
LEGATT, David 36
LEIGH, Lavinia 236
LEVERT, Dr 31 Emeline 31 Henry
  B 31
LEWIS, 205 293 Anna 195 Annie
  195 Daniel W 195-196 219
  Edw 76 Edward D 195 Emma
  195 Fannie 195 Jane 167 John
  195-196 Luke 77 Mary 195
  Sallie 166 195 243 Sallie D 195
  Sarah 195 Watson 139 141
  176 195 Watson Jr 187 195
  243 Watson Sr 166 194
  William 42
LEWTER, Jiles 107 John T 216
  246
LILES, 114-115 Edwin 107 Jo 114
  Jos T 100 Joseph T 113
LILLINGTON, Alexander 13
LILLY, Lewis 42
LINCOLN, Abraham 89 212 226
  343 Pres 179
LINTAL, Joseph 77

LITTLE, 205 235 300 Alexander
  231 George 39 41 48 58 77 96-
  97 153 George Jr 97
  Homarselle S 153 Penelope 97
  Thomas P 118 161 327 Thos P
  97 Thos Person 97 William 56
  58 96-97 153 William Jr 96
  William Person 97 Wm 316
  Wm P 97 Wm P Jr 97
LIVERMAN, Edmond 77 Josiah 36
LOCK, John 11
LOCKHART, George 17 Lillington
  17
LONG, 300 Harry W 59 64 85
  168 329 Jno 76 Nehemiah 64
  67 Sarah 64
LOUIS, XVI King Of France 121
LOWE, Starkey 284
LUDWELL, Philip 13
LUKE, Capt 218 J M C 218 John
  19
LUTON, Sam 76 Thos 76
LYON, A A 284 C F 61 164 Cicero
  F 217 Lt 217-218
MACON, Gideon 199 Nathaniel
  96 199 Priscilla 199 Wm 77
MADDREY, H C 323
MADDRY, Annie 252 H C 229
  243 287 324-325 H Carter 252
  K R 217 Mrs H C 252
MADISON, James 84 105 343
MAGET, Bessie 251 Ida 274 James
  221 James H 176 John E 176
  251 274 297 Malissa Anne 297
  Sally 85 Sarah 175-176
MAGGET, John 77
MAHONE, Gray 107
MAJETTE, Blanche 292 J G 153
  292 333-334 James 85 292
  Joseph G 199 286 Mr 293
  Penelope 85 William J 263 292
MANEY, 84 104 205 Annie 113
  Annie R 110 117 Bettie 113
  120 David 111 Elizabeth M 45

MANEY (cont.)
59 110 Elizabeth Meredith 103
110 Frank 112 Gen 112
George 111 Henry 110-111 113
253 James 19-20 36 47 64 77
91 109-111 113 122 198 253
300 317 James D 112 James II
83 110 James III 110 118
James IV 103 110 James V 110
Judge 111-112 Martha 110
Mary 110 198 Mrs James 91
Peggy 77 110 Priscilla 110
Rebecca 120 Sallie H 110
Susanna 83 110 Thomas 91
109-113 117 120 124 133 139
318 328-329 William 110-111
113 253
MANLEY, Gabriel 77 Moses 42
Southam 42
MANLY, Charles 147 340 Gov 183
MANNEY, 111
MANNING, 300 Daniel 263 John
106 W H 322
MANSARD, Anna 197
MARSH, Geo 77 S E 296 331
MARTIN, Alexander 339-340 Gen
133 Gov 15 38 Josiah 14 50
339 Leonard 133 318
MASHBORN, Charity 78 Matt 77
Wm 77
MASONGILL, Daniel 77
MASSENBURG, Elizabeth 157
James P 221 Mary Hare 246
Wm 157
MATTHEWS, Edmond 78 Farmer
77 Giles 78 James H 261
Maggie 127
MAYNE, Robert 77
MCANGES, Cora 195 W D 195
MCCALL, J D 283
MCCLAMMY, Herbert 283
MCDADE, Addie C 275 P H 275
MCDOWELL, 302 A 150 Archer
263 Archibald 182 191 262 Dr
182 James 18 Ruth R 150 Sallie
191 T D 209-210 W O 262

MCFARLANE, Walter 77
MCGLAGHON, W D 220
MCGLAUGHON, Geo 77 James
77 John 42 Luke 106 151 297
MCGLAUHON, Elisha 77
MCGLOUGHON, Luke 256
MCKEEL, Michael 42
MCKENNY, Mary 172 Mr 172
MCKENZIE, J W 283
MCKINLEY, William 344
MCMULLEN, P H 323
MEARES, Mary Thomas 199 W B
199
MEBANE, 260 John T 225 Julia M
225
MERCER, W C 321
MEREDITH, 300 Capt 92 253
Elizabeth 148 Elizabeth R 32
Lewis 32 64 78 91 93 168 198
Lewis M 148 Mary 84
MERRIFIELD, Dora M 257
Thomas J 257
MERRIMON, A S 231 242 254
272 Judge 231
MEWBORNE, S G 284
MILLER, Jno 77 Thomas 12
William 340
MINTS, Elisha 106
MITCHELL, Arthur 256 Bettie 237
C W 237 284 G W 333 Geo H
256 297 322 Geo W 286
George H 232 323 J H 268 333
J R 243 J S 224 James L 237
James Lawrence 329 James R 60
330 James S 156 237 262 278
287 327 Jas R 315 Jesse H 256
286 297 Jno 237 John 156
John P 60 237 Lila 268 Mary
237 Mary Green 156 Miles 229
Nancy 156 Pauline 237 Sallie
237 243 Sheriff 279 W J 237
W W 161 170 193 228-229
236 262 278 William J 237
William W 327 Wm 77
MODLIN, Dempsey 77 J T 217
MONGOMERY,John 58 Robert 58

MONK, Nottingham 42
MONROE, James 343 W C 284
MONTGOMERY, 205 300
  Amanda C 127 B J 318-319
  Bridger J 127 136 139 145 148
    184 328 Elinder 78 Fannie 295
    G W 141 184 Gen 133 Geo W
    142 319 George W 127 146
    149 244 251 Georgie 244
    Georgie W 225 Harriet 184
    John 18 49 84 John C 106 127
    184 Kerr 127 148 Martha 127
    Mary 84 127 Nancy C 127
    Robert 57 78 84 90 93 107 118
    127 307 316 328-329 Robt
    317-318 W M 187 W P 218
    William M 127 250 295 297
    328 William Meredith 127
    William Preston 127 Wm M
    161 229
MONTIER, Gilbert 132
MOORE, 205 259 299-300 303
  313 Aaron 77 Albert 190
  Alfred 164 190 Allen 106 149
  164 190 Augustus 94
  Bartholomew Figures 67 Britton
  26 248 Britton S 138 Caroline
  138 248 Dr 144 Edward 78
  140 Elizabeth R 93-94 129
  Emily Bland 225 Ester 124
  Esther 145 G C 145 167 184
  224 229 Godwin C 31 137 142
  147 225 245 258 262 319 327
  Godwin Cotton 144 Henry 190
  J G 145 J W 192 324 James 13
  17 37 77 James A 161 James
  Wright 31 124 259 John 19
  149 164 190 John W 85 118
  132 145 149 200 219 258 298
  313 315 John Wheeler 329
  Juhan G 219 Julia 144 Julian G
  216-217 225 Lawrence 77 Maj
  92 164 246 258-260
  Marmaduke 42 Mary 24 59 67
  Maurice 39 49 Mrs Jesse 239
  Samuel 101 109 140 161

MOORE (cont.)
  164 170 187 190 Thomas 145
  William 145 Willis 77 Wm 77-
  78
MOREHEAD, J M 210 John M
  340
MORGAN, 66 300 Eliz 77 Gen 54-
  55 Hardy 77 Jacob 77 James 42
  78 John 42 P H 272 322
  William 124 William P 108
  Willis 77 Wm P 139
MULLEN, James 77 Jno 77
MURAT, Joachim 125 Prince Of ?
  124-125
MURFREE, 205 300 Capt 40 Col
  44-45 58-59 64 Elizabeth 104
  Elizabeth M 45 110 Elizabeth
  Meredith 103 Fannie Priscilla
  104 Fanny N D 104 Hardy 24
  37 39 42-44 57-58 64-65 77 90-
  91 93 103-104 110 126 199
  269 303 316 John H 126 Maj
  44 Martha 110 Mary 24 59
  199 313 Mary Noailles 104
  Matthias B 104 Matthias
  Brickle 45 199 Sallie H 110 W
  H 124 William 19-20 23 40-41
  43 48 59 65-66 86 316-317 326
  William H 45 103 298 328
  William Hardy 45 59 90 315
  329 William Law 67 103
  William Law Jr 104 William
  Law Sr 104 Wm 24 26 39 77
  91 Wm H 92 110 118 139 318
  Wm Law 103
MURPHY, 300 Edw 271 Mary
  270-271
MURRAY, James 236 Pattie 236
  Wm 42
MUSE, Wm B 123
MYRICK, 205 300 303 Ann O
  157 Charles E 158 David 157
  Dr 158 Elizabeth 157 Helen
  157 225 James L 157 221 John
  D 157 John S 158 Julia 116
  Julia R 158 Lawrence Baker 158

MYRICK (cont.)
  Lucy A 157 Mary 157 Mcclure
  157 Sue J 117 Susan J 53 119
  158 224 T N 224-225 Thomas
  N 98 116 157-158 Vrginia 157
  W B 157 Walter 140 Walter B
  107 141 157 221 Walter B Jr
  157 Walter D 158
NASH, Abner 339
NEAL, 300 Ann O 157 Annie E
  190-191 Edw S 185 190
  Edward 161 Fannie 191 Francis
  191 Geo W 120 191 John B
  190 263 Maj 190-191 Mary S
  191 Mrs Edw 53 Prof 120 191
  Sallie 263 Sarah T 191 Thomas
  106 191 Thomas N 190 Walter
  H 121 191
NELSON, J L 283
NEWSOM, Charles 78 Edw H 142
  Hosea 78 Joel 78 John 78 John
  F 279 332 M E 140 Marcella
  177 Michael B 177 W D 232-
  233 323
NEWSOME, Annie 152 J E 153 J
  F 333 Jno F 322 John F 329
  Joseph 152 263 Michael E 153
  William D 332
NEWSON, 140
NICHOLS, Jno 78 John 195 Nat
  78 Willis 36 Wm 78
NICHOLSON, Sallie 119 Samuel
  119 176 Sarah 176
NICKINS, James 78 Malichi 78
NIEPEE, Joseph Nicephore 130
NOLLEY, E W 219 Emmett W 149
  Fannie 150 Francis 149 Geo W
  149 Julia 150 M J 219
  Marcellus 149 Susan 150
NORFLEET, E B 140 Judith 52
  Marmaduke 52 Miss 197
  Mourning 99
NORTHCOTT, Andrew J 295-296
  332 Anthony 78 Bertie 295
  Elizabeth 296 James 256 295-
  296 John 48 78 295

NORTHCOTT (cont.)
  John A 295-296 331 Mamie
  296 Nancy 295
NORVELL, Benj 78 Mary 78
NOWELL, Dempsey 78 Seth 229
  William 141 Wm 139
O'BRADY, Thomas 86
O'BRIEN, 300
O'BRYAN, Dr 133 Lawrence 123
  184
O'DONAL, Miss 275
O'DWYER, 87 130-131 267 300
  Dr 92 115 128 130 145
  Thomas 92 124 184 235 Thos
  198 313
OATIS, Fannie 150 Mr 150
ODOM, Jacob 78
OLIVER, Andrew 105
OLMSTEAD, S R 207
OLMSTED, S R 201
ORANGE, Henry 78
ORMES, Samuel 17-18
OUTLAW, Col 197 David 50 134
  192 197 George 134 Lewis 78
  Thomas 78 134 Thos 21 Wm
  78
OVERBY, Maggie 165 Paul 165
  Thomas 165
OVERTON, Elisha 106 H H 218 J
  E 308 Jacob 106 James 78
  Nath'l 78
OWEN, John 340 Mary 262 Miss
  237
PACE, William 20
PANTER, Edw 79
PARHAM, E E 183
PARKER, 125 300 A I 60 286 292
  333-334 Abigail 79 Alfred Isley
  294 Annie L 234 Augustine
  295 C W 292-293 334 Carey
  W 298 Daniel 79 David 298
  David A 220 Demsey 37
  Elizabeth 294 Ephraim 79
  Fannie 101 H B 97 101 235 H
  T 218 Hester 294 Ike 294 Isaac
  36 J B 221 J D 332

PARKER (cont.)
  James 106 272 322 Janie J 294
  Jno 79 John 65 Joseph 293
  King 101 L A 308 Lilly 164
  Martha 294 Mary C 293 Mrs A
  I 47 237 262 Mrs David 296
  Mrs Redmond R 91 Oler S 298
  Oris 27 109 229 298 P P 217
  Pattie 60 294 Peter 27 79 Peter
  P 298 Priscilla 292 R S 332
  Robert 108 234 Robert S 232
  236 Sam 79 Samuel 107 Sarah
  164 294 Silas 79 139 171 298
  Silas II 298 Soloman 323
  Solomon 242 W Carey 164
  William 107 William Carey
  216-217 Willis 294 Wm 79
PARTEN, Henry 78 Hubbon 78
PATTERSON, George 17
PATTIE, Martha A 199
PAYNE, Peter 18 R L 284 Wm A
  107
PEAL, Ann 78 Daniel 79 Dempsey
  78 Edw 78 Thomas 78
PEARCE, Daniel 79 Isaac 106 Job
  79 Jordan 70 79 Mattie A 99 S
  F 99 Samuel J 150 Susan 150
PEARSON, Chief Justice 268
  Richmond M 255
PECK, Mary 98
PEEBLES, Etheldred 267 Howell 67
  Jno T 175 John 108 Lucretia
  267 R B 267 281 283 Robt 67
  Turner 267
PEETE, 300 George W 161
PELTIER, Prof 130
PENDER, 114 Jethro 79 113-114
PENTECOST, Hugh O 175
PERKINS, Mary S 191 Robert 191
PERRY, 205 299 Abner 41 60 78
  90 297 318 Abner J 91 161
  186 326 Andrew T 91 Capt
  193 Celia 79 Elisha 79 Emma
  195 Ezekel 78 Freeman 240 J J
  190 J W 190 307 James 79
  Jesse A 216 John B 91

PERRY (cont.)
  Joseph J 195 239 Joseph W 239
  329 Josiah 240 Julia 266 Mrs
  Abner 60 Patrick 161 331 Patsy
  91 Preston 186 326 Simeon 78
  Susan 297 W A 266 W J 234
  266 William J 331 Wm 79 Wm
  N 140 161
PERSON, Mary Ann 96 Thomas
  96 Thomas J 292
PETE, Hugh 307
PETERSON, Ann 154
PETTIGREW, J J 247
PETTY, 302 Prof 182 W O 182
PHELPS, Dempsey 79
PICOT, Antoinette 122 153 Capt
  122 219 Guy C 153-154 J H
  109 118 120 153 Julian H 121
  218-219 290 298 L J 153 Louis
  121 Louis J 154 Marietta 121
  Peter B 325 Peter Blount 330
  Peter O 121 Prof 121
PIERCE, Franklin 343 James 42
  Thomas 42
PINCKNEY, C C 88
PINNER, Milbry 79 Rachel 79
PIPER, Maria 241
PIPKIN, 300 Anne Maria 123 Dr
  123 Georgie 244 Georgie W
  225 Isaac 32 36 53 123 127
  147 162 218-219 225 228 231
  243-244 251 326 Martha 127
  251 Martha A 162 Mary
  Ellenor 123 Sue Frank 127
  Thomas W 244
PITT, William 38
POLK, James K 121 343 L L 277
  Leonidas 148 Miss 148 Pres
  169 William 148
POLLOCK, Thomas 14 Thos 16
POOL, John 242 247 S B 219
POPE, Leo XIII 312
POPE, Nathan 107
PORTER, Abram 78 Benj 225
  Epinetus 225 Jno 79 William
  234 Wm 79

POTTER, Henry 197
POWELL, Anna 78 Augustine 295
  Charles 79 Dempsey 78 Exum
  42 James M 245 Jesse 308 Jesse
  C 187 Shadrick 78 William 295
  Willie Pauline 295
PRAT, John 17-18
PRESCOTT, 9
PRETLOW, Bettie 202 Joseph 202
  Mary 202 Mary H 202 Mary
  Hare 246
PRIOR, Maj 247 Roger 247
PRITCHARD, Jeter C 280 John
  Lamb 87
PROSSER, Gabriel 90
PRUDEN, 205 299 Bettie 99
  Charles N 219 Elizabeth 155
  James 177 John 180 Lodswick
  108 Marcella 177 Martha G
  177 Nathaniel 177 W D 161
  170 178 180 229 245 W D Sr
  99 William Dorsey 329 William
  Dossey 177
PRUET, Mary 78
PURDIE, Alexander 176 Dr 176
  John H 176 Sarah 175-176
PURNELL, Wm 107
PURYEAR, R C 210
PYLAND, Wm 108
QUEMBY, Jesse 79
QUINTON, Sarah 164
RABY, Joel 79
RALEIGH, James 106 Walter 10
RAMSAY, Allen L 106 Henry 129
  148 Henry A 133 Temperance
  148
RAMSEY, 94 300 Martha A 94
  Temperance 95
RANDOLPH, Mary A 159
RANSOM, 254 Amy 199 Edmond
  321 Gen 193 198 James 199
  James II 199 James III 199 M
  W 242 247 272 306 Martha A
  199 Matt W 146 199 280
  Matthew W 193

RANSOM (cont.)
  Matthew Whitaker 198 Pattie A
  198 Priscilla 199
RASBERRY, James Jr 106 Margaret
  79 Wm 79
RASCOE, A S 283 Alex 80
RAWLES, Absalom 80 Jesse 80
  Wm 79
RAWLS, Mariah 79
RAY, J Frank 283 John E 270
  Stephen 42
RAYNER, 205 299 Amos 80 147
  Kenneth 142 147 190 201 210
  246 315-316 319 330 Mr 148
  Mrs 148
RAYNOR, Amos 171
REA, 187 205 300 Daniel 97-98
  Daniel Jr 98 Fannie 101
  Hannah Peck 99 James 98-99
  250 Joseph 108 Joseph G 97-98
  106 Julia 98 Margaret 98 100
  159 Margaret L 168 Martha 98
  Martha Ann 96 Mary 98 Mary
  Ann 100 Mrs 130 Nancy 98
  100 Rachel 98 Sally 98
  Sampson 98 100 168 Sampson
  III 168 William 97-98 100-101
  108 119 133 288 William Jr
  100 William Sr 159 Wm 79
  168
READ, Hamilton 79
READE, E G 227
REAMS, John 218
REED, D W 197 William 14 233
  247 332-333
REID, David S 197 340 Dr 100
  Emily B 100 Walter 100
REINHARDT, J F 283
REVEL, Hezekiah 241 Silas 80
REYNOLDS, Jesse 79 Thomas 79
RHOADS, Abram 79
RIBAULT, John 10
RICE, Mrs E F 271 Nathaniel 14
RICKS, Edwin 218
RIDDICK, 205 300 Abraham 142

RIDDICK (cont.)
　Abram 109-110 235-236 Alfred
　296 Anne Maria 236 Cora 195
　Cornelius B 183 Fannie 195 J
　D 236 333 James 37 48 178
　236 296 James A 187 Joseph
　103 116 Lavinia 236 Martha G
　177-178 Mary E 296 Pattie 236
　Samuel A 221 236 Thomas 195
　Virginia R 236
RIDER, Nancy 80
RIDLEY, 205 300 Day 39-40 52
　170 316 Nathaniel 40 Thomas
　79 Timothy 141 146 170 327
　Timothy Sharp 40
RIDPATH, 9
RILEY, Benj 79 Wm 80
RINDAL, Joseph 79
ROADS, Wm 80
ROBBINS, 254 Josiah 106
ROBERSON, Mr 93
ROBERTS, Benj 198 Benjamin 198
　Benjamin Jr 198 Elizabeth 198
　Esther 198 Esther Wilkinson
　198 Jonathan 198 253
　Jonathan Jr 198 Jonathan Sr
　198 Lavinia 198 Lavinia Esther
　Wilkinson 199 Martha 198
　Mary 110 198-199 Thomas V
　142 146 198 Thomas Vaughan
　198 Thos V 319 W P 151 Wm
　79
ROBERTSON, Josephine 156
ROBINSON, L D 283
ROGERS, 114 Alberta 291 Bill 114
　J M S 291 James 80 Jonathan
　80 288 Sarah 288 William 107
　113 William W 330 Wm W
　315
ROMAN, Matthew 14
ROOKS, Dempsey 79 Joseph 79
ROOSEVELT, Theodore 344
ROSBERRY, William 36
ROUNTREE, A J 172 Miss 172
ROWAN, Matthew 339

RUFFIN, Susan 250 Thomas 148
　209 219
RUSH, Martha 168 William 168
RUSSELL, Daniel 284 Daniel L
　341 Jonathan 105 Thomas 79
RUTLAND, Elizabeth 31 James 21
　31 James Sr 36 Parthenia 145
　Shadrack 145 Wm 79
SANDERFORD, James 80 John 80
　Nancy 80
SANDERS, Bartha 176 David 80
　Jemima 175 John H 175 John P
　80 Lemuel 107 Nathan 80
SAULS, Miss 234
SAUNDERS, Asa 218 Miss 177
　Sarah 195 W L 180 Winnifred
　156 Wm 80 Wm L 23
SAVAGE, Alexander 196 Leroy J
　248 R R 153 287 Rowena 153
　Toy D 154 Wm V 154
SAWYER, Lemuel 103
SCALES, 254 Alfred M 341
SCALLY, Samuel 17
SCARBOROUGH, Benj 107 C W
　119 291 Jesse 107 John C 182
　302
SCHOFIELD, Gen 222
SCHULE, 130
SCOTT, Andrew 96 Dred 200 Gen
　241 310 George 96 James 96
　241 John 81 93 95 105 241
　Martha Ann 96 Mary 32
　Virginia 241 William 96
　Winfield 96
SCRBOROUGH, Anna 291
SCULL, 299 E D 167 195 Edw 80
　Elisha 80 J J 148 James S 140
　John 80 106 Nannie 167
　Parthenia 294
SEALL, Jno 107
SEARS, Annie 252 Benj 308 Dr
　252 Edgar G 253 John 80
　Jonathan 69 W H 129 252-253
　William H 252
SEHON, John L 113 Maj 113

SENTER, Gov 112
SESSOM, 299
SESSOMS, 205 Ann 80 Charles C 190 D V 229 263 319 Daniel V 139 Daniel Vanpelt 105 189 Elisha 139 Eliza 189 Elizabeth 189 H B 190 Jos W 190 Joseph W 249 Rachel 80 W W 140 171 190 William 189 William Wynns 239 Wm 106
SEVIER, John 63
SEWARD, W H 89
SEWELL, Dempsey 80 Jacob 106 Jethro 106 Richard 81 William 107 Wm 80
SEYMOUR, Francis 22
SHARP, 205 299 Annie 167 Capt 216 Caroline 136 Charles L 167 245 Col 167 Cunningham 107 E H 134 136 E Hunter 136 Eleanor 166 Elisha H 139 166 Elisha Hunter 133 Elizabeth 25 85 167 Elleanor 176-177 Fannie 167 Gemona 80 H C 136 167 313 Henry C 245 Henry Clay 331 Hunter 167 196 316 Isaac 81 J B 166 187 J Bembery 245 J Bembury 167 Jacob 25 133 139 166-167 187 330 Jacob H 134-136 Jacob II 245 Jacob Sr 166 James 167 323 Jamima 32 166 Jane 167 195-196 John 167 260 327 331 John B 236 Nancy 85-86 166 Nannie 167 195 Patsy 123 S III 166 Sallie 133 166 Sally 136 Sarah 25 32 133 166 Sen 133 Starey 166 Starkey 25 32 81 85-86 123 133 140 167 170 195-196 216 218 229 246 330 Starkey I 166 326 331 Starkey II 166 Starkey III 166 176-177 Starkey IV 167 196 Thomas B 140 142 171 Thomas Blount 86 166 Thomas H 216 245 Thomas L 136

SHARP (cont.)
Thos B 166 Thos H 136 Thos L 134 Timothy 40 William 61 136 167-168 228 245 328-329 Willie 135 Wm 167
SHARPE, 205 Elisha H 318 Fannie 243 Jacob 319 Starkey 319 Starkey II 145 148 Starkey III 243 Thomas B 319 Thos H 167 William 219
SHAW, Edw 141 Henry M 198 242 John A 61 John S 61 Lt 61 Mary R 135 Matilda 60 Mr 62 N L 218 Norman L 218 W B 242 W P 61 135 219 258 322 324 W P Jr 61 William 60 William P 61 Wm B 321
SHEPHERD, 218 James E 217 Providence 80 Sarah 153 Solomon 153 199 William Biddle 136 William S 217
SHERMAN, Gen 226 W T 221
SHEWCROFT, Silas 106
SHEWINAFT, Wm 80
SHIELDS, R H 235
SHORT, William 19-20 110
SHUBRICK, John T 167 Mrs Dr John T 167 Mrs John T 196 Wm B 167
SIKES, Britton 106
SIMMONS, Charles 52 Elizabeth 86
SIMONS, Eliz 245 Elizabeth 167 John 166 195 Joshua 80 Miss 167 Nancy 194-195 Obediah 80 Sallie 166 195
SITZGRAVES, Judge 197
SKETCHLY, Harriet 87
SKINNER, 235 Charles 20 Dr 97 Harry 278 James 80 107 John 65 Mrs Dr Charles 97 T G 286 322 Thomas G 272
SLADE, Miss 121
SLATER, Thos 17
SLAUGHTER, 201 205 J B 187 229 289 319 324 328

SLAUGHTER (cont.)
  John A 219 John Blount 194
  Joseph B 319 328 Joseph
  Blount 193 224 329 Michael
  36 Wm 194
SMITH, 197 205 262 300 303
  Abram 80 Alexander 106
  Annie 266 Annie E 191
  Benjamin 340 Chief Justice 149
  166 186 272 Daniel L 241
  Garrison 100 James 80 Jennie
  241 John 80 Joseph 20 Judge
  229 304 Kirby 226 L L 281 283
  Mary Olivia 234 Mrs Judge 234
  Nancy 85 100 166 Olivia O
  166 R L 283 Richard H 190
  Sallie 191 Sipha 139 145 319
  332 Thomas 13 81 95 W N H
  50 161 165 170-171 187 189
  192 194 197-198 200 209-210
  227 234 236 255 268 315-316
  328 William 58 84 William L
  85-86 William N H 319
  William Nathan Harrell 85 329
  Wm 49 Wm L 166 Wm N H
  319
SNIPES, E F 287 E T 231 233 257
  278 285-286 322-323 332-333
  Edgar Thomas 307 Isaac F 285
  323
SORRELL, James 81 Wm 81
SOTHEL, Seth 13
SOUTHALL, 205 300 Annie R
  110 117 Daniel 115 120 124
  149 Emily Bland 225 Emma
  120 Fannie 158 James H 116
  Jno W 99 140 John W 110 116
  133 141 158 187 193 236 Julia
  116 Julia R 158 Mary 116 Mary
  A 289 Mary W 116 Rebecca
  120 Rev 115-117 149 Sarah C
  116 Seth 115 149 Sue E 99
SOWELLS, Sarah 267
SPARROW, Mary 195

SPEIGHT, John 36 Richard Dobbs
  Jr 340 Richard Dobbs Sr 340
  W W 322
SPICEY, Daniel 80
SPIER, 300
SPIERS, 115 205 B T 100 165 167-
  168 319 Benj 271 Brackney T
  330 Douglas 169 221 H Mcd
  169 James 105 113 Jim 114
  Lewis T 236 Lucy 169 Margaret
  L 168-169 Margeret 100 Norma
  I 271 Tyrone 169 William 169
SPIKES, Thomas 80
SPIRES, Absalom 80 Elisha 80
STALLINGS, 100
STANCELL, 267 Mrs R H 288
STAR, William G 183 243
STARKEY, Edward 167 John 80
  154 167
STEELE, 254
STEPHEN, Wm 37
STEPHENS, Alexander H 212 Ann
  80
STEPHENSON, Nancy 295
STEVENS, R L 284 Samuel 12
  Thad 320 William 37
STEWART, W H 320
STOKES, Montford 340
STONE, David 50 340
STORY, J B 296 John 80 Parker
  296 Rosa 296
STRICKLAND, Drew 80
SULLY, Ellen 137 Thomas 137
SUMNER, 205 299 David E 128
  318 Dempsey 18 Eliz 80 Jethro
  128 John 18 Josiah 29 48 326
  Luke 128 Margaret 128 Mary
  80 Moses 29 36 80 326 Robert
  17 24 29 34 36 40 47 68 128
  316-317 327
SWAIN, David L 340 Gov 92
SYKES, Joseph 20
TARLETON, 54 Col 55
TAYLOE, 299-300 David 171

TAYLOE (cont.)
　　James 171 Jonathan 171
　　Jonathan II 171 Langley 171
　　220 229 332 Leander 171 W S
　　171 229 William H 327
TAYLOR, 129 Boaz 81 Chief
　　Justice 128 Dorsey 218
　　Elizabeth 155 Hillory 220 238
　　Hilory 278 Isaac 107 140 148
　　278 Isaac Lafayette 218 John 36
　　155 John Lewis 128 133
　　Margaret 128 Miles 81 Mr 278
　　Richard 40 Richard J 155 219
　　Sallie 237 Samuel 18 W E 219
　　W P 149 219-220 237-238 323
　　W W 308 William P 277
　　William T 155 Williford 81
　　Zachary 343
TEASTER, William 107
TENNESSEE, John 81
THACH, Benj 197
THOMAS, Abraham 139 155-156
　　299 Abram 141 Benj 81 Geo H
　　199 Isaac 81 James 155 John Q
　　156 216 Josephine 156 Josiah
　　81 Martha 156 Mary 156 Mary
　　Green 156 Nancy 156 R P 28
　　Rascius P 156 Samuel 20
THOMSON, Eliz 81
THORNE, Thomas 106
TIFTON, John B 81
TILDEN, Samuel J 254-255
TILEY, John 81
TOLAR, Julia 150
TOMLINSON, J 284
TRADER, 300 Betsy 244 D C 244
　　Henry G 244 J M 229 James M
　　31 231 244 330-331 John 244
　　John B 245 Martha 271 Mary
　　244 Mary E 245 Rachel 81 W
　　H 244 William 244-245
TRAVIS, Joseph 142-143
TRITT, Thos 81
TROY, R P 183
TRYON, Gov 38 William 14 22
　　339

TUCKER, Henry Saintgeorge 257
TURNER, Benjamin 142 James 20
　　340 Miss 291 Nat 142-143 189
　　Thos 17
TYLER, Hellen 81 Luther R 220
　　Samuel 81
TYNER, Arthur 107 267 Drew 267
　　Lucretia 267 Lucy 267 296
　　Mary 267 Mildred 267 Nich Jr
　　36 Nicholas 267 Nicholas II
　　297 Nicholas Jr 267 Nicholas
　　Sr 267 Priscilla 267 Sarah 267
　　William 267
TYNTE, Edward 13
USHER, B 131 Barney 131
VAIL, Edwin 18
VALENTINE, Alex 81 Daniel 29
　　161 187 194 229 David 81
　　Isaac 81 Lemuel 141 W D 170
　　187 194 328 William D 328
　　William Darden 329
VANBUREN, Martin 343
VANCE, Bob 254 Gov 97 166 222
　　238 Z B 254 272 280 306 341
　　Zebulon B 223 Zebulon Baird
　　198
VANN, 205 300 A C 327 332 A G
　　187 229 Albert C 151-152
　　Albert G 151 Ann 154 Annie
　　152 Auquilla 152 Bettie 237 C
　　S 323 Chairman 161 Charles
　　154-155 Charles Spurgeon 153
　　330 Col 155 Cordie 151 Darius
　　154 Harriet 151 Henry B 152-
　　153 Homarselle S 153 J J 151 J
　　M 145 Jesse B 151 224 237-
　　238 256 319 Jesse Thomas 155
　　Jno 108 154 Jno E 315 John 36
　　139 145-146 148 150-155 183-
　　185 238 318-319 327 John A
　　151-152 184 186 224 228 233
　　237 252 319 326 328 331 333
　　John E 153 292 323 325 333
　　John Eley 330 John Jesse 329
　　Momoiselle S 97 Mrs T E 171
　　274 Rachel 154 Rensselear 151

VANN (cont.)
   Richard T 151 Rowena 153
   Sallie 237 Sarah 153 T D 122
   187 Thaddeus E 151-152
   Thadeus E 332 Thomas 154
   Thomas J 151 237 Tilman 153
   Tilman D 97 141 151 153-154
   161 247 296 William 36 151-
   152 154 Willie 154 296 Wm A
   225
VANPELT, Daniel 36 Elizabeth 189
   Henry B 189 331 John 36 81
   Sarah 81
VASSAR, Robert 81
VAUGHAN, 205 300 303 Annie
   100 Benj 107 Betsey 293 Bettie
   238 C T 293 Charles T 250
   Col 287-289 Elisha 188 Hilary
   107 J B 286 333 J E 221 James
   67 107 John 81 107 288 John
   N 100 221 293-294 307
   Lemuel 107 Martha 198 Mary
   C 293 Mary Louise 188 Mrs E
   B 296 Nellie H 150 305 Polly
   99 Rosa 257 Sallie 198 Sarah A
   288 T J 68 Thomas J 288 U 98
   Uriah 68 98 100 146 176 187
   198 238 257 287-288 293 305
   William 65 68 250 288-289
   293 Wm 81 263
VELENTINE, Daniel 187
VENABLE, A W 210
VICK, Arthur 107 Britton C 218
   Elias R 218 Lilly 172 Mary 172
   177
VILAS, W F 263
VINSON, Demsey 142 Drew 86
   Drewry 187 Elisha 81 J C 221
   286 333-334 J Henry 293 James
   81 John 107 John C 292
   Martha 293 Mary W 293 Mrs J
   C 293 Nehemiah 107 Peter 81
   Shad 81 Wm 81
WADDELL, 254
WADDILL, 205 Annie 177 199
   John 199-200 John Jr 200
   Margaret 199
WADILL, John 118
WAIT, Pres 182
WALKE, Isaac 250 Linda 250
WALKER, 205 Caroline 136
   Henderson 14 Hunter 136 Jos
   45 Joseph 41 Patsy 82
WALTERS, 92 Lewis 91 93 108
   318 Mills 106
WALTON, Anne 85 Bembury 127
   Celia 127 Isaac 85 James 167
   195 Nancy C 127 Nannie 167
   195 Timothy 18 85 William
   127 Wm 105 127
WARD, 299 A C 284 Ann J 149
   Anne 258 Anne J 258 E L C
   335 Isaac Hill 82 James 149
   258-259 Mary 275 Michael 36
   Miss 134 259
WARNER, 120 Mr 119
WARREN, 300 Col 118 Elizabeth
   252 Etheldred 117-118 138 246
   270 Jordan 82 Margaret R 118
   Martha 25 138 246 Obediah
   82 Priscilla 270 Robert 20 117-
   118 138 297 Sallie 59 Samuel
   107 117-118 246 T K 221
   Willis 115 Willis C 330
WASHINGTON, George 54 83 88
   117 132 343 James 18-20 24
   67 Stephen 140
WATSON, 299 Micajah 82
WAYNE, Gen 43-44
WEAKS, Arthur 81 Julian 82 Wm
   82
WEAVER, Esther 145 224 John
   106 Ned 82 R T 145 Richard T
   224
WEBB, Benj 82
WEBSTER, Daniel 344
WEED, Joseph 217 Mrs 91
WEIRSDOTZ, Anna 99

WELCH, David Jr 107
WELLBORNE, Samuel 107
WELLS, 300 Brooks 293 C D 13
　James 142 Martha 293 Mary
　293 Samuel 102 115
WEST, James 82 John 82 Peter 17-
　18 34 36 Thos S 108
WESTON, Elizabeth 252 Jesse 82
　Jordan 82 Miss 60 Thomas 60
　106
WESTRAY, Sallie M 31
WHEDBEE, J L 322 Lavinia 236
WHEELER, 66 131 205 300 303
　313 Col 137 Ellen 137
　Ephraim 108 137 Francis 137 J
　H 137 Jabez 108 137 John 87
　108 116 123 137 143-144 148
　171 John H 145 316 318-319
　John Hill 136 144 329 Joseph
　137 Julia 137 144 258 Julia M
　225 Junius B 137 170 Martha
　171 Mary 137 Mr 41 Mrs John
　124 S J 219 260 Samuel J 137
　200 225 Sarah 116 137 148
　Sarah C 116
WHITE, Alex 82 Henderson 82
　Mary E 268 Mr 195 Rufus 322
　Theo 279 322 William 92
WHITEHEAD, Paul 183
WHITEY, John 141
WHITFIELD, Wm W 106
WHITLEY, 300 Ann 82 George
　107 James 82 William 36
WHITNEL, Thomas 17 Thos 17
WHITNEY, W C 263
WIGGINS, Henry 106 Joshua 82
　Sarah 82 Wm 82 Wright 82
WILES, Joshua 83
WILKINS, James 81 Richard 82
　Wm 82
WILKINSON, Commodore 94
　Esther 198 Henry 13 Lucy 94
WILLEY, James 82
WILLIAM, Lord Craven 10
WILLIAMS, Abner 108 Addie C
　275 Amanda 171

WILLIAMS (cont.)
　Annie 195 Anthony 106
　Aromitta 171 Arthur 16 B B
　275 B F 275 286 333-334 Ben
　82 Benj 107 Benjamin 340
　Benjamin B 220 Charles 81
　Col 224 Constant 82 Daniel
　107 David 107 Eldridge 171-
　172 Eliz 82 Elizabeth 275
　Francis 275 Geo 82 140 George
　A 307 Gilstrap 36 82 H L 141
　Hardy 108 Harriet 171-172
　Henry L 152 161 171-172 274
　J T 274-275 Jack 275 James A
　171 Jesse 37 Jno 275 John 275
　Martha E 171 Mary 60 171
　275 Miss 171 Nathan 19 82
　Peter 90 307 Rev 275 Richard
　82 171 Roland 19 Rowland 17
　Sarah 82 Warner 82 Whit 82
　William 17 82 106 267
WILLIAMSON, Benj 67 Francis
　172 Mrs Francis 172 Priscilla
　W 270
WILLIFORD, John 81
WILLOUGBY, William 69
WILLOUGHBY, Henry 69 John
　69 82 William W 170 Willie
　106
WILLS, D P 183
WILSON, 300 John G 142 236
　253 Matthew 82 Scarbrook 34
WINBORN, John 41-42
WINBORNE, 111 205 288 300
　303 305-306 334 Arabella 295
　B B 25 279 283 316 325 333
　Benj 108 Benj B 314-315 323
　Benj B Jr 305 Benjamin 305
　Benjamin Brodie 329 Bob 247
　Caroline 138 248 Elisha 25 93
　124 138 202 246 270 327
　Harry 248 Henry 23-25 32 34
　42 45 49 57-58 63 81 85-86
　138 195 202 246 297 317 327
　332 Isabella 176 James 81 83
　Jessie 201 John 25 44 81 83

WINBORNE (cont.)
  139-141 188 194-195 299
  Josiah 81 83 Judge 277 Judith
  25 Lemuel 107 Maj 202 246
  284 Martha 25 117 138 270
  Mary H 202 Micajah 305
  Micajah T 26 31 138 161
  Micajah Thomas 247 Mrs B B
  288 Mrs Elisha 124 Mrs R W
  288 Nancy 195 Nellie H 150 R
  H 138 R W 325 Richard 26
  138 161 247 Robert H 26 247
  Robert Henry 247 Robert W
  248 256 323 Robert W Jr 257
  Robert Warren 25 330 Roger
  M 257 Rosa 257 S D 24 26-27
  45 97 138 170 187 228-229
  233 248 257 297 332-333 S P
  202 Samuel D 202 216 245-
  246 Samuel P 248 297 Samuel
  Pretlow 201 Sarah 25 133 166
  Sarah A 25 93 Stanley 305 307
  Stephen 107 Thomas 20 25 49
  81 93 138 140 202 246 327
  Thomas III 187 Uriah V 305
  Watson 299 Watson S 176
  294-295 William 20 25 68 195
  William J 188
WINESDALE, Charles 130
WINN, 29
WINNS, Geo 27 Rose 27
WINSLOW, Warren 340
WINSTON, Francis D 302 Gov
  302 P H 192 P H Jr 305
WISE, Annie L 234 Christianna
  234 George W 234 June M 234
  Lula 235 M M 220 235
  Marshall M 234 Mary Olivia
  234 Mollie 235 Mrs W B 124
  Olivia O 166 Sallie 234 Sarah
  234 W B 216 221 W D 234
  William 234 William B 234
  William Bartelle 234 Wm B
  161 Wm Bartelle 166 225
WITHERINGTON, J 106
WOMBLE, Mary 197

WOODARD, J S 283
WOODHOUSE, J M 322
WORRELL, 300 Betsy 172 Charles
  W 172 Cyrus E 171-172 Cyrus
  E Jr 172 E C 68 95 190 192
  198 253 Edward 172 Elisha
  172 Harriet 172 I W 217 J A
  172 236 James 107 171-172
  James A 171-172 John 35 John
  Wesley 171-172 Julian 172 Lilly
  172 Martha 171 Mrs Charles
  W 172 Mrs John Wesley 172
  Rebecca 172 Rhoda 82 Richard
  82 172 Richard Jr 172 Walter
  172
WORTH, Gov 230 240 Jonathan
  228-229 341 Joseph 330
WORTHAM, Benj H 107
WORTHINGTON, 303 Arcada 82
  Denny 260 329 H L 217 Mary
  82 R H 116 200 260 Sarah 82
WRIGHT, Henry 82 James 40 48
  316 Jane 82
WYNN, 29 253 300 Calvert 163
  Col 220 W B Jr 162 Wm B
  163
WYNNE, 29 Benj 36 Edmond 29
  Peter 29 Thomas 29
WYNNS, 29 205 300 303 Aaron
  114 Annie 252 Benj 17-18 20
  23-24 26-27 36 46 105 107 162
  317 Benj III 28 Benj Jr 24 27-
  28 32 36 317 Benj Sr 24 317
  Benjamin 28-29 39 68 83-84
  125 159 162 252 327
  Benjamin IV 28 Benjamin Jr 57
  327-328 330 Col 46 164 David
  107 Gen 90 103 110 Geo 316
  George 16 24 27-28 36-37 39
  41 56-57 83 86 107 159 317
  327 331 George Jr 27-28
  George Sr 28 George W 253
  Henry 107 J M 29 123 225
  229 J T 333 James 125 James D
  84 125 139 141 162 James
  Dean 28 162 James M 29 31

WYNNS (cont.)
46-47 163 187 219-220 224
298 319 James Madison 162
James Thomas 252 Jas D 318
Jennie 163-164 225 Jno A 82
John 16-17 27-28 John A 27-28
332 Margaret 98 159 Mary 98
116 159 Matthew 28 83 Mr
126 Peter 24 107 317 Polly 252
Sarah A 252 Sheriff 162-163
Susan 162 Susanna 110
Thomas 28 41 56-58 83-84 88
91 110 118 123-124 126 159
162 315-316 Thomas P 29 162-163 Thos 28 317-318 W B 161
William 17 27-28 47 49 57 83
106 252 317 326-327 332
William B 28-29 84 139 162
185 249 326 Wm 28 Wm B
116 162 Zilpha 47

YANCEY, 300 A P 187 A Poma
328 Antonio 171 Antonio P 86
170 Antonio Poma 329 James
M 86 128 171

YATES, Jesse J 187

YEALLOBY, Geo 83

YEATES, 201 205 254 Charles M
241 Edw 241 George 241 J J
232 241 333 James 241 Janie
241 Jennie 196 241 Jesse 83
241 Jesse J 50 96 164 196-197
218-219 231 240 315 319 328
Jesse Johnson 329 Maj 241
Maria 241 Mrs Virginia 96
Sarah 83 Virginia 241 William
Scott 241 Wm 107

www.ingramcontent.com/pod-product-compliance
Lightning Source LLC
Chambersburg PA
CBHW050832230426
43667CB00012B/1967